*To Heather Jeeves*

# THE
# INDIAN
# MUTINY

# THE
# INDIAN
# MUTINY

Julian Spilsbury

Weidenfeld & Nicolson

LONDON

First published in Great Britain in 2007
by Weidenfeld & Nicolson

1 3 5 7 9 10 8 6 4 2

© Julian Spilsbury 2007

Every effort has been made to contact the owners
of material reproduced in this book. Any omissions drawn to
the pu                                                    ns.

A CIP catalogue record for this book
is available from the British Library.

ISBN    978 0 297 84651 2

Typeset by Input Data Services Ltd, Frome

Printed in Great Britain by Butler and Tanner Ltd,
Frome and London

Weidenfeld & Nicolson

The Orion Publishing Group Ltd
Orion House
5 Upper Saint Martin's Lane
London, WC2H 9EA

The Orion Publishing Group's policy is to use papers that
are natural, renewable and recyclable products and made
from wood grown in sustainable forests. The logging and
manufacturing processes are expected to conform to the
environmental regulations of the country of origin.

www.orionbooks.co.uk

# CONTENTS

# List of Illustrations

# List of Maps

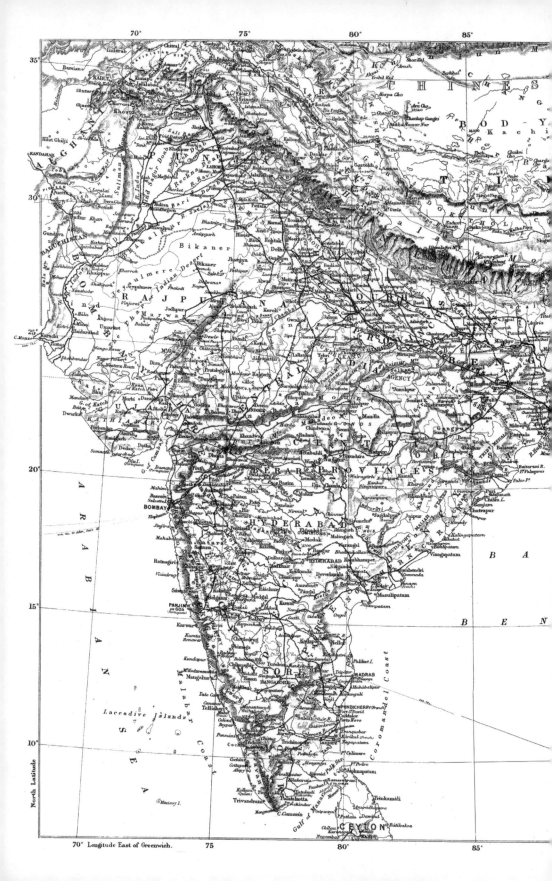

MAP OF
NORTH-WESTERN
AND CENTRAL INDIA

*Of the Railways shown in the Map
the line between Allahabad and
Cawnpore was available for the
use of Government in 1858.*

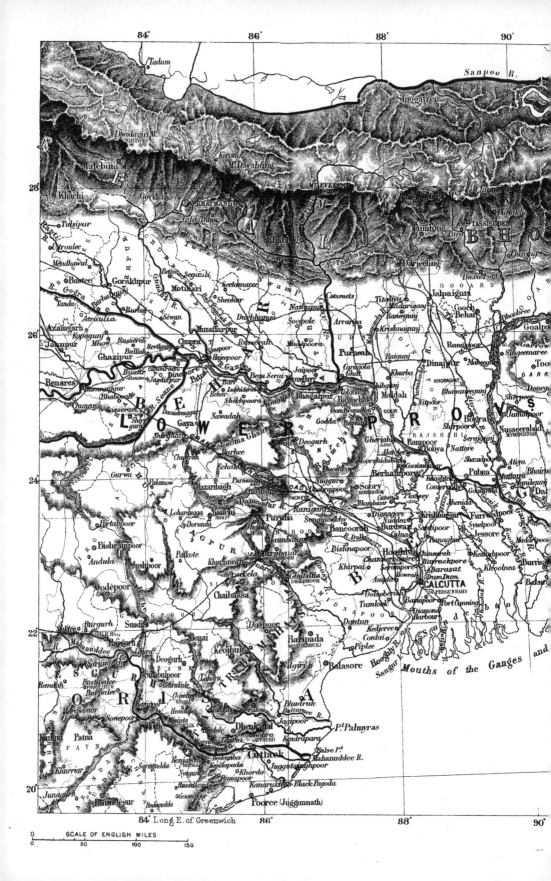

SCALE OF ENGLISH MILES

84° Long. E. of Greenwich

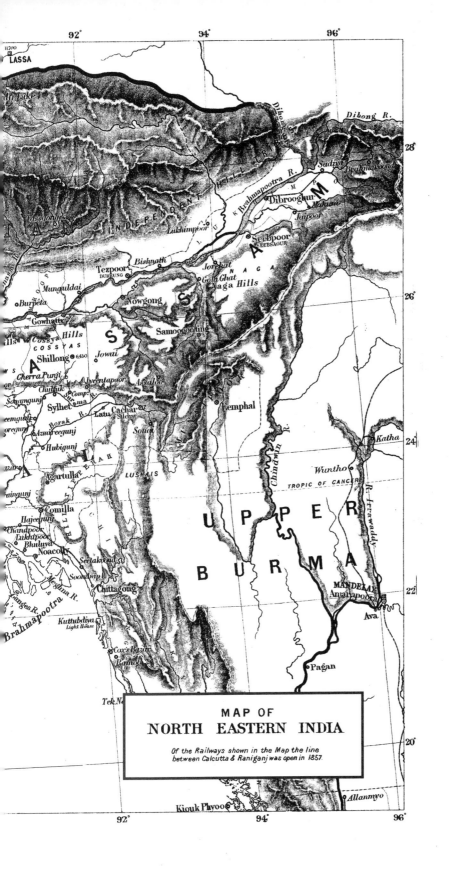

MAP OF
NORTH EASTERN INDIA

Of the Railways shown in the Map the line
between Calcutta & Raniganj was open in 1857.

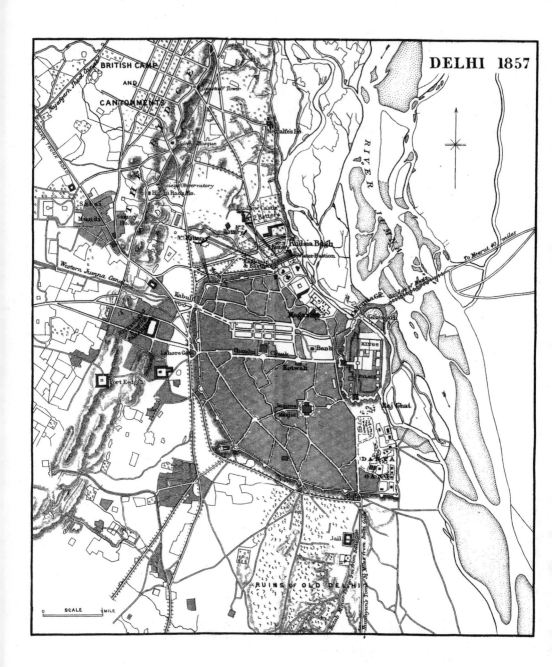

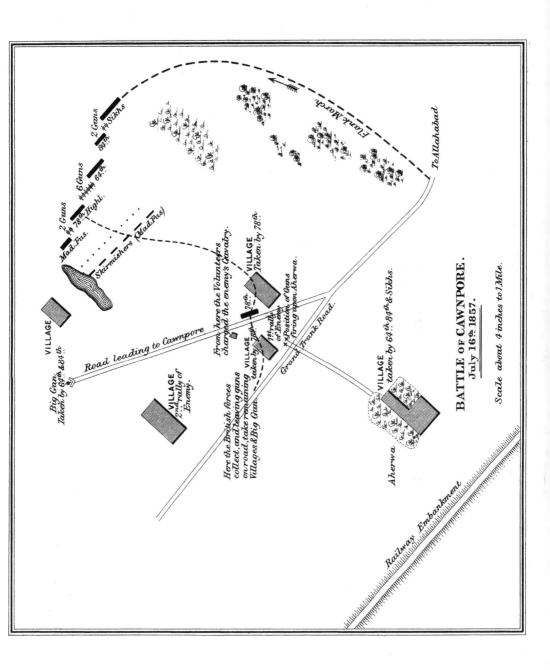

BATTLE of CAWNPORE.
July 16th 1857.

Scale about 4 inches to 1 Mile.

Flank March

To Allahabad

2 Guns ## Sikhs
82th
6 Guns ## 64th
2 Guns
Mad. Fus. 78th Highl.
Skirmishers (Mad Fus)

VILLAGE
Big Gun
Taken by 64th & 84th

Road leading to Cawnpore

VILLAGE
2nd rally of
Enemy.

VILLAGE
Taken by 78th

From here the Volunteers
charged the enemy's Cavalry.

78th
1st rally ×× Position of Guns
of Enemy firing upon Aherwa.
VILLAGE
taken by 78th.

Here the British forces
collect, and leaving guns
on road, take remaining
Villages & Big Gun.

Grand Trunk Road.

VILLAGE
taken by 64th 84th & Sikhs.

Aherwa

Railway Embankment

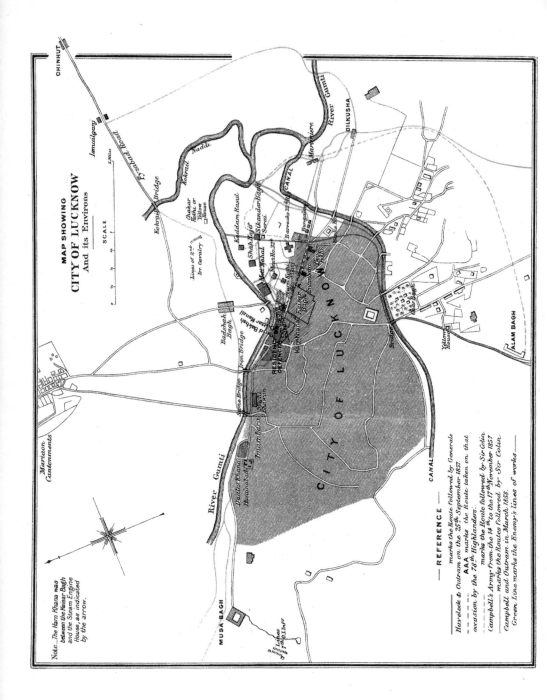

**MAP SHOWING**
**CITY OF LUCKNOW**
And its Environs

SCALE

— REFERENCE —

———— marks the Route followed by Generals
Havelock & Outram on the 25th September 1857.
AAA marks the Route taken on that
occasion by the 78th Highlanders:
–––– marks the Route followed by Sir Colin
Campbell's Army from the 14th to the 17th November 1857
———— marks the Routes followed by Sir Colin
Campbell and Outram in March 1858.
——— Green Line marks the Enemy's lines of works ———

Note. The Ham Khana was
between the Kaisar Bagh
and the Steam Engine
House, as indicated
by the arrow.

CITY OF LUCKNOW

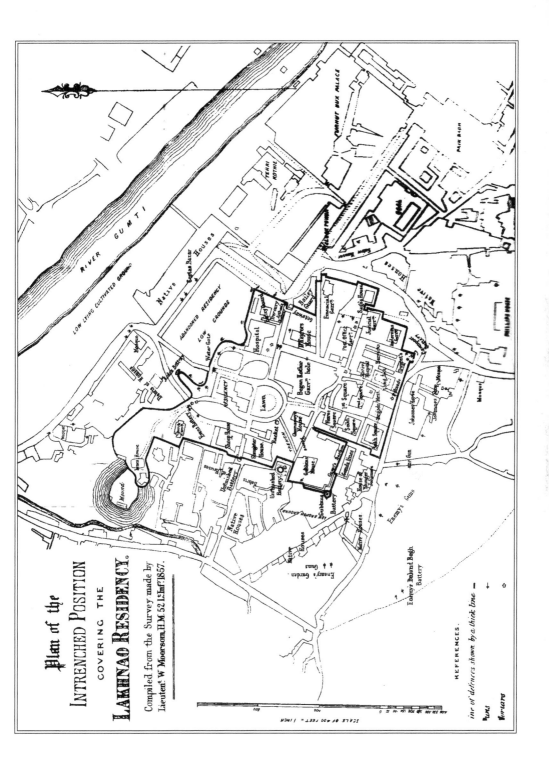

Plan of the
INTRENCHED POSITION
COVERING THE
LAKHNAO RESIDENCY.

Compiled from the Survey made by
Lieutenant W. Moorsom, H.M. 52 Lt.Infy. 1857.

SCALE OF 400 FEET = 1 INCH

REFERENCES.

line of defences shown by a thick line

Guns

Mortars

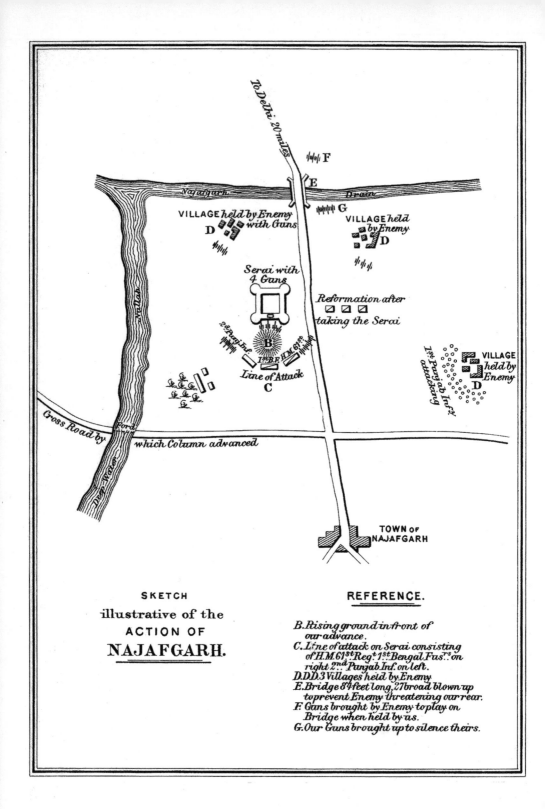

To Delhi 20 miles

F
E
Najafgarh   Drain
G

VILLAGE *held by Enemy*
*with Guns*
D

VILLAGE *held*
*by Enemy*
D

Serai with
4 Guns

*Reformation after*
*taking the Serai*

2ᵈ Punj Infy
B
1ˢᵗ B.F.  H.M. 61ˢᵗ

*Line of Attack*
C

1ˢᵗ Punjab Infy
attacking

VILLAGE
*held by*
*Enemy*
D

Nullah

Cross Road by   Ford
*which Column advanced*

Deep Water

TOWN OF
NAJAFGARH

SKETCH
illustrative of the
ACTION OF
NAJAFGARH.

REFERENCE.

B. *Rising ground in front of*
   *our advance.*
C. *Line of attack on Serai consisting*
   *of H.M 61ˢᵗ Regᵗ 1ˢᵗ Bengal Fusᵗˢ on*
   *right 2ⁿᵈ Punjab Inf. on left.*
D.D.D. *3 Villages held by Enemy.*
E. *Bridge 84 feet long, 27 broad blown up*
   *to prevent Enemy threatening our rear.*
F. *Guns brought by Enemy to play on*
   *Bridge when held by us.*
G. *Our Guns brought up to silence theirs.*

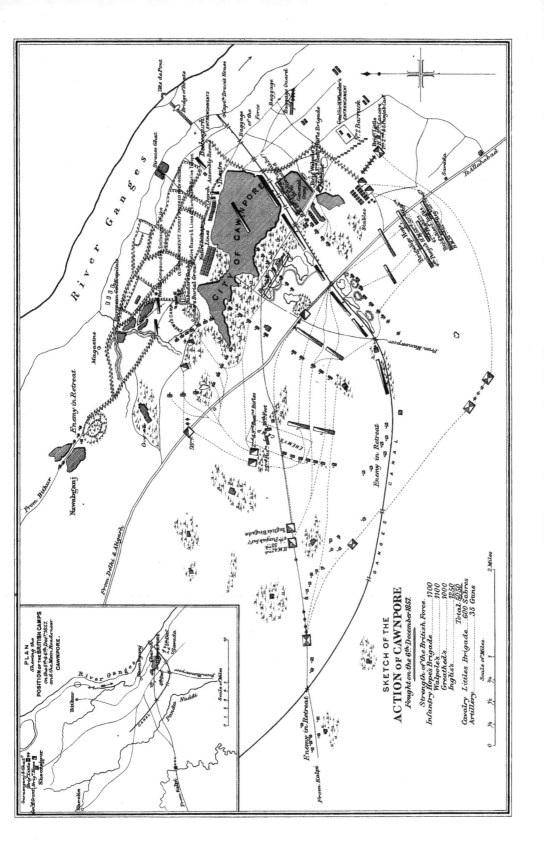

SKETCH OF THE
ACTION OF CAWNPORE
Fought on the 6th December 1857.

Strength of the British Force.
Infantry Hope's Brigade........1100
Walpole's........................1100
Greathed's.......................1000
Inglis's.........................1250
                    Total 4450
Cavalry Little's Brigade...600 Sabres
Artillery........................35 Guns

Scale of Miles

PLAN
Shewing the
POSITION OF THE BRITISH CAMPS
on the 5th & 6th Dec.r 1857.
and the Main Road near
CAWNPORE.

Scale of Miles

# Acknowledgements

For help and support during the preparation of this book, I am indebted first and foremost to my mother. Thanks are also due to staffs of PSW Alcester, Warwickshire, the National Army Museum and the British Library; to Patrick Mercer MP; Alan Waters; Ian Drury and Penny Gardiner, Weidenfeld & Nicolson; and for his kind permission to quote from the memoirs of Richard Barter, R. J. B. Snow.

# Author's Note

British and Indian regiments were all, in the mid nineteenth century, designated by number. British regiments can be recognized by the prefix HM (Her Majesty's) followed by their number, e.g. HM 86th Foot. Native regiments are indicated by a suffix: BNI (Bengal Native Infantry), e.g. 19th BNI, or NI. Regiments from the Bombay and Madras Presidencies have the Presidency name added in full, e.g. 24th Bombay NI.

# I

## Signs and Portents

'I wish for a peaceful term of office; but I cannot forget that in the sky of India, serene as it is, a small cloud may arise, no larger than a man's hand, but which, growing larger and larger, may at last threaten to burst and overwhelm us with ruin.'

So spoke Lord Canning, at the banquet given to him by the Court of Directors of the East India Company, prior to his departure for India to take up his post as Governor General. The Directors could be forgiven, in February 1856, when Canning took over from his predecessor, Lord Dalhousie, for thinking that his term of office would indeed be peaceful. The Honourable East India Company had arrived in India as traders in the seventeenth century, firstly in Madras, and later in Bombay – known as 'John Company' or 'Kampani Bahadur' to the natives (Bahadur being a title of respect implying courage). By the eighteenth century, with the anarchy that accompanied the decline of the Mogul Empire, the Company found itself fighting for survival against the French, and various native princes, themselves eager to profit from the weakening of the power of the Emperor at Delhi. To fight these wars the British relied largely on Indian troops – sepoys (from the Turkish '*sipahi*', meaning soldier) – whom they trained on European lines, using European weapons. Wars for survival turned to wars of conquest. After Robert Clive's victory at the Battle of Plassey in 1757, the British – in the form of the East India Company – gained Bengal, becoming, in effect, an Indian ruler, subject to the Emperor. Over the next hundred years the

Company, by a combination of intrigue, negotiation, treachery and, when occasion demanded, brute force (this last provided by its sepoy army, backed by smaller numbers of British troops), had become rulers of most of India. The Mogul Emperor, formerly a puppet of Maratha princes, became a puppet of the British. By the 1850s the Company had ceased trading altogether and existed solely to run the civil and military affairs of India, as agents of the British Government. The Government had the final say in the appointment of the Governor General, who ruled the Bengal Presidency from Calcutta and exercised authority over the governors of the two other Presidencies – Madras and Bombay.

The military situation, by 1856, seemed especially promising. After a disastrous incursion into Afghanistan in 1842, the British had settled for conquering northern India right up to the Afghan frontier, and maintaining good relations with its amir, Dost Mohammed. Humiliated in Afghanistan, the British had almost immediately annexed Scinde rather in the mood – as the conqueror of Scinde, Sir Charles Napier put it – of a man who, insulted in the street, goes home and kicks the cat. Then in two bloody and hard-fought wars, in 1845–6 and 1848–9, they had conquered the Sikhs – whose European-trained army, the *Khalsa* (meaning 'the Pure') had proved the equal of their own – and annexed the Punjab. The destruction of the *Khalsa* meant that the last independent native power was no more. The entire subcontinent from the mouths of the Ganges to the Indus was under the Company's *raj* (rule).

The East India Company's Bengal Army in 1857 (Bombay and Madras had their own armies) consisted of 151,361 men of all ranks, of whom the great majority – 128,663 – were Indians. The European troops – the Bengal Horse Artillery and the Bengal Fusiliers – were organized on similar lines to the regular British 'Queen's' regiments, and recruited from the Company's military headquarters at Warley, in Essex. As with the Queen's regiments, Ireland proved a fertile recruiting ground. The bulk of the Bengal Army, though, was made up of sepoys – serving in the seventy-five infantry regiments and ten of cavalry. These were men of warrior caste if they were Hindu (as roughly three-quarters of them were) and martial traditions, if Muslim. Writing in *The Indian Army* (1834) Sir John Malcolm, who had a lifetime's experience of Indian soldiering, wrote comparing the Bengal and Madras Dragoons:

The latter are all Mohammedans and a considerable proportion of the Bengal cavalry are of the same race. The fact is, that with the exception of the Mahratta tribe, the Hindoos are not, generally speaking, so much disposed as the Mohammedans to the duties of a trooper; and though the Mohammedans may be more dissipated and less moral in their private conduct than the Hindoos, they are zealous and high-spirited soldiers, and it is excellent policy to have a considerable proportion of them in the service, to which, experience has shown, they often become very warmly attached.

Of the Bengal infantry he wrote:

They consist largely of Rajpoots, who are a distinguished race among the Khiteree, or military tribe. We may judge of the size of these men when we are told that the height below which no recruit is taken is five feet six inches. The great proportion of the Grenadiers are six feet and upwards. The Rajpoot is a born soldier. The Mother speaks of nothing to her infant but deeds of arms, and every action and sentiment of the future man is marked by the first impressions that he has received. If he tills the ground – which is the common occupation of this class – his sword and shield are placed near the furrow, and moved as his labour advances. The frame of the Rajpoot is always improved (even if his habits are those of civil life) by martial exercises; he is, when well treated, obedient, zealous and faithful.

A warning note comes from Albert Hervey, a captain in the Madras Army, writing only a few years later:

Treat the sepoys well: attend to their wants and complaints; be patient and, at the same time, determined with them; never lose sight of your rank as an officer; be the same with them in every situation; show that you have confidence in them; lead them well, and prove to them that you look upon them as brave men and faithful soldiers, and they will die for you. But adopt a different line of conduct – abuse them; ill-treat them; neglect them; place no confidence in them; show an indifference to their wants or comforts – and they are very devils!

As well as cavalry and infantry, there was also a corps of Native engineers and a regiment of Native artillery. In addition to these there were twelve regiments of Irregular cavalry (men who provided their own horses and weapons) and various Irregular corps (Sikh battalions, Irregular horse, and cavalry recruited in the newly conquered Punjab), as well as 'Provisional' battalions recruited from the warlike hillmen, Gurkhas and Afghans, and the troops of the Oude and Gwalior contingents.

Each Native regiment had a full complement of European officers, shadowed by an equal number of Native officers, the senior of whom was junior to the newest-joined European subaltern. At its best, the relationship between officers and men was good. Sita Ram, who enlisted in the Company's army in 1812 and served until 1857, remembered: 'When I was a *sepoy* the Captain of my company would have some of the men at his house all day long and he talked with them. Of course many went with the intention of gaining something – to persuade the company commander to recommend them to the Colonel for a promotion, or to obtain this or that appointment in the regiment – but far more of us went because we liked the *sahib* who always treated us if we were his children.' In retrospect it seems like a golden age – with the colonel or captain seated on his verandah in the cool of the evening chatting happily with the '*baba logue*' or 'dear children' as they were known; and officers participating in Hindu ceremonies, piling their swords alongside the sepoys' muskets to be blessed by the holy man.

As the century progressed, however, problems began to emerge. Garrison life in India could be stultifying for a young man possessed of talent – detached service in an Irregular corps, or the civil service of Scinde, the Sutlej provinces or the Punjab, offered better pay, prospects for advancement and a more worthwhile existence. By 1857, one thousand officers of the Bengal Army were on detachment, weakening the bond between officers and sepoys. Those that remained were often the duller or less enterprising officers, who had come to India because it was the only place where they had any 'interest'. 'Interest' – friends or relatives in high places – was vital to an ambitious young man in the nineteenth century, and even to an unambitious one who wanted a comfortable life. Such men often hated India and its people. 'I regret much to say that it is too often the case that our European officers, and more particularly those in the junior ranks of the army, do not treat them as they should be treated,' wrote Captain Albert Hervey, an officer in the Madras Army. 'People come out to India with but very indifferent ideas regarding the natives. They think that because a man is black he is to be despised. And thus we find young officers, on first commencing their military career, talk about "*those horrible black nigger sepoys*" or some such expressions. They look down upon them as brute beasts; they make use of opprobrious language towards them; and lower themselves so far even as to curse and swear at them!' The arrival of increasing numbers of 'memsahibs' as the century progressed meant increased numbers of married officers who – retreating into domestic life – distanced themselves still further from their men. Promotion in the Bengal Army was strictly by seniority – so that many of its senior officers were long past the age at which they should have been pensioned off. William Hodson, a young officer who had served in the Sikh wars, wrote of his commanders: 'The officer who so disgraced the service at Chilianwallah was not able to mount a horse without the assistance of two men. A brigadier of infantry, under whom I served during the three most critical days of the late war, could not see his regiment when I led his horse by the bridle until its nose touched the bayonets; and even then he said faintly, "Pray, which way are the men facing, Mr Hodson?"'

Because it recognized that such old men were poor judges of efficiency, the Government had taken from them the power of promotion – among the Native officers, too, promotion was strictly by seniority. This had also lowered the prestige of the commanding officer in the eyes of his men. Nor was the sepoy in awe of the British soldier as he once had been – the defeat in Afghanistan in 1841–2 had seen to that – and it was whispered abroad that the Company's *iqbal* (luck) had deserted it. The British soldier may have enhanced his reputation by the defeat of the Sikhs and the conquest of the Punjab, but this too brought problems. Many British officers had noticed a tendency among the sepoys to hang back during the bitter fighting against the Khalsa – partly due to a long-standing fear of the Sikhs, partly, it was felt, due to a reluctance to see the last independent native state defeated. It was not that they loved the Sikhs – quite the contrary – but the conquest of the Punjab meant that Britain's forces in India could sheath their swords for lack of argument. If the sepoys were no longer needed in India, many thought, where would the sahibs want to use them next? The answer seemed obvious – overseas in Persia, China or Burma. To a high-caste Hindu, crossing the 'black water' was unthinkable – the common messing arrangements on board ship would make it impossible to avoid violating their caste, with its complicated eating arrangements. An indication of how strict these rules were is provided by an anecdote heard by Captain Maude of the Royal Artillery:

When we were in Madras in '54 we heard then the following story relating to caste as having quite recently happened there: 'A native woman was one day bringing the dinner for the Sepoys in Fort St. George. It consisted of a huge covered pot or saucepan full of cooked rice. There was a young European sentry at the Fort Gate, whose orders were to forbid the entry of any spiritous liquors. He stopped the woman and asked her what was in the saucepan. As neither party could understand the other, he lifted the lid and looked in. Whereupon the woman, knowing that his action had defiled the food, promptly threw it all in the Fort ditch, and so the poor fellows lost their dinner.'

In his first year of office, Lord Canning directed that all recruits for the Bengal Army should in future, like Madras sepoys, be attested on joining, with an obligation – taken under oath – to serve wherever they were required. This did not directly affect the men already in the ranks but – since service in the regiments was to a great extent hereditary – it would affect their families.

Curiously, these rules did not seem to have been as rigorously applied in the Madras Army. It was a commonplace among the British that Madras sepoys could be transported by sea. 'The Moslems and Hindoos in our part of India', wrote Albert Hervey of the Madras Army, 'are not so foolishly punctilious regarding their religious prejudices as are those of Bengal and Bombay. This is the advantage that the Madras Army has over those of the sister Presidencies. Our sepoys put aside those prejudices when the service is concerned, as an old *subadar* [native officer of a company] one day observed to me: "We put our religion into our knap-sacks, sir, whenever our colours are unfurled, or where duty calls."' Some allowance must be made for the natural prejudice of the officers of the Madras and Bombay Presidencies (the 'Mulls' and 'Ducks', as they were called) when discussing the 'Quai hai's' of the senior, Bengal, Presidency. One English traveller was told by a British officer of the Bombay Fusiliers that there were three things wrong with the Bengal Presidency: 'First the inferiority of the Bengal Horse Artillery system; second that the Benga-lees were guilty of the base effeminacy of drinking beer out of champagne glasses; third that in pig-sticking they threw the spear at the boar.' Even allowing for this rivalry it was generally agreed among senior officers that discipline in the Bengal Army had slackened – since 1833 Indian soldiers could not, like their British counterparts, be flogged – and that its sepoys, its 'dear children', were becoming spoilt children. 'They were petted and pampered like children,' wrote one observer, 'or as if they had been Praetorian cohorts, with whom it rested to bestow or withhold the imperial title and power. No wonder, then, that they became inflated with an idea of their vast importance, and considered themselves the real masters of the state. Their self-complacency gradually overstepped all bounds, and, like all mercenary armies, they threatened to become more formidable to their employers than to the enemy.'

Some of their grievances were real enough, though. Before, its annexation, service in desert Scinde, or the equally dry, dusty Punjab, was alleviated by extra allowances (*batta*) paid on active service or outside the Company's territory. After these states became British provinces the Government decided – with impeccable civil servants' logic – that as they were no longer outside the Company's territory, payment of *batta* should cease. The sepoys' reward for victory, then, was a substantial pay cut. Worse, the annexation of the Punjab brought new recruits into the army – the hated Sikhs. The sepoys of Oude or Rajputana regarded Sikhs as uncouth, smelly (because of the curds with which they dressed their long hair) savages. Yet, as was their way with peoples who had given their armies a hard fight, the British seemed to have taken to them. It was the same with the Gurkhas and Afghans who had started to appear in the Company's army – to some extent the anger of the sepoys was that of a spurned lover.

One annexation may be said to have done more damage than all the others – that of Oude in 1856. Oude – until then, outside British territory – was the home of 60 per cent of the Bengal Army's sepoys. Service in the Company's army gave an Oude sepoy and his family one highly prized privilege at home – in the courts. Native justice was slow, uncertain and corrupt. An Oude sepoy on furlough, however – or a member of his family – had a right of petition to the British Resident at Lucknow, which made that official, in effect, a powerful and influential advocate on his behalf. This right of petition was highly prized. When Sita Ram announced to his family that he wished to enlist, his mother was horrified – as a Brahmin, she wanted him to become a priest. His father, to Sita Ram's surprise, made no objections: 'At this particular period of which I now write a lawsuit was impending over my father, about his right to a mango grove of some 400 trees, and he thought that having a son in the Company Bahadur's service would be the means of getting his case attended to in the law courts of Lucknow; for it was well known that a petition sent by a soldier, through his commanding officer, who forwarded it to the Resident *sahib* in Lucknow, generally had prompt attention paid to it, and carried more weight than even the bribes and party interest of a mere subject of the King of Oude.' With the annexation of Oude, and the sending of the Nawab into exile in Calcutta, this right was abolished: English judges replaced native officials and the great advantage enjoyed by sepoys and their families disappeared. G. B. Malleson – later a historian of the Mutiny – was at Cawnpore, on the border of Oude, when the annexation took place: 'Never shall I forget the agitation which prevailed in the sipahi [sepoy] guard over my official quarters when the object of the expedition oozed out. Most of those forming it were Oude men, and I had to use all the influence I possessed to prevent an outbreak. My native subordinates in the Commissariat department assured me that a similar feeling was being manifested in the lines of the sipahis.' The annexation of Oude, he wrote, was felt by every sepoy to be a personal blow, 'because it deprived him of an immemorial privilege exercised by himself and his forefathers for years, and which secured to him a position of influence and importance in his own country'. From being a respected and privileged member of a warrior elite, it must have seemed to many sepoys that they were slowly being reduced to the status of that most despised of creatures – the British private soldier.

It was not just the army that was disaffected. Canning's immediate predecessor, Lord Dalhousie, had been a reformer – keen to bring to the peoples of India the benefits of modern Western notions of government. The Settlement Act introduced a new system of land taxation, which weakened the power of the *talukdars* (village headmen) who raised the money from the landholders, or *zamindars*. Many *talukdars* were also *zamindars* in their own right, and the system was complicated, haphazard and corrupt, with title to land often being based on weak or non-existent foundations. The British attempted to bring order and justice to this system, but reform brought resentment. If some among the peasantry benefited, others higher up the social scale lost out. The Rajah of Mainpuri, to quote just one example – a loyal servant of the Crown – lost 138 out of 189 villages, which his family had possessed for over a hundred years. Huey 'The Kingfish' Long, Governor of Louisiana, once quipped, 'One day the people of this state are gonna get good government – and they ain't gonna like it.' There were many in Upper India who weren't liking it now – a more just, more 'modern' system of landholding was no more popular with *talukdars* and *zamindars* than equality before the law had been to sepoys. On the part of both native civilians and sepoys this was to be essentially a conservative revolt; they wanted their old India – and their old army – left as it was.

The fact was that British India was increasingly being ruled by a new breed of men. The old breed – like the old generals now rightly regarded as long overdue for retirement – for all their faults, had one redeeming virtue: a sincere love for India and its ways. Many of them had taken Indian wives. A portrait of the distinguished soldier, Sir David Ochterlony – twice Resident at the Court of the Mogul Emperor at Delhi – shows him seated in native dress watching a nautch dancer, smoking his hookah, attended by some of his thirteen Indian wives. Only the portraits of red-coated relatives on the wall proclaim that this isn't a portrait of some Hindu rajah or Muslim nawab. True, there were still some – like Sir Henry Lawrence, formerly in the Punjab, soon to be at Lucknow – who were sympathetic to native sensibilities and urged the need for reform, if it must take place at all, to take place slowly. For the most part, though, the reformers were driven by contempt for all things native. Lord Macaulay described Hindu culture thus: 'Medical doctrines that would disgrace an English farrier – Astronomy, which would move laughter in girls at an English boarding school – History abounding in kings thirty feet high, and reigns thirty thousand years long, and geography made up of seas of treacle and oceans of butter.' It was his belief – and he was by no means alone – that Indians should be educated to create 'a class of persons, Indian in blood and colour, but English in taste, in opinions, in morals, and in intellect'. No doubt the reformers were sincere in their desire to bring good government to India's masses, but the potential effects of such rapid change on a deeply conservative people were largely disregarded. Western innovations such as the telegraph system, steamboats and the railways – designed to drag India into the nineteenth century – were often misunderstood, and regarded with deep and fearful suspicion.

For the Victorians, material and spiritual improvement went hand in hand. Until 1813, the Company had kept Christian missionaries out of the country, feeling that they were potentially a disruptive and divisive force. The Company had come to India to trade, with no notion of improving the locals. In that year, however, by the power of the Evangelical lobby in Parliament, the Company was forced against its better judgement to lift the ban. By 1833 – by which time the Company had ceased to trade altogether and was nothing more than the British Government's agent for running India – it had lost the power to license missionaries. The proliferation of missionaries and mission schools that followed led to the widespread belief among Indians that the ultimate aim of the British was to convert them all to Christianity. The ruthless suppression of Thuggee (a widespread cult, worshippers of Kali, who strangled and robbed travellers), human sacrifices and suttee (widow-burning) – practices that, however much feared and disliked, all had religious sanction – seemed to furnish proof of this. The actions of certain Evangelically minded Company officers – civilian and military – who preached openly to the natives in their charge, seemed to confirm it.

With the arrogance of power came forgetfulness of the foundations of that power – for to some extent India was ruled with the consent of those princes who had, for reasons of their own, allied themselves to the British or at the least acquiesced in their *raj*. Lord Dalhousie's removal of the Nawab of Oude on the grounds of his unfitness to rule must have seemed an alarming precedent. More alarming still was the Doctrine of Lapse – whereby the Company took it upon itself to annex princely states whose ruler died leaving no legitimate heir. Among Hindu rulers, adoption was commonly resorted to in order to ensure succession and the performance of all-important funeral rites, but the Company had ruled that recognition of adoption was an indulgence that 'should be the exception, not the rule, and should never be granted but as a special mark of favour and approbation'. Under the Doctrine of Lapse, the British had from 1842 to 1857 gathered in Satara, Sambalpur, the Punjab, Jhansi and Nagpur. Friendship, even alliance, with the British was, it appeared, no guarantee of safety to a native prince. By the 1850s a number of those formerly well-disposed to the British – notably the Rani of Jhansi and the Nana Sahib – were in protracted and bitter dispute with the Government over matters of inheritance.

The extent to which the events of 1857 were the result of an organized conspiracy remains a matter of debate. What is certain is that particular individuals had been actively subverting British rule. One such was Ahmed-Ullah, the Maulvi (learned man) of Faizabad. After the annex-ation of Oude this learned and charismatic holy man made a tour of what were then called the North-West Provinces of India, visiting Agra, Delhi, Meerut, Patna and Calcutta. When he returned to Oude in April 1857 he was arrested, found guilty of circulating seditious literature and preaching jihad against the British, and condemned to death. At the time of the Meerut outbreak he was awaiting execution in Faizabad. There is little doubt, also, that agents of the exiled King of Oude were active in that province, not least among the many thousands thrown out of employment by his deposition, and that some among the advisers of the Rani of Jhansi and the Nana Sahib were whispering that the time had come to sweep the British out of India.

It was a time of signs and portents. In the summer of 1856 the British authorities were puzzled by the emergence of the 'chapatti movement'. Starting, some said, in Delhi – though more probably in Oude – this took the form of messengers running from village to village. Each messenger would seek out the elder of the village and give him six chapattis, telling him to make six more and deliver them to the next village. This movement spread across Upper India throughout the year – the Indian Government had no organized intelligence service at the time, but those who enquired into the cause or meaning of the phenomenon could get no answers. Most natives seem to have been as ignorant of its meaning as the Europeans – after the outbreak, it was interpreted by the latter as a sort of 'fiery cross', a warning to the natives to ready themselves for rebellion, but not all were so sure. Robert Dunlop, a civilian administrator, was in no doubt: 'The transmission of little cakes from one district to another is supposed by the Hindoos to effect the removal of epidemic disease ... a similar transmission of cakes had taken place on a former occasion when a murrain attacked the cattle of the districts bordering Oude, and the disease was supposed to be stayed as the said cakes reached the holy flames of Hurdwar.' Dunlop maintained that most of the agitation taking place against British rule at this time was by Muslims and that the transmission of cakes was a Hindu practice, adding: 'Its real origin was, doubtless, a superstitious attempt to prevent any return of the fearful visitation of epidemic cholera which devastated the North-West Provinces the year before, and still lingered in scattered spots.' Whatever the truth – and Dunlop's was a minority opinion – both natives and those Europeans who were aware of the chapatti movement took it as a sign that something was about to happen.

More alarming was the distribution of lotus flowers – a Hindu symbol of war – among the sepoy regiments at about the same time. A man would come to the cantonment bearing a lotus flower and present it to the senior Native officer. The flower would then be passed from hand to hand in the regiment – each man would look at it saying nothing and then pass it on. When it reached the last man in the regiment he would take it on to the next military station. This occurred throughout the stations of the Bengal Army.

This was a tempest long foretold – by some. As early as 1844 Lord Hardinge, on arriving as Governor General, had declared that he had no apprehension about any enemy he was likely to encounter, except the Bengal Army. Sir Thomas Metcalfe, British Representative at Delhi, once said 'that some fine morning all the Europeans in India would get up with their throats cut'. There had been mutinies before – generally in the hot season when the men spent all day on their cots and the officers slept in their bungalows. At Vellore, in 1806, sepoys had mutinied over the issue of new leather headgear and the banning of religious face markings and jewellery – fourteen British officers and 115 enlisted men died before it was suppressed. At Barrackpore, in 1824, when sepoys of the 47th NI refused to march to the coast for embarkation for Burma, British troops fired on them and the regiment was dispersed and disbanded. Yet despite further mutinies in 1844, 1849, 1850 and 1852 – all of them, it should be said, isolated incidents involving individual regiments – the sepoy army was considered by most Europeans as being both the sword and shield of the Company's *raj* in India. Whether the Mutiny was the result of a well-organized conspiracy remains a matter of debate. Certainly there were many outside the Bengal Army who saw its discontent over pay and conditions, and its fears over religion, as the means to turn the *Gora Log*'s (Europeans') strongest weapon against them. That process had already begun – all that was needed now was a catalyst, and that was not long in coming.

It started – as explosions often do – with a cartridge. The cartridge in question was to fire the .577-inch bullet from the army's new Enfield rifle. This weapon had already been issued to British troops at home and to some in India. Its accuracy and power were a great improvement on the smoothbore 'Brown Bess' currently issued to most British and all Native troops in India. Tests with the smoothbore musket in 1841 had shown that its range varied from 100 to 700 yards – at 150 yards three shots out of four hit a target 12 feet by 3 feet. Beyond that no hits were scored. With the new Enfield, a reasonable shot could score a high percentage of hits up to 200 yards, could hit a target 6 feet square at 500 yards, and a target 8 feet square with every other shot at 1,000 yards. Preparations were now in hand to issue Native troops with the new rifle.

The problem with the Enfield, however, was that its rifled barrel made the cartridge harder to ram down the barrel. For this reason the cartridge was greased, and it was the nature of the grease – or what was thought to be its nature – that upset the sepoys. The problem first surfaced in January 1857, at the Bengal Army's musketry school at Dum Dum (later birthplace of the notorious expanding bullet) – 6 miles north-west of

Calcutta. A low-caste *classie* (workman) one day asked a Brahmin grenadier of the 2nd NI for a drink from his *lotah* (water pot). When the request was indignantly refused the *classie* replied, 'You think much of your caste but wait a little: the *sahib-logue* will soon make high and low caste on an equality; as cartridges smeared with beef fat and hog's lard are being made up in the magazine, which all sepoys will be compelled to use.' The very thought appalled both Hindu and Muslim soldiers – especially as the cartridge had not only to be handled, but also needed to have its wrapping torn between the teeth before it was rammed down the barrel. When Major Bontein, the officer in command at Dum Dum, paraded the troops there and asked if there were any objections, two-thirds of Native officers declared that the new cartridges were offensive to their religion.

The Government was not slow to react. General Anson, the commander-in-chief, instituted enquiries that suggested – in the case of the batches of ammunition sent from England – that there might well have been some truth in the story. He at once recommended that the Government send out no more made-up ammunition for the Enfields. From now on Native troops could buy beeswax and oil at the bazaars and grease their own cartridges. By then, however, the sepoys had noticed that the paper in which the new cartridge was wrapped had a glazed appearance. On 6 February General Hearsey, commanding the division at Barrackpore – 24 miles from Calcutta – reported to the Government: 'A most unreasonable and unfounded suspicion has, unfortunately, taken possession of the native officers and sepoys at this station, that grease, or fat, is used in the composition of this cartridge-paper; and this foolish idea is now so rooted in them, that it would, in my opinion, be both idle and unwise to attempt its removal.' The previous day a sepoy lieutenant, or jemadar (native lieutenant), of the 84th NI had told Lieutenant Allen of that regiment that the four Native regiments were ready to break out in open mutiny. He said he had been invited to a meeting for planning – and suggested that Allen come along and listen. Allen went down at the appointed time but could see no evidence of sedition. The jemadar said the meeting had been cancelled because of suspicions that the British were aware of the planned outbreak.

On 9 February General Hearsey paraded his men and spoke to them in his fluent Hindustani.

Energetically and explicitly I explained in a loud voice to the whole of the men the folly of the idea that possessed them – that the

Government and their officers, wished to interfere in their caste or religious prejudices, and impressed upon them the absurdity of their, for one moment, believing that they were to be forced to be Christians. I told them the British were Christians of the Book, *i.e.*, Protestants; that we admitted no proselytes but those who, being adults, could read and fully understand the precepts laid down therein; that if they came and threw themselves down at our feet, imploring to be made 'Book-Christians', it could not be done; they could not be baptised until they had been examined in the tenets of the Book, and proved themselves fully conversant in them; and then they must, of their own good-will and accord, desire to become Christians of the Book ere they could become so.

The Native troops had seemed satisfied with this declaration at the time, but two days later Hearsey was writing to Headquarters that the Europeans at Barrackpore were 'dwelling upon a mine ready for explosion'; after watching the sepoys he was convinced that 'their minds had been misled by some designing scoundrel'.

The next development took place at Berhampore – 116 miles north of Calcutta – on 24 February. Here a detachment of the 34th NI – known, in the manner of Indian regiments after its founding officer, as the *Bradshaw-ka-Pultan* – one of the regiments that had been harangued by Hearsey, marched in to Berhampore to form part of the garrison. As was traditional the regiment was welcomed and entertained by men of the 19th NI – the *Ung-ka-Pultan*. The following day, the 25th, Colonel Mitchell, the officer commanding, ordered an issue of ammunition. Although this was old ammunition – in blue paper, issued before the Enfield rifle was even heard of – the 19th refused to put it in their pouches. At length the regiment was intimidated by the presence of Native artillery and cavalry into accepting the ammunition, but that night the men burst open the huts where their weapons were kept and seized them – with shouts of defiance. Mitchell had no choice but to wait until morning when – in negotiation with the sepoys – he agreed to withdraw the still loyal artillery and cavalry if the sepoys would make submission.

The Commander-in-Chief, General Anson, an aristocratic British regular and Waterloo veteran who lacked Indian experience, was in Simla for the hot season. The Government, however, aware of the danger, immediately sent the Oriental Company's ship *Bentinck* towards the

Irrawaddy to fetch one wing (half a battalion) of HM 84th Foot back to India. Now having returned to their duty, the errant 19th NI were ordered down to Barrackpore – as were a wing of HM 53rd Foot (Shropshire) and two troops of European artillery. The previous Governor General, Lord Dalhousie, had pleaded that he would not be responsible for the safety of the Indian Empire if any more European troops were withdrawn from India. Despite this, four more regiments had been sent to Persia after he had left the country. There was now only one British to ten Native regiments between Calcutta and Agra.

Back at Barrackpore, troops of the 34th NI were openly declaring that the men of the 19th NI – now marching back to the station to learn their fate – deserved to be honoured, not punished, for their defence of their religion. On the evening of 29 March a soldier of this regiment – Mangal Pandy – intoxicated with *bhang* (Indian hemp) and other drugs, marched round the regimental lines armed with musket and sword calling on his comrades to revolt. The Adjutant, Lieutenant Baugh, and Sergeant Major Hewson moved to disarm him, calling on the guard to help but they, under their jemadar, merely looked on. Ducking behind a field gun, Pandy shot at Baugh and brought down his horse; Baugh fired his pistol at Pandy and missed. Before Baugh could draw his sword, Pandy rushed at him and cut him down with his *tulwar* (native sword). Sergeant Major Hewson rushed forward in time to stop Pandy finishing the officer off, but was himself knocked to the ground from behind with a musket by one of the guard. Both men were only saved by Baugh's orderly – a Muslim, Shaikh Paltu – who grappled Pandy by the waist and held him, while the two Europeans ran for their lives. One of the guard even shot at them, but missed. By now the commanding officer of the 34th, Colonel Wheler – one of those officers who considered it his Christian duty to convert his men – had arrived on the scene, as had Brigadier Charles Grant. Neither succeeded in restoring order. At length General Hearsey galloped up, accompanied by his two sons, both officers in Native regiments. Informed that the guard would not obey orders he answered, 'We'll see about that!' and rode over to them. A Native soldier warned him that Pandy's musket was loaded – 'Damn his musket', was Hearsey's reply, and to his son, 'If I fall, John, rush on him and put him to death.' He then pointed his cocked revolver at the guard and announced, 'Listen to me. The first man who refuses to march when I give the word is a dead man. Quick march!' As Hearsey, followed by a reluctant guard, advanced on him, Pandy – perhaps realizing his mutiny had failed –

turned his weapon on himself, wounding himself, but only slightly. The guard then carried him off to gaol.

The following day the jemadar of the guard and Pandy – whose name was to become the British nickname for all mutineers – were tried and hanged in front of the Native lines. When, on 31 March, the 19th NI arrived in Barrackpore they found HM 53rd and 84th Foot and two batteries of European artillery as well as the Governor General's Cavalry Guard drawn up on the parade-ground waiting for them. These stood on one side of the parade-ground, they and their comrades of the 34th NI stood on the other. The Governor General's sentence – that the 19th NI, which had been raised in 1776, was to be disbanded and its name struck from the Indian Army List – was read out. In the face of the European guns, the men piled their arms, handed over the regiment's dark green silk colours, and were given what pay they were owed. Many of the Native officers wept openly, while others protested that men of the 34th had subverted them and that they would willingly march against them if ordered. Many cheered General Hearsey as they left, for the leniency of their treatment – they had even been reimbursed for the cattle and boats that had brought them and their families down from Bharatpore. Their claim to have been led astray by the men of the 34th rings true – not one man of the *Ung-ka-Pultan* was ever, subsequently, found in arms against the Government.

No action was taken against the 34th NI at that time and it was generally felt that the worst had passed – a vessel was even chartered to take HM 84th Foot back to Rangoon. Incendiary fires, however, were now nightly occurrences at stations across Upper India, and the distribution of chapattis and lotus flowers continued unchecked.

On 24 April in Meerut – the 'pleasantest station in the Presidency' according to Hugh Gough – the skirmishers of the 3rd Light Cavalry, Gough's own regiment, were called out to learn the new loading drills. The regiment's colonel, George Monro Carmichael-Smyth, had ignored the urgings of a number of his officers not to hold such a parade. Lieutenant Craigie – who, with his wife, Lieutenant Mackenzie and Mackenzie's sister, were to end up hiding in a Hindu temple – wrote to the Adjutant the night before the parade: 'Go at once to Smyth and tell him that the men of my troop have requested in a body that the skirmishing tomorrow morning may be countermanded, as there is a commotion throughout the native troops about cartridges, and that the regiment will become *budnam* [disreputable] if they fire any cartridges ... We have none of the objectionable cartridges, but the men say that if they fire any kind of cartridge at present they lay themselves open to the imputation ... of having fired the objectionable ones.' Cornet John McNabb – whose mutilated body was later recognized by Hugh Gough only from his incorrect lace – wrote to his mother on the last morning of his life: 'There was no necessity to have the parade at all or to make any fuss of the sort right now. No other Colonel of Cavalry thought of doing such a thing, as they know at this unsettled time their men would refuse to be the first to fire these cartridges ... and that next parade season, when the row had blown over, they would begin to fire as a matter of course, and think nothing of it.' Carmichael-Smyth was an obstinate man, not overly or even adequately popular with his officers. He was also ambitious. Possibly he felt that if his regiment were the first to accept the new cartridges – and the 3rd were considered a crack regiment, 'the old and steady 3rd' – it would further his ambitions. Whatever his reasoning, he ignored his officers – arguing that to cancel the parade would be to show fear of the men – and the parade went ahead.

The skirmishers were an elite within any cavalry regiment, and Carmichael-Smyth was convinced that once informed that the drill had been amended – sepoys could now tear the end of the cartridges with their fingers rather than biting them – his men would obey. Ninety men were on parade that morning. When ordered to take three cartridges each, the men refused to do so. The Havildar-Major (Senior Native NCO) then showed the men the new drill. 'I then ordered the cartridges to be served out to the ninety men on parade,' wrote Carmichael-Smyth. 'The first man to whom a cartridge was offered said he would get a bad name if he took it. I said to him, "You see the Havildar-Major has taken and fired one." He replied, "Oh, the Havildar-Major!" in a manner to signify that his position obliged him to do it, adding, "If all men will take the cartridges, I will." He assigned no reason for not taking it, but still refused to do as I ordered him.' Carmichael-Smyth had no better success with the next man, or the next. Only five men – three Muslims and two Hindus, all NCOs – accepted the cartridges. The parade was dismissed, the Colonel rode off and the eighty-five men who had refused to take the cartridges were confined to their lines.

'Oh why did you have a parade?' said General Hewitt to Carmichael-Smyth on hearing the news. 'My division has kept quiet and if you had only waited another month or so, all would have blown over.' A court of inquiry was held the following day, and a week later – a week in which huts burned every night – the Judge Advocate General recommended a court martial. Held on 6, 7 and 8 May the court martial – fifteen Native officers, six Muslims and nine Hindus – found all eighty-five troopers guilty of mutiny. In contrast to the lenient treatment meted out to the 19th NI, the troopers were sentenced to ten years' imprisonment with hard labour. A recommendation for clemency on the grounds of the men's previous good character was rejected by General Hewitt, and on 9 May the division was paraded to see the sentence carried out.

The entire garrison – the 11th and 20th NI, the 3rd Light Cavalry, and the European troops HM 60th Rifles, the 6th Carabiniers, a troop of horse artillery, a company of foot artillery and a light field battery – were assembled in a hollow square formation on the European parade-ground. The European troops were armed and loaded. The prisoners were marched into the centre – their sentences were read out and they were stripped of their uniforms, their boots were removed and their ankles shackled. 'We *stood* for 2 hours and more while the sentence was being read, and the irons put on,' wrote Cornet McNabb in what was to be his last letter. 'When the sentence was read the men in the ranks behaved very well, with the exception of a few who wept for their brothers, and fathers among the mutineers. When the irons were put on they were marched past the whole parade, and when they passed us of course they began to cry, and curse the Colonel, and throw away their boots, almost at him, but they blessed Craigie, and called out that "they hoped he would be a prince and a Lord".'

It is hard to exaggerate the depths of this humiliation to men like these – not just cavalry troopers but followers of a proud and hereditary warrior tradition. These were men who had served the British in Afghanistan and charged alongside Her Majesty's 16th Lancers against the Sikh squares at Aliwal. Now they were stripped of all that made them men, paraded in chains like common criminals and condemned to work the roads like Untouchables. At the gaol there were heart-rending scenes. Hugh Gough went down after the parade, to settle the condemned men's pay.

Shall I ever forget the scene? It made the strongest impression on me, though I was but a thoughtless subaltern. We found our men imprisoned in one large ward; at first they seemed sullen or impassive, until it entered their comprehensions that it was all a sad reality, that they were now being paid up and discharged from an honourable service, into which as it were they had been born; for in those days the career of a soldier descended from father to son, and men were born into their profession – a profession which in the good old days of John Company was considered the most honourable a man could belong to; soldiers were held in the highest esteem in their villages, had prior legal rights to any others, and were looked up to by all ... Once they began to realise all they were losing, and the terrible future before them, they broke down completely. Old soldiers with many medals gained in desperately fought battles for their English masters, wept bitterly, lamenting their sad fate, and imploring their officers to save then from their future; young soldiers, too, joined in, and I have seldom, if ever, all my life experienced a more touching scene.

'When they were being paid,' wrote McNabb, 'one man said, "Oh give it to my wife", another, "Oh give it to my brother; what good is it to me; I am a dead man now."' Although horrified at what had happened to his regiment – 'It is a great pity that it has happened in my regiment ... and brought on us in such a useless manner. It is the *first* disgrace the regiment had ever had.' – Cornet McNabb was thankful that this dreadful business had happened where it did. 'It is lucky that this had happened in Meerut where there are so many European troops, for if it had been at a small station I would not have given much for the officers' lives. But here there are Cavalry, Infantry and Artillery, all English, who would cut them up in no time.' He could not have been more wrong.

# 2

# Meerut

On the afternoon of Sunday, 10 May 1857, Mrs Muter, as was her habit, was preparing to attend Evensong in the garrison chapel. Lieutenant Gough, as was his, was playing with his pet bear. They were in Meerut, in India's North-West Provinces, 'One of the pleasantest and most favourite stations in the Presidency,' as Lieutenant Gough wrote. 'There was a great deal of sport and gaiety, which all subalterns like, and I confess I took my full share of both. The regiments in the garrison were singularly sociable; and in the midst of fun and gaiety, which was to most of us the apparent object of life, there was little thought or apprehension of anything so serious as war breaking out. The Punjab had been completely pacified, our frontiers appeared unusually quiet, and, seeing all things the same around us, our martial spirit distinctly lay low.' At six o'clock, Mrs Muter, wife of Captain Muter of HM 60th Rifles, set off for the garrison church. It had been scorchingly hot from early in the morning, which perhaps explained why the native servants had mostly been conspicuous by their absence – both in barracks and private houses – for much of the day. Other than this there was nothing to suggest that it was anything other than a normal Sunday in this, one of Britain's largest garrison towns, or cantonments, 30 miles north of Delhi. True, there had been murmurings during and after the punishment of the eighty-five men of the 3rd Light Cavalry – one of the East India Company's Indian regiments – the day before, but it was felt that the incident was now closed and that the discontent among the sepoys would soon blow over.

Mrs Muter arrived at Meerut's garrison church at about 6.30 that evening:

> I . . . waited outside the door, expecting every moment to hear the sound of a gay march which so strangely heralds the approach of a body of soldiers to divine worship; but – I listened in vain. A dull sound, very different from that I had expected, came over the stillness of Nature; but I little heeded the holiday-making in the bazaars, holiday-making as I then thought it . . . A gentleman accosted me. 'You need not be alarmed, but an outbreak has taken place requiring the presence of the troops, so there will not be a service in the church this evening.' 'A slight disturbance would not stop the service,' I replied; 'therefore I will wait a little.' But when the clock struck seven, the hour to commence, and no congregation was assembling, I called to my friend and requested him to tell my husband, should he arrive, that he had advised me to return home. Up to this I was seated with my back to the cantonment in a little pony carriage, but the moment the horses' heads were turned I saw the Native lines in a blaze, and in some alarm, but not in the least understanding the gravity of the position, I gave the order to hasten home.

Driving back to her bungalow, Mrs Muter 'beheld the horizon on fire as if the whole cantonment were in flames. Entering the broad road that leads to the bazaar I saw it was crowded with men. Two of the European Artillery were hurrying up, pursued by a throng of natives hurling everything they could get at the wounded and unarmed Englishmen. So intent were they on this occupation that I was allowed to pass unhindered into a road leading to my house.'

As Mrs Muter had been setting off, Lieutenant Hugh Gough – as orderly officer – had been dressing for duty. The first he knew of the native lines being on fire was when his servants told him. Moments later a Native officer of his own regiment – the 3rd Light Cavalry – came galloping up accompanied by two orderlies crying that the sepoys were killing their officers and that the sowars (Native cavalry) were arming and mounting. At once Gough mounted his own horse and, with the officer and the two men, rode off towards the 3rd Light Cavalry's lines. On the way they passed the lines of the 20th BNI:

> These lines, usually a scene of perfect discipline and neatness, with rows of mud barracks neatly thatched, with the quarter-guard ready to

turn out, and with groups of well-dressed and happy contented sepoys lounging about, were now the scene of the most awful confusion; the huts on fire, the sepoys (in each regiment over a thousand strong) having seized their arms and ammunition, dancing and yelling to each other, and blazing away into the air and in all directions – suddenly a maddened crowd of fiends and devils, all thirsting for the blood of their officers, and of Europeans generally.

Seeing the white officer riding past, some of the sepoys fired a ragged volley in his direction – without effect – so Gough led his party down towards his own regiment's lines.

A comrade of Gough's, young Lieutenant Mackenzie, also of the 3rd Light Cavalry, had not gone to church that evening: 'I was quietly reading a book in my own bungalow when my bearer Sheodeen suddenly rushed into the room, declaring that a *hulla-goola* (in our vernacular a riot) was going on in the lines, that the sepoys had risen, and were murdering the Sahib logue [people]. Not for an instant did I believe the latter part of his story, even though the frequent and rapid reports of fire-arms, which broke the quiet of the Sabbath evening, made only too clear the truth of the first.' Mackenzie assumed that the noise was the result of regimental rivalry: 'The thought that flashed through my mind was that our men of the cavalry were attacking the native infantry in revenge for the sneers with which we all knew these others had freely, since the punishment parade, lashed their submissive apathy in witnessing, without an attempt at rescue, the degradation of their comrades. Sooth to say – so strong is the tie of camaraderie – my sympathies were all in the wrong direction; and I would secretly have rejoiced to have seen the insult avenged.'

Putting on his uniform and sword and mounting his horse, Mackenzie rode down towards the regimental lines. The first thing he saw was the regiment's English quartermaster sergeant running up the road from his house in the lines:

'Oh God, sir!' he exclaimed, 'the troopers are coming to cut us up!' 'Let us then stick together,' I answered; 'two are better than one.' For a moment he hesitated. Then, looking back, the sight of a small cloud of dust rapidly approaching from the distance overcame his resolution, and he rushed through the gate into the grounds of my bungalow, and scaled the wall between them and those of the next house. Instantly a small mob of *budmashes* (rascals), prominent among whom I recognised my own night watchman, attacked him. The chowkidar thrust at him with his spear as he was crossing the wall, and cut open his lips. To my joy he fired one barrel of a gun which he carried with him, and shot the brute dead. He then dropped on to the ground on the other side, and disappeared from view ... I rejoice to say he escaped with his life.

If, like most of the British officers of the Company's army, Mackenzie still held to his belief in the loyalty of 'Jack Sepoy', he was swiftly disillusioned:

At this moment an infantry sepoy, armed with a sword, made a sudden swoop with it at my head. I had not drawn my sword, and had only time to dig a spur into my horse's flank, and force him almost on to my enemy. This spoilt his stroke, and his *tulwar* fortunately missed its aim, and only cut off my right shoulder cord. By this time I had pulled my weapon out of its scabbard, but the sepoy declined any further swordplay, and promptly climbed out of a wall out of my reach. As I turned from him and looked down the road to the lines, I saw that it was full of cavalry troopers galloping towards me.

These were Mackenzie's own men. He had seen *badmashes* – the scoundrels and the scum of the bazaars – attack the sergeant and had had a close encounter himself with an infantryman of another regiment, but surely his own troopers could be trusted?

Even then it did not occur to me that they could have any hostile intent towards myself, so I shouted to them to halt. This they did, and surrounded me; and, before I knew what was happening, I found myself warding off, as well as I could, a fierce onslaught from many blades. A few moments would have sealed my fate, when, providentially ... Lieutenant Craigie emerged from his gate a little further down the road, and came straight to my help. The diversion saved me. The troopers scattered past us, and made off towards the European lines. It was only too clear now that a mutiny, and that of the most serious kind, was in full swing.

Meanwhile, Hugh Gough had actually reached the 3rd Light Cavalry's lines. 'There I found everything in the utmost disorder: the men had thrown off all control and discipline, and were wildly excited; most of them were mounted and were galloping to and fro, the lines were being burnt, and there was a general rush to the magazine, where the men helped themselves to the ammunition – regardless of it being the "unclean cartridge". As for any efforts to bring them to a sense of their duties or obedience to my orders, they were absolutely useless.' Gough had always been a popular officer, and at first his men were content simply to ignore his shouted orders: 'After a time, however, the disregard of my authority changed to open mutiny; there were shouts of "Maro, Maro!" ("Kill him, kill him!") and a few men, chiefly recruits, fired pistol shots at me.' The officer and orderlies who had accompanied him down to the lines urged him to leave, as did a number of his sowars who, while still refusing to obey his orders, seemed reluctant to kill him. 'Seeing all was lost, and that my power as an officer was absolutely gone, and acting on the earnest, in fact forcible, solicitation of the better disposed (for they took my horse's head and forced me to leave), we decided to make the best of our way to the European lines.' Gough and his three companions rode off pursued by the angry shouts of the men who, twenty-four hours earlier, it had been his pride to command.

Gough's road to the European lines – where there was safety behind the bayonets of HM 60th Rifles and the guns of the European-recruited Bengal Horse Artillery – took him through the native bazaar, which, he found, 'such was the singularly unanimous outbreak of fanatical and race feeling – was up in arms; the roads were covered with foes, and we had literally to cut our way, pelted with stones, through hundreds of men, armed with *tulwars* and *lathies* [iron-bound cudgels]. But our speed saved us and we got through safely, though bruised and beaten.' Gough recalled his shock at seeing 'the very hell of fury and hatred through which we passed – men who had hitherto always salaamed to almost all Europeans now thirsting for their blood!'

Instead of going straight to the European lines, Gough rode to the house of Mr and Mrs Greathed, the civilian Commissioner and his wife. An angry mob was already swarming up the road from the bazaar, intent on murder. The Greatheds' servants assured Gough that their master and his memsahib had already fled. In fact, they had concealed them on the roof – reckoning that they were safer there than anywhere else. As Gough rode off the Greatheds watched him go, wondering whether their servants could be trusted, or whether they might turn them over to the mob and join in the looting themselves. They need not have worried – as the mob set fire to the house, one servant pretended to betray his master and led the crowd off in the wrong direction, while others escorted the Greatheds to safety.

Meanwhile, Gough made his way,

> still escorted by my loyal native officer and his two sowars, to the Artillery lines, where having brought me in safety, they made their final salute and left me, notwithstanding my earnest entreaties and persuasions that they should remain with me – the native officer averring that his duty was with his regimental comrades, and whether for life or death they must return to the regiment ... A braver or more loyal man I have never met, and, whatever his faults may have subsequently been, in his mutiny against his salt and his military allegiance, all will allow his loyalty to me was beyond praise, and I can never forget him, or how he risked his life again and again to save mine.

Hugh Gough had learned what many were to learn that night, and many more in the weeks and months to follow across northern India – that the carefully nurtured bond between Indian sepoys and their British officers had been shattered. The officers of the 20th NI had been the first to discover this terrible truth. A number of them had been sitting talking in their commanding officer's bungalow when they had been called down to the native lines. The prostitutes of the bazaar had been taunting the sepoys with their failure to defend their religion and free their comrades. The sepoys had replied that they were going to mutiny that evening and kill every European on the station. Soon a rumour swept the lines that the European troops were coming to disarm them. The arrival of a crowd of *badmashes* from the bazaar fanned the flames, and by the time the officers arrived on the scene it was already out of control. Ordered to disperse the mob, the grenadiers of the 20th NI refused to move. Moments later a trooper of the 3rd Light Cavalry rode into the lines shouting that the British were coming. At once the sepoys broke open the bells of arms and commenced firing their muskets wildly in all directions. Colonel Finnis (the brother of the then Lord Mayor of London), the commanding officer of the 11th NI, rode over from his regiment's lines in an attempt to restore order. As he harangued the men of the 20th he was shot in the back, fell, choking, from his horse and was hacked to pieces. Within minutes the 11th, too, were up in arms. The officers of both regiments – many of whom had wives and children who were now their first concern – then fled, some spared by their own men who held their fire and urged them to run.

There followed scenes of slaughter that were to embitter the conflict that followed and affect relations between Indians and British for much of the rest of the century. Neither age nor sex nor rank was spared the fury of the mutineers. The commanding officer of the 20th and six of his officers hid in a latrine in the grounds of the bungalow of Colonel Carmichael-Smyth, of the 3rd Light Cavalry – all were discovered and slaughtered. Having escaped the sabres of the 3rd Light's troopers, Lieutenants Mackenzie and Craigie's thoughts turned, like those of many others that night, to their loved ones. As Mackenzie wrote:

> Our duty was plain, though very hard to perform, for at this moment Lieutenant Craigie's wife and my sister were on their way together in his carriage to the church, situated in the European lines, and our first natural impulse was to gallop after them. But they had started some little time previously, and we hoped that they had already reached their destination, and were in safety among the British troops. Military discipline sometimes tries a soldier to the utmost; and now we felt that wife and sister must be left in the hands of God, and that our place was among the mutineers on the parade-ground.

In fact, the two young ladies on their way to church had encountered an English soldier – of the 6th Dragoon Guards – running for his life towards them, pursued up the road by a howling mob of natives. At great personal risk the two women halted their carriage, dragged the man in and, as the rioters beat at the sides of the vehicle with *lathies*, galloped off down the road in the direction of the Craigies' bungalow. The crowd pursued them on foot for some distance, slashing at the hood with their *tulwars*, before being shaken off.

Back at the Craigies' bungalow the two women found Lieutenant Craigie's weapons – three double-barrelled guns – and placed them to be at hand when, or if, the menfolk returned. They did not load the guns – they did not know how, and the soldier they had rescued was in a state of nervous collapse. After that there was nothing they could do except watch as bungalow after bungalow went up in flames as the mob drew nearer. Soon they were watching in helpless horror as first the stables and then the house of their immediate neighbour, Captain Chambers, adjutant of the 20th NI, were torched. Charlotte Chambers – one of the beauties of the station and heavily pregnant – was forced out on to the verandah by the flames, where her throat was cut by a Muslim butcher, whom she had a few days earlier reprimanded for supplying bad meat. As a final horror the man cut her unborn baby from her body and laid it upon her chest. Moments later the mob was clamouring at their own gates.

Meanwhile, Mrs Craigie's husband and Miss Mackenzie's brother – true to their duty – had reached the parade-ground of the 3rd Light Cavalry: 'We ... found ourselves in a scene of the utmost uproar,' wrote Mackenzie. 'Most of the men were already mounted, and were careering wildly about, shouting and brandishing their swords, firing carbines and pistols in the air, or forming themselves into excited groups. Others were hurriedly saddling their horses, and joining their comrades in hot haste.' There seems to have been a reluctance to kill their own officers on the part of many, though not all, mutineers – Colonel Finnis, the only officer of the 11th NI to die, was shot by men of the 20th. Enough of the officer–soldier bond survived in this army to ensure that in many cases officers, especially popular ones, were spared. This was the case with the 3rd Light. Mackenzie recalled:

Nearly every British officer of the regiment came to the ground, and used every effort of entreaty, and even menace, to restore order, but utterly without effect. To their credit be it said the men did not attack us, but warned us to be off, shouting that the Company's Raj was over for ever! Some even seemed to hesitate about joining the noisiest mutineers; and Craigie, observing this, was led to hope that they might be won over to his side. He was an excellent linguist, and had great influence among them, and eventually managed to get some forty or fifty troopers to listen to him and keep apart in a group.

Hearing that the gaol was being attacked and the prisoners released, Craigie and another officer, Lieutenant Melville Clarke, led the troopers off towards the scene. Mackenzie rode with them: 'The roads were full of excited natives, who actually roared approbation as we rode through them, for they evidently did not distinguish in the dusk the British officers, and took the whole party for a band of mutineers.' Nearing the gaol, the party broke into a gallop:

Already the sepoys and the mob had begun their destructive work. Clouds of smoke on all sides marked where houses had been set on fire

... I was horror-struck to see a palanquin-gharry – a sort of box-shaped venetian-sided carriage – being dragged slowly onwards by its riderless horse, while beside it rode a trooper of the 3rd Cavalry, plunging his sword repeatedly through the open window into the body of its already dead occupant, an unfortunate European woman. But Nemesis was upon the murderer. In a moment Craigie had dealt him a swinging cut across the back of the neck, and Clarke had run him through the body. The wretch fell dead, the first sepoy victim at Meerut to the sword of the avenger of blood.

Craigie's killing of the trooper angered the men who had until now followed him: 'Shouts of "Maro! Maro!" ("Kill him! Kill him!") began to be heard among them, and we all thought the end was approaching. However, none of the men attacked us, and in a few minutes we reached the gaol, only to find that we were too late. The prisoners were already swarming out of it; their shackles were being knocked off by blacksmiths before our eyes and the gaol guard of native infantry, on our riding up to it, answered our questions by firing at us ... there was nothing to do but ride back to the cantonment.'

Mackenzie now obtained Craigie's permission to go and look for his sister and Craigie's wife: 'I lifted my sword and shouted for volunteers to come to save my sister, and some dozen of them galloped after me. As hard as our horses would gallop we tore along. Every house we passed was in flames, my own included and my heart sank within me.' Craigie's house alone was not burning when he reached it – a large double-storeyed building, in very extensive grounds, surrounded, as was then usual, by a mud wall. The mob that had stormed the gates and swarmed over the mud wall while Mrs Craigie and Miss Mackenzie cowered in the house and prepared themselves for death, had been halted temporarily by the household servants who ran to confront the crowd, waving their arms and shouting to them to remember what kind of man Craigie was – a 'friend of the people' they called him. The delay was just sufficient for Mackenzie and his troopers to come galloping into the compound. 'I ... brought the ladies down to the door of the house,' wrote Mackenzie, '... and calling to me the troopers commended their lives to their charge. It is impossible to understand the swift torrents of feeling that flood the hearts of Orientals in periods of intense excitement. Like madmen they threw themselves before the ladies, seizing their feet, and placing them on their heads, as they vowed with tears and sobs to protect their lives with their own.' This incident is just one of many – that night and later – that show the confused state of mind of so many pulled in different directions by ties of caste, religion, comradeship and soldierly loyalty. The same men who minutes earlier had been about to kill Mackenzie – crying '*Maro! Maro!*' – now swore, and swore sincerely, to defend his sister with their lives.

Although their ordeal was far from over, the Mackenzies, brother and sister, and the Craigies were among the lucky ones – others died horribly. Amelia Courteney, the wife of the hotelkeeper at Meerut, was murdered in her carriage as she rode to church, as was the unknown lady in the *palkhi-gharry*, whom Craigie had so swiftly avenged. Another neighbour of the Craigies, Mrs Captain Macdonald, whose husband had already been shot on the parade-ground of the 20th NI, was smuggled out of her house – with her children – by her servants. The *ayah* (children's nurse) and the *dhobi-wallah* (laundryman) hid her in a hut and gave her and the children native clothes – then the *chowkidar* (watchman) escorted them in the direction of the Artillery School in the European lines. When they were stopped by a crowd the *chowkidar* bravely asserted that Mrs Macdonald was his sister-in-law, but the covering was removed from her face and, as the servants bustled the children to safety, she was murdered. Lieutenant Mackenzie's housemate John McNabb was hacked to death by *badmashes* from the bazaar. McNabb had ridden to church with Hugh Gough that morning, and both were dressed in regimental frock coat and white overall trousers. McNabb's coat had the wrong kind of lace – Gough had pointed it out to him, warning him not to let the Colonel see it. After church McNabb had gone to visit friends in the artillery lines, returning home via the bazaar. It was only by his great height and incorrect lace that his badly lacerated body could be identified. Two veterinary-sergeants attached to the 3rd Light Cavalry were murdered. One of them, Veterinay Sergeant Dawson, and his wife were both in bed with smallpox. As the mob approached, they came on to the verandah of their home in their night-clothes. Dawson fired a shot into the crowd before being shot dead, but the mob, being too afraid of infection to attack Mrs Dawson, threw lighted firebrands at her until her clothes caught fire.

Mrs Douglas Muter, meanwhile, having avoided the mob chasing the two artillerymen, arrived at her house: 'Our servants were assembled at the gate in a flutter of alarm, the Khansamah (answering to a house steward) at their head. He declared he could no longer be responsible for any property, and bringing the silver in use, he returned it to my charge. At the same time he advised me to conceal myself – a proposal I regarded as an insult.' Before she could be insulted any further, her conversation with her servants was interrupted by a sergeant of her husband's regiment, HM 60th Rifles. The sergeant had been sent by her husband 'with directions for me to proceed to the Quarter Guard. He told me the Native force had broken into revolt, that they were shooting down every European they met, and that the English troops were moving on the bazaars.' Mr Muter's servants, commanded by her *khansamah*, now surrounded her with drawn swords and escorted her to the safety of the European lines where the British regiments were now assembling.

Mrs Muter's story was not, as we have seen, an isolated incident. Amid the horrors of the Meerut massacres, in which, by sunrise, some fifty European men, women and children had been slaughtered, there are numerous stories of natives – servants or sepoys, townsmen or villagers – risking their lives to save the lives of fugitives. Some no doubt acted out of a conviction that the British would soon restore order, or in hope of eventual reward; others, however, saved European lives despite believing that the Company's *raj* was ended forever. Mrs Muter's *khansamah*, for example, having gone to great lengths to escort her to safety, 'made me a grand salaam, and on his return to our bungalow, though in ordinary times scrupulously honest . . . he forced open some cases recently soldered, preparatory to our intended departure for the Hills, believing that neither Colonel Muter nor I would ever return alive to the house, and proceeded to make a selection from the contents'.

The slaughter was not confined to Europeans. For many among the native population, this was an opportunity to settle old scores. Anglo-Indians and Indian Christians were slaughtered, too, as well as those – such as the moneylender class, the *banias* – who were perceived as having done well out of British rule, and Native Government officials. Gungapershad, the *tehsildar* (native tax collector) of the Meerut District, who had had an English education at the Government College at Bareilly, was conducting business in his office when he heard that the sepoy regiments were mutinying, but he refused to believe it. Soon, however, he saw a crowd coming from the city: 'A 3d Cavalry trooper was seen proceeding at full gallop towards the new gaol. He was heard saying, "Brothers! Hindoos and Mussulmans! make haste to join with us in the religious war to which we are going." Then another followed, and in a very short interval some fifty passed, all going towards the new gaol, and a good number of sepoys accompanied them.' As a Government official, Gungapershad stuck to his post armed with a sword and rifle, and watched as the house of a Mr Blunt and the Civil Court were looted and burned. Then the mob – troopers, sepoys, *badmashes* and released prisoners – turned its attention to him:

First two of the 3d Cavalry Sowars advanced towards the Tehsil, and enquired where I, the Tehsildar, was, and on being pointed out, they threatened me, and demanded the keys of the Treasury, which I refused, when they advanced with drawn swords towards me. I shot one of them with my rifle, and loading again from behind the wall, I also shot the other. When their comrades saw them falling, the whole gang, some hundreds, rushed in shouting 'Ali! Ali!' and 'Nare Hyduree!' with drawn swords and muskets, and then I saw resistance was of no use, and everyone ready to kill me. I jumped down the Tehsil wall, and, taking flight, concealed myself in the house of a native gentleman. Here I heard they looted the Tehsil Treasury, and my house and the Tehsil; burnt my English books, maps, property and instruments, and all Government records and papers, the Commissioner's (the late Mr Greathed's) house, the Civil Court, and in fact all the adjoining public buildings.

Back at the Craigie house, Lieutenant Mackenzie had taken his sister and Mrs Craigie upstairs and loaded the guns: 'One of them I placed by itself against the wall. Long afterwards in quiet England, my sister ... told me that both she and Mrs Craigie well understood the sacred use to which that gun was, in the last resort, devoted, and that the knowledge comforted and strengthened them.' All around them were the sounds of burning timber, the yells of the mob and the rattle of musketry – the whole scene being lit by the flames of the houses all around: 'As I stepped out on to the upper verandah I was seen by some of the mob who were wrecking the opposite house. "There is a feringi!" they cried; "let us burn this big *kothi*! [house]." And several of them ran forward with lighted brands to the boundary wall; but on seeing my gun levelled at them they thought better of it and recoiled. More than once this happened. It seemed only a matter of time before our house should be set on fire at one point or another.' With this in mind Mackenzie prepared to move with the ladies to a small, strongly built Hindu shrine: 'If I could only get my charges and the guns and ammunition safely across the open space between us and that building, I felt sure of being able to hold out till help should come; for surely help would soon come! Were not the 6th Dragoon Guards, the 60th Rifles, and the Horse Artillery Batteries within a couple of miles?' As Mackenzie was pondering this Lieutenant Craigie arrived, having escaped with one or two other officers from the parade-ground, 'carrying with them the now forever-disgraced standards of the regiment'. Together Craigie, Mackenzie, the two ladies and the Carabinier they had rescued now ran across to the shrine. Safe at least from being burnt out in this 10-foot-square stone building with loophole-like slits for windows, they awaited their fate. The troopers who had so far protected them were growing more restless:

> A young recruit who had, not long previously passed the riding school in the same squad with myself, presently came to me as I was standing among a group of the men outside our stronghold . . . and warned me to beware of the havildar-major, who had, he said, at that moment, been urging the others to kill me. It may well be imagined that I took very good care afterwards to keep a watchful eye on that non-commissioned officer, and to let him see by a touch of my hand on the hilt of my sword that I was quite ready for any suspicious movement on his part. Soon afterwards he and a few other rode out of the gate and we saw them no more.

Shortly afterwards one of Craigie's servants came up to the shrine to report that a crowd of *badmashes* were coming in at the gate: 'He implored us to give him one of the guns, and let him go fire at them. Whether wisely or not, we did so; and almost immediately afterwards we heard a report, followed by yells and groans. In a few moments the bearer returned, and gave us back the gun, saying that he had fired into "the brown" of the advancing mob, and brought one of them down, and the rest had fled.' Hour after hour they waited, but no help came. At last, with the uproar around them dying down, they saddled up the Craigies' carriage and, placing the ladies and the carabinier inside with the guns and riding alongside themselves with drawn swords, they galloped out of the compound, sweeping through a hesitant group of troopers and over the body of the man the faithful servant had shot, 'who was afterwards identified as a Mussulman butcher, a class of men who were among the most bloodthirsty actors on that night'. After a helter-skelter dash across the plain that separated the Native cantonment from the European lines, the party spied the light of a port-fire – used to ignite the charge of an artillery piece – near the stables of the Carabiniers:

> Craigie and I galloped forward, shouting 'Friend! Friend!' at the utmost stretch of our lungs. And well it was we did so: for we found, at a point where a bridge crossed a nullah [ditch], a picquet with a gun trailed up the road; and the subaltern in command told us he was on the point of firing at our rapidly approaching group when our voices reached him. At last – with deep gratitude – we felt that our dear ones were once more safe among our own countrymen. The wife of a sergeant of the carabineers very kindly gave the ladies shelter for the rest of the night; and Craigie and I shifted for ourselves *al fresco*.

Craigie and Mackenzie had not been the only ones looking to the European lines for rescue. Meerut had the biggest European garrison in India; many who died that night must have done so while waiting to hear what Mrs Muter described as 'the heavy tramp of an English battalion on the march, which can be distinguished at once from the movement of any other body by one accustomed to the sound'. So what had the British garrison been doing while the sepoys and sowars rose in arms and the mobs ran riot? As soon as he had heard of the outbreak Brigadier Archdale Wilson – a man already looking forward to his retirement – had ordered the artillery and the Dragoon Guards to parade on the parade-ground of HM 60th Rifles. The Dragoon Guards (the Carabiniers) – a regiment that contained a high proportion of half-trained recruits, only half of whom possessed broken horses – the artillery, also mainly recruits, and the 60th Rifles, a first-class regiment at full strength, were soon assembled and ready for action. The artillery ammunition had been secured by Lieutenant Alfred Light, who commanded the depot of the Bengal Horse Artillery – an entirely European unit, largely composed of Irishmen. It was the practice in India at the time for all important posts requiring a permanent guard, such as magazines or treasuries, to be manned by sepoys to protect Europeans from the effects of the sun. At the first sign of trouble Light took six of his gunners down to the magazine to take it over from the sepoy guard. The Native guard sergeant when summoned refused to hand the magazine over – Light placed his hand on the man's shoulder and said, 'You must do so.' By way of answer the man stepped back a pace and fired his musket from the hip at point-blank range. He missed, and Light rushed forward and grappled with him. Both men fell to the ground, the European gunners and sepoys firing at each other over their bodies. Several sepoys were killed before the remainder fled and Light got to his feet, dusting himself off, having left his opponent dead with a broken skull.

If the European troops were now ready for action, however, its commanders were not. Archdale Wilson – as he was to demonstrate more than once in the coming year – was not the most decisive of commanders. Once he was joined by his divisional commander, General W. H. 'Bloody Bill' Hewitt, all hope of swift action was lost. A fat, benign, indolent 67-year-old, Hewitt was, in the opinion of many, well overdue for retirement, and the situation in which he found himself seems to have overwhelmed him. So while all the horrors of Indian communal violence were unleashed on Europeans and Indians alike, the British garrison confined itself to a few random volleys in the direction of the burning bungalows (which nearly killed Lieutenant Galloway of the 3rd Light Cavalry who was hiding in an outhouse), the odd round shot directed into a nearby tope of trees, and a misdirected reconnaissance by the Carabiniers. Captain Rosser of that regiment had ridden to Archdale Wilson asking for permission to take some of his men down the Delhi road. Wilson replied that there was no evidence that the mutineers were heading in that direction and that most of them would probably disperse to their homes. In any case, Hewitt added, their first duty was to protect European civilians and the city from the *badmashes* – not pursue mutineers the Lord knew where, with a force half of whom were barely trained and unacclimatized to the heat of India. Although Hewitt and Wilson were to be much criticized for their inaction on the night of 10 May, there was some justice in their arguments. Most of the rebels, though, did not disperse to their homes. They were marching en masse down the road to Delhi, the Mogul capital, and home of the last Mogul Emperor, now styled 'King of Delhi', 30 miles distant. As they did so the European garrison stood-to-arms throughout the night, surrounded by the flames of the burning bungalows, listening to the sounds of looting and murder coming from the native city. Was this an isolated outbreak, many of them wondered, or the start of a general uprising? Or, as Mrs Muter asked herself, 'Was the Native Army in revolt? Had the threatened storm come so soon, and was the instrument, so carefully sharpened by our Government, at its own throat?'

# 3

# DELHI

Far from 'cutting them up', as Cornet McNabb had predicted in his final letter, the European garrison had watched helplessly while the mutineers burned their lines and the European bungalows, massacred those Europeans they could find, looted the city and marched off towards Delhi. Here in the magnificent red sandstone palace built by his Mogul ancestors – a city within a city – lived Bahadur Shah II, the last Mogul Emperor, now King of Delhi. A puppet of the British as his predecessors had been puppets of the Marathas, he was generally content, at the age of 82, to enjoy his British pension, play with his pet animals and birds, cook, write his poetry and sport – as best he could – with his concubines. He had his differences with the British, however, over his pension and the succession. The British were growing tired of maintaining the fiction that this old man in a Red Palace within a Red Fort was, in truth, the Padshah, Shah of Shahs, Sovereign of the world, the Shadow of God. They had stopped making the four-yearly *nuzzurs* (payments of tribute) to him and agreed to increase his pension – 100,000 rupees (£10,000) a month – only if he gave up the palace and title. This pension, though generous, was insufficient to maintain the household and dependants, amounting to some 12,000 people, who inhabited the palace. The succession was an even more vexed question – as far as the British were concerned there wasn't going to be one. When his heir apparent, Dara Bakht, had died in 1849, the British Resident had negotiated an arrangement with the next heir, Fakir-ud-Din, that on his father's death he would retain the title of prince, but give up the palace. When

Fakir-ud-Din died – possibly poisoned – Bahadur Shah pressed the claim of Jawan Bakht, his son by his favourite wife, Zenat Mahal. He had pressed this claim before, and as they had done before, the British rejected it – after Bahadur Shah, it seemed, there would be no King of Delhi.

Such was the state of affairs when the mutineers from Meerut approached the city on the morning of 11 May. First to arrive – at 8 a.m. – were twenty men of the 3rd Light Cavalry, who rode in over the Bridge of Boats, killed the tollkeeper and a passing European, and then made straight for the King's Palace (see map 4, p. xviii). Gathering under a window at the royal palace, where the King had traditionally shown himself to his people, they called up to him 'Help, Oh King! We call for assistance with our fight for the faith!' The King's immediate reaction was to call for the commander of his bodyguard – a British officer, Captain Douglas – and ask him what this demonstration meant. Douglas replied that he did not know, but that he would go down and speak to them. The King fearfully pleaded with him not to risk his life and – his pleas being backed by the King's physician, Hakim Ahsanullah Khan – Douglas contented himself with calling down to them from the balcony that their presence at the palace was an annoyance to the King and that they should go away at once. The troopers then rode south to the Raj Ghat Gate and entered the city. Sir Theophilus Metcalfe, the Joint Magistrate of Delhi – son of Sir Thomas Metcalfe, who had prophesied the throat-slitting that had just commenced – had also seen, from his office window, the arrival of the mutineers. He rode at once to the magazine, 500 yards from the palace, to warn Lieutenant Willoughby, and ask whether two guns could be placed to cover the bridge. This proved impossible – there were no draught animals to drag the guns – so Metcalfe proceeded to the Calcutta Gate. By now a larger body of the 3rd Light Cavalry had arrived from Meerut, followed – at a run – by numbers of sepoys. These also headed straight for the Calcutta Gate, only to find it closed against them. The Commissioner, Simon Fraser had – together with Captain Douglas and Mr Hutchinson, the Collector – closed and barricaded it against them. Like the earlier party these mutineers turned south to look for another entrance, upon which Fraser sent Metcalfe off in his buggy to secure the Water Gate against them.

It was too late. The sepoys guarding the palace that morning were from the 38th Native Infantry. This was the regiment that had, five years earlier, defied Lord Dalhousie's order to sail to Burma. No doubt with this 'victory' still in mind, they were ripe for revolt, and no sooner did the Meerut mutineers appear at the entrance to the palace compound than they were admitted by the guard. From his apartments the King watched in growing alarm as the Meerut mutineers poured into the palace compound to the cheers of the 38th NI Guard and his own servants. At the Calcutta Gate, Fraser and the Europeans with him now found themselves confronted by a large and hostile mob led by troopers of the 3rd Cavalry. Having attempted, and failed, to reason with the troopers, Fraser took a musket from one of the King's guard, fired into the crowd and then dashed through it in his buggy. Captain Douglas jumped down into the moat and was carried, badly shaken, by some still loyal attendants back to the palace. Here he was met by Fraser and Hutchinson. Within moments the three men found themselves surrounded by the King's servants – as Fraser tried to reason with them, he was cut down. Douglas and Hutchinson died with him and the mob proceeded to rampage through the palace, killing Mr Jennings the chaplain, his daughter and a young lady, Miss Clifford, who was staying with them. There then began, throughout the city, a repeat of the events of Meerut the night before. At the Delhi Bank, the manager Mr Beresford and his family were slaughtered – their throats cut with pieces of broken glass. The staff of the *Delhi Gazette* were massacred; the compositors and printers were hacked to pieces, and the presses thrown into the river. All across the city mobs killed any European, Christian or Eurasian they could find.

Theophilus Metcalfe, who had set off in his buggy to close the Water Gate, never reached it. Halfway there he found himself confronted by a crowd that, like the one that had assembled at the Calcutta Gate, had dressed in 'holiday garb' – clearly in expectation of some great event. Some troopers of the 3rd Cavalry rushed at Metcalfe, slashing at him with their sabres and cutting the hood of the buggy. Jumping from the buggy, Metcalfe ran towards a troop of Mounted Police – his own men – and ordered them to charge. Not a man moved. Knocking their commander from his saddle, Metcalfe mounted the horse himself and galloped back to his office. Learning there of the death of his companions from the Calcutta Gate, Metcalfe then toured the city hoping to secure the lives of any Christians he might find. It was while thus engaged that he heard news which might, it seemed, offer hope to them all – Delhi's garrison, the Native Brigade, was marching in good order, under its European officers down from the cantonment.

*

Delhi's garrison – based on Delhi Ridge, 2 miles from the city (see map 4 on page xviii) – consisted entirely of Native troops; the 38th, 54th and 74th NI and Captain de Teissier's battery of Native artillery. Only that morning their commander, Brigadier General Graves, had paraded the brigade to read to them the proceedings of the court martial of Mangal Pandy. If some present suspected that they heard murmurings of sympathy for the convicted man, the confidence of the British officers in their 'Jacks' remained unaffected. The parade over, the officers retired to refresh themselves. Among them was Lieutenant Edward Vibart of the 54th NI.

> The British officers of my own regiment (54th NI) for the most part retired to the regimental mess-house, where, after partaking of a light breakfast, called in India *chota haziree*, and laughing and conversing together until nearly eight o'clock, we separated for the day and returned to our own houses. About an hour later the orderly havildar of my company came running up to the bungalow to report that the regiment had received orders to march down instantly to the city, as some troopers of the 3rd Light cavalry had that morning arrived from Meerut, and were creating disturbances. Hurrying on my uniform, and ordering my pony to be saddled, I without loss of time galloped down to the parade-ground, where I found the regiment falling in by companies and preparing to start.

Graves had no hesitation in sending his men down to the city. There could be no doubt that the outbreak at Meerut was an isolated incident, and the European garrison – the 60th Rifles, the Carabiniers and the artillery – must surely be hot on the heels of the mutineers, who would soon be crushed between them and his own men. To this end he ordered Colonel Ripley of the 54th Native Infantry to take his regiment down to the city to confront the mutineers. Watching them march by was Mrs Peile and her husband, Lieutenant Peile of the 38th NI. This was to have been their last week in India, which they were spending with the regiment's surgeon, Dr Wood, and his wife. Having that morning received news of the arrival of the Meerut mutineers, the Peiles and the Woods had gone to the house of Mrs Patterson – whose husband was Major Patterson of the 54th NI. 'In the verandah we met Major Patterson, dressed in uniform, from whom we heard that his Regiment had been ordered down to the City to quell the disturbance, and we shortly after saw them pass the house, and from their cheerful appearance, and determined look, we congratulated ourselves on having such a brave set of fellows, as we thought, to go forward and fight for us.' Colonel Ripley marched his men down the road towards the Kashmir Gate – the main entrance to the city for troops or travellers descending from the Ridge. The guns being slightly delayed, he left two companies to wait for them – and took the remainder on. At the head of his men, Ripley entered the city by the Kashmir Gate, which was held by men of the 38th NI, whose comrades had already risen in revolt at the King's Palace and joined in the massacre of Europeans there. Inside the gates they were confronted by a large mob, headed by troopers of the 3rd Light Cavalry, who at once attacked the mounted officers. The sepoys of the 54th, called upon to assist their officers, either shot the officers themselves or fired in the air. Men of the 38th NI Guard when called upon by their commander to fire, merely laughed at him. In seconds Colonel Ripley fell mortally wounded and four of his officers – Smith, Burrows, Edwards and Water-field were dead.

With the two 54th companies left behind to wait for the guns was Lieutenant Edward Vibart:

> After a delay of about twenty minutes we were joined by the two guns, then proceeded on as fast as possible to the city. We were still some distance off when the sound of musketry was distinctly heard; and now, as the church tower came into view, we could plainly see, from the smoke arising around it, that our regiment was actively engaged in that locality. Pushing on with all speed, we shortly after met Captain Wallace of the 74th NI, the field officer of the week, coming out of the Cashmere Gate and riding back to the cantonments. He implored us for 'God's sake' to hurry on as fast as possible, as all the 54th officers were being shot down by the cavalry troopers, and their men were making no effort to defend them.

Ordering the companies to halt and load, Patterson then led his force through the Kashmir Gate: 'The two guns ... advanced through the gate, followed by the infantry. At this moment the body of our unfortunate Colonel was carried out, literally hacked to pieces. One arm just below the shoulder was almost severed. Such a fearful sight I never beheld. The poor man was still alive, and, though scarcely able to articulate, I distinctly gathered from the few words he gasped out, that we had no chance against the cavalry troopers, as our own men had turned against us.' Ripley was carried, still alive, up to the Flagstaff Tower.

The Kashmir Gate, close by the Kashmir bastion, had two arched entrances – one for entry, one for exit. Inside the gate was a small enclosure – normally guarded by fifty sepoys and a European officer. The European officer's quarters comprised a two-roomed house up a ramp on top of the bastion. It was this enclosure – known as the Main Guard – that Vibart now entered: 'On looking out into the open space in front of the church, a few cavalry troopers in their French-grey uniforms were seen galloping back in the direction of the palace. Lieutenant Wilson brought a gun round to bear on them, but they were out of sight before he had time to fire. As for the men of my own regiment, I could not imagine what had become of them. Not a sepoy was to be seen; they had all vanished.' It was decided to hold the Main Guard and await events. Two guns were sited so as to command the approaches from the church – St James's Church, sometimes known as Skinner's Church after its founder the Anglo-Indian freebooter, James Skinner. Sepoys were deployed in support of the guns, with more on the ramparts. The 38th NI had provided the original guard for that day. These men, who had refused to fire while Colonel Ripley and his officers were murdered, were still at the Main Guard, and chatting now with Vibart's men. Vibart had few illusions about the 38th: 'The guard of the 38th NI on duty had, just before our arrival, refused to fire on the cavalry mutineers, when called upon to do so by Captain Wallace and Lieutenant Proctor, in order to save the life of our poor colonel as he was being pursued and cut down right in front of their eyes. They even taunted these officers in mutinous language, and said that now the time had arrived to take revenge on people who had tried, as they asserted, to subvert their caste and religion.' Not strong enough to disarm or disperse them, however, and unwilling to test his own men's loyalties to the limit, Vibart and his colleagues endured an anxious time, speculating on the fate of their colleagues:

At length some of us advanced beyond the inner gates, when the first thing I saw was the lifeless body of Captain Burrows lying close by the gate of the churchyard. Assisted by a couple of sepoys I carried him into the Main Guard and laid him on a *charpoy* [native bedstead]. Other bodies were now observed scattered about the place. Five were at length found and brought in, also a sepoy shot through the arm. These were poor Burrows, Smith, Edwards, and Waterfield, all of my own regiment. The fifth was one of the European sergeants attached to the corps; and he was the only one left alive. A ball had shattered his leg, and he had another frightful wound on his head. Since then I have witnessed many painful sights, but I shall never forget my feelings that day as I saw our poor fellows being brought in, their faces distorted with all the agonies of a violent death, and hacked about every conceivable way. Only a couple of hours previously we had been laughing and chattering together, utterly unconscious of the danger which threatened us; ... it instinctively occurred to us that it was only a question of a few hours, more or less, when we too should share a similar fate.

From the cantonment Mrs Peile, with her own little boy, Mrs Wood and Mrs Patterson and her two daughters had been advised to go up to the Flagstaff Tower:

Here on arrival we were told that poor Colonel Ripley was lying at the bells of arms, dreadfully wounded. We proceeded immediately to the place where he lay, to see if we could render him any assistance. We found him lying on a bed of very rough manufacture, and a sergeant's wife brought us a nice soft *rezaie* [quilt], which we folded once or twice double, and laid him upon it. This appeared to comfort his wounds, and after we had applied some lavender-water to his temples he seemed much better, and talked to us. He was, of course, in great agony, and begged the native doctor to give him a dose of opium to deaden his sufferings, and, after some persuasion, the doctor did so. The Colonel was then so much better, that he pointed to one frightful wound in his left shoulder, and told us that the men of his own regiment had bayoneted him.

Having done what they could for the Colonel, the ladies returned to their homes to gather what belongings they could. 'On reaching home,' wrote Mrs Peile, 'our servants begged us not to remain in the house, as it was fully understood that the bungalows were to be burnt at night. Thinking, however, we might save our clothes, and other little articles which for years past I had been gathering together, Mrs. Wood and I packed our boxes, and ordered our servants to hide them in the fowl-house, and we took our jewel-cases with us. When we left the bungalow it was about two o'clock p.m.'

Down at the Main Guard – inside the Kashmir Gate – as reports came in that the 11th and 20th Native Infantry had arrived from Meerut, Vibart's men, who had been fraternizing with the 38th, became more and more restless:

> Their hesitation, no doubt, to commit themselves at this period may be attributed partly to the fact that the regiment as a body was not yet wholly imbued with the spirit of disaffection, and partly to the feeling of uncertainty as to whether the British troops were not already on their way from Meerut to succour Delhi. Indeed, the sepoys themselves were very anxious to be informed on the latter point, and kept repeatedly inquiring when we thought the *Gora Log* [British soldiers] would arrive. To have shown any mistrust of their fidelity at such a moment, however, would have been fatal, so we kept speaking cheerfully to the men and assuring them of the certainty of troops coming to our aid ere long; in fact we had no reason to doubt but that sooner or later assistance would be forthcoming, could we only hold out long enough.

Presently two officers, Osborn and Butler, made their appearance from the direction of the city – and Vibart learned more of what had happened to Colonel Ripley and his officers:

> The latter [Butler] was besmeared with blood, and was faint from a blow he had received on his head from a large brickbat. We now learned some particulars of the events of the morning. It appeared that no sooner had the regiment advanced through the Cashmere Gate into the open space in front of the church than they were assailed by about twenty troopers dressed in uniform. These men shouted out to the sepoys that they had no intention of hurting them, but they had merely come to slaughter the accursed Feringhees. Our officers were then sabred and shot down. In vain did they call on their men to fire on the troopers: these miscreants, on the contrary, immediately joined with the insurgents, and some of the cowardly traitors actually bayoneted Colonel Ripley after he was unhorsed and cut down. In the midst of this confusion Osborn and Butler escaped down one of the streets.

Eventually reinforcements arrived at the Kashmir Gate – not the British forces from Meerut that Vibart and his colleagues were hoping for, but more sepoys: 150 men of the 74th NI under Major Abbott, and two guns under Lieutenant Aislabie:

> Their arrival was hailed with delight; and now, to make the state of affairs look brighter still, and to our no small surprise, some two hundred of the men of my regiment who had so treacherously disappeared in the morning, abandoning their officers to their fate, entered the Main Guard, bringing the regimental colours with them. From their statements it appeared that the onslaught of the cavalry troopers had been so sudden and unexpected, and they were so totally unprepared (their muskets not even being loaded, owing to our poor Colonel thinking the bayonet would be enough for all purposes) that they were seized with panic in the confusion that ensued, and had separated in all directions. They further added that they had been tampered with by the insurgents, but had refused to listen to their overtures. How far this was true it was impossible to judge; but there is no denying that we all felt a good deal cheered by their return, and really began to hope that matters might not, after all, turn out so bad as we had anticipated at first.

However, although the men remained outwardly respectable, their behaviour was causing increasing worry to the small number of British officers, Vibart included:

> They stood about in groups talking to each other in an undertone, and I overheard one young sepoy of my company distinctly refuse to go on duty on the bastion when ordered to do so. I at once went up to him, and laying my hand on his musket, said I would take his duty myself, thinking to shame him out of what I then imagined was his cowardice; but he roughly disengaged himself and slunk back into the crowd ... On another occasion an officer asked a non-commissioned officer why the native troops at Meerut had risen in rebellion against the *Sirkar* [Government], on which he replied 'Why not? The Commander-in-Chief is up at Simla, eating his dinners, and pays no heed to our complaints.' ... it was evident from his reply that the men's minds were rankling under some fancied sense of injustice, and that they had not the slightest intention of making

any effort to defend us in the event of being attacked by the insurgents from Meerut.

As the hours passed a number of ladies who had escaped from various parts of the city arrived: 'All those ladies who had taken refuge with us naturally remained in the utmost state of alarm and perturbation, and as we had no means of sending them to cantonments they were forced to remain in the densely crowded enclosure of the Main Guard throughout the scorching heat of the day, without food or sustenance of any kind.' The heat was affecting the dead, too – and steps were taken to remove them from the confines of the Main Guard: 'Major Abbott observing the bodies of our unfortunate officers who had been killed in the morning's encounter with the cavalry troopers, lying in a corner of the Main Guard, suggested the propriety of sending them back to the cantonments. The only conveyance available was an open bullock cart, so after placing the bodies inside, and covering them over with the skirts of some ladies' dresses procured from a house just inside the enclosure ... the driver was despatched in his errand.' Up at the Flagstaff Tower Mrs Peile saw the cart arrive: 'The people at the Flagstaff,' she wrote,

> were in a great state of alarm ... and numbers of gentlemen and merchants from the city, assisted by several ladies, were bringing in boxes upon boxes of powder, caps and bullets, which were all being lodged at the top of the Tower. Our alarm was still further intensified when a cart drawn by bullocks shortly after arrived at the Flagstaff, which it was whispered contained the bodies of the unfortunate officers, who had been so brutally killed in the city. The cart was covered over with one or two ladies' dresses, to screen the dead from view; but one of their arms was distinctly noticed by myself as it was hanging over the side of the cart. Some now advised leaving for Kurnaul, a distance of about seventy miles from Delhi; but several ladies present declaimed against going, as their husbands had been absent since morning. Alas! one or two of these ladies were then widows, although they knew it not. One young lady, whose poor brother was lying in the cart outside the Flagstaff, was enquiring of several of the officers if they had seen him, she little thinking that he was numbered among the dead.

Officers rode down from the Flagstaff to the Kashmir Gate looking for information on the enemy, but there was none to be had. Messages came, too, from within the city – Mr Galloway of the Civil Service sent to inform them he was at his post at the Treasury, sword in hand, but that his sepoy guards were of a very sullen disposition. Their own troops being no better, the officers at the Main Guard could offer him no assistance. Nor could they respond when appealed to from a location perhaps even more vital to the maintenance of British rule in Delhi – the Magazine.

Five hundred yards from the palace, and surrounded by high walls, was the Magazine, filled with munitions and occupied that morning by Lieutenant George Willoughby, Lieutenants Forrest and Raynor of the Commissariat Department, Conductors Buckley, Shaw, Scully and Crow, and Sergeants Edwards and Stewart. Willoughby who commanded there had been consulted, it will be remembered, by Theophilus Metcalfe earlier that morning about the feasibility of deploying two guns to command the Bridge of Boats. In the meantime, sure that the Magazine would be one of the rebels' first targets, he set about making it as defensible as possible in the time allowed him. 'The gates of the Magazine were closed and barricaded,' wrote Lieutenant Forrest, Willoughby's second-in-command,

and every arrangement made for a vigorous defence of some hours at least. Inside the gate leading to the park we placed two six-pounders double charged with grape, one under Sub-conductor Crow, the other under Sergeant Stewart, who stood by them with lighted matches in their hands. Their orders were that if any attempt was made to force that gate both guns were to be fired at once, and they were to fall back on that part of the Magazine where Willoughby and myself were posted. The principal gate of the Magazine was similarly defended by two guns, with *chevaux de frise* laid down on the outside. For the further defence of this gate, and the Magazine near it, two six-pounders were so placed as either to command the gate or a small bastion in its vicinity. Within sixty yards, in front of the office and commanding two cross-roads, were three six-pounders and one twenty-four-pounder (howitzer) which could be so managed as to act upon any part of the Magazine in the neighbourhood. All these guns were loaded with double charges of grape. Arms were now placed in the hands of the native establishment. They took them reluctantly, and it soon appeared that they were not only in a state of excitement, but also of insubordination, particularly the Mussulman portion, for they flatly refused to obey the orders issued by the Europeans.

Knowing that unless relieved they could not hold out for long against the forces likely to be coming against them, Willoughby and his men resolved to blow up the Magazine, at the last, rather than let such a store of guns and powder fall into the hands of the mutineers: 'After the above arrangements had been made a train was laid communicating with the powder magazine, and ready to be fired by a preconcerted signal, which was that of Conductor Buckley raising his hat from his head on the order being given by Willoughby.' The arrangements for the defence had hardly been completed when members of the King's guard came down from the palace:

> The guards ... demanded possession of the Magazine in the name of the King of Delhi. To this no reply was made, and immediately after the Subadar of the native infantry guard on duty came and informed Willoughby and myself that the king had sent down word to the mutineers that he would without delay send them down scaling ladders from the palace for the purpose of scaling the walls; and shortly afterwards they arrived. On these being erected against the walls the whole of our native establishment deserted us by climbing up the sloped sheds on the inside, and descending the ladders on the outside. The enemy now appeared in great numbers on the wall.

These were largely sepoys of the 11th and 20th NI from Meerut, who attacked Willoughby's position in overwhelming numbers. Even so the guns took their toll. 'We opened a fire of grape on them, and kept it up as long as a single round remained. Every shot went crashing through them and told well.' The two Conductors – Buckley and Scully – distinguished themselves, wrote Forrest:

> The former, assisted only by myself, loaded and fired in rapid succession the several guns above detailed, firing at least four rounds from each gun, and with the same steadiness as if standing on parade, although the enemy were then some hundreds in number, and kept up a continuous fire of musketry on us from within forty or fifty yards. After firing the last round Conductor Buckley received a ball in his right arm, and I at the same time was struck in the left hand by two musket-balls, which disabled me for a time. It was at this critical moment that Lieutenant Willoughby gave the signal for the firing of the Magazine. Conductor Scully, who had from the first evinced his gallantry by

volunteering for this dangerous duty, now coolly and calmly, without hesitation, and yet without confusion, set fire to the several trains. In an instant, and with an explosion that shook the city and was distinctly heard at Meerut, the Magazine blew up. The wall was thrown flat upon the ground, and it is said that some hundreds of the enemy were buried under the ruins or blown in the air.

Conductor Scully and four others died instantly – Willoughby and Forrest were blown in the air but landed burned, blackened and alive. Lieutenant Raynor and Conductor Buckley also survived and in the confusion made their escape. Among the mutineers, the casualties – never recorded – were believed to number in the hundreds. For the British, the blowing up of the Delhi Magazine was to become one of the emblematic moments of the Mutiny – the first act of defiance against the forces arrayed against British rule and a sign that if the rebels had so far had it all their own way, it would not always be so. Even Forrest was forced to admit that the material value of the defence was less important than the moral: 'It does not detract in the least from the merits of this gallant defence that the blowing up of the Magazine did not prevent large quantities of stores from falling into the hands of the enemy. It was not a precautionary measure, but a deed of defiance and daring ... Numbers of the enemy were slain by the explosion, and it was a great service even in the stores it did destroy. And was not a noble example here shown? Such deeds are never in vain.'

The explosion at the Magazine startled Edward Vibart and his companions, still waiting anxiously at the Kashmir Gate:

About 4 p.m. guns were heard booming in the direction of the Magazine, but no-one could conjecture what had happened. We were not long, however, kept in suspense, for after some thirty rounds had been fired in rapid succession, a terrific explosion rent the air, shaking the foundations of the Main Guard to its centre. Bugles were blown, the assembly sounded, and all was confusion and dismay, everybody rushing here and there, some pacifying the ladies, other trying to get the men together, none of us knowing what to make of it. Presently a dense column of smoke and dust ascended to an immense height, and we rightly guessed that the Magazine was blown up.

A few moments later Willoughby and Forrest arrived at the gate, Forrest bleeding from a wound in the hand. Captain Gordon of the 74th tried to get together a party of his sepoys to go into the city to search for more survivors, but the men refused to move. A few minutes later an order came from Brigadier Graves, on the Ridge, recalling the men of the 74th and the two guns under Lieutenant Aislabie. 'On receipt of this order,' wrote Vibart, 'Major Patterson, Mr. de Gruyther [the Deputy Collector], and several others strongly remonstrated against its being carried into effect; for it was obvious that if the 74th left it would have been impossible to hold the post against any attack, as it was evident that our men were not to be trusted, and our confidence in them was utterly shaken. Major Abbott, however, contended that having received a specific order, he could not but obey it.' The Deputy Collector said he would ride up to the cantonments and point out to the Brigadier the necessity of the 74th staying put, but Lieutenant Aislabie felt that he had no choice but to obey his orders – and with the two guns set off up to the Ridge.

They got no further than the crossroads leading up to the Flagstaff Tower – the point on the Ridge that overlooked the Kashmir Gate. There they were met by a picket of the 38th who fired on Lieutenant Aislabie. Aislabie turned and rode for his life – and the sepoys and Aislabie's gunners turned the guns round and began marching them back down towards Delhi. Captain de Teissier, the battery commander, who had seen all this from the Flagstaff Tower, rode down to tell them to halt. He, too, was greeted by a volley, which wounded his horse in three places. Minutes later the two guns arrived back at the Kashmir Gate. Edward Vibart saw them arrive:

On seeing them re-enter the Main Guard without an officer we were all greatly astonished, and on Major Abbott asking the drivers why they had returned, they gave some evasive reply. Meanwhile several of the 38th Sepoys kept entering the enclosure in parties of threes and fours, and we could observe our men getting very restless and uneasy. Some time having now elapsed since the departure of the Deputy-Collector on his errand to the Brigadier, Major Abbott determined to wait no longer. He accordingly fell-in the 74th detachment, ordering at the same time the two guns, which had just returned, to follow him out of the Main Guard. The order to march was then given, when, thinking it would be a good opportunity of getting the ladies who had taken shelter with us up to cantonments, we began assisting them on to one of the gun wagons. At this critical juncture, and just as Major Abbott had passed through the Cashmere Gate with about half his men, and the guns were about to follow, some of the 38th Sepoys rushed at the gate and closed it; their next act was to discharge a volley right amongst a group of officers, and their example was, as far as I could see, rapidly followed by all the other sepoys inside the enclosure.

It seems as if the explosion at the Magazine had acted as a sign to all the Native troops in the Main Guard – the already mutinous 38th, the restless 54th and 74th and Aislabie's gunners – that the rebels had penetrated to the heart of the city. 'A scene now ensued that baffles description,' wrote Vibart,

> and of which I can convey but a faint idea. Almost at the first discharge I saw Captain Gordon fall from his horse; a musket-ball had pierced his body, and he fell without a groan within a few feet of where I was standing. The next moment I saw Mrs Forrest hastily dismount from the gun wagon on which she was seated and jump across his prostrate body. It seems some sepoys had advanced towards her in a threatening manner, and, shooting a wounded conductor, who was sitting by her side, dead on the spot, had compelled her to alight. The horrible truth now flashed on me – we were being massacred right and left without any means of escape!

Outside the walls Major Anderson of the 74th – leading his men up to the Flagstaff Tower as ordered – heard the shooting from the Main Guard. 'It is the men of the 38th killing their officers!' his men told him. He ordered them to turn back, but they refused. 'It is too late,' they cried, 'they are all dead by this time; we won't let you go back to be murdered ... Pray fly for your life; we cannot protect you any longer.'

Inside the Main Guard was pandemonium – the only way of escape for the officers and ladies (who included Mrs Forrest, wife of the defender of the Magazine, and her two daughters) was up on to the ramparts. Vibart was one of those who led the way:

> Scarcely knowing what I was doing, I made for the ramp which leads from the courtyard to the bastion above. Every one appeared to be doing the same. Twice I was knocked over as we all frantically rushed up the slope, the bullets whistling past us like hail, and flattening themselves against the parapet with a frightful hiss. To this day it is a perfect marvel to me how any one of us escaped being hit. Poor Smith

and Reveley, both of the 74th, were killed close beside me. The latter was carrying a loaded gun, and, raising himself with a dying effort, he discharged both barrels into a knot of sepoys, and the next moment expired. Osborn, of my own corps, was shot through the thigh as he ran up scarcely two paces in front of me, and every second I expected to feel a bullet through my own body as well.

Once up on the ramparts there was some shelter from the sepoys' fire, but the only way out of the city was over the walls:

The embrasures of the bastion were at length reached, and into these we all crowded. Some officers leaped without hesitation into the ditch, a drop of some twenty-five feet, and then scrambled up the counterscarp. Amongst these I noticed Lieutenants Willoughby, Butler and Angelo. Poor Osborn's look of despair I shall never forget, as he bound up the wound in his leg with a handkerchief, and then dropped off the parapet into the ditch. I heard him shout out to us to follow, and the next moment I saw him climbing the opposite bank. Myself and the rest were in the act of following his example when despairing cries for help were heard proceeding from some ladies who had taken shelter in the officers' quarters, situated on the top of the bastion. Running back at once, we found them in a state bordering on distraction, and the Misses Forrest were weeping over their mother, who had been shot through the shoulder. The bullets all this while came whistling in through the windows of the house, and delay was hazardous in the extreme.

Seeing some of the sepoys running out into the city to loot the Treasury, one officer thought that the Main Guard might soon be empty:

Wilson of the Artillery, thinking there was possibly a chance of our being able to descend to the courtyard and effect our escape by means of the Cashmere Gate, went out to reconnoitre. A bullet through his cap, however, caused him to beat a hasty retreat, and it was then seen that a number of sepoys still remained in the enclosure, some of whom commenced pointing the guns in our direction. We were at a loss what to do. To take the ladies into the ditch and scale the counterscarp seemed an impossibility; to stay longer in our present position was to court certain destruction. Words are unable to express adequately the agonising suspense of that moment; all chance of escape seemed utterly cut off.

By now the Native gunners had unlimbered their guns and turned them on the Europeans crowded on the ramparts.

Instinctively we all rushed out and crowded once more round an embrasure; all at once, bang went a gun in the courtyard below, and the same instant a round shot passed within a few feet of our heads, expediting our movements in no small degree. Quick as lightning we fastened our sword-belts together; some then jumped into the ditch, whilst others remained above to assist the ladies to descend. One by one they were dropped in this manner over the parapet, those below catching them in their arms to break the fall as much as possible. One very stout old lady, whose name I did not know then, but afterwards ascertained to be Mrs. Forster, commenced to scream, and refused to jump. At this instant another shot from the gun crashed into the parapet a little to the right, covering us with splinters. It was madness to waste time in expostulation; somebody gave her a push, and she tumbled headlong into the ditch beneath.

The ditch – like that around all fortified places – had steep slopes on either side:

An almost perpendicular bank rose before us, to scale which with delicate ladies appeared a hopeless task indeed. Meanwhile a few sepoys were observed peering over the rampart; but, as we instantly took cover by retreating close to the inner wall or 'escarp', it was impossible for them to depress their muskets sufficiently to shoot us. After a short while of extreme suspense their heads disappeared, and we surmised they must have gone with the rest of their comrades to join in plundering the Treasury, from which direction the sound of firing now came. With beating hearts we commenced the ascent of the counterscarp. Again and again did the ladies reach the top, when the earth, crumbling away beneath their feet, sent them rolling back into the ditch. Despair, however, gave us superhuman energy, till at length we all succeeded in gaining the summit. We now quickly ran down the short glacis, and plunged into some thick shrubbery that grew at the bottom. Here we stopped to take breath; but the sound of voices proceeding from the high road, which ran close by, induced us to hurry off again as fast as possible. It was evident, however, that the powers of endurance of poor Mrs. Forster, the stout old lady to whom I have already alluded, were fast failing. She had been grazed by a bullet in the temple, and the severe fall she experienced in tumbling head foremost from the parapet into the ditch had partially stunned her. Every effort was made to rouse her, but without success. As a last resource, two of the strongest of our party attempted to carry her, but, being now in a state of collapse, her enormous weight rendered such a feat impossible, especially as the belt of brushwood through which we were forcing a passage was overgrown with thorny bushes and thick underwood, without a semblance of a pathway. In the meantime those in front had advanced some distance through the thicket, and the two officers in immediate attendance on the poor lady were left in the rear. Finding at length that she had become unconscious, and that their united efforts to carry her were unavailing, they were reluctantly com-pelled to leave her where she fell. Truly it was a most sad predicament; but I think there is little doubt, from the statements of those who last saw her, that the unfortunate woman's life was practically beyond human aid, and that she never again regained consciousness. May God have mercy on her soul!

Vibart and his party – the few survivors of the massacre at the Main Guard – now straggled on through the bush in the direction of the cantonments.

At the Flagstaff the sound of the explosion – loud enough as Forrest said to be heard at Meerut – was greeted by sepoys gathered at the Flagstaff Tower with cries of '*Deen! Deen! Deen!*' ('Faith, Faith, Faith!' – the war cry of the Muslim sepoy). Only minutes earlier – while Brigadier Graves was haranguing his remaining men, urging them to be true to their salt – a crowd armed with *tulwars* and *lathies* had come out of the city and up the hill towards the Flagstaff. A European taking post beside the two remaining guns on the Ridge had caused the crowd to waver and turn back – but significantly the sepoy gunners had not stirred. Clearly – although they had not yet turned on their officers – these men could not be relied upon to protect the Europeans in the event of an attack from the city. It was at this point that Captain Tytler of the 38th came up to Graves and argued for a retreat to Karnal. Tytler had gathered a loyal remnant of the 38th, who he was sure would protect them all. Other officers were for making a stand at the Flagstaff Tower, which was even now being fortified; Tytler was certain that if they stayed put they would be massacred, as had the Europeans inside the city. After many hesitations – and hesitation seems to have been a hallmark of the senior officers caught up in the initial outbreaks – Graves agreed to Tytler's plan. What was intended as an orderly retreat, however, with European men and women in carts and carriages, escorted by sepoy infantry and two guns, quickly degenerated into a helter-skelter flight. 'A fearful scene presented itself at the Tower,' wrote Mrs Peile. 'Carriages of every description were in waiting, but as I had gone up to the Flagstaff with Mrs Patterson, and my husband had ridden, I was left without any conveyance. Everybody, with the exception of one or two ladies and gentlemen were by this time fairly off on their way either to Kurnaul or Meerut. One gentleman, seeing me standing by, offered me a seat in his carriage, and as I had my little boy with me, I placed him in with him, hoping to follow with Mrs Wood.' Not knowing where her husband was – in fact, he was tending to the wounded Colonel Ripley – she eventually started off with Mrs Wood and Mrs Patterson and her two daughters in two buggies.

The experiences of the European fugitives from Delhi were to be repeated over much of what was then called the North-West Provinces of India in the next few weeks. Plunged overnight from being an unassailable, untouchable ruling elite, they found themselves isolated and hunted – alone or in small groups – subject to the cruelties, the mercy or sometimes the mere whim of the native population. The immediate result of the removal of the Company's *raj* was anarchy in the countryside – an anarchy in which the possession of white skin could mean either salvation or instant death. Fanny Peile's adventures are typical. She and her companions had not travelled far when they encountered Mrs Wood's husband – the surgeon of the 38th – being carried on a bed. He had been shot in the face by a sepoy of his own regiment. Transferring him to one of the carriages, they asked the Brigade Major how their evacuation was to be managed – he answered, 'The best way you can.' Lieutenant Peile left to rejoin his regiment's quarter guard, hoping to persuade them to accompany the officers and their ladies to Karnal, so Fanny and the Woods set off alone – the two ladies being the last to leave the station. They had not gone far when some men approached and warned them not to proceed further as all the Europeans ahead of them had been murdered. That this was untrue they had no way of knowing, and so when a neat well-dressed boy who said he was a servant of the 38th's quartermaster offered to guide them via some fields, they followed him. Soon they were surrounded by large numbers of men demanding rupees. Fanny told them to go to her house and help themselves to what they wanted:

> They particularly enquired where our house was situated, and I explained it to them as well as I could. They, however, fancied we had money with us, and insisted on my showing them the seat of the buggy, and they searched every corner of it; but still I managed to keep my jewel box. I was driving, with Mrs. Wood by my side, and the hood of the buggy being down, the vile wretches had a capital opportunity of standing up behind, and with the number of tulwars and sticks which they had, could have killed us in a very short space of time. Mrs. Wood had a black velvet head-dress on, and as it had some bugles about it, it glittered a great deal in the moonlight; and when they saw this, they lost no time in tearing it from her head, and at the same time struck her rather heavily with one of their sticks.

Fanny kept driving until they regained the Grand Trunk road, where they met the two guns that had accompanied the earlier refugees up the road towards Karnal.

> A cavalry man was riding by the side of the guns, and at first I was inclined to think that aid had reached us from Umballa or Meerut; instead of which, it was the guns returning to the city. I called out to the trooper, fearless at the time of being murdered, to assist us by directing us to the safest road. The answer I received was – 'Go that way' (pointing to Kurnaul) 'you will get murdered! Come this (pointing to Delhi) and you will meet the same fate!' We were then quite close to the gunners and the dreaded trooper; but in fact they offered us no insolence.

Deciding to shelter in the Company's gardens nearby, they were hidden by the gardener in a thatched hut, but soon another party of robbers, fifty strong, found them.

> We kept quite still, thinking they might leave us; but we heard them determine on breaking the lock, which was soon effected, and into the

hut they rushed. I went up to one of them and implored him to save us. He asked for what we had. I told him we had lost everything we possessed; but until he had searched us, he would not give credit to what we told him. Certain it was, for everything to my bonnet and cloak had been taken, and the carriage and buggy horses ridden away, whither we knew not. They were not satisfied with taking our horses, but broke up the carriage and buggy in our presence.

For the next six days the two ladies wandered from village to village meeting with varying receptions from the occupants. At the first village they tried the villagers gave them bread, and milk for the doctor, and hid them in a cowshed:

Soon after daylight one of the women ran to the shed and begged of us to remain quiet as some sepoys were just entering their village. I at first thought she wished to frighten us, and the first thing I did was look over the mats which formed the door, and sure enough there stood a sepoy, and had he been standing with his face towards the shed in which we were secreted he must have seen me. He was, however, standing talking to the old man of the village, and was making a request for carts and bullocks to assist in taking away the officers' property. He was dressed in every way like a sepoy, with the exception of pantaloons; in place of the latter article of dress he had on the *dhotee*, usually worn by the natives of India. The man appeared in a great hurry to get rid of the sepoy, for he gave him bullocks and carts in a very short space of time.

The predominant attitude among the villagers in all the fugitives' accounts seems to have been fear – the lot of peasants in any war. There was much to fear: the fury of the sepoys if they hid or assisted European fugitives, the fury of the British if they did not. The sepoys might claim that the Company's *raj* was over for good and the rule of the Moguls had been restored but, in a country where communications were slow, how could they be sure that the British were not gathering their strength elsewhere? Whether loved by the natives or not, the rule of the Company had brought order to a region that had known little but anarchy for many years before. Now that that rule had been removed – whether permanently or not remained to be seen – there were many with scores to settle, old communal religious or caste enmities to revive, and many simply in search of plunder. The removal of debts was another strong motivation, either by burning Government records and offices or simply slaughtering the creditor. The reassertion of old landownership claims, overturned in British courts was another. Most villages were walled, loopholed and gated with strong watchtowers, and now, lined with matchlock-wielding inhabitants who blazed away impartially at all comers. By night the country sounded like a war zone – which in many areas it was.

One of the most feared groups in the area between Delhi and Meerut were the Goojurs. R. E. W. Dunlop, the Deputy Commissioner at Meerut – who was at this time shooting in the Himalayas, blissfully unaware of the events unfolding at his station – described the Goojurs thus: 'These men, a sect of Hindoos located only in the neighbourhood of the Meerut district, have long been noted as inveterate robbers. They are cattle stealers by profession, and, like most of the predatory tribes, take employment (whenever they can find officials foolish enough to trust them with it) as watchmen, or village police.' Now they thronged the roads, making many of them impassable. Dunlop added, however: 'They have nevertheless no ill will against the English Government. They plundered the mutineers as readily as the Europeans, if found in as defenceless a condition.' It was probably Goojurs who robbed Fanny Peile and her companions on the first evening of their flight and twice more on their journey. More than once she had to beg for her life – once by offering up her wedding ring and another time her dress, which, after some consideration, was returned to her. If plunder was the main aim of most of the hostile natives encountered on the road, there was an ever-present danger from parties of sepoys who were scouring the countryside in search of the fugitives, with the object of taking them back to Delhi.

Eventually, after being sheltered by kind villagers who gave them bread and milk, and hot water to wash the Doctor's shirt, and even made them a wooden pipe through which the Doctor – whose lower jaw was shattered by a musket ball – could drink, Mrs Peile was reunited with her husband. He, too, had wandered at large for days and had been robbed of everything but a shirt and his socks. At last, after finding shelter with the Rani of Balghur, they managed to get a message to Karnal and, after several more days of travel and hardship, reached safety. Dr Wood survived his wound and the Peiles heard from the people into whose carriage Fanny had bundled her son, that the boy was safe and well at Meerut.

Others were not so lucky. Lieutenant Willoughby, the commander of the Delhi Magazine, having survived the explosion and the massacre at the Kashmir Gate, escaped across country along with six other men – one of whom was Lieutenant Osborn, who had survived the 54th's massacre of its own officers and been shot in the thigh while running up the ramp at the Main Guard with Edward Vibart. At the first village they came to they were fed and sheltered, but Osborn was unable to go on and they were forced to leave him hidden in a ravine, promising to send help as soon as possible. Near the second they were met by a crowd led by a Brahmin by the name of Kana, who called upon them to make him a present. As the party had only one carbine and one or two swords between them – their only means of protection – they declined. In the fracas that followed this demand Willoughby put a bullet through the chest of Kana, upon which the inhabitants of five neighbouring villages converged on the party and – enraged by the killing of a Brahmin – cut them to pieces. R. E. W. Dunlop, who later investigated the incident, wrote: 'The act of Lieutenant Willoughby . . . has since been commented on in very unjust terms, on the plea that submission to the demand might have saved the lives of the party. There is much, however, to admire in that stern courage which has no dread of numbers. Had Willoughby been a man to surrender his arms to villagers, he never could have blown up Delhi Magazine.' Osborn – who had been left behind with a shattered thigh – was, ironically, the only survivor. Stripped of everything but his pith helmet by Goojurs, he was found by a native woman who fed him for three days and had him carried to Meerut.

Willoughby's second-in-command at the Magazine, Lieutenant Forrest, was another of those who had jumped from the walls of Delhi along with Edward Vibart, whom we last saw stumbling through the bush towards the cantonment with a mixed party of officers and ladies. Having reluctantly abandoned old Mrs Forster, they headed for Metcalfe House – the superb mansion built by Sir Thomas Metcalfe, late Resident at the King of Delhi's Court, and now owned by his son Sir Theophilus, himself a fugitive. Here they were sheltered in a cellar by Sir Theophilus's *khitmutghar* (butler, or waiter) – who seemed much distressed at his master's failure to return home – and given food and beer. They were a mixed party, Vibart recalls:

It will be as well here to enumerate our party. The ladies we had brought with us from the Main Guard consisted of Mrs. Forrest and her three daughters, the youngest a sweet little girl of nine years of age, Mrs. Fraser, and Mrs. Forster. The latter, as I have related, was no longer with us, so there were five ladies in all. The gentlemen also numbered five, viz. Salkeld, of the Engineers ... Proctor, of the 38th NI; Lieutenant Forrest, the husband of Mrs. Forrest; Wilson of the Artillery; and myself – making altogether a party of ten. There was also a native servant of Salkeld's who had followed us out of the Main Guard and seemed disinclined to leave us.

The *khitmutgar* told them that the mob was now close behind and that they must leave.

As we left our hiding place and issued forth from a door leading down to the bank of the river we saw the whole extent of the cantonments in a blaze of light as if every house had been set on fire. It was scarcely more than half a mile distant and we could distinctly hear the hoarse shouts of the mutineers, mingled with volleys of musketry and discharges of cannon. It appeared to us to matter very little whether we remained or not – either way we were sure to be captured; and I don't suppose there was one amongst our little party who expected to live through that terrible night. Meerut, the nearest British station was thirty-eight miles off, and situated as we were, what possible hope was there of reaching it in safety?

Vibart and his party headed for the Jumna River:

Poor Mrs. Forrest ... had been severely wounded in the Main Guard, and though she suffered much pain in her shoulder, and could proceed but slowly, she uttered no complaint, but walked out heroically. Each of us took charge of a lady, and I had little Miss Forrest to my share. The poor little child kept asking all kinds of innocent questions, not being able to realise the fearful events that had occurred. In this manner we trudged on for about half an hour, when suddenly a bright streak of fire rose up behind us. To our horror we perceived it was Metcalfe's house on fire!

After crossing the Jumna the group – ragged, starving and scorched by the sun – endured the same privations and dangers as Mrs Peile and her companions. At one point, resting at night in some scrub jungle, they had a close encounter with a band of sepoys:

I was just on the point of dropping off to sleep, when suddenly some one shook me by the arm, exclaiming that the sepoys were upon us. To start to my feet and seize the gun which lay by my side was the work of a second; the next moment served to reveal the peril we were in. Not a hundred yards distant, and coming in a direct line towards us, we perceived a body of some eight or ten sepoys, two of whom were mounted on ponies. The imperfect light of dawning day was just sufficient to show us that they were armed, though only about half were dressed in uniform. They were making apparently for Delhi by a country track, and were bearing down straight for the spot where we lay concealed. This fact showed them to be stragglers from Meerut. We had barely time to creep under the bushes and hide ourselves as well as we could when they were upon us. We watched them in breathless anxiety, not daring to move and scarcely to breathe. Not for untold wealth would I pass such another moment of agonising suspense. Now they slowly pass in Indian file within a few feet of us. Surely we must be observed? But no; they are moving on. Can it be that they have not perceived us? Ah! they see us now, for one of them stoops and picks up something from the ground, and whispers to his comrades, and then all come to a sudden halt. Alas! our water bottle had betrayed us! In our hurry and confusion we had left it lying in the open, and one of them, in stooping to examine it, had undoubtedly caught sight of some of our party as we lay amongst the brushwood ... They were standing within a few paces only of where I lay concealed, and I watched with an intensity of suspense too acute for words. There was complete silence, broken only by the low mutterings of the sepoys, and we distinctly heard them remark that people were hiding among the bushes. I involuntarily cocked my gun, and, filled with apprehension as to what they would do next, I inwardly resolved, in the event of any threatening movement being made toward us, to shoot the foremost man dead. After a brief interval, which in the extreme tension of that supreme moment seemed interminable, and during which I clearly saw by the gold regulation necklace he was wearing that the party was led by a native officer, we saw them, to our unbounded astonishment, silently move off, and after proceeding about a hundred yards further come to another halt. They now leisurely seated themselves on the ground, the two mounted men dismounting from their ponies and joining the group. Waiting to look no longer, we hastily rose from our crouching position and fled precipitately in the opposite direction. To our unspeakable relief no attempt was made to follow us, and we could once more breathe freely.

Vibart puts the sepoys' inaction down to either a disinclination to tangle with an unknown number of Europeans in the dark, or the fact that these men were simply less inclined than some of their comrades to spill the blood of the defenceless.

Vibart's description of his party's state that night vividly portrays the sufferings undergone by the women caught up in these events. Unlike their husbands – the soldiers amongst whom were, after all, dedicated to a life of privation and danger – they had until that night led the most sheltered of lives. Yet when the crisis came – like Mrs Craigie and Miss Mackenzie snatching a lone trooper out from under the noses of the mob, or Mrs Peile thrusting her 'dear boy' into a stranger's carriage and bartering with her wedding ring for her own and her companions' lives – the women proved capable of acting with a courage and decision that was not, at the time, expected of their sex.

> There sat the poor Misses Forrest, their dishevelled hair hanging down their backs, without a particle of covering for their heads. There lay the unfortunate mother, her head resting in the lap of one of her daughters, and, though suffering excruciating pain from the gunshot wound in her shoulder, yet never uttering a word of murmur of complaint. Mrs Fraser sat close by, bewailing the untimely end of her little babe, who, she imagined, together with her sister, had perished in the Main Guard, both having been lost sight of in the panic and confusion which ensued when the firing commenced. Subsequently, however, it transpired that a Christian drummer belonging to the 54th had hidden them under a dark archway, and after the sepoys had left the enclosure conducted them unharmed to cantonments, whence, together with some of the other residents they had escaped in a carriage to Kurnaul. The little girl, however, died from exposure and want of proper nourishment. The rest of our party lay all about, under the best shelter we could find, keeping a sharp look-out to see that we were not surprised.

Like the Peiles', Vibart's party's journey involved many kindnesses, some cruelty and some treachery from the villagers; meetings, in this case with Colonel Knyvett and Lieutenant Gambier of the 38th NI and a European merchant, Mr Marshall; and an encounter with the Goojurs in which they almost suffered the same fate as Willoughby:

> We found ourselves getting gradually surrounded by fierce looking men, armed with spears and bludgeons. These were no more than the dreaded Goojurs themselves. Their numbers increased rapidly, and in whichever direction we looked, we observed others, similarly armed running towards us. At length, when they had completely hemmed us in, they gave a fearful shout, and rushed upon us with demoniacal gestures. We stood back to back and made a vain attempt to beat them off; but being ten to one, we were soon overpowered. One rascal laid hold of my sword, and tried to wrench it out of my hand. In vain I resisted; a blow from behind stretched me on my back, and ere I could recover myself, I was mobbed by some half a dozen others. In the midst of this *melee* I saw Colonel Knyvett levelling the gun he was carrying point-blank at the head of one of the wretches as he stood whooping and yelling by way of inciting on the rest. Fortunately, some one shouted out to him not to fire; so, deliberately removing the caps, he gave it up. It was as well we permitted ourselves to be disarmed, for, had we continued the struggle, our lives would undoubtedly have been sacrificed. Having once got us down, they set to work stripping us of everything. Studs, rings, watches etc., all were torn off. They did not even spare my inner vest, and one of the ruffians actually snatched away the piece of cotton cloth which was wrapped round my head. I trembled with foreboding as I saw the unfortunate ladies in the grasp of these savages. One of them had her clothes literally torn off her back, whilst others were treated with similar barbarity. At last, when they had appropriated everything, leaving only our shirts and trousers, and the ladies their upper garments, the entire band retreated a short distance and commenced quarrelling over the spoil.

Ignored by the Goojurs and guided by a fakir to another village where there were some *chupprassies* (Government police), they thought they had reached safety, but were to be bitterly disappointed. 'By the time the police-station was reached we were nearly dead-beat; but here we were received with supreme indifference. In fact, the demeanour of the *chupprassies* was the reverse of reassuring: they merely looked on in sullen silence, and on our venturing to remind them that, as paid servants of the Government, they were bound to afford us all the protection in their power, they told us, with a sneer, that the British *raj* was no longer in existence. They further informed us that the station of Meerut was in flames, and nearly all the Europeans killed.' At length the men persuaded them to bring out some *charpoys* for the ladies but a threatening crowd soon gathered: 'Growing bolder and more insolent, they insisted at last on searching each individual of the party, including the ladies, as nothing would dissuade them from the belief that we had money and valuables concealed about our persons. It would take up too much space to describe all the indignities we were forced to submit to at the hands of these scoundrels, or to relate in what conflicting hopes and fears the remainder of that never-to-be-forgotten afternoon passed away and evening arrived.'

Help arrived in the form of a more sympathetic group of villagers, who led them away and hid them for several days from bands of sepoys who were now scouring the countryside in search of them. They endured hot nights and days lying concealed in a fakir's hut. Soon they were joined by two more refugees: 'We received another addition to our party by the arrival of two poor sergeants' wives, each carrying a baby in their arms. They had been wandering about, poor creatures! ever since the day of the outbreak at Delhi, not knowing what had become of their husbands, and having been robbed of all they possessed except the clothes on their backs. At some of the villages they had passed through, they had experienced much indignity and abuse, whilst at others they were fed on unleavened cakes and an occasional draught of milk.' A native barber surgeon came and tended Mrs Forrest's wound:

> After thoroughly cleansing it from all the sand and dirt which had collected, and extracting certain portions of her dress which the bullet had carried into the wound in its passage, he caused boiling *ghee* [clarified butter] to be passed completely through it, and after this painful process had been repeated two or three times, a cloth was bound over both orifices of the wound. Next day it assumed a more healthy appearance, and finally commenced to suppurate; and although the treatment I have described was of a somewhat heroic nature, I believe it effectually prevented mortification from setting in, and was the means of saving this brave and gentle lady's life.

Although safe from hostile villagers for the present they were not yet out of danger: 'We were hourly harassed,' wrote Vibart, 'by ever-recurring reports of the *Telinga Log* [sepoys] having been seen scouring the neighbourhood in search of fugitives, and we were thus kept in a continual state of dread, lest we should be discovered.' Even so, it proved difficult to get anyone to carry a message. 'We ... made a vigorous attempt to get a letter from us taken to the general officer commanding at Meerut; but no one seemed inclined to comply with our request, in spite of the rich bribe we offered. At last, after great difficulty, we succeeded in persuading a native to risk the attempt, and Gambier, having written a few lines in French with a stick for a pen, we saw the former conceal it about his person and shortly after depart.'

At last news reached them that the sepoys had given up the hunt and departed. Even better news was to follow: 'While we were congratulating ourselves on this piece of good fortune, a messenger arrived from Hurchundpore, a walled town situated some five miles further on the road to Meerut, saying his master a Mr. Cohen, hearing of our miserable plight, had sent him to express his sympathy at our situation, and begging us to take shelter with him.' If Vibart wondered why the natives hadn't informed them of Mr Cohen's existence before – he came to the conclusion that the villagers had intended to keep them as long as possible and sell them to the highest bidder, British or sepoy – he was in no mood to complain. By daybreak they were on their way by cart to Mr Cohen's home. Cohen was a German who had come to India to trade, had married an Indian woman and adopted Indian ways.

We were cordially welcomed by the old man and his two grandsons ... It appeared they owned several villages round about, for which they paid a certain sum to the Government. The old man himself had lived here all his life – so long, in fact, that he had almost forgotten his own language, and had become thoroughly native in his habits; but his two grandsons were somewhat different in this respect, and lived more in the European fashion. We were soon refreshed with a hot cup of tea, after which clean clothes were brought, and we proceeded to divest ourselves of the soiled rags we were wearing and enjoy the luxury of soap and water. A room was set apart for the ladies of the party, and they too managed to procure a change of apparel, in the shape of some clean *koortas* and snowy white *chuddahs* of fine nankeen, which latter they wore over their heads and draped over their shoulders in native style, and really looked so spruce and tidy in their novel costume, when they joined us at breakfast, that we could scarcely recognise them as the poor forlorn creatures of yesterday.

Meanwhile at Meerut, news had filtered through of refugees from Delhi; General Hewitt had received a letter – in French – telling him of one such party. Lieutenant Mackenzie, of the 3rd Light Cavalry – who had stood ready to shoot his sister and Mrs Craigie on the night of the outbreak – offered to go in search of them. Hugh Gough, now attached to the Carabiniers heard of it, too: 'Young Mackenzie of our regiment had already volunteered to take a party of the men who had remained loyal, and proceed to their rescue but ... the general had objected to so young an officer going by himself. I at once volunteered to accompany him, and my offer was accepted.' There wasn't much time to prepare, and stuffing a few biscuits in their pockets, they set off. The information they had was vague in the extreme and the conditions – heat, parching thirst and wells few and far between and mostly brackish – were harsh. 'At most of the villages the inhabitants turned out against us, and here and there shots were fired at us. But we held to our search, and slowly and by degrees tracking the fugitives, through information scantily and unwillingly given by the villagers, we ran them to ground towards evening, they having taken refuge in a large village called Hurchundpore. As we approached this village, a very large and fortified one, we could see the inhabitants lining the walls. Knowing for a certainty that our fugitives were there, we could not understand these signs of hostility.'

Meanwhile, Edward Vibart and his party of fugitives were enjoying Mr Cohen's hospitality:

At four o'clock p.m. a plentiful repast was set before us, and, to our no small astonishment, several bottles of beer were produced, followed, when dinner was removed, by a bottle of excellent Cognac. We were all sitting round the table, quietly talking over our recent adventures and hairbreadth escapes, and looking forward with light hearts to setting out next day on our journey to Meerut, when all of a sudden a tremendous shout was raised without, followed by such a terrible commotion amongst the townspeople that we were utterly dumbfounded to conceive the cause of so much uproar and confusion. Our ignorance was not of long duration, for soon there arose a cry amongst the excited multitude which, as it became gradually louder and more distinct, filled us with terror and dismay. 'Badshah ka fouj!' they shouted, 'Badshah Dehli ka fouj aya!' ('The King's troops, the King of Delhi's troops have come!'); and there sure enough, on looking out, we saw some forty troopers, dressed in the French-grey uniform of the mutinous 3rd Cavalry, drawn up in line just outside the walls and demanding admittance.

It seemed their luck had changed again – the mutineers had found them. 'The first thing we called for was to be supplied with arms; the next thing we did was to throw off the clean clothes we had on and jump into our former old ones. How far this exchange was likely to benefit us I know not; but certain it is that in a space of a very few seconds we were once more clad in the filthy garments of the previous day, and stood ready to meet the worst.'

Meanwhile, outside the town, Gough realized what had happened: the loyal troopers of the 3rd – in their French-grey tunics – had been mistaken for mutineers. 'I rode forward with Mackenzie and a trumpeter, halting our party some way off. Some of the leading inhabitants came out to parley. Seeing two British officers, they became to a certain extent friendly.' The townspeople allowed the two officers in, but not the troopers. Mackenzie and Gough rode in: 'surrounded by armed men on all sides, whose disposition, judging by their talk and gesticulations, seemed to us far from friendly, the moment was an anxious one. At last, after much delay and passing through narrow lanes, we came to the gates of a *serai*, or walled enclosure, in which the principal house of the village stood. As we entered we realised, to our intense relief and delight, that we had been successful and our search was at an end.' The relief was mutual: 'In the midst of all this excitement,' wrote Edward Vibart, 'two European officers were observed riding up the street, and as they were followed very quietly a few paces in the rear by the troopers themselves, we came to the very natural conclusion that they were friends and not enemies. And now the rush that was made by one and all to greet them as they rode up to the house! I was not long in recognising both officers to be old friends – Gough and Mackenzie, of the 3rd Cavalry, whose acquaintance I had already made in the course of frequent visits to Meerut.'

'Grouped in the centre of the enclosure,' wrote Gough, 'was a large party of our fellow-countrymen and women, who hailed our advent with an intensity of joy and relief which it is impossible to describe.' The fugitives were astonished, wrote Vibart, that their desperate message had found a response so soon. 'In reply to our queries as to how they had succeeded in finding us out, they informed us that the messenger we had despatched only reached Meerut on the evening of the previous day – that is to say, forty-eight hours after his departure – and that as soon as they ascertained our whereabouts they volunteered, with the remnant of their regiment which had remained faithful, to come out to our rescue, and had accordingly started the same night.' The whole party was conveyed to Meerut – and safety – the following day. 'There was only one sad heart among our party,' Vibart recalled, 'and that was Mrs Fraser. She had been looking forward to meeting her husband, who was in charge of the Sappers and Miners in Meerut, and fancying what his delight would be on welcoming her again, when alas! the first thing she heard was that he had been shot by his own men.'

Back in Delhi, Sir Theophilus Metcalfe escaped from the city – via the Lahore Gate – in native disguise. Conveyed by the native *thannadar* (superintendent of police) to the house of a *zamindar*, Bhur Khan, he spent three days in hiding on the roof of the *zenana* (women's quarters) until his host warned him that he must move him on. Bhur Khan took him to a small cave near by where he left him with a pitcher of water, some native bread and a sword and pistol. Next day he heard voices outside the cave and two troopers of the 3rd Light Cavalry came up with a third man, who was heard saying, 'I am sure he is here. Come in with me through this opening.' Metcalfe recognized the voice as that of his office orderly. As the first man came into the cave – blinded by the transition from blazing light to darkness – Metcalfe killed him with his sword then ran out into the open. The other two men fled in opposite directions and Metcalfe took one of their horses and made his way to Jhaijar, 35 miles north of Delhi. Metcalfe's father had saved the Nawab of Jhaijar's father from the confiscation of his principality. The Nawab, however, seemed reluctant to shelter the son of his father's friend and sent him on his way with an escort of soldiers. Not trusting these men, Metcalfe slipped away from them, hid among some sleeping villagers while they searched for him, and later made his way to Karnal and safety.

Meanwhile, in Delhi, the King had assumed the dignity of Mogul Emperor urged on him by the mutinous sepoys who thronged the *Diwan-i-Khas* (Hall of Audience). He had played for time at first – sitting in his private quarters while sepoys and *badmashes* rampaged through the gardens of the palace and the streets of the city, hunting out and slaughtering Europeans and Christians. Surely, he thought, British troops from Meerut would arrive soon, but time passed and no such force arrived. Captain Douglas, who had gone to convey the message to the newly arrived mutineers that they were disturbing the King, had not returned and now never would. All the British who surrounded him were dead, in hiding or on the run. It is difficult not to sympathize with Bahadur Shah, raised to Imperial dignity on the sword-and-bayonet points of a mutinous soldiery, like some reluctant Roman senator elevated by the Praetorians, with the threat of death if he refused. Whether or not he was actually so threatened, it was clear from the start that his new army would bring him no real power. To them he represented a rallying point behind which – they hoped – the deeply conservative peoples of India would gather. His legitimacy could cloak their rule, as it had that of the British and, before them, the Marathas. On 12 May he called a council of advisers and appointed a governor for the city with the task of restoring order. Delhi had been looted by the sepoys, aided by the mobs swelled with released convicts. He would still have played for time – his physician, Ahsanullah Khan, managed to get a message off to the Lieutenant Governor of the Punjab appealing for British aid – but his family would have none of it. For the Queen, Zenat Mahal, these events offered the fulfilment of a long-held dream, a dream that two Governors General had thwarted: the succession of her son Jawan Bakht. If the British would not allow him to occupy his father's throne then they – with the help of this modern, European-style army that they had raised and trained – would be driven into the sea. Her stepsons, too – even if the eldest of them, Mirza Mogul, had no desire to see Jawan Bakht on the throne in his place – knew well that the existence the British had planned for them was just as impotent, but even less gilded than that of their father. Better to swim with the new tide, and await events, while doubtless planning an early exit for Jawan Bakht in due course. Accordingly, Mirza Mogul accepted the post of commander-in-chief and lesser military titles went to his brothers.

Despite all this, the mutineers' leaders were suspicious of the King and acted swiftly to implicate him more deeply in their revolt. A number of Europeans had, on 11 May, taken refuge from the mob in the King's Palace. One English lady had even been sheltered by the Queen herself in the *zenana* until a group of sepoys demanded of the King – in a scene that characterizes the relationship between the 'Sovereign of the World' and his new army – that she be handed over to them. The King complied, making the sepoys promise not to harm her, but she was taken down to the main bazaar and there shot. The remaining fugitives – some fifty or so, mostly women or children – were held near the Lahore Gate, where they were fed at the King's expense. After four or five days the mutineer leaders decided to bring them out for execution. According to Mubarak Shah, appointed a police official in Delhi at the time: 'The King wept and besought the mutineers not to take the lives of helpless women and children, saying to them: "Take care – for if you commit such a deed the vengeance and anger of God will fall on me – Why slay the innocent?" The mutineers refused to listen and replied: "We'll kill them and in your Palace so whatever be the result you too shall be considered *one* in this business and you will be thought equally guilty by the British."' The captives were led out, a rope was thrown around them – as was the usual way of herding large numbers of prisoners – and under a peepul tree in a courtyard, they were hacked to death by members of the King's household.

Shortly after the announcement of the revived Mogul Empire a royal proclamation was issued. 'To all Hindus and Mussulmans, Citizens and servants of Hindustan, the Officers of the Army now at Delhi and Meerut send greeting: It is well known that in these days all the English have entertained these evil designs – first, to destroy the religion of the whole Hindostani army, then to make the people by compulsion Christians. Therefore we, solely on account of our religion, have combined with the people, and have not spared alive one infidel, and have established the Delhi dynasty on these terms.' The proclamation went on to appeal to all Indians to unite in the struggle – while, of course maintaining the social order – and to post the proclamation far and wide. These words were intended as a call-to-arms to all the peoples of India, but words – like everything else in India at the time – travelled slowly. They travelled less slowly for the British, though, and – even as the newly restored Mogul Emperor was settling uneasily on his silver throne – their hated new technology was starting to work in their favour.

# 4

## REACTIONS

The telegraph office at Delhi lay outside the city walls – halfway between the Flagstaff Tower and the Kashmir Gate. As was the practice throughout India it had been closed for most of the day on Sunday 10 May, as was the office at Meerut. On Saturday the 9th the officials at Meerut – 'gossiping' down the line – had conveyed to their colleagues in the Delhi office the excitement caused by the disarmings, but there had been no official communication. Such was the complacency felt by the authorities at Meerut that they had felt no need to warn the Europeans at Delhi of the tension in the town. At 4 p.m. on Sunday the 10th the Delhi office had been opened as usual, and it was found that communications between it and Meerut had been interrupted. This was not uncommon – the line to Meerut crossed many rivers, where problems regularly occurred. Mr Todd, the assistant in charge, had crossed to the far side of the Bridge of Boats over the Jumna and found all well with the line up to that point – clearly the fault lay further up the line towards Meerut. In fact, the Meerut mutineers had cut the line, but Todd – like everyone else in Delhi – was unaware of any outbreak and assumed it was a routine fault. He resolved to go out first thing next morning to attempt to restore communications.

He set out at 8 a.m., but he never returned. It is believed that he was the lone European the mutinous 3rd Light Cavalry encountered on the Bridge of Boats, pulled out of his *gharry* (trap) and killed. He left behind him in the office his wife – now, though she did not know it, a widow – and two young assistants, Brendish and Pilkington. As the day wore on,

69

messengers came in from the offices of the *Delhi Gazette* informing them of the arrival of the mutineers and, later, that the sepoys of the Delhi garrison sent to oppose them had mutinied, too, and shot their officers. Shortly afterwards a wounded officer, making his way up from the Kashmir Gate to the Flagstaff, had confirmed the news and urged them to run – as did a number of fleeing native shopkeepers. At length they were able to persuade a frantic Mrs Todd to come with them, but before they did – true to their duty – they sent one crucial message. The line to Umballa and on to Lahore was open – no mutinies having yet occurred in that direction – and before leaving the office Brendish signalled: 'We must leave office, all the bungalows are on fire, burning down by the sepoys of Meerut. They came in this morning. We are off. Mr C. Todd is dead, I think. He went out this morning and has not yet returned. We learned that nine Europeans are killed.'

This message, received at Umballa and passed to Sir Henry Barnard, commander of the Sirhind Division, was flashed across the Punjab to Lahore and Peshawar on the North-West Frontier, enabling the authorities there to take swift action to prevent similar outbreaks. On 12 May a young staff officer – Sir Henry Barnard's son – rode from Umballa to Simla in the hills, where the Commander-in-Chief had gone shooting. That same day in Calcutta – at the other end of India – the Governor General, Lord Canning, received a telegram via Agra, informing him of the events at Meerut. If the initial rounds of this conflict had gone to the mutineers – possessed as they were of the element of surprise – the technological edge possessed by the British now began to even the odds. In the opinion of Sir Robert Montgomery, Judicial Commissioner of the Punjab, thanks to the action of two young men left isolated while all around them fled, 'The electric telegraph saved India'.

More detailed telegrams on 14, 15 and 16 May informed Lord Canning in Calcutta of the seizure of Delhi, the massacre of the Europeans and the raising of the standard of a revived Mogul Empire. Canning seems to have understood at once that what faced him was the possibility that the whole Bengal Army might soon rise in revolt. His immediate response was to telegraph the Governor of Bombay for the speedy return of troops of the Bombay Army from their recent campaign in Persia. Another telegraph was sent to the commander-in-chief of the Bengal Army, General Anson, at Simla, ordering him to gather the forces available to him and march at once on Delhi, and a third was sent to Sir John Lawrence in the Punjab, conferring on him full powers to act as he thought fit. Of the troops immediately under Canning's hand in or near Calcutta, HM 84th Foot's ordered move to Rangoon was cancelled and another regiment summoned from Moulmein, also in Burma. A message was sent to Lord Harris, Governor of Madras, ordering him to send up two European regiments without delay. Knowing that an expedition was on the sea heading for China, Lord Canning – on his own responsibility – telegraphed Lord Elgin and General Ashburnham ordering them to divert their troops to Calcutta. Canning's priorities from the start, then, were the speedy recapture of Delhi – which he rightly saw as the linchpin of the revolt – and the summoning of British reinforcements from wherever they might be procured.

If Lord Canning was aware of the potential dangers of the Meerut rising, this does not seem to have communicated itself to other members of his Government. The merchants of Calcutta – a mixture of British, Europeans (mainly French and German) and Americans – approached the Government with an offer to form a Volunteer corps. 'The situation is full of peril,' they wrote, 'you are short of men, you have to control a large population in Calcutta, and you have within call but two English regiments; there are three native regiments at Barrackphur, ready to emulate the conduct of their comrades at Mirath [Meerut], why not utilise our services? We can furnish a regiment of infantry, a regiment of cavalry, and a battery of artillery; our interests and your interests are identical: use us.' They were blandly assured by the Calcutta Home Secretary, Mr Cecil Beadon, 'Everything is quiet within six hundred miles of the capital. The mischief caused by a passing and groundless panic has already been arrested; and there is every reason to hope that in the course of a few days tranquillity and confidence will be restored throughout the Presidency.' As a statement of the exact opposite of the truth this could scarcely be bettered. In the next five days news came in of risings at Ferozepore, Aligarh, Bulandshahr, Itwah and Mainpuri – and discouraging reports arrived from Lucknow, Cawnpore, Agra and Benares.

When Canning reviewed the situation in the light of this news, what he saw would have daunted a lesser man. Between Dinapore (see map 2 on page xiv) and Calcutta there were no British Regiments. HM 10th Foot were at Dinapore, and at Calcutta he had two British Regiments; HM 84th and HM 53rd Foot. At Benares there were no European troops save a handful of gunners. The same was true of Allahabad, and Cawnpore, on the border of Oude. In Oude itself, likely to take the lead in any general revolt, Sir Henry Lawrence at Lucknow had just one regiment, HM 32nd Foot, to hold the whole province. At Agra, similarly, there was only one regiment of the Company's European troops – beyond that Delhi was in rebel hands. Meerut was secure and, further north, Anson had three British regiments on the spurs of the Himalaya. How things stood with Sir John Lawrence in the newly conquered Punjab – where the bulk of the British troops in India was concentrated – Lord Canning had no way of knowing. What he did know was that if the Punjab were now to rise – and the Sikhs had been the Company's most recent and most formidable foe – the whole of the British position in India would be at risk. In short, there now existed a whole swathe of Northern India where British rule was at best precarious, at worst non-existent. Within that central belt the British were either on the run or huddled behind their fortifications.

Calcutta, Canning believed, was safe, but the whole country from Benares to Meerut was for the time being out of his control and the Punjab was an unknown quantity. If Delhi was not retaken and order restored in that central belt soon, then the Punjab, too, might rise. To this end, as soon as he was able, Canning began pushing troops north, starting, on 20 May, with detachments of HM 84th Foot to Benares and Cawnpore. On 23 May the 1st Madras European Fusiliers – known for their pale blue cap-covers and neck-guards as 'Neill's Blue Caps' – arrived and were likewise sent on to Benares, under their colonel, James Neill. In the first week of June HM 64th Foot and the 78th Highlanders arrived from Persia – their commander, General Henry Havelock, was still at sea. A wing (half a battalion) of HM 35th Foot arrived from Moulmein, and a wing of HM 39th Foot and a company of artillery from Ceylon. Before the Mutiny it had been whispered among the disaffected in the native lines and bazaars that the British soldiers outside India were all dead, killed by the Russians in the Crimea. Some even believed that the *Gora Log* (British) had moved to India en masse, and that if those in India were killed the world would be rid of them forever.

Any rebel standing on the quays of Calcutta and watching the reinforcements arriving, even at this early stage, would have been cruelly disillusioned. In June three more battalions of infantry and three companies of artillery arrived – a further three battalions arrived the next month with two more companies of artillery, and two more battalions in August. Troops continued to arrive in steadily increasing numbers; three battalions in September; eight in October – on average a brigade each month until November, when eleven battalions and three cavalry regiments arrived (another three were to follow the next month) with five artillery companies (to be followed by another eight in December). All this lay in the future, though, and the earliest arrivals, in June, arrived in a city in which early complacency had given way to near panic. Among the earliest arrivals was F. C. Maude of the Royal Artillery. Maude had taken his battery 'out into the country for a few days pic-nic' when, 'In the afternoon of the 6th June, 1857, our lotus-eating life [in Ceylon] was suddenly disturbed by the arrival in Back Bay, Trincomalee, of the *Semiramis*, a frigate belonging to the East India Company, which brought the astonishing news that the Sepoy Mutiny had broken out, and that every European soldier was to proceed immediately to British India.'

Maude and his battery arrived in Calcutta in time to witness what went down in that city's history as 'Panic Sunday'. On 16 June a rumour reached Calcutta that the sepoys at Barrackpore had mutinied and were marching on the city. In fact, the Mutiny had been forestalled when – with the 78th Highlanders, a wing of HM 32nd Foot and a battery of artillery – the formidable General Hearsey had disarmed the sepoys at Barrackpore, but before the truth reached Calcutta its citizens, in Maude's words 'gave heed to the various rumours of which the air was rife, their hearts became as water and melted within them, neither did there remain any courage within them. They rushed on board the ships in the Hooghly, crowded Fort William, and said and did many other foolish things for which, however, it is hardly fair to blame them too heavily now.' Colonel G. B. Malleson (later a historian of the Mutiny), who was in Calcutta on the day, saw the plain in front of Fort William 'covered with fugitives, some riding, some in carriages of sorts, some in palanquins, some running, some walking – men, women, and children all making for the nearest fort gate. It was a sight once seen never to be forgotten.' While other – previously complacent – souls lost their heads, Lord Canning kept his, and executed a measure he had been contemplating for some time. 'The King of Oude who had lately been deposed by Lord Dalhousie,' wrote Maude, 'occupied a splendid palace at Garden Reach, on the left bank of the Hooghly, where his *zenana* and menagerie were the talk of the town. A great part of the plotting that led to the terrible outbreak was believed to have been hatched in this hot-bed of Mussulman intrigue; Ali Nukkee Khan, the ex-King's able Premier, being one of the main-springs of the conspiracy.' Canning's spies had kept him well informed, and the arrest of the ex-King and his *vakeel* (man of business) was resolved upon. The *vakeel* was arrested outside the palace, condemned to hang the next day, and confined in Fort William.

'At midnight on Saturday the 15th June,' wrote Maude,

> every European capable of bearing arms was marched silently out of Fort William, and disposed strategically, around the Royal residence, on its land side. The *Zenobia* had also noiselessly slipped from her moorings at Calcutta and anchored off the Garden Reach Palace, upon which her guns ('double-shotted' as was the fashion) were carefully pointed. The writer had charge of the four field guns, which we took down with drag ropes and laid them so as to command the respective gateways. So complete was the surprise that the two officers appointed for this capture found the King asleep in bed. The moment was critical, for the Park was known to be swarming with desperate fanatics armed to the teeth. One or two of the King's wives were very warlike and urged him to resist; but a short and stern colloquy, enforced by the sight of loaded revolvers, together with a peep at the frigate opposite his windows, proved sufficient to induce the King to dress himself speedily, and he was forthwith conducted to the carriage prepared for him, arriving at his quarters in Fort William before sunrise.

It had been a daring stroke, which involved leaving Fort William in the hands of the 43rd Bengal Native Light Infantry who – had they chosen to mutiny at this time – could have closed the gates of Calcutta's main stronghold to the British. Canning, however, in Maude's words 'had the talent of knowing exactly whom to trust and when to strike'. The 43rd remained true to their salt throughout the Mutiny. 'On our return to the Fort,' wrote Maude, 'we found that the wily Vakeel, who lay under sentence of death in the guard-room, perceiving that the coast was clear, and probably with the connivance of friends had made himself scarce; nor was he ever afterwards heard of by the authorities.' Considering his remarkable escape from a locked guardroom, it is tempting to speculate on the *vakeel*'s real role in the betrayal and arrest of the ex-King of Oude.

On India's North-West Frontier, Sir John Lawrence, Chief Commissioner of the Punjab, was at Rawalpindi when he heard the news of the Meerut outbreak. He at once saw Delhi as the key to the uprising and impressed this view – via Lord Canning at Calcutta – on the commander-in-chief, General Anson. These were among the first of a series of letters and telegrams that Lawrence was to send in all directions –

giving orders, bracing the timid, urging on the backsliders and dispensing advice – throughout the emergency. Passing through Simla on his way to Meerut, the civil servant Robert Dunlop met a lady – one of many – who sang the praises of Sir John: 'who not only got through Herculean labours himself, but sternly forced all malingerers to do their duty, who, with the authority of a master mind, flashed message after message of abrupt command wherever the electric shock was necessary. One of the earliest victims of the struggle had sunk, she said, killed by an attack of Lawrence's telegraphic messages.'

Lawrence's first task was to secure the Punjab itself. With the revolted 'central belt' to his south-east, and a currently peaceable but untrustworthy Afghanistan to his north-west, his position was not enviable. He was lucky in his subordinates, who were perhaps the most remarkable group of men ever produced by British India. The Punjab was – prior to the Mutiny of 1857 – the point of maximum danger and difficulty, and it is perhaps unsurprising that it had, in the previous few years, attracted the boldest and the best. His brother, Sir Henry Lawrence – now nervously watching the sepoys in his station at Lucknow, the capital of Oude – had a gift for recruiting such characters, and their names dominate the story of the Mutiny almost from the outset.

Youth was on their side. Frederick Roberts – a young officer of the Bengal Horse Artillery, who was in Peshawar at the time – writing in later years recalled: 'Fortunately for India, there were good men and true at Peshawar in those days, when hesitation and irresolution would have been fatal, and it is worthy of note that they were comparatively young men – Edwardes was thirty-seven, Nicholson thirty-five; Neville Chamberlain, the distinguished commander of the Punjab Frontier Force ... was thirty-seven; and the Brigadier Sidney Cotton, though much older, being sixty-five, was not only exceptionally young for his years and full of energy and intelligence, but actually much younger than the average of General officers commanding stations in India.'

The firm and resolute actions of the men who ran the Punjab make a bracing contrast with the confusion and hesitancy that prevailed – with a few honourable exceptions – south of the Sutlej. The first act of Edwardes – together with Nicholson – on hearing of the Mutiny was to send to the post office and lay hands on all native correspondence. 'The letters they thus secured,' wrote Roberts, 'showed but too plainly how necessary was this great precaution. The number of seditious papers seized was alarmingly great; they were for the most part couched in figurative and enigmatical language, but it was quite sufficiently clear from them that every Native regiment in the garrison was more or less implicated and prepared to join the rebel movement.' One letter from a portion of the 55th NI stationed at Attock – an important ford on the Indus – addressed to the 64th NI at Peshawar, reads: 'The cartridge will have to be beaten on the 22nd instant. Of this you are hereby informed. This is addressed to you by the whole regiment. Oh, brothers! The religion of Hindoos and Mohammedans is all one; therefore all you soldiers should know this. Here, all the sepoys are at the bidding of the jemadar, soubahdar-major [sic], and havildar-major. All are discontented with this business, whether small or great. What more need be written?' Another, written by a subadar-major of the 51st NI, said: 'In whatever way you can manage it, come into Peshawur on the 21st instant. Thoroughly understand that point; in fact, eat there, and drink here!' It was clear from this correspondence that none of the Hindustani sepoys could be trusted.

At a conference held in Peshawar on the morning of 13 May, which Frederick Roberts attended, the assembled soldiers and soldier-civilians, in the absence of the Chief Commissioner, assessed the military situation. The first question addressed was how to secure the Punjab with the 15,000 British troops and eighty-four guns available to them, against a force of 42,000 sepoys with sixty-two guns. Native troops formed the majority in most stations, and in others there were no European troops at all. Two of the Commissioners, Roberts wrote, had a radical solution to the manpower problem. 'Edwardes and Nicholson gave it as their opinion that the only chance of keeping the Punjab and the frontier quiet lay in trusting the Chiefs and the people, and in endeavouring to induce them to side with us against the Hindustanis. They undertook to communicate, regarding the raising of levies and fresh troops, with their friends and acquaintances along the border, who had proved such staunch allies in 1848–9 when we were fighting with the Sikhs.' At this meeting it was also agreed that a 'Movable Column' be formed, prepared to move in any direction in which it might be needed.

Sir John Lawrence, when he heard of Edwardes' proposal to enlist frontier men, was unsure (it was the only measure of the 13 May meeting with which he disagreed), but allowed himself to be persuaded. At first, though, there seemed no great willingness to enlist. 'Nicholson encountered considerable difficulty in raising local levies,' wrote Roberts, 'and there was a general unwillingness to enlist. Our disasters in Kabul in 1841–2 had not been forgotten; our cause was considered desperate, and even Nicholson could not persuade the men to join it.' It was clear that this state of affairs must not be allowed to continue and some decisive measures must quickly be taken, or there would be a general rising along the frontier. Decisive action was taken: at Lahore the Chief Civil Officer, genial, rotund Robert Montgomery, nicknamed 'Pickwick', had already disarmed the sepoy regiments there on 13 May – three of infantry and one of cavalry. On 22 May it was decided to do the same in Peshawar. As elsewhere, this had to be done in the teeth of opposition from the regiment's British officers: 'The officers were quite aghast,' wrote Roberts of the moment they received the order. 'They were persistent and almost insubordinate in expressing their conviction that the measure was wholly uncalled-for, that the sepoys were thoroughly loyal, and that, not-withstanding what had occurred in other places, they had perfect confidence in their men.' In spite of that confidence, under the guns and muskets of European troops four out of the five Native regiments were ordered to lay down their arms. The fifth was spared, because it was well officered and had shown no signs of disaffection. Also spared, because they brought their own horses and weapons so were considered to have more commitment to the service, were the two regiments of Irregular cavalry. The effect of the disarming in the Peshawar valley was almost immediate. 'As we rode down to the disarming,' wrote Herbert Edwardes later, 'a very few Chiefs and yeomen of the country attended us; and I remember judging from their faces that they came to see which way the tide would turn. As we rode back, friends were as thick as summer flies, and levies began from that moment to come in.' That night the Subadar-Major of the now disarmed 51st NI – the man who had written the second letter quoted (see page 76) – deserted and headed for the hills, taking 250 men with him. If he had hoped for a welcome from the hillmen, wrote Roberts, he was disappointed: 'However welcome 250 muskets might have been to the Afridis, 250 unarmed sepoys were no prize; and as our neighbours in the hills had evidently come to the conclusion that our *raj* was not in such a desperate state as they had imagined, and that their best policy was to side with us, they caught the deserters, with the assistance of the district police, and made them over to the authorities. The men were all tried by Court Martial, and the Subadar-Major was hanged in the presence of the whole garrison.'

Having identified the recapture of Delhi as the primary British object-ive, John Lawrence knew that this would have to be done at the expense of the Punjab and with the help of British troops currently holding it. It was a huge risk – the Punjab had only been finally annexed eight years earlier after the costly British victories of Chillianwallah and Gujerat. He had accepted Edwardes' advice that as well as denuding the province of its British garrison it would be necessary to raise fresh troops from along the frontier. This principle was soon extended to the Sikhs themselves – those same Sikhs who had until recently been the British Army's bitterest enemies. If they now took their opportunity to throw off the British yoke, and throw in their lot with the sepoys, all of British India north of Dinapore might be lost, but Lawrence now embarked on one of the greatest gambles in the history of the British Empire.

He was helped by a number of factors. To appeal to the Sikhs in the British *raj's* hour of need was, on the face of it, a hopeless task. However, if the Sikhs had no great love for the British they had a bitter hatred – tinged with contempt – for the 'Purbiyas' (from the Persian for Easterners) of Oude and Bihar, who formed the bulk of the Company's sepoy army. They deeply resented the fact that they had been conquered by the British, aided by men whom they considered to be their inferiors as soldiers. The Khalsa, the famous and formidable Sikh Army, had marched against the British in 1845 with the intention of sacking Delhi – if the British were now marching on Delhi themselves there was no shortage of former Khalsa men willing to enlist and march with them. Some Sikh soldiers were already serving under British officers; more would soon enlist. The British had, in their time as administrators of the Punjab, brought a measure of good government – a welcome relief after the almost continual anarchy that had followed the death of Ranjit Singh, the almost legendary Sikh leader, in 1839. Under Sir Henry Lawrence, Sir John's elder brother (whom he had replaced in circumstances that had caused some bitterness between them), British district officers had established a bond of trust between themselves and the peasants. Moreover, the Sikhs – like the men of the hills – seem to have assessed the situation across the Sutlej and concluded that, in the end, the British would win. Today what the British call the Indian, or Sepoy, Mutiny is known in India as the First National War of Independence. It was no such thing – if for no other reason than that there was no real 'national' feeling. As Robert Dunlop wrote at the time: 'Many in England seem to class all tribes of Indians together, whereas the Hillmen and Sikhs are less like the Poorbeas than Englishmen are like Russians or the men of European Turkey.' The troops that Lawrence – with an eye to the strategic 'big picture' and a gambler's cool-headedness – began sending south, were to consist of large numbers of such 'Sikhs and Hillmen'. First to be despatched in the direction of Delhi were the Corps of Guides – a mixed force of Afghans and Gurkhas, under Captain Daly. Soon after, from the Punjab Frontier Force, went the 4th Sikhs and the 1st Punjab Infantry (Coke's Rifles) as well as a squadron each of the 1st, 2nd and 5th Punjab Cavalry, and the 2nd and 4th Punjab Infantry.

So intent was Lawrence on succouring attempts to take Delhi – at the expense, if necessary, of his own province – that he even considered doing a deal with the Amir of Afghanistan, and evacuating Peshawar. Dost Mohammed, who had expelled the British from Afghanistan in 1842, had since proved to be the reliable neighbour he had only ever wished to be. He had shown no sign, so far, of seeking to capitalize on British woes, but like many further south, was watching to see which way the tide would flow. The recovery of Peshawar – lost to Ranjit Singh some years earlier – was a project dear to his heart. Lawrence's plan – if events in the south required still more British troops – was to withdraw across the Indus and allow the Dost to reoccupy Pehsawar. Lawrence understood that the adherence of the Sikhs depended on success in the south, and he was willing – in order to achieve that success – to take even this drastic step. It was a nice calculation. Certainly such a withdrawal would free more British troops who could be sent south. On the other hand, it would be an admission of weakness that might bring the Sikhs – and the Afghans – in on the wrong side. Edwardes was against it from the start. 'Pashawar', he wrote to Lawrence, 'is the anchor of the Panjab, and if you take it the whole ship will drift to sea.' Nicholson and Brigadier Cotton agreed with Edwardes; Lawrence remained obdurate, and the argument dragged on well into June when Lord Canning ended all debate in a telegram from Calcutta: 'Hold on to Pashawar to the last.'

By 27 May the Movable Column – consisting of HM 52nd Light Infantry, Dawes' troop of horse artillery, Bourchier's battery of European field artillery, a wing of the 9th Bengal (Native) Light Cavalry, and the 35th NI – had assembled at Wazirabad. In command, as brigadier, was Neville Chamberlain, with Frederick Roberts as his staff officer. Chamberlain – already a distinguished Frontier fighter – had been appointed over the heads of officers senior to him, which caused problems at first. Roberts' first job was to inform Colonel Campbell of the 52nd that Chamberlain had arrived to take over command of the force.

I found the Colonel lying on his bed trying to make himself as comfortable as it was possible with the thermometer at 117 degrees Fahrenheit. We had not met before, and he certainly received me in a very off-hand manner. He never moved from his recumbent position, and on my delivering my message, he told me he was not aware that the title of Brigadier carried military rank with it; that he understood that Brigadier Chamberlain was only a Lieutenant-Colonel, whereas he held the rank of Colonel in Her Majesty's army; and that under these circumstances, he must decline to acknowledge Brigadier Chamberlain as his senior officer.

It took a message from Sir John Lawrence, explaining that it was necessary for an officer of Indian experience to command the force (Campbell was new to India) and that Colonel Campbell could, if he wished, remain with his Headquarters at Lahore when his regiment marched, before Campbell agreed, reluctantly, to serve under Chamberlain. Roberts regarded Campbell as 'at heart . . . really a very nice fellow and an excellent officer', but felt there was another reason for his reluctance to serve under Chamberlain: 'The Brigadier was a servant of "John Company", while Campbell belonged to the "Queen's service". From the time of the establishment of the local army there had existed an absurd and unfortunate jealousy between officers of the Queen's and Company's services . . . This ill-feeling influenced not only fellow countrymen, but relations, even brothers, if they belonged to the different services, and was distinctly prejudicial to the interests of the Government.'

Ruffled feathers having been smoothed, the Movable Column set off – first for Lahore. 'As a general rule we marched between 12 and 1 a.m.,' wrote Reginald Wilberforce of the 52nd Light Infantry,

our band playing us out of camp on the Trunk Road with 'The girl I left behind me': then the order was given to 'March at ease', 'March easy'. The men used to sling their firelocks over their shoulders and smoke their pipes. The band used to go on playing, and when the bandsmen were tired, our bugle band would take it up and play away. When they had finished, some individual, somewhere in the centre of the regiment, would start a song, and so the hours whiled away until 'coffee shop'. Half way along the line of march we always halted for half an hour; the men had rum served out to them, and the officers used to have coffee as well as other things. One of the favourite songs was of a most revolutionary character; it had about 30 verses and a long chorus. I forget the song but I recollect that 'Confound our officers!' had a place in the chorus, and used to be lustily shouted. At first the men would not sing this song – they thought it would hurt our feelings, but it had so good a tune that every night one of our Captains would call for it.

The march would then continue – with more music – through the night, arriving at camp, which was already set up and waiting, just as the sun rose.

The first thing to be done was a good wash, to get rid of the dust of the march, and then everyone turned in to sleep. At first we used to sleep on our beds, but we soon gave this up, the heat was too great, 130 Fahr. We used to sleep under our beds and keep the heat of the sun off ... About 12.30 we began to get up, and 1 to 1.30 found us all gathered together in the big mess tent, the temperature of which, by the aid of *tatties* [wet grass screens] we managed to keep down to 120 for breakfast. [After breakfast] ... some of us, and I always among the number, used to get on our ponies about 3 p.m. and scour the surrounding country in search of antelope, nylghau, or even the familiar pariah dog; the two former we tried to shoot; I think we once got a blue bull; the latter – and they never failed us – we used to try to stick with spears ... At 6 p.m. there used to be a short parade, and at 7.30 we were all gathered together round the mess table for dinner. While that meal was in progress camp was struck and the camels loaded to be sent forward in readiness for the next day. The mess tent was the last to be taken down. After dinner we lay down on the ground, wet or dry, to smoke our pipes and get some two hours' sleep before resuming the march.

At Lahore, 'Pickwick' Montgomery having already disarmed the sepoys there, the only problem came from the sepoys present with the column. Spies informed Roberts in the night that the sepoys of the 35th NI were planning to mutiny and that some sepoys had already loaded their muskets. The regiment was paraded at dawn and two men were found to have loaded muskets and were placed under arrest. Chamberlain decided to revive an obsolete custom – the Drum Head Court Martial – and, to demonstrate impartiality, appointed Native officers to form the tribunal. Chamberlain was fortunate in having on hand the 1st Punjab

Infantry (Coke's Rifles) a regiment composed of Sikhs and Afghans, and rightly considered to be of unshakeable loyalty. The prisoners were found guilty of mutiny and sentenced to death. Chamberlain ordered that they should be blown from guns in the presence of their comrades as a deterrent and an example.

Blowing away from the mouth of a cannon was a traditional military punishment in India, much practised by the Moguls, and one that in the present emergency the British resorted to with alacrity. As well as being spectacular – though Roberts points out that it was also humane, as death was instantaneous – it was offensive to the religious sensitivities of Hindus and Muslims alike. A Colonel Hamley, who had witnessed the execution of some mutinied sepoys of the 55th NI in Peshawar, described the process:

> All the troops, European and native, loyal and disaffected, were drawn up on parade, forming three sides of a square; and drawn up very carefully, you may be sure, so that any attempt on the part of the disaffected to rescue the doomed prisoners would have been easily checked. Forming the fourth side of the square were drawn up the guns (nine-pounders), ten in number, which were to be used for the execution. The prisoners, under a strong European guard, were then marched into the square, their crimes and sentences read aloud to them, and at the head of each regiment; they were then marched round the square, and up to the guns. The first ten were picked out; their eyes were bandaged, and they were bound to the guns, their backs leaning against the muzzles, and their arms fastened to the wheels. The port-fires were lighted, and at a signal from the artillery major the guns were fired. It was a horrid sight that then met the eye: a regular shower of human fragments – of heads, of arms, of legs – appeared in the air through the smoke; and when that cleared away, these fragments lying on the ground – fragments of Hindoos and fragments of Mussulmans, all mixed together – were all that remained of those ten mutineers. Three times more was this repeated; but so great is the disgust we all feel for the atrocities committed by the rebels, that we had no room in our hearts for any feeling of pity; perfect callousness was depicted on every European's face; a look of grim satisfaction could even be seen in the countenance of the gunners serving the guns.

Hamley claimed that this form of punishment was the only one that held any terror for the native:

If he is hanged or shot by musketry, he knows that his friends or relatives will be allowed to claim his body, and will give him the funeral rites required by his religion; if a Hindoo, that his body will be burned with all due ceremonies; and if a Mussulman, that his remains will be decently interred, as directed in the Koran. But if sentenced to death in this form, he knows that his body will be blown into a thousand pieces, and that it will be altogether impossible for his relatives, however devoted to him, to be sure of picking up all the fragments of his particular body; and the thought that perhaps a limb of some one of a different religion to himself, might be burned or buried with the remainder of his own body, is agony to him.

Frederick Roberts witnessed the punishment parade at Lahore:

The troops were drawn up so as to form three sides of a square; on the fourth side were two guns. As the prisoners were being brought to the parade, one of them asked me if they were going to be blown from guns. I said, 'Yes.' He made no further remark, and they both walked steadily on until they reached the guns, to which they were bound, when one of them requested that some rupees he had on his person might be saved for his relations. The Brigadier answered: 'It is too late!' The word of command was given; the guns went off simultaneously, and the two mutineers were launched into eternity. It was a terrible sight, and one likely to halt the beholder for many a day; but that was what was intended.

After moving on to Multan, where his column disarmed the two sepoy regiments there, Chamberlain continued to Amritsar where he received a telegram summoning him to join – as adjutant general – the field force that was preparing to advance on Delhi. To replace him Lawrence had nominated John Nicholson, who would join the column at Jullundur. To select an officer with the regimental rank of captain, on civilian service, and appoint him to such a command – with the rank of brigadier general – is yet another measure both of Lawrence's audacity and of the seriousness with which he viewed the situation. That Nicholson was given the *rank* of brigadier general rather than the *appointment* of brigadier seems to have satisfied Colonel Campbell's sense of *amour-propre* – and the two men got on well from the start.

In contrast with the rest of the Punjab, affairs at Jullundur had been mishandled. Three Native regiments had been allowed to mutiny and march off to Delhi with their arms and treasure under the noses of a European garrison – a replay of events at Meerut. The British garrison had now set off in a half-hearted pursuit and the Commissioner, Major Edward Lake, had accepted the offer of a local prince, the Rajah of Kapurthala, to provide a garrison. The reputation of the British had suffered, however, as Roberts discovered: 'There was no doubt as to the loyalty of the Rajah himself, and his sincere desire to help us; but the mismanagement of affairs at Jullundur had done much to lower our prestige in the eyes of his people, and there was no mistaking the offensive demeanour of his troops. They evidently thought that British soldiers had gone never to return, and they swaggered about in swash-buckler fashion, as only Natives who think they have the upper hand can swagger.'

When Nicholson arrived on 20 June to take over his command, a *durbar* (court assembly) was held at Lake's house to pay a compliment to the Rajah and his commanders. There, Roberts witnessed a scene that showed him – and the natives – the calibre of man they were dealing with in John Nicholson.

At the close of the ceremony, Mehtab Singh, a general officer in the Kapurthala Army, took his leave, and, as the senior in rank at the durbar, was walking out of the room first, when I observed Nicholson stalk to the door, put himself in front of Mehtab Singh and, waving him back with an authoritative air, prevent him from leaving the room. The rest of the company then passed out, and when they had gone, Nicholson said to Lake: 'Do you see that General Mehtab Singh has his shoes on?' Lake replied that he had noticed the fact, but tried to excuse it. Nicholson, however, speaking in Hindustani, said: 'There is no possible excuse for such an act of gross impertinence. Mehtab Singh knows perfectly well that he would not venture to step on his own father's carpet save barefooted, and he has only committed this breach of etiquette to-day because he thinks we are not in a position to resent the insult, and that he can treat us as he would not have dared to do a month ago.' Mehtab Singh looked extremely foolish, and stammered some kind of apology; but Nicholson was not to be appeased, and continued: 'If I were the last Englishman left in Jullundur, you' (addressing Mehtab Singh) 'should not come into my room with your shoes on'; then, politely turning to Lake, he added, 'I hope the Commissioner will allow me to order you to take your shoes off and carry them out in your own hands, so that your followers may witness your discomfiture.' Mehtab Singh, completely cowed, meekly did as he was told.

Nicholson's demeanour seems to have impressed the natives; after that, wrote Roberts: 'Their manner at once changed, all disrespect vanished, and there was no more swaggering about as if they considered themselves masters of the situation. If Mehtab Singh had to learn the hard way what kind of man John Nicholson was, most others knew him by reputation.' Reginald Wilberforce overheard a conversation between two British privates the day Nicholson arrived: '"Jack, the General's here." "How do you know?" "Why look there; there's his mark."' The "there" his fellow soldier was told to look at was a pair of gallows, each of which was adorned with six hanging mutineers, while close by were several bullock carts, all filled with Sepoys who had revolted, and who were waiting for their turn.' An Ulsterman from Lisburn, the son of a doctor, John Nicholson had served eighteen years with the East India Company's army – eleven of them as a civilian administrator. He had seen action in the First Afghan War, where he had had the no doubt formative experience of finding the dead body of his brother – killed by the Afghans – with his genitals cut off and stuffed in his mouth. In the First Sikh War he had served on the Commissariat, and in the Second he had commanded a party of Pathan levies acting as a political and intelligence officer to the then commander-in-chief, Sir Hugh Gough (father of Lieutenant Hugh Gough, who survived the mutiny at Meerut and rescued Edward Vibart and his friends). After the Sikh wars – as one of Sir Henry Lawrence's circle – he became Commissioner for Bannu on the North-West Frontier. Although technically a civilian, administrative post, Nicholson's job – in a troublesome province peopled by warlike and hostile tribesmen – involved long hours in the saddle at the head of his hand-picked force of Multani horsemen, punitive raids and often the dispensing of ruthless Jedburgh-style justice. Nicholson's policy of strict-but-fair justice meted out with an iron hand won him the admiration of the tribesmen who declared that the early Muslims must have been like him – and that he was a true Hakim (master). Among the feats that drew their admiration was his method of hunting leopards – riding swiftly round the animal on a pony, in ever-decreasing circles, before despatching it with a sabre. 'The sound of his horse's hooves,' one native said, 'is heard from Attock to the Khyber.' Such was Nicholson's fame that one group of Hindus even proclaimed him an avatar of Vishnu and – under the name 'Nikalseyn' – worshipped him. Nicholson, a devout, Bible-reading Ulster Protestant, was appalled, and when they came to adore their deity in person, thrashed them all soundly – an action that only increased their devotion.

Frederick Roberts, who had worked with him in Peshawar, had complete confidence in the column's new commander: 'He seemed always to know exactly what to do and the best way to do it. This was the more remarkable because, though a soldier by profession, his training had been chiefly that of a civilian – a civilian of the frontier, however, where his soldierly instincts had been fostered in his dealing with a lawless and unruly people, and where he had received a training which was to stand him in good stead. Nicholson was a born commander, and this was felt by every officer and man with the column before he had been amongst them many days.'

Reginald Wilberforce, with the 52nd, wrote his impression of the column's new commander: 'He was of a commanding presence, some six feet two inches in height, with a long black beard, dark grey eyes with black pupils (under excitement of any sort these pupils would dilate like a tiger's), a colourless face, over which no smile ever passed, laconic of speech.' Nicholson took great care to establish a reliable intelligence system, making good use of his own Irregular cavalry. 'Nicholson', Wilberforce wrote, 'brought with him from the frontier, a motley crew called the "Mooltanee Horse"; . . . they came out of personal devotion to Nicholson, they took no pay from the Government, they recognised no head but Nicholson, and him they obeyed with a blind devotion and a faithfulness that won the admiration of all who saw them. These men some 250 in number, mounted on their wiry ponies, surrounded the column like a web; they rode in couples, each couple within signalling distance of the other, and so circled the column round for many a mile.'

From Jullundur, Nicholson marched his column to Phillaur, from where, having disarmed the two Native regiments there, he moved to Amritsar. Here he heard that a wing of the 9th Cavalry and the 46th NI had mutinied at Sialkot. A number of cavalry officers and civilians had been murdered but the infantry had saved their officers – even offering two of them generous pay if they would stay with the sepoys and command them at Delhi. Nicholson lost no time in disarming the other wing of the 9th, which was present with his column, before mounting as many of HM 52nd and 180th Punjabis as he could on pony carts and force-marching them to intercept the rebels, who were on their way to Delhi. During this march Wilberforce observed an example of Nicholson's powers of observation, as well as his ruthlessness:

In marching along the road, two bowed-down wretched-looking men, with bundles on their backs, had ... passed close by the regiment. Some half-hour afterwards Nicholson, attended by his Brigade-Major, his Aide-de-camp, and some Pathans, came down the road at a hand-gallop to overtake the column; as he passed the two men he turned slightly round, and, pointing to the two apparently innocent-looking men, said to the Pathans who were following, *Maro!* The order was instantly obeyed; the unerring eye of Nicholson had detected the Sepoy, the harmless-looking bundles they were carrying were native swords, and these were being taken to Goodaspore to arm an irregular cavalry regiment which had been disarmed by Nicholson the previous day.

Captured mutineers were now either shot, bayoneted, sabred or – when time allowed – hanged. One of Nicholson's first acts on assuming command had been to ban the practice of blowing away from guns – he considered it a waste of powder.

The threat to the column was not just external, as Wilberforce and his brother officers of the 52nd discovered one evening:

One night we were all waiting for our dinner and none appeared, messengers were sent to the cooking tent, but only brought back word that dinner was coming, till about half an hour after the appointed time, Nicholson, who always dined with us, came on the scene, with 'I am sorry gentlemen, to have kept you waiting for your dinner, but I have been hanging your cooks!' We soon learnt the story. One of the cook boys, whose conscience revolted at wholesale murder, went to Nicholson and told him that the soup was poisoned with aconite. Nicholson kept the boy safe until just before dinner was to be served, when he sent for and arrested the cooks. The soup was brought in with the cooks. Nicholson told one of the cooks to eat some; the cook protested, on the ground of caste. Nicholson knew that a Mussulman had no caste, and peremptorily ordered the cook to swallow some, telling him at the same time that he, Nicholson, knew it was poisoned; of course the cook denied this. Nicholson then had a small monkey brought in, and some of the soup poured down its throat. In a few minutes the truth of the cook boy's story was seen – the little monkey was dying of poison. Sentence of death was at once passed, and a few minutes afterward our regimental cooks were ornamenting a neighbouring tree.

The Movable Column caught up with Sialkot rebels trying to cross the Ravi River. Shrapnel and grape-shot from the guns of Dawes' battery and three guns of Bourchier's drove them back to the river, hotly pursued by the Punjabis. Nicholson's exhausted gun teams dragged the guns to the water's edge, from where they raked the swimming sepoys with grapeshot. Those who escaped took refuge – with one gun – on an island. The following morning the 52nd were ferried over and landed out of sight of the sepoys. Nicholson himself led the charge – which resulted in the annihilation of the rebels – cutting the rebel gun commander in two with his sword. Perhaps unsurprisingly, Nicholson's sword, too, was the stuff of legend as Wilberforce recorded:

> Nicholson had the reputation of being the best swordsman in India, and his sword had the credit of being the best sword in India. It was presented to him by the Sikh nation ... when the Sikhs had decided on presenting Nicholson with the best sword that could be found, they invited their people to send to Peshawur swords to select from ... At length by a process of elimination, the number was reduced to three, all of which appeared to be equally excellent. Nicholson was then invited to take his choice of the three swords, and chose a straight one. Native swords are very seldom straight – they are generally curved. It was generally supposed that this sword was grooved inside and contained quick-silver, so as to increase the force of a direct blow.

Wilberforce had, too, the opportunity to see the devotion that Nicholson aroused among the Sikhs:

> John Nicholson was worshipped by the Sikhs. Their religion admits of repeated incarnations, and this noble, sad-faced man was thought by them to be their god veiled in human flesh ... During the time Nicholson was with the column, it was a common sight of an evening to see the Sikhs come into camp in order that they might see him; they used to be admitted to his tent in bodies of about a dozen at a time. Once in the presence, they seated themselves on the ground and fixed

their eyes upon the object of their adoration, who all the while went steadfastly on with whatever work he was engaged in, never even lifting his eyes to the faces of his mute worshippers. Sometimes, overcome perhaps by prickings of conscience, or carried away by feelings he could not control, one of them would prostrate himself in prayer. This was an offence, against the committal of which warning had been given, and the penalty never varied: three dozen lashes with the cat-o'nine-tails on the bare back. This they did not mind, but on the contrary, rejoiced in the punishment, for they used to say: 'Our god knew what we had been doing wrong, and therefore punished us.'

It wasn't only Sikhs; Wilberforce described Nicholson's personal bodyguard:

Nicholson's personal attendant was a huge Pathan, black whiskered and moustachioed; this man never left his side, he slept across the doorway of Nicholson's tent, so that none could come in save over his body. When Nicholson dined at mess this Pathan stood behind his chair with a cocked revolver in one hand, and allowed none to hand a dish to his master save himself. The story of this man's devotion was that, years before, in one of the many frontier skirmishes, when Nicholson was surrounded by the enemy, this man's father saved Nich-olson's life with his own by throwing himself between Nicholson and a descending sword which must have killed him, and further, in another of these skirmishes, this man was taken prisoner and carried off, when John Nicholson, single-handed, gave chase, and cutting his way through, bore him away in safety across his saddle bow.

In order to reinforce British prestige – which had suffered in recent weeks – Nicholson had ordained that all natives must 'salaam' (salute) passing British troops. This was rigidly enforced. Wilberforce tells of an orderly officer with the Movable Column confronted in the night by travellers on an elephant. The officer ordered the natives to dismount and salaam – there was hesitation and a rattle of arms, but the officer stood his ground until the occupants of the elephant's howdah did as they were ordered. The following day the officer was summoned to Nicholson's tent.

The General was sitting, writing at his table; near him stood a native magnificently dressed, with a clear olive complexion, black beard and whiskers. Nicholson said: 'You met an elephant on the road this morning, and made the riders get down and salaam to you; why did you do it?' 'Your order, Sir that no natives should pass a white man riding, without dismounting and salaaming.' Nicholson turned to his companion and said something in a language unintelligible to the young officer, and then turning to him said, 'You owe your life to this gentleman, for his attendant would have shot you, but he prevented him.' The stranger said something in the same unintelligible language to Nicholson, who then said, 'You can go, but before you do so, I may tell you what he has just said to me: "No wonder you English conquer India when mere boys obey orders as this one did!"'

The stranger, it emerged, was an emissary from Dost Mohammed – the Amir of Afghanistan – assuring loyalty to Nicholson and offering support in the form of troops if necessary. 'The fact of the Dost sending the message to Nicholson instead of to Sir John Lawrence, the Lieut.-Governor of the Punjaub,' wrote Wilberforce, 'shows how much Nicholson was thought of, even by those who were not under English rule.'

By 24 July Nicholson was back at Lahore, where Sir John Lawrence gave him new orders. Nicholson was to take the Movable Column, which would be reinforced en route by 2,500 men – 400 of HM 61st Foot, 200 of HM 8th Foot, 100 European gunners, the remainder being Sikhs and Baluchis – and march to join the force assembling under the Commander-in-Chief, the Hon. George Anson, for the recapture of Delhi.

# 5

# THE MARCH ON DELHI

General Anson's first action on receipt of the news from Meerut was to alert the three European regiments close at hand in the hills – HM 75th (Stirlingshire) at Kasauli, the 1st Bengal Fusiliers at Dagshai and the 2nd at Subathu. The 75th he ordered to march at once on Umballa and the other two to be ready to march at a moment's notice. Having sent orders for HM 61st to secure the fort at Ferozepore, HM 81st that at Govindgarh, and two companies of HM 8th to secure Phillaur on the Sutlej, Phillaur was to be the rendezvous point for a small siege train – which was to march down from Ludhiana – and its escorting troops. Among these were to be a Gurkha battalion – the Nasiri Battalion – that Anson ordered down from Simla, and the 9th Irregular Cavalry. Having issued these instructions, Anson set off himself for Umballa on 14 May. The mutineers had chosen the hottest time of year for their rising, a time that made for hard marching, even at night, when marches were conducted – the troops lying up during the heat of the day. It was especially punishing for European troops who, since the rebels seem to have opted early on for static warfare – holding significant strongpoints – would be doing most of the marching. The practice was for the troops to set out at 9 p.m. and march through the night, halting before sunrise. Writing in retirement in Ireland, Richard Barter described the weather during the hot season:

> None in this country can form an idea of what this really is: the nearest approach to it is the hot room of a Turkish bath, but the hot wind

differs from this by bringing out no moisture, but withering the skin like parchment until it crackles, and the mouth and the throat become parched and the lips split from the fierce furnace-like blast. We threw water over one another from the bhisti's [water carrier's] water bags and saturated our turbans and clothes, but in ten minutes we were as dry as tinder, and towards noon all but the sentries dropped off into a queer state which could not be called sleep, till the fierce sun went down and the wind had ceased, when the Assembly sounded and we were once more upon the long dusty road.

The heat and the stress of the situation soon claimed its first casualty. Shortly after daybreak on their first day on the plains Barter – as adjutant – was summoned by his colonel, in a towering rage about the baggage carts not being 'dressed' – aligned like soldiers on a parade-ground. At first, Barter thought the Colonel was joking, then realizing he was in earnest, he summoned the doctor – who pronounced the Colonel 'mad as a March hare'. Sent back to Umballa, the Colonel was escorted back to the hills in the care of his wife's maid, who was sent down for the purpose.

The situation at Umballa, where Anson arrived on 15 May, was far from encouraging. While aware, as he was, of the moral effect of the rebels' seizure of Delhi and the importance of its swift recapture, Anson felt that the forces at his disposal were too small. Lord Canning in Calcutta and Sir John Lawrence in the Punjab were telling him, by letter and telegraph, that he was wrong. Canning seemed to think the small number of siege guns beginning the slow tramp down from Ludhiana more than sufficient for the task. Lawrence was of the opinion that Anson had only to appear before Delhi and the city would open its gates. Never in its history had the city offered significant opposition to an attacking army – Lord Lake had captured it with comparative ease in 1803 and the fact that its walls had been strengthened since by British engineers, and that it was now manned by many thousands of British-trained sepoys with British small arms and artillery, was discounted. 'Reflect on the whole history of India,' Lawrence wrote. 'Where have we failed when we have acted vigorously? Where have we succeeded when guided by timid counsels?' All true enough, no doubt, and a bracing change from the vacillation that had prevailed, for example, at Meerut, but Anson had a point. In the time-honoured traditions of British military admin-istration the army's permanent transport establishment had been abol-ished, sold off in 1854 on grounds of economy. By 18 May his force had no tents, no transport, no artillery reserve ammunition and only twenty rounds of ball cartridge each – the main magazine, currently guarded by Native troops, was at Phillaur, eight marches away. The heads of several departments – Commissariat, Medical, Transport, Ordnance, Ammunition – were telling Anson that an immediate move towards Delhi was impossible for at least a fortnight.

If that were not enough, there were three sepoy regiments at Umballa whose men were becoming increasingly restless. Sir John Lawrence – in yet another of his innumerable telegrams – urged Anson to disarm them at once. Anson – painfully aware of his lack of Indian experience – succumbed to the siren voices of the regiments' own officers who, like so many officers of the Bengal Army, persisted in believing that the outbreaks at Meerut and Delhi were untypical. Their 'Jacks' were steady, they insisted; what was more, they had been promised that they would not be disarmed, and no good would come of breaking that promise. Richard Barter, a lieutenant with HM 75th who had now arrived at Umballa, like many 'Queen's Officers', had his doubts. His officers soon abandoned the mess they shared with the 9th Lancers to sleep in the barracks with the men. They were often turned out two or three times a night to deal with incendiary incidents and attempted attacks by the sepoys of the 5th and 68th Native Infantry but, Barter noted, 'During the daytime these men were models of fidelity and the Commander-in-Chief who had followed us from Simla used to have evening parades of them at which they were speeched to and praised, while they themselves swore Colours to be true to the Company behadoor [*sic*].' The three sepoy regiments kept their arms and were readied to march on Delhi with the column that was assembling.

For march they would. Under intense pressure applied from both ends of the subcontinent, Anson felt he had no choice but to march for Delhi almost at once. First, however, he needed to open communications with Meerut. For this task he chose a man who was already mired in controversy and was to court a deal more – as well as becoming one of the heroes of British India. William Raikes Hodson, 24, the son of a Gloucestershire clergyman, had already seen service in the Sikh wars in the East India Company's infantry, though by nature and instinct he was a cavalryman. His talents were recognized early on by Sir Henry Lawrence – then British Resident at Lahore, capital of the recently conquered Punjab. As one of Lawrence's young men, Hodson had been employed as an administrator in the new province, 'initiating me into the mystery of "political" business, and thus giving me more knowledge of things and persons Indian than I should learn in a year of ordinary life'. Particularly to his taste were the Sikhs and hillmen he encountered in his work and when, under Harry Lumsden, it was proposed to form a corps of such men, infantry and cavalry, to scout and police the new frontier, Hodson jumped at the offer of a command. The Corps of Guides – one of the earliest units to be dressed entirely in khaki (named from the Persian word for dust) – quickly established itself as an elite among Britain's Indian forces, and Hodson proved an inspired, and inspiring, leader of Native cavalry. When Lumsden went home on long leave in 1852, Hodson took over command. Overbearing to the point of arrogance, Hodson had – among Europeans, at least – a gift for making devoted admirers and bitter enemies. Soon rumours were rife of feuds and dissensions within the ranks of the Guides' officers and men. When a new commander took over, questions were asked about the regiment's accounts and Hodson was accused of fraud and suspended. A court of inquiry cleared him – his accounting was chaotic rather than crooked – but the questions about his probity and character, fuelled by personal animosities, remained. Hodson had been lobbying Anson for a new command when the Mutiny broke out at Meerut. For Hodson, the timing could not have been better – a man of his undoubted talents could not be allowed to sit idle in these desperate times. Anson appointed him assistant quartermaster general, placed him in charge of the Intelligence department, and ordered him to re-establish communications with General Hewitt in Meerut.

Meerut was cut off from all communication with Umballa, the countryside around it being, as Edward Vibart and the other fugitives had discovered, in a state of anarchy. The senior officers in Meerut – Archdale Wilson and General Hewitt – had spent the time since the outbreak of the Mutiny ten days earlier, fortifying their position against attack. On 20 May, accompanied by a troop of Sikh horse provided by the loyal Rajah of Jhind, Hodson set out and reached Karnal, 76 miles from Meerut. The following night an officer on picket duty in Meerut was discussing their isolated state with a colleague:

> I said 'Hodson is at Umballa, I know; and I'll bet he will force his way through, and open communications with the commander-in-chief and ourselves.' At about three that morning I heard my advanced sentries firing. I rode off to see what was the matter, and they told me that a

part of the enemy's cavalry had approached their post. When day broke
in galloped Hodson. He had left Karnal (seventy-six miles off) at nine
the night before with one led horse and an escort of Sikh cavalry, and,
as I had anticipated, here he was with despatches for Wilson! How I
quizzed him for approaching an armed post at night without knowing
the parole! Hodson rode straight to Wilson, had his interview, a bath,
breakfast, and two hours' sleep, and then rode back the seventy-six
miles, and had to fight his way for about thirty miles of the distance.

Within seventy-two hours of setting out Hodson was back at Karnal –
telegraphing the information he had gained to Anson. 'The pace pleased
him, I fancy,' Hodson wrote to a friend, 'for he ordered me to raise a
force of irregular horse, and appointed me commandant.' This force,
originally intended to be 1,000 strong, then later increased to 2,000, was
to become the most famous Irregular cavalry unit raised during the
Mutiny, and, in time, one of India's most famous regiments – Hodson's
Horse. Hugh Gough from Meerut, who was shortly to become Hodson's
adjutant, gives his first impression of the kind of men Hodson was
recruiting:

> It was always necessary to bear in mind that these men were utterly
> undisciplined and untaught soldiers according to our ideas, being either
> raw recruits, or disbanded soldiers of the old Khalsa army, who had
> fought against us in the Punjab some eight years previously. They were
> indifferent riders, as Sikhs usually are (till taught), and at least half of
> them used with one hand to clutch hold of the high knob in front of
> the Sikh saddle as they galloped along. They had no knowledge of drill
> or of our words of command; in fact, all I attempted to teach them
> were 'Threes right', 'Threes left' (never Threes about!) and 'Form Line,'
> 'Charge'. However, with all their want of knowledge and training, they
> had plenty of pluck, and their success lay in that, combined with
> readiness and goodwill for any amount of work.

Gough was one of those who fell under Hodson's spell: 'A finer or more
gallant soldier never breathed,' he wrote. 'He had all the true instincts of
a leader of men; as a cavalry soldier he was perfection, a strong seat on
horseback (though an ugly rider), a perfect swordsman, nerves like iron
and with a quick, intelligent eye, indefatigable and zealous, and with
great tact. He had the all-round qualities of a good soldier.' Among those

who met Hodson on his return to Karnal was Charles Thomason of the Bengal Engineers, an old friend of Hodson's. After a wash and brush up and breakfast, Hodson passed on to those present what he had learned of the outbreak at Meerut and concluded: 'Well, here we are; the wires cut north, south east, and west; not a soul can interfere with us, we have the cracking of the nut in our own way, and here we are "jolly as a bug in a rug!"' Clearly the Mutiny, and the consequent state of anarchy, had come to Hodson – as to many others on both sides – as a Godsend. 'Cool *insouciance* was one of Hodson's great characteristics,' wrote Hugh Gough, 'whether in the heat of action, or sitting at mess, he always seemed the same – nothing appeared to put him out.' All Hodson's Indian experience up until now seemed to have been leading to this crisis: 'He had a wonderful knowledge and command of the native language, and was a thorough master of the idioms, phrases, and accents peculiar to the different districts through which we were campaigning; and by this knowledge, and his own keen commanding way of applying it, he was able to obtain the surest and best information.'

Anson's force, gathering at Umballa, was now composed of HM 9th Lancers, the 75th Highlanders, the 1st and 2nd Bengal Fusiliers, two troops of horse artillery and another Native regiment, the 60th NI, in addition to the three sepoy regiments of doubtful loyalty. The whole force was divided into two small brigades under Brigadiers Halifax and Jones. With the 9th Lancers was Lieutenant Colonel James Hope Grant – a popular commander who had been commissioned into the regiment in 1826 and had, unusually for those times, remained with them ever since. He had served on the staff of Waterloo veteran Lord Saltoun in the First China War of 1842, chosen because Saltoun, a keen violinist, wanted someone to accompany him and Grant was an accomplished cellist. There was no doubting his ability, however. For his service on this campaign he was awarded a majority without purchase (i.e., promoted without payment). Having served with his regiment in the First Sikh War, he commanded it in the Second, again gaining promotion without purchase. Hope Grant was to command all the cavalry in Anson's force.

At Nagphat – one march from Delhi – Anson's force was to link up with a force from Meerut under Archdale Wilson, to consist of two squadrons of the Carabiniers, one wing (a half-battalion) of the 60th Rifles, Scott's Light Field Battery, which included two 18-pounders with European crews, Tombs's troop of Bengal Horse Artillery, two companies of Native sappers and miners and fifty troopers of the 4th Irregular Horse.

Both forces would then push on towards Delhi. By 25 May most of these troops were on the march – no small achievement for a commander-in-chief who was sickening before he left the hills. Already the force was beset by that scourge of British armies in India – cholera. 'To give an idea of the deadly nature of the cholera at this time,' wrote Barter,

> I may give an instance, which struck me the more as the young man who died of it belonged to the Company to which I formerly belonged and of which I was in temporary command when appointed Adjutant. He was moreover both a countryman and protege of my own, a smart painstaking young soldier in a fair way of doing well in the Service. The man I allude to was Lance Corporal Sweeney of No 2 Company. One evening about 4 p.m. I was talking to his Captain (Dunbar) when Sweeney came up with a report that two of the men of the Company were dead of cholera and were to be buried at 6 p.m. Under such circumstances and in a tropical climate burial follows fast upon death, and there were no coffins as may be imagined, the bodies being consigned to earth wrapped in their bedding. When Dunbar returned from the funeral I remarked, 'So there are two more of the old Company gone.' He replied: 'Ah! yes, three more; I buried poor Sweeney with the other two.'

No respecter of youth and health, cholera was no respecter of rank either. On 26 May, having arrived at Karnal, General Anson was struck with cholera – and in the early hours of the following morning, he died. Anson's successor was Sir Henry Barnard – who had most recently been chief of staff to General Simpson in the Crimea. Less concerned than Anson by his lack of Indian experience, almost his first act was to pack the unreliable Native regiments off: the infantry to Rohtuk – where they subsequently mutinied – and the cavalry to Meerut. Richard Barter was not sorry to see them go. On the march down from Umballa the sepoys had been discreetly guarded by the European regiments: the 75th, for example, were ordered to march at all times in rear of the 68th NI so as to guard against any treachery on their part. These orders had not been made known to Colonel Seaton, commanding officer of the 68th NI, who was also column commander, but when he attempted to alter the order of march the situation was explained to him. It was much to his displeasure. Seaton and his officers, like most other officers of the Native army had, even now, implicit confidence in the fidelity of their regiment.

This faith was hard to shake. 'I well recollect the evening the 68th marched away from Kurnaul,' wrote Barter, 'my sympathising with one of the Captains of the Regiment on his going away with such a set, and his reply to me was: "I assure you, Barter, we feel quite as safe with our 'Jacks' as you do with your Europeans." The next time I saw him he had run the gauntlet of fire of these "woffadars" who had done their best to massacre him and his brother officers, fortunately without success.'

On the 27th, without waiting for the siege train, Barnard's force set off for Bagpat. Brigadier Halifax had also died of cholera, his place being taken by Brigadier Showers. Barnard's plan, which he assured Sir John Lawrence he would devote 'every energy' to achieving, was to collect a force before Delhi, secure the bridge at Bagpat and establish secure communications with Meerut. This last was easier said than done. The events at Meerut seem to have paralysed General Hewitt, who devoted most of his energies to rendering Meerut itself impregnable. As the fugitives from Delhi could testify, anarchy reigned outside the reach of British guns. Despite this, the Meerut column set off the same day and, after three days' march, arrived at Ghazi-ud-Din Nagar, one mile short of the Hindun River, and 15 miles from Delhi. Wilson had been informed of native rumours that the sepoys intended to contest the crossing of the Hindun, but this was considered unlikely. It was a surprise, therefore, when at 4 p.m. a picket of the 4th Irregulars came galloping in, crying that the enemy was close at hand and advancing, information reinforced by a round from an 18-pounder that bounced through the camp shortly afterwards.

At once two companies of the 60th Rifles advanced at the double to clear the bridge, which they found defended by a strong force of sepoys who lined the bank and part of the sandy riverbed, along with artillery deployed to the right of the bridge. As the Rifles advanced along the causeway that led to the bridge they came under fire from the mutineers' guns. Scott's guns and the two 18-pounders replied. In this, the first clash of the British and their own sepoys, the latter fought well and held their ground until they became aware – on their left – of the Carabiniers and the horse artillery splashing across the stream that was the Hindun at this time of year. At this point – as the 60th fixed swords and charged – they gave way, and fell back to a walled village. Again the 60th went in with the bayonet – a rifle officer wrote home: 'As the riflemen charge ... the word is passed, "Remember the ladies! remember the babies!" and everything flies before them. Hundreds are shot down or bayoneted. The sepoys, it is true, fight like demons; but we are British, and they are natives.'

The extreme heat prevented any pursuit, with the result that by midday the following day the sepoys were back, occupying a ridge to the right of the British position. A two-hour artillery duel followed, after which Wilson, sensing that the enemy's fire was slackening, ordered a general advance. The sepoys did not wait to receive it – after firing a few rounds of grape they marched away up the Delhi road leaving the Meerut Brigade exhausted – with some fifty casualties, including Lieutenant Perkins of the artillery killed – but satisfied that they, who had been the first to suffer from the sepoys' revolt, had also been the first to draw blood. Next day, 1 June, the Meerut column received reinforcement in the form of the 2nd (or Sirmoor) Battalion of Gurkhas commanded by Major Charles Reid. Fresh orders for a march to Bagpat arrived on the 4th – the Meerut Brigade set off, arriving there on the same day. The following morning the two columns met at Alipur – to be joined by the siege train that had been pushed on from Phillaur. All was set – if Lawrence and Lord Canning were correct – for a triumphal march through the thrown-open gates of Delhi.

The mutineers had other ideas. Scouts informed Barnard that they had established a strong position at Badli-ke-Serai, a collection of old walled houses and gardens – the homes of former officials of the Mogul Court – 6 miles to the north of Delhi. At midnight on 7 June he gave orders for all three columns to advance. The enemy position was a good one. To their right were the serai and the walled village, filled with infantry and protected in front by a swamp. On their left, on a low ridge, a sandbag battery had been constructed for four heavy guns and an 8-inch mortar. The ground all around the position was swampy and intersected by watercourses.

As the lights of the enemy camp became visible Hope Grant took the cavalry – three squadrons of the 9th Lancers, ten horse artillery guns and some Jhind horsemen under William Hodson – to turn the enemy's left flank. The horse artillery in Grant's command were from the Bengal Horse Artillery. Known as the 'Red Men' from the red plumes that cascaded down from their full-dress brass helmets these men were the elite of the Company's artillery, and only the best officers – such as the skull-cracking Major Light or young Frederick Roberts – could aspire to 'getting their jacket', the right to wear their splendid braided tunic. Pulled by horses – rather than bullocks or elephants like most artillery in India –

and moving almost as fast as cavalry, their job was to gallop up towards the enemy and deliver grapeshot at close range, usually as the prelude to a charge by the cavalry. This mobile artillery could be rushed to any point in the battlefield and – like Marmont's horse gunners at Marengo – turn defeat into victory in a matter of minutes.

Guiding Grant at this point was Hodson's friend Charles Thomason, who at the outbreak of the Mutiny was acting as deputy superintendent of the West Jumna Canal, which ran a mile to the left of the enemy's position: 'I led Sir Hope Grant past the bridge by which we should have recrossed the canal to take the enemy fairly on his left flank. We were, however, brought up by a watercourse in which our guns seemed to be helplessly stuck, when the report of the first gun of the Badli-ke-Serai battle broke the silence immediately upon the left. It might have been the morning gun, but for the unmistakable scream of the round-shot directed against our main column advancing along the Grand trunk road.'

This main column was now advancing to attack the enemy frontally – the 1st Brigade under Showers to the left of the road, the 2nd under Graves to the right. On the road itself were the four heavy guns, a troop of horse artillery and part of a field battery. Near by on a small mound stood General Barnard and his staff, including – in the way of nineteenth-century British armies – his son, William. The British guns, which had already started to deploy for action, were soon replying to the enemy's fire. In the artillery duel that ensued, however, the enemy's numbers and heavier weight of shot began to prevail. The British artillery was soon taking casualties. To make things worse, the heavy guns' bullock drivers fled with their beasts and a wagon blew up. The skill of Indian gunners was to prove a feature of the coming campaigns. There was a long history and an established tradition of artillery in Indian warfare – and the gunners were to prove one of the most effective elements in the rebel forces. Almost their second shot slammed through Barnard's cluster of officers, killing two – Colonel Chester, Adjutant General of the East India Company's army and his ADC Captain Russell of the mutinied 54th NI – a former Delhi fugitive.

Richard Barter, with the 75th, was halted close by. Chester was a great favourite with all and his mortal wounding at the outset of the battle was demoralizing:

Both horse and man lay dying side by side: a shot had evidently alighted on the holster pipes, smashing the horse's back and cutting it open, at the same time disembowelling the rider. The horse was rolling in agony and the poor old Colonel lay on his back, his helmet off and his grey hair stained with blood and earth, calling in a faint voice to Captain Barnard, the A.D.C. who was kneeling by his side. He said, 'Lift me up, Willie, and let me look at my wound.' Barnard did so and on seeing it the old man said, 'That will do boy, go to your father.' How he could speak at all was a puzzle to me for the whole of his stomach lay on the ground beside him as if it had been scooped from the back, and yet I heard afterwards that he lived for a quarter of an hour. Close to the Colonel lay Captain Russell and his horse, both mortally wounded ... It was a sad picture of war under the rising sun that June morning.

Now, with his own artillerymen dropping fast, Barnard had recourse to something that was also a feature of Indian warfare – and which generally proved unstoppable – the British bayonet charge. Even when it resulted in heavy casualties to the attacker – as with General 'Paddy' Gough's 'Tipperary tactics' against the Sikhs – Indian troops seem to have been psychologically averse to standing when confronted by the levelled bayonets of European troops. It was not a question of courage – the courage of the mutineers was undoubted and to be demonstrated time and again. It seems more to have been a cultural objection to the weapon. Robert Dunlop, now hurrying down to take up his post as Deputy Commissioner at Meerut (and volunteer cavalryman) had considered the question thoroughly.

Often and often I have seen natives executed, of all ages, of every caste, and every position in society, yet never have I seen one of them misbehave at the scaffold; they died with a stoicism that in Europe would excite astonishment and admiration; yet the very same men behave in some instances with the rankest cowardice in the field; crowds of them routed, and ignominiously put to flight by merely handfuls of Europeans, few of whom, whatever their conduct in battle, would walk to execution with equal indifference. I have heard this difficult question in metaphysics being put to one of themselves. 'It lies in the legs,' he replied, 'the whole fault is in the legs; often when we have made up our minds to die, and hear the cheer of the "Goras" (pale faces), our legs carry us off against our will.'

No doubt with this in mind, Barnard ordered Showers to assault the main battery. Showers selected the 75th to make the assault, with the 1st Europeans in support. Although they were now lying down, with their officers dismounted, the 75th were already taking casualties. Enduring an enemy bombardment with no way of replying was a severe test of nerve – the order to attack came as a relief. 'The order came "The 75th will advance and take that battery." In an instant the line was up. I remounted my horse, and on we went.' Rifles 'at the shoulder' as though on parade, the 75th advanced on the battery – the entire fire of the enemy's round shot now concentrating on them. As they closed on the enemy, wrote Barter, casualties mounted:

> I remember one in particular taking a man's head off, or rather smashing it to pieces and covering my old Colour Sergeant Walsh of No 2 Company with blood and brains so that it was some time before he could see again. The coolness of a little Drummer boy, a mere child, who was acting as bugler to one of the Centre Companies surprised me. His turban had got undone from some cause or another and he was too much engaged trying to look between the ranks at what was in front to notice it. I called to him, telling him he'd soon lose it altogether if he didn't mind, upon which he halted, and kneeling down, replaced it with as much care as if he was going to be inspected, instead of perhaps going to be killed; and running after us took up the step and his place in the line with a smile as if to say, 'I think it's all right now, sir.'

It was at this point that Brigadier Showers – riding in front of the centre of the regiment – gave the seemingly inexplicable order for the regiment to 'Double' forward. Barter, fearing that it was too early for the men to break into a run, and that the men would be 'blown' before they reached the enemy's battery, ventured to object: 'The old Brigadier told me to see his orders carried out and be silent and I soon saw how wise and judicious they were, for having gone a hundred yards or so the quick time was again taken up and we were spared a good deal of round and grape shot which flew over our heads, the Enemy not having depressed their guns.' When they were within 150 yards of the battery the men of the 75th could see the rebel infantry in line before them. The sepoys were blazing away wildly with their 'Brown Besses' and their officers, running among them, could be heard shouting 'Take low aim! Take low aim!' If the enemy's musketry was largely ineffective at that range, the grape was taking its toll.

'The Colours carried by Ensigns Pym and Row were in tatters,' wrote Barter,

a shell had burst straight between them and torn the silk to ribbons. Gaps were made in the different companies only to be filled up at the next moment; to the enemy it must have seemed like an awful Nemesis, not a sound to be heard save now and then a suppressed shriek of pain as someone was freshly wounded, followed by the sharp word of command, 'Close up men,' and 'Mind your dressing.' I saw a Shrapnel shell burst exactly in the faces of one of the companies of the right wing. It tore a wide gap and the men near it involuntarily turned away from the fire and smoke. I called out, 'Don't turn men, don't turn,' and was at once answered, 'Never fear Mr. Barter, sir, we ain't agoing to turn.' And on they went, quietly closing the gap made by their fallen comrades.

Soon the regiment was within charging distance:

The time had at length arrived to end all this and Brigadier Showers turning round in his saddle addressed a few short words of praise to the Regiment; he then galloped round the left flank and riding up to me enquired for the Colonel. I pointed him out on my right, and he said, 'Tell him to give the word, prepare to charge.' In a moment the order was given: '75th, prepare to charge,' and down went the long line of bayonets, while the line seemed to extend as each man sought more room for the play of the most terrible of all weapons in the hands of a British Soldier; a few more paces to steady the line then came the word to 'charge'.

As with the 60th's riflemen at the Hindun, so for the men of the 75th, fired up – like all the European troops – by tales of the atrocities committed at Meerut and Delhi. This was a moment they had been waiting for.

The long hoped-for time had come at last. We had the brutal murderers face to face now in an open field, and a wild shout or rather a yell of vengeance went up from the Line as it rushed to the charge. The Enemy followed our movements, their bayonets were also lowered and their advance was also steady as they came on to meet us, but when that exultant shout arose they could not stand it, their line wavered and undulated, many began firing with their firelocks at their hips and at last as we were closing on them the whole turned and ran for dear life followed by a shout of derisive laughter from our fellows. In three minutes from the word to charge the 75th stood breathless but victors in the Enemy's battery.

Moments later General Barnard rode in and, taking Colonel Herbert by the hand, this Crimea veteran told him that in all his service he had never seen anything so noble as the advance or so brilliant as the charge. Carrying an enemy battery by frontal assault was a desperate business and the 75th got off comparatively lightly, with a loss of nineteen officers and men killed and forty-three wounded. One of the enemy's defensive measures may have contributed to the low butcher's bill. The flooding of the ground in front of the battery may have impeded the advancing British, but it had the unintended effect that the rebels' grapeshot stuck in the mud, rather than ricocheting up and killing more men. Even so, the ground made it difficult for those few who, like Barter, were still mounted. Richard Barter had been forced, like all the other officers, to dismount and charge on foot.

> We had just commenced the rush, when I felt a blow under my left knee, which completely numbed the limb and I fell forward on my face and hands; on recovering I found that I had been wounded; I tried to stand but couldn't and so sitting down I tied my black silk neckerchief tight above the wound and I then felt the bullet heavy in the calf of my leg, where, after glancing off the bone, it had gone down. The numbness caused by the blow had prevented any pain and after pressing it slowly up for a little time I had the satisfaction of forcing the ball back through the hole by which it had entered and I then put it in my pocket.

The enemy fell back to the serai at the rear of their position. The ground before the battery was strewn with the 75th's dead and wounded, the latter including Richard Barter:

> Amongst the killed was Lieutenant Alfred Harrison, an old school-fellow of mine. He lay a little to my left front on his back with his sword still clenched in his right hand and under his body, as if in falling he had made a half-turn round; he was pointed out to me by one of

the wounded men near, and I crawled to him on my hands and knees. His eyes were turned back in his head so that only the whites were visible and he was gasping for breath and totally insensible. I couldn't see where he was wounded, but putting my left hand under his head I lifted him up and threw some water on his face, speaking to him and asking if he knew me, but there was no reply. I took off his necktie and as I did so his head fell back and he was dead. On taking my hand from under his head I found some of his brains were in it, and I then saw that he had been shot through the head and right side, as with his sword raised he had taken a pace or two in front of the Company he was commanding and was cheering the men on while looking towards them. In a few moments after four Sergeants came by order of Colonel Herbert and carried me into the battery we had just captured.

The enemy, having rallied at the serai, commenced firing on the battery they had abandoned. The men of the 75th went on to storm the main entrance to the serai: 'Our fellows ... dashed at the large iron-studded gate, thinking of course that it was barred at the other side; but this the Enemy by some oversight had forgotten to do, and the gate flying open with the rush of so large a body of men caused most of our fellows to tumble on their faces inside, by this means escaping a volley fired at them at close quarters by the Sepoys drawn up within. The 75th were quickly on their feet and bringing the bayonet into play soon left not a man alive.' Some rebels ran up a winding staircase into the gateway – there was only room for one man at a time to go up, but the men of the 75th pushed their way up on to the walls from where, with their bayonets, they forced the sepoys to fall to the road below. A fakir who had stood by, loading a firelock, seemingly lost in meditation, was taken out and hanged from a peepul tree. 'These were the gentry,' said Barter, 'who acted as go-betweens to the Native Regiments and by their teaching spread and encouraged disaffection. So the meditative dodge did not save this fellow.'

By this time Graves' brigade had passed round the swamp and was threatening the enemy's right, and Hope Grant with his cavalry and horse artillery had overcome the watercourses. It hadn't been easy, but the sound of the heavy cannonade that was punishing their comrades on the main road had spurred them on.

The few sappers that we had with us were struggling to get the guns across the watercourse, but the sound of the guns did more than our sappers, hard though they were working. 'Horse Artillery to the front!' was the word of command, and over the guns went. It was at this time that I found Hodson at my right, followed by the 9th Lancers who were escorting the guns. 'Come along Charlie, the fun has begun!' Away we started, he on a beautiful chestnut and I upon a poor old artillery caster. We rattled along the right bank of the canal till we came to the first bridge, when Hodson said to me, 'Will that bridge carry the guns?' 'Can't say,' was my reply, 'and I have no time to calculate,' and so we crossed and found ourselves in the rear of the enemy's position. We now had to go back on the left of the canal, giving it a wide margin in order to get into action. To do so we had to overcome the obstruction of more than one watercourse. We seemed again hopelessly stuck in crossing one of these – the battery, or rather the *troop* as we called it in those days, of Turner's Horse artillery consisting of three 6-pounders, the latter being apparently immovable.

Just then Lieutenant M. G. Geneste, another Bengal Engineer officer, rode up. Being well mounted, he led the way. Thomason heard him shout: '"Come along!" and [he] took the watercourse at a jump, and after him went one gun. Seeing the success of Geneste's manoeuvre, I thought I would try with my old artillery caster, and over he went with another gun behind him. I believe somebody else brought over a third gun in the same way ... within a few minutes we found ourselves just under the serai with all three of the six-pounders.' As the horse gunners poured grape into the serai Hodson was keen to lead a charge, but the officer commanding the Lancers had strict orders to support the guns. Frustrated, Hodson rode off looking for a fight – he soon found one. 'He had not gone a very short distance from us,' wrote Thomason, 'when he found himself confronted by one of the enemy with a shield and tulwar. I shall never forget Hodson's face as he met this man. It was smiles all over. He went round and round the man, who in the centre of the circle was dancing *more Indico*, doing his best to cut Hodson's reins. This went on for a short time, when a neat point from Hodson put an end to the performance, and he himself vanished into space.'

Hodson's choice of the 'point' to despatch his opponent is interesting. The point-versus-edge debate is as old as the cavalry itself – both had their advocates. Captain Louis Nolan – who carried the fatal order to the Light Brigade at Balaklava and was the first to die in the charge – had been very impressed, on a visit to Hyderabad, with the razor-sharp edges of the Nizzam's troopers' swords. In a recent battle against the Rohillas they had sliced off heads, arms and legs. When he asked about their training the reply was: 'We never teach them any way, Sir: a sharp sword will cut in anyone's hand.' Native swords were kept in wooden scabbards and only drawn for action, whereas the British sabres – in metal scabbards, which blunted the edge – were constantly being drawn on parades. This may perhaps explain the British cavalry's preference for the point, but whatever the reason it did – when troopers in the heat of battle remembered to use it – give them an advantage over Indian cavalry. Robert Dunlop, who gained his experience later in the campaign as a volunteer cavalryman, recorded his conclusions. 'A native cannot cope with a good fencer using the small sword, but will very likely beat him if he keeps to cutting only.' Dunlop recommends the wearing of a light steel arm-guard – which he calls 'The Wallace Guard' – from elbow to wrist on the left arm: 'As it is concealed by the sleeve of the coat, and as a good native swordsman could cut through the unprotected arm and cleave the skull with facility, he does not check or change his blow on seeing the arm raised. But at the same moment that he discovers from the jar to his wrist, that "you must have had some iron under your sleeve," he finds that he has himself got something similar transfixing his own body.' When attacking another horseman, Dunlop recommends a last-minute swerve to the right: 'On horseback it is usual for two opponents to close sword-arm to sword-arm; but when using the guard, it is better, after approaching in the usual way on nearing you adversary, to incline a little to the right, so as to pass on his left. The cut any native will give is probably No. 1 or No. 6, either of which is easily received on the left arm, of course dropping the rein, and giving a cross point at the same time.'

Hodson himself was a superb *sabreur* – not for nothing was he nicknamed 'The Company Blade'. 'In a fight he was glorious,' wrote an officer who served with him. 'If there was only a good hard scrimmage he was as happy as a king. A beautiful swordsman, he never failed to kill his man; and the way he used to play with the most brave and furious of these rebels was perfect. I fancy I see him now, smiling, laughing, parrying most fearful blows as calmly as if he were brushing off flies, calling out all the time, "Why, try again now"; "What's that?" "Do you call yourself a swordsman?" etc. The way that in a pursuit he used to manage his hog-spear was miraculous.'

At length, the 9th Lancers did charge. Cornet A. S. Jones and a handful of troopers captured a 9-pounder gun, sabred its crew and turned it on the enemy. Colonel Yule – in command of the Lancers – killed three men with his own hand. Beaten in front, with Hope Grant's guns and cavalry attacking their left and Graves' brigade threatening their right, the rebels streamed away up the Delhi road, abandoning their guns. British casualties were fifty-one killed and 131 wounded – the rebels left a thousand dead and thirteen guns, two of which were 24-pounders, behind them. Although the men were tired, Barnard pushed them on. From the crossroads just beyond the enemy's position Barnard could see the Delhi Ridge. Forming his force into two great columns – one led by Archdale Wilson with Brigadier Showers' brigade in support, the other led by Barnard himself with Graves' brigade in support – he led his column to the left towards the ruined cantonment and sent Wilson with the second up the main Delhi road. Fighting its way through gardens and enclosures, Wilson's column reached the western edge of the Ridge while Barnard's column, after coming under fire from enemy artillery, made a left sweep, climbed the Ridge and then passed down its length from the Flagstaff Tower to Hindu Rao's House where, at 9 p.m., both columns were reunited.

Also reunited on the Ridge were Charles Thomason and his old friend William Hodson. 'He was a picture,' wrote Thomason, 'and told me he had had real sport, and looking towards the Jumna bridge, he said "Oh for another Sobraon!"' Hodson was referring to a battle in 1846 when, after a hard day's fighting, the British had killed many thousands of the Khalsa – the Sikh Army – as they attempted to escape across a bridge of boats. It is ironic that many of the Sikhs who now formed a vital part of Barnard's Delhi force were old Khalsa men. Men who in 1845 had crossed the Sutlej crying 'To Delhi! To Delhi!' intending to capture it from the British and their sepoys, had now finally arrived – only now they would fight alongside the British against the sepoys. Sikhs who had manned the Khalsa's formidable artillery would soon be manning British guns side by side with their former enemies. If the mutineers were buoyed by the prophecy that the Company's rule would end one hundred years after Plassey, the Sikhs had their own prophecy. Also a hundred years earlier a Sikh guru – about to be executed in Delhi by the Mogul Emperor –

had prophesied that the Khalsa would one day sack Delhi and end the line of the Moguls. Surely now, the Sikhs felt, the prophecy would be fulfilled.

Almost the first thing the British found at the Flagstaff Tower – where the Europeans at Delhi had gathered to make a stand less than a month earlier, and from whence they departed on their nightmare flight to Meerut and Karnal – was the cart containing the bodies of the officers who had been murdered at the Main Guard. They were reduced to skeletons now, and only the regimental buttons on their white uniforms showed who they had been.

Rising 60 feet above the city the Ridge covered the main British line of communication back to the Punjab. Its left end rested on the Jumna, at which point it was nearly $2\frac{1}{2}$ miles from the city walls. At its other end – the British right – it was about 1,200 yards from the walls. It was, as Frederick Roberts described it, 'not only a coign of vantage for attack, but a rampart of defence'. Having defeated the rebels in the open field and driven them from the Ridge, Barnard decided against following them as they retreated into Delhi. Critics felt that a great opportunity was lost to seize Delhi by a *coup de main*, but the stand made by the rebels at Badli-ke-Serai, had convinced Barnard that the gates of the city would not be thrown open to him as Sir John Lawrence had fondly imagined. The size of the enemy's garrison – some 20,000 sepoys and 114 guns – made him reluctant to drive his understrength, exhausted force into a prolonged bout of street-fighting with the danger of being outflanked and overwhelmed. Such a result, he knew, would be disastrous to British rule in India. Nor did it help that his Chief Engineer, Major Laughton, arrived with his Persian wife, twenty camels and ten carts' worth of belongings, but with no plan for the capture of the city. His own force – 3,000 British troops, one battalion of Gurkhas, twenty-two field guns and some sepoys of questionable loyalty – would only be able to attack one-seventh of Delhi's perimeter. In fact, for most of June and July, the British on the Ridge would be not the besiegers, but the besieged.

On 9 June two batteries were established – each for one 18-pounder and an 8-inch mortar – on either side of Hindu Rao's House, to counter the enemy's heavy artillery on the Kashmir and Mori bastions. That same day reinforcements arrived in the form of the Corps of Guides – three troops of cavalry and six companies of infantry under Captain Daly. Writing to his wife, Major Anson of the 9th Lancers described them thus: 'The Corps of Guides is a sight to see. Their dress is highly peculiar, and the men are chiefly of two sorts, viz., the tall powerful swarthy Afghan, and the short, muscular, olive-skinned Goorkha. They are the admiration of the camp, having marched 580 miles in twenty-two days – a feat unparalleled in the records of Indian marching.'

One of the first officers to greet them was their former commander, William Hodson. 'It would have done your heart good,' he wrote to his wife, 'to see the welcome they gave me, cheering and shouting and crowding round me like frantic creatures. They seized my bridle, dress, hands, and feet, and literally threw themselves down before the horse with the tears streaming down their faces.' Anyone who still believed that Hodson had been disliked by his men had their answer: 'Many officers who were present,' he continued, 'hardly knew what to make of it, and thought the creatures were mobbing me; and so they were, but for joy, not for mischief.' No sooner had the Guides arrived than they were sent into the action. All morning the guns of the Kashmir and Mori bastions had been cannonading the British positions – now the rebels were attacking the Ridge along its entire length. In support of the pickets, the Guides cavalry – 150 sowars under Quintin Battye – were rushed forward. After giving another quick cheer for their beloved Hodson, already – with his Jhind horsemen – closely engaged with mutineer cavalry, they plunged into the fight, and were soon knee to knee with the enemy. Robert Dunlop, who was not present, later recorded an incident from that fight:

A Ressaldar of these men I heard, on that day had a single combat with a native officer of the 3rd Light Cavalry, when riding out on the plain, between the ridge on which our camp was pitched and the city. The Ressaldar, a Mussulman Wulytee, or Afghan, went forward to meet his rival of the rebel host. Asiatics never thrust with their swords, but after a few rapid cuts and guards, the head of the mutineer regular was swept from his body, and the Guide seizing the bridle of the dead man's horse, a powerful stud breed, plundered by its late owner from the Government, and springing into the saddle, turned to his men, as he lifted the dripping sword over his head, and exclaimed, 'Allah-u-Akbar! and by the blessing of the Prophet, may we all get mounted in a similar manner.'

The Guides were to add further lustre to their name during the siege, with the loss, three times over, of all their officers. The attrition started early; pursuing the enemy too close to the walls, Lieutenant Quintin Battye was wounded by a round shot and carried from the field. Fresh-faced and small in stature – he generally took the female parts in the amateur dramatics that were so much a part of Victorian garrison life – Battye was a popular officer. When he died twenty-four hours later, whispering '*Dulce et Decorum est pro Patria Mori*', he was much mourned throughout the Delhi force.

Exposed as they were on the Ridge, the Delhi force suffered terribly from the heat – on 13 June it was so intense that the gunners could not handle the shot to load the guns. Life on the Ridge was a constant battle against the elements – a particularly hard one for men pushed to the limits by constant duty on the pickets, vedettes and batteries. 'A tattee seems to make a wonderful difference to the coolness of a tent when a good strong hot wind is blowing,' wrote Major Anson of the 9th Lancers. 'I have been under my bed for five hours to-day, lying on such a hot mattress and breathing such hot air, but I suppose I am getting fairly used to the heat, for I do not feel it as much as I did.' When off duty the Engineer officers used to wrap wet towels round their heads and shelter under one camp table. Hope Grant found his own remedy: 'During the terribly hot weather beer was my great standby. In fact I scarcely think I could have existed without this balmy nectar – it put such vigour and strength into my sadly exhausted frame. We were also very fortunate, during the first three months, in procuring an ample supply of Bass and Alsopp's best brew, as all the houses in the north sent as much as they could – knowing the uncertainty of being able to retain it in the state the country was in.'

Despite the heat, and the need for constant vigilance, the British soon settled into a routine of life replicating as far as possible that pleasurable life in cantonments: the life of a ruling elite, which they were fighting to restore. In off-duty moments they indulged in their usual pastimes – horse races, cricket and football matches, played in the cool of the evenings, rackets at the courts at Metcalfe House, fishing in the canal and uproarious bathing parties in the *jhil* (swamp) behind the camp on Sunday mornings. Officers would read letters, newspapers and magazines from home – eagerly awaiting the next episode of *Little Dorrit*. There was singing and music – the Engineers even got up an instrumental quartet. Another reminder of the regular life of the outside world was provided by one of the many refugees from Delhi who were with the force. Captain Tytler of the 38th NI had now come back in command of the military treasure chest. Somehow he had managed to bring his wife with him – probably the only European lady on the Ridge. On the 21 June she gave birth to a son. The boy – named Stanley Delhi Force Tytler – was received by the troops as a good omen. The day after his birth his father heard one soldier say to another: 'Now we shall get our reinforcements; this camp was formed to avenge the blood of innocents, and the first reinforcement sent to us is a new-born infant.' Reinforcements arrived the next day.

Anyone who felt that the rebels were so demoralized by their 'licking' at Badli-ke-Serai that they would cower behind their walls awaiting the next British move were soon disabused of the notion. On 11 June the rebels issued out of the city and attacked the British position frontally and in the rear. Despite penetrating into the heart of the British camp, however, they were driven out through Metcalfe House where, from then on, a British picket was established. On the same day another rebel force attacked through the suburbs of the Sabzi Mandi and Hindu Rao's House. Although they were driven off with considerable loss, one Native regiment took the opportunity to desert to the mutineers. This was just one of a series of sorties in which the rebels attempted to turn the British right flank by attacking Hindu Rao's House, and Barnard's heavy batteries there.

The British were not the only ones being reinforced – on 12 June, the 60th NI, having mutinied at Rohtuk, came into Delhi and the following day attacked the Ridge. There was a pattern in these events. Just as with the conduct of mutinying regiments – killing or driving off officers, ransacking the Treasury and marching to Delhi – so their arrival in Delhi followed a predictable course. The new arrivals would be paraded before the King, swear loyalty and the next day – or sometimes the same day – be sent out against the British on the Ridge to test their mettle and commitment to the cause. British observers soon learned that the arrival of new contingents of sepoys – often marching over the Bridge of Boats with their British colours flying and their bands playing British marches – was the harbinger of a fresh attack.

Despite Barnard's reservations, a plan for a surprise attack – devised by the younger Engineer officers, Lieutenants Greathed, Maunsell and Chesney, without the knowledge of the Chief Engineer – was deemed feasible. The idea was for all the available troops to assemble at 1 a.m., approach the walls in silence in three great columns and enter the city via the Kashmir Gate, the Lahore Gate and, by escalade, somewhere between the two. The columns would then fight their way into the heart of the city and unite. On the night of 13 June the columns were assembled and orders were issued – for the first time – to the column commanders. Brigadier Graves' contingent of three hundred men, however, was found to be missing – it was on picket at Metcalfe House and had received no orders. By the time the men returned and had been issued with ammunition the sun was rising. The attack was cancelled, which many thought a good thing. The plans for exploitation of any success were vague, and once inside the walls the men would have had to fight in labyrinthine streets, against superior numbers and with no reserves, while the camp and the sick were left to the mercy of any counter-attack. Frederick Roberts was in no doubt: 'The failure to give effect to the young Engineers officers plans,' he wrote, '... may be looked upon as a merciful dispensation of Providence which saved us from what would almost certainly have been an irreparable disaster.' The fact was that with the huge disparity in numbers, the Delhi force on the Ridge was more besieged than besieger.

As well as attacks on the Ridge the rebels attempted to set up batteries outside the walls. On 17 June Charles Reid and his Gurkhas, from Hindu Rao's House, and Tombs's horse gunners from the camp, succeeded in destroying one such battery. The following day the rebels, newly reinforced by the mutinied Nasirabad Brigade, with six guns, attacked the British camp in the rear. Both sides incurred heavy losses. Yule of the 9th Lancers was killed and Becher, the Quartermaster General, was wounded. The rebels held the ground they had gained until the following morning.

Two days later the enemy came out in large numbers wearing their British uniforms with bands playing – some of them played 'God save the Queen' – and attacked the British positions all along their length. While the British were thus occupied, a part of the rebels' force – cavalry, artillery and guns – passed unnoticed through the suburbs and gardens on the British right, and by evening were a mile and a half to their rear. The only British troops available to meet this new threat were 250 troopers and twelve guns under James Hope Grant. 'On seeing my small force,' he wrote, 'they opened a heavy fire upon us, to which we responded with equal vigour. It was wonderful to see how the shot and shell fell among us without doing much harm: a grape-shot tore a pistol out of my holster-pipe, and I never saw it again.' Hope Grant's guns, though, were able to make little impression against the enemy's heavier weight of shot – and were soon in danger of being overrun by their infantry. Daly brought the Guides up just as Tombs's troop was about to be overwhelmed. 'Daly if you do not charge,' shouted Tombs, 'my guns are taken.' With only a dozen or so Guides, Daly charged into the undergrowth, scattering the enemy – he returned a few minutes later with a bullet through his shoulder, but the guns were saved. Hope Grant saw another two guns in similar peril:

> I therefore collected a few men together and charged the enemy. A sepoy within 5 yards of me fired at my horse, and put a bullet through his body, close to my leg. It was singular he did not aim at me; but in all probability he thought it best to make sure of killing the horse, and that then to a certainty, the rider would fall into his hands. I felt that my poor charger had received its death wound, yet he galloped on 50 yards through the throng of rebels, and then dropped down dead. I was in rather an awkward predicament – unhorsed, surrounded by the enemy, and, owing to the darkness, ignorant in which direction to proceed – when my orderly, a native sowar of the 4th Irregulars, by name Rooper Khan, rode up to me, and said, 'Take my horse – it is your only chance of safety.' I could not help but admire his fine conduct. He was a Hindostanee Mussulman, belonging to a regiment the greater part of which had mutinied; and it would have been easy for him to have killed me and gone over to the enemy; but he behaved nobly, and was ready to save my life at the risk of his own. I refused his offer; but taking a firm grasp of his horse's tail, I told Rooper Khan to drag me out of the crowd.

Two guns were lost to the rebels, but were recaptured by three hundred riflemen and fusiliers who had just arrived on the scene. It was 11.30 p.m. before the enemy was beaten off, at a cost of three officers and seventeen men killed. Among them was Lieutenant Colonel Yule of the Lancers, who was found with both thighs broken by musket balls, another ball through his head and his throat cut – four of his lancers lay around him. Hope Grant returned to the camp weary and wounded and was only restored by a draught of his favourite 'elixir'. 'I threw myself exhausted on the ground, and the only thing which revived me was a glass of beer, given me by Lieutenant Drummond, attached to the Rajah of Jheend's horse.'

The following morning Hope Grant tried to reward Rooper Khan:

I called him to my tent (he was a fine-looking fellow, of tall stature, about twenty-five years of age), and after praising him for his gallant behaviour, I offered him some little money; upon which he drew himself up with great dignity, salaamed and said, 'No, sahib, I will take no money; but if you will get my commanding officer to promote me, I shall be very grateful.' I answered him that I would make a request to that effect, but urged him also to receive the money. He reluctantly took it and left the tent; but the next morning I received a note from his commanding officer, Major Martin, returning the rupees, and stating that Rooper Khan could not be prevailed upon to accept them. Major Martin promoted him; and in consequence of my favourable mention of him, Sir Henry Barnard awarded him the second-class order of merit.

On 23 June – the 100th anniversary of the Battle of Plassey – native prophecy had said that British rule would end. It was also the first day of a new moon – auspicious for Muslims, and Ruth Juttra, a Hindu holy day. In order to fulfil the prophecy, the rebel commander in Delhi ordered a big attack to drive the British off the Ridge. The brunt of the attack was borne by the British right, by Reid's Gurkhas and the 60th Rifles. Reid's Gurkhas – on permanent duty at Hindu Rao's House – had been subjected to constant attempts by the mutineers to subvert them and bring them over to the rebel cause. 'Come over!' the rebels would cry – to which the Gurkhas would reply 'Yes, we are coming!' and charge out with their *kukris*. Despite the British force being reinforced on the 23rd – by a company of the 75th, four of the 2nd Bengal Fusiliers, four horse artillery guns, some Native cavalry and Punjabi infantry and horse – the fighting went on until nightfall. Much of it was centred on the Sabzi Mandi suburb, where the Gurkhas distinguished themselves. Hope Grant recorded an incident that took place during the street-fighting of that day: 'A sepoy was seen at the window of a house by some Goorkas, who crept up and lay in wait underneath. As they expected, the unfortunate fellow again put his head out of the window to ascertain how matters stood, when the Goorkas seized him by the hair, and with a large kokry, or knife which they carried with them, severed his head from his body in an instant.' The Guides, too, played their part, wrote Grant, in driving the rebels out of the village: 'Fifty of the scoundrels had shut themselves up in a house into which the Guides forced their way. The mutineers threw down their arms and begged for quarter; but the hatred which existed between the Sikhs and the Hindostanees put this out of the question, and every one of the latter were slain.' If the British now regarded even loyal sepoys with suspicion, new bonds were being formed. British soldiers and Sikhs fraternized when off-duty, and the Gurkhas became great favourites – especially with the 60th Rifles. Robert Dunlop, visiting the siege lines, noticed this: 'They shared their grog, and walked about arm-in-arm, interchanging sentiments on the world at large in a compound dialect of Oordoo, mixed with Nagree and Sanscrit phrases, and British, mixed with a good deal of the barrack-room classics.'

Although the British had succeeded in beating off the rebel attacks with heavy losses – they lost over one thousand men on 23 June – their own casualties from wounds, sickness and exhaustion were a severe drain on an already inadequate force. On 24 June Neville Chamberlain had arrived to take up the post of adjutant general, bringing with him reinforcements that brought the total British force to 6,600 men of all arms, but on the same day the arrival in Delhi of the Rohilkhand mutineers – a cavalry regiment, four battalions and eight guns – brought the rebel forces up to 30,000. New recruits were being enrolled in the Punjab – five new regiments by the end of June, to rise to eighteen battalions by the beginning of October, as well as 14,000 Irregular horse and foot – but for the time being reinforcements from that quarter were few and far between. Although the rebels had by the beginning of July been driven from the Sabzi Mandi, the British were in no position to launch an assault, and had established only a partial blockade. Their batteries – 1,500 yards from the walls – controlled the Kashmir and Kabul gates, but five other gates were free for the enemy to use; new rebel contingents arrived, marching over the Bridge of Boats, with their colours flying and their bands playing.

On 1 and 2 July the rebels received the substantial reinforcement of the revolted Bareilly Brigade, consisting of four sepoy regiments, a cavalry regiment, a horse battery and two heavy guns. Its commander was Bakht Khan, a subadar of artillery, whom the King immediately made com-mander-in-chief of the whole rebel army. Robert Dunlop, then a vol-unteer cavalry officer in Meerut, was of the opinion that the Bareilly Brigade could have been prevented from reaching Delhi by firm action on the part of the Meerut garrison. The rebels had been about to cross the Ganges at the ghaut of Ghurmukhtesar, and Dunlop approached General Hewitt with a proposal to contest the crossing:

> I tried to rouse the worthy old general to letting us go down with a couple of hundred men and two guns to the Ghaut. He replied by calling a council of war, which, of course, 'did not fight.' ... I think now, as I thought then, that we could have driven the enemy, though about 2,500 from the Ghaut; but even had we failed, our lives would have been well expended. It was advisable, in so early a stage of the struggle, to show these men what Englishmen could dare to do; and it must be remembered that the assault of Delhi, which was arranged for the night of the day on which the Bareilly brigade marched over the Jumna Bridge, with their Christian bandsmen playing 'Cheer, boys, Cheer,' was postponed for months by their arrival.

Whether Dunlop – a civilian – was right about the prospects of such a small force being able to stop the formidable Bareilly Brigade is open to question, but he was right about the projected assault. Major Laughton had at last been removed from his post as Chief Engineer to the Delhi force and had taken his Persian wife and camels to the hills. His temporary replacement was Captain Alexander Taylor, an altogether more vigorous character who at once urged on Barnard the necessity of attempting an assault. Every day Delhi remained in rebel hands, he argued, the British position in the whole of India grew worse. British casualties were increasing – the onset of the rains at the end of June brought little relief and increased sickness – recruiting in the Punjab was as yet a trickle rather than a flood, and unless the Sikhs heard of a victory soon, a rising might follow. Taylor proposed a plan for a *coup de main* similar to that of 13 June, only with five columns instead of three. General Barnard, sickening and suffering from an inability to sleep, had already been considering withdrawing the whole force to Agra, but allowed himself to be talked into this desperate measure. The arrival of the Bareilly Brigade, however, and doubts about the loyalty of the Native troops, caused its cancellation.

On the same day there arrived from the Engineer Depot at Rurki a small contingent of sappers and miners. Its commander, Colonel Richard Baird-Smith, who had heard of the projected assault and had rushed on so as to be able to participate in it, now took over as Chief Engineer. Together with Captain Taylor, he infused a new spirit of aggression into higher British counsels. Baird-Smith at once urged on Barnard a renewal of the planned *coup de main*. Barnard asked for time to consider the matter – by the time Baird-Smith returned, however, the General, stricken by cholera, was too ill to see him. 'The next morning (6th July),' wrote Hope Grant, 'I learned that poor Sir Henry Barnard had been seized with cholera, and had been carried off by it after an illness of six or seven hours. Like General Anson, he had little pain, and had wasted away, at the last quite unconscious. His son told me that after he was taken ill his mind wandered, and he kept continually saying, "Tell Grant to take out all the cavalry. Tell Reed I have sent up the 60th to support him." The following day we buried him in the old cemetery within our lines.'

Chief command passed to Major General Reed, who, being too old and too ill to accept any responsibility, temporized over any new plans for attack. Baird-Smith busied himself taking surveys of the British position, starting with the siege artillery. What he found – two 24-pounders, nine 18-pounders, six 8-inch mortars and three 8-inch howitzers, with enough ammunition for one day's concentrated fire – was hardly encouraging. The rebels – with almost unlimited ammunition – could bring thirty guns and twelve mortars to bear on any threatened point. Realizing that Reed would not authorize a *coup de main* attempt and that any assault would have to await reinforcements and more and bigger guns, Baird-Smith set out to strengthen the position on the Ridge. Over the next few days his sappers destroyed most remaining bridges over the canal, which the enemy had used in their earlier attacks, cleared the Ridge of brushwood and improved the defences of the outposts and batteries.

The rebels persisted in their attacks. Their initial attack – the usual rite of passage for newly arrived contingents – having been repelled, the Bareilly Brigade made a second attempt on 9 July. They were assisted by the 8th Irregulars who – since their French-grey uniform was the same as that of the so far loyal 9th Irregular Cavalry – approached a post manned by the 9th at the rear of the British camp. The two regiments were closely linked and there were many friendships between the sowars so the men of the 9th allowed the sowars of the 8th to pass through the post unmolested. In seconds the rebel Irregulars charged into the British camp, the only opposition – a picket of the Carabiniers composed of young recruits – was swept away. Near by were two guns of Tombs's troop of horse artillery, commanded by Lieutenant Hills. Frederick Roberts described what followed: 'The moment Hills saw the enemy he shouted,

"Action front!" and in the hope of giving his men time to load and fire a round of grape, he gallantly charged the head of the column single-handed, cut down the leading man, struck the second, and was then ridden down himself.' It had been raining and Hills was wearing his heavy cloak, which probably saved his life, as it and his jacket and shirt were badly slashed. As the enemy passed him, Hills ran to recover his sword. 'He had just found it,' wrote Roberts, 'when he was attacked by three men, two of whom were mounted; he fired at and wounded the first man; then caught the lance of the second in his left hand, and ran him through the body with his sword. The first assailant coming on again, Hills cut him down, upon which he was attacked by the third man on foot, who succeeded in wrenching his sword from him.' As Hills lay on the ground with the sowar standing over him about to deliver the death blow, his commander Major Tombs rode up and – from 30 yards away – shot the man dead.

Meanwhile in the camp, wrote Hope Grant, 'Our men quickly turned out in their shirt-sleeves, some with swords, some with rifles, and succeeded in killing 30 of the rebels.' While the fight continued in the camp, Tombs and Hills were tending to their wounded gunners when they saw a sowar running back towards the Sabzi Mandi. Hills ran out to engage him. 'Let me alone,' shouted the man, 'or I'll kill you, as you killed our leader, my father.' Hills feinted a cut, then as the man parried, attempted a lunge, but overbalanced. The sowar sidestepped and cut Hills to the head – he was about to finish him off when Tombs ran up. The sowar cut at Tombs's head, beating down his guard and cutting his forage cap, while at the same moment Tombs ran him through the body. In a few minutes the rebels had ridden through the camp and back towards the Sabzi Mandi, pursued by Hope Grant and his cavalry. Even during the pursuit it was difficult to discern friend from foe. Hope Grant saw a party of some eighty grey-coated Native cavalry near the Ochterlony Gardens.

> I sent my aide-de-camp, Augustus Anson, to ascertain their identity, and he brought me back word that they were a detachment of our own cavalry. Captain Hodson also rode up to them, accosted them, and marched with them for some distance, under the impression that they belonged to one of the Hindostanee regiments in camp. They entered into most friendly conversation with him, and told him, I think, that they were a party of 9th Irregulars. All of sudden, however, they put

spurs to their horses, galloped off like wild-fire, giving us the slip completely; and we then discovered for the first time that they were some rebel cavalry.

The rebel cavalry's raid was followed by a major attack on the Sabzi Mandi, which was only beaten off after hard fighting, leaving five hundred sepoys dead on the ground. The cost to the British, though – which they could ill afford – was 233 killed. As a result of the treachery of the 9th Irregulars it was decided soon after to disarm all Hindustani troops on the Ridge, with one or two notable exceptions – Hope Grant ensured that Rooper Khan kept his sword and weapons. For their actions that day both Lieutenant Hills and Major Tombs were awarded the Victoria Cross.

Further rebel attacks – on 14 July on Hindu Rao's House, on the 16th by the newly arrived Jhansi mutineers, and on the 18th – were all driven off, but each time with heavy British casualties, including Neville Chamberlain who, leading from the front during the fighting on the 14th, was wounded in the shoulder and rendered *hors de combat* for the next few months. When, on 17 July, General Reed stood down due to ill health, his replacement, General Archdale Wilson, immediately proposed withdrawing the entire force across the Jumna. Baird-Smith urged him to continue the siege, remain on the defensive and order up a siege train from Ferozepore. This would bring the British guns up to a total of sixty-three. These, together with Nicholson's Movable Column, now making its way to join the Delhi force, would make the siege of Delhi – a siege, so far in name only – a reality.

The first day of August – *Bakhra Eid* – was sacred to Muslims as the date of Abraham's intended sacrifice of his son (Ishmael rather than Isaac, according to Muslim teaching). It was customary for the King of Delhi, accompanied by huge crowds, to visit a large serai outside the walls and sacrifice a camel or goat in honour of Ishmael, and the day was considered propitious by all Muslims. A major assault on the British positions was prepared. On 31 July a strong rebel force marched up the left bank of the Jumna intending to cross the river at Bagpat and, from the left rear, block British communications from the north, thus starving them out. Another force of 6,000 men with sixteen guns was to cross the canal on the British right and attack the British from the rear, while the main body of the rebel army was to attack the British positions frontally. It was a good plan and the weather was favourable. For the past two weeks the almost incessant rain had ceased, and the previously swampy ground had firmed up enough to allow the passage of artillery. 'All the morning of the 1st August mosques and Hindu temples were crowded with worshippers offering up prayers for the success of the great attempt,' wrote Roberts. The rebel force, intending to attack the British rear, constructed a bridge across the canal strong enough to bear the weight of guns, but no sooner had part of the cavalry crossed over than a huge storm broke, the waters of the canal rose and the bridge was washed away. This force fell back to Delhi – the cavalry who had already crossed, fearing to attack the British camp unsupported, made their way back to the city by a circuitous 16-mile march.

Nothing daunted, the main rebel body attacked in the afternoon. 'The rebels, mad with excitement and fanaticism, issued in countless numbers from the city gates,' wrote Roberts, 'and shouting the Moslem battle-cry, advanced and threw themselves on our defences.' Baird-Smith's work on the Ridge's defences had not been in vain. Wave after wave of rebel attacks broke on the British breastworks. 'They were driven back by our deadly volleys,' wrote Roberts,

> but only for a moment; they quickly re-formed and made a fresh attack, to be stopped again by our steady, uncompromising fire. Time after time they rallied and hurled themselves against our breastworks. All that night and well into the next day the fight continued, and it was past noon before the devoted fanatics became convinced that their gods had deserted them, that victory was not for them, and that no effort, however heroic on their part could drive us from the Ridge. The enemy's loss was heavy, ours trifling, for our men were admirably steady, well protected by breastworks, and never allowed to show themselves except when the assailants came close up. We had only 1 officer and 9 men killed and 36 men wounded.

Rebel losses were about 1,500.

Both sides now settled down to a waiting game – the rebels, for further reinforcements to render a British assault on the city impossible or for cholera to force a British withdrawal; the British, for Nicholson's column and the siege train – 13 miles long, hauled by oxen and elephants – about to start plodding its ponderous way down from Ferozepore. While the British consolidated, however, and turned hopeful eyes towards the

Punjab, dire news arrived from another part of India, from a city nearly 300 miles away whose name was to become for the British both a watchword and a battle-cry – Cawnpore.

# 6

## CAWNPORE

Cawnpore, on the right bank of the Ganges – which separates it from Oude – is 270 miles south-east of Delhi. The headquarters of a division, it was the largest station in that swathe of India most affected by the mutinies – and in large parts of which, for the time being, the Company's rule was suspended. In 1857 its garrison consisted of the 1st, 53rd and 56th Regiments of Native Infantry, the 2nd Light Cavalry and sixty-one European gunners, armed with six guns – one 24-pounder and five 9-pounders. The station was also home to the families of HM 32nd Foot, then garrisoning Lucknow, the capital of Oude. Its commander was Sir Hugh Massey Wheeler, a soldier of the old school – he had an Indian wife – who had served in India with distinction for fifty-four years.

Believing from the first news of the outbreak at Meerut on 14 May that his command was in danger, Wheeler set about putting it in a posture of defence. To this end, on the very day he heard of the Mutiny, he began construction of an earthwork into which – in the event of any similar outbreak at Cawnpore – he could move all Europeans, Eurasians and Indian Christians. His selection of a site was to be criticized at the time and since. Based around two barrack buildings in open ground near some other, half-finished barracks, what came to be known as 'Wheeler's Entrenchment' was well placed to receive aid from Allahabad, the most likely source of relief. Wheeler was later criticized for not basing his defence around the Magazine – a strong stone building nearer the river, but this was 7 miles away and to enter it would require a doubtless straggling column of civilians to pass the native lines and the town.

Work on the entrenchment was slowed by the hardness of the ground at this season, but Sir Hugh pushed his workforce hard. Spies were bringing him news of nightly meetings in the lines of the 1st NI and the 2nd Light Cavalry. It was not anticipated that the sepoys, if they did mutiny, would turn on the European population. In all likelihood, thought Sir Hugh, they would march for Delhi – the rallying point for the rebel cause. Throughout his preparations and the arming and victualling of the entrenchment, Wheeler maintained close contact with Mr Hillersdon, the Collector of Revenues, at Cawnpore, who was himself in close touch with the Rajah of Bithur, Dhondu Pant.

The Nana Sahib, as Dhondu Pant was commonly called, was one of the adopted sons of the last Peshwa – the lord of all the Maratha princes – Baji Rao II. Baji Rao had been dethroned by the British in 1818 and granted a pension for life of 8 lakhs of rupees (800,000). He took up residence at Bithur and adopted the Nana Sahib as his son – to a childless high-caste Hindu, adoption was a way of ensuring that after death the correct funeral rites would be carried out. Before his death, Baji Rao petitioned the British Government that his adopted son might, in due course, inherit the title of Peshwa and the pension. The Government refused the notion of the Nana Sahib inheriting the title, and reserved the issue of the pension until such time as the Peshwa died. When he did die, in 1851, the then Governor General, Lord Dalhousie, turned down the request for the pension – even though it was backed by the British Commissioner responsible for the ex-Peshwa's estate. With a large household – left him by his adoptive father – to support, the Nana Sahib was determined to fight for his father's pension. Bypassing the Governor General, the Nana decided to appeal to the East India Company at its headquarters in London. He sent there, as his agent, Azimullah Khan. Intelligent, charming and witty, Azimullah enjoyed some social – and amorous – success in London's drawing rooms, but his charm was lost on the East India Company's Court of Directors. In their answer to the Nana Sahib's petition, they declared 'that the pension of his adoptive father was not hereditary, that he has no claim whatever to it, and that his claim is wholly inadmissible'. If the Court were within their rights by Western standards there was, in the eyes of the Nana Sahib and many thousands of natives, a superior moral obligation owing to a man whose father had been overlord of most of western India.

On his way home – bearing the Court of Directors' reply – Azimullah

Khan visited Constantinople and from there went on to the seat of war in the Crimea. He was a witness to the ill-fated British assault on the Redan at Sebastopol on 18 June 1854 and was treated to the sight of redcoats being mown down in swathes and running for their lives. On his return to Bithur he remained the Nana's adviser. Even without his pension, the Nana Sahib was far from poor – his adopted father left him the equivalent of 4 million pounds sterling. He lived in some style at his palace in Bithur and frequently and lavishly entertained British officers and civil servants and their ladies. Sometimes he would urge his guests to take up the question of his pension with Queen Victoria if the opportunity ever arose. It was noticed that he refused all social invitations from the British.

When the news of events at Meerut first arrived at Cawnpore, the Nana Sahib assured Hillersdon of his support, offered his palace as a safe refuge for Hillersdon's family, and promised 1,500 of his own men to take the field against the Cawnpore sepoys if they did rise. According to Captain Mowbray Thomson of the 53rd NI, it was at about this time that Azimullah Khan came down to view the entrenchment. 'Azimoolah met Lieutenant M. G. Daniell, of our garrison and said to him, pointing toward our entrenched barrack: "What do you call that place you are making out in the plain?" "I am sure I don't know," was the reply. Azimoolah suggested it should be named the fort of despair. "No," said Daniell; "we will call it the fort of victory." "Aha! Aha!" replied the wily eastern, with a silent sneer that betrayed the lurking mischief.' Reluctant though the British may have been to trust the Nana Sahib, they had little choice. It was looking increasingly likely that the Cawnpore sepoys would indeed break out; when, on 21 May, Wheeler was told that the 2nd Light Cavalry would rise that night, he began moving the women and children into the entrenchment, and attempted to do the same with the contents of the Treasury. The sepoys on guard there, however, refused to part with the money and Wheeler agreed that both the Treasury and the Magazine should be guarded by three hundred matchlock men and two guns sent by the Nana Sahib. The following day eighty-four men of HM 32nd Foot arrived, sent down from Lucknow, in post carriages, by Sir Henry Lawrence. Both sides now settled down to wait. While the bulk of the Europeans – and Wheeler himself – had now moved into the entrenchment, the British officers of the Native regiments continued to sleep in the regimental lines, to show their confidence in their men.

The prospect seemed much brighter, when, during the three days of 31

May and 1 and 2 June, fifteen men of the 1st Madras Fusiliers (European) arrived, together with a hundred of HM 84th Foot, the first element of these regiments hurried up from Calcutta by Lord Canning. It seemed to Wheeler that as communications to the south-east were open and with British troops starting to arrive, the sepoys would think a rising too hazardous. So confident was he that he sent fifty men of the 84th on up to Lucknow. Communications with Calcutta, however, did not stay open – mutinies at Allahabad, Benares and Dinapore soon left Cawnpore isolated. On the evening of 3 June half of a battery of the 3rd Oude Native Artillery under Lieutenant Ashe – which had been patrolling the road from Cawnpore to Agra – came into the entrenchment. The Native troopers accompanying the guns, Ashe reported, had mutinied and the battery had been forced to retreat. The guns – two 9-pounders and a 24-pound howitzer – were incorporated into the entrenchment's defences, but the European troops regarded the Native gunners with a wary eye.

On the night of 4 June the Native troopers of the 2nd Light Cavalry mutinied. Wheeler – forewarned – had already forbidden the European officers to sleep in the lines, so the troopers contented themselves with setting fire to the sergeants' bungalows and riding to the Treasury, where they were confronted by the soldiers of the Nana Sahib. Within minutes both bodies of men were cooperating in loading the treasure – amounting to £170,000 – on to elephants and carts. Soon they were joined by the sepoys of the 1st NI, who had at least refrained from killing their officers – they had begged them to return to the entrenchment saying that they meant them no harm, but that their allegiance was ended. The mutiny at Cawnpore followed the usual pattern – treasury, magazine, gaol. At the Magazine a British warrant officer tasked with blowing it up in the event of a rising was prevented by the sepoy guard, and at the gaol the worst criminal elements were unleashed on the empty station. The Europeans huddled in the entrenchment watched as flames lit up the night all around them.

In the morning four officers of the as yet uncommitted 53rd and 56th set off towards their lines, only to be fired on by their men. Shortly afterwards, Native officers arrived to report that the men could not be relied upon. At 9 o'clock the sepoys of these regiments arrived before Wheeler's position and formed into columns as though for an attack. Three rounds from a cannon inside the entrenchment were sufficient to drive them off towards Nawabganj, where they joined their comrades of the 1st NI. Ironically, the fact that the mutineers had taken the Treasury gave Wheeler cause for optimism – the mutineers had nothing to gain from storming the entrenchment. The bulk of them were now at Nawabganj on the Delhi road and there was every chance that they would now march off to Delhi to join the wider rebellion. Wheeler, however, had reckoned without the Nana Sahib.

In the light of his later conduct, it was generally assumed that the Nana Sahib had been intent on treachery from the start, although at least one commentator, J. W. Sherer, believed that his initial design in coming to Cawnpore had been to earn his pension by making himself invaluable to the British in their hour of need. Whatever the truth, when the leaders of the mutinous sepoys came to him and – placing his foot on their heads declared him their leader – the Nana Sahib accepted their homage. There is no doubt that Azimullah Khan was at his elbow, perhaps whispering in his ear that the redcoats – as he had seen – were not invincible in battle. The four mutinous regiments had demanded to be led to Delhi, and actually marched off in that direction. The Nana Sahib, however, like other Maratha princes, had no desire to serve that monarch who had, until the arrival of the British, been their puppet. In Delhi he would be one of many vassals; in Bithur he could exercise kingly power. The first step to this was the destruction of the British. As the rebels encamped for the night at Kalianpur the Nana's agents went to work among the regiments. They persuaded the rebels that the first step – before any march to Delhi – was the annihilation of the British. They had scotched the snake, not killed it, they argued, and it would be a mistake to allow the British to survive, possibly to regroup in their rear. On the morning of 6 June, the mutineer army returned to Cawnpore. On arrival there the Nana pitched camp in the centre of the station and, with beat of drum, declared himself the Peshwa – the Maratha title last held by his adoptive father. Subadar Tika Singh of the 2nd Light was appointed his general of cavalry, and Subadar Ganga Din and Jemadar Dalganjan Singh of the infantry were appointed his two brigade commanders, with the rank of colonel. Two standards were hoisted – one of Mohammed and one of Hanuman the Monkey God – to satisfy both Hindus and Muslims among his following. Among the advisers of the Nana Sahib was Ramchandra Panduranga, who had adopted the name Tantia Topi – a Deccan title meaning 'commander'. Tantia had served the Nana as aide until the outbreak and was now employed in raising troops. He was soon to prove a more able commander than any of those the Nana had just appointed –

and to win fame, or notoriety, as the most able and persistent opponent of the British *raj*.

Wheeler, having thought that the threat to his entrenchment had vanished, now learned that it had reappeared with redoubled force. The following day – 7 June – he received a letter from the Nana Sahib announcing his intention to attack the entrenchment, and as an earnest of his bad faith two guns began at once to fire upon the British. 'The bugle-call sent every man of us instantly to his post,' wrote Thomson, 'many of us carrying in our ears for the first time the peculiar whizzing of round shot, with which we were to become so familiar. As the day advanced, the enemy's fire grew hotter and more dangerous in consequence of their getting the guns into position.' Thomson also witnessed the first casualty of the siege – a gunner called McGuire, killed by a round shot. 'Several of us saw the ball bounding toward us, and he also evidently saw it, but, like many others whom I saw fall at different times, he seemed fascinated to the spot.' By the following day – the same day on which General Barnard's army took possession of Delhi Ridge – three more guns had joined in. By the 11th the rebels had in position three mortars, two 24-pounders, three 18-pounders, two 12-pounders, two 9-pounders and one 6-pounder. These kept up a cannonade night and day. On the first day, Thomson had noted,

> The shrieks of the women and children were terrific; as often as the balls struck the walls of the barracks their wailings were heart-rending, but after the initiation of the first day, they had learnt silence, and never uttered a sound except when groaning from the horrible mutilations they had to endure. When night sheltered them, our cowardly assailants closed in upon the intrenchments, and harassed us with volleys of musketry. Waiting the assault that we supposed to be impending, not a man closed his eyes in sleep, and throughout the whole siege, snatches of troubled slumber under the cover of the wall, was all the relief the combatants could obtain.

Sorties were mounted against the adjacent unfinished barracks, which, wrote Thomson, were often occupied by parties of rebels:

> From the windows of these barracks they could pepper away upon our walls, yelling defiance, abusing us in the most hellish language brandishing their swords, and striking up a war-dance. Some of these

fanatics, under the influence of infuriating doses of *bhang*, would come out into the open and perform, but at the inevitable cost of life. Our combined pickets always swept through these barracks once, and sometimes twice a-day, in chase of the foe. They scarcely ever stood for a hand-to-hand fight, but heaps of them were left dead as the result of these sallies ... In some of these charges we occasionally bagged a prisoner or two ... they expressed sorrow for their conduct, and attributed the mutiny to the *hawa*, meaning thereby an invisible influence exercised over them by the devil. It is a curious circumstance, that the Hindoos associate almost all calamity with the wind, and in not a few parts of India, the name by which the Mutiny has been designated is the devil's wind.

Soon the Nana's forces were being augmented by mutineers and volunteers from Allahabad and from Oude – to oppose this force Wheeler had 210 British soldiers and a hundred officers and civilians, mostly railway engineers, tradesmen and clerks. In addition, there were some Christian drummers, a handful of loyal sepoys from the 53rd and 56th, who had made their way into camp, making a total of 450 combatants. The rest of the population of the entrenchment consisted of 330 women and children, many of the latter being half-caste schoolchildren. There were four weeks' worth of supplies within the entrenchment, whose walls were only 4 feet high, not even bulletproof at the top, and which was overlooked from several directions. Things went wrong from the start – overcrowded, baked by the heat and exposed to a vicious crossfire by day and night the garrison suffered terribly. Almost at once the disposal of the dead became a problem. A small well outside the walls, not far from the unfinished barracks, provided the answer – and the dead, after lying on the verandah of the barrack building during the day, were carried out at night and lowered into it. The only water supply in the compound was a single well on to which by day the rebels concentrated their fire. It was soon ordained that each man would draw his own water and at night, when the fire slackened, there were crowds about the well. 'Even in the dead of night,' wrote Mowbray Thomson,

the darkness afforded but little protection, as they could hear the creaking of the tackle, and took the well-known sound as a signal for instantly opening up with their artillery upon the suttlers. These were chiefly privates, who were paid as much as eight or ten shillings per bucket. Poor fellows! their earnings were of little avail to them; but to their credit it must be said, that when money had lost its value, by reason of the extremity of our danger, they were none the less willing to incur the risk of drawing water for the women and children.

Constant blasts of grape soon destroyed the well's winding gear, so Mr John MacKillop of the Bengal Civil Service undertook to draw water up – 60 feet – by hand. 'He became self-constituted captain of the well …', wrote his friend Captain Thomson. 'He jocosely said that he was no fighting man, but would make himself useful where he could, and accordingly he took this post; drawing for the supply of women and children as often as he could.' Not everyone, Thomson regretted to record, rose to the occasion:

> One officer of high rank, and in the prime of life … never showed himself outside the walls of the barrack, nor took even the slightest part in the military operations. This craven-hearted man, whose name I withhold out of consideration for the feelings of his surviving relatives, seemed not to possess a thought beyond that of preserving his own worthless life. Throughout three weeks of skulking, while women and children were daily dying around him, and the little band of combatants was being constantly thinned by wounds and death, not even the perils of his own wife could rouse this man to exertion.

The rebel cannonade soon rendered the barracks almost useless as shelter – and many were forced to burrow into the walls of the entrenchment. Before long, every able-bodied man or woman was needed to keep watch on the walls. 'The execution committed by the twenty-four pounders they had was terrific,' wrote Thomson, 'though they were not always a match for the devices we adopted to divert their aim. When we wanted to create a diversion, we used to pile up some of the muskets behind the mud wall, and mount them with hats and shakos, and then allow the sepoys to expend their powder on these dummies while we went elsewhere.' Under ceaseless bombardment, however – as well as musket and matchlock fire, heat exhaustion and disease – casualties mounted. Mr Hillersdon, the Collector, was killed by a round shot. His wife died a few days later when a piece of the hospital roof – brought down by a shell – fell on her while she was in labour. Another round shot took off the head of Lieutenant Wheeler, Sir Hugh's son, as he lay wounded in the barracks. Colonel Williams of the 56th NI died of apoplexy; his wife of her wounds. Colonel Ewart of the 1st NI was severely wounded early in the fighting. Mr MacKillop, the 'captain of the well', was mortally wounded at his post. 'It was less than a week after he had taken this self-denying service,' wrote Thomson, 'when his numerous escapes were followed by a grape-shot wound in the groin, and speedy death. Disinterested even in death, his last words were an earnest entreaty that somebody would go and draw water for a lady to whom he had promised it.' The constant crying of the babies and children, said Thomson, drove many soldiers to risk – and some to lose – their lives trying to get water for them. 'The men could scarcely endure the cries for drink which were almost perpetual from the poor little babes, terribly unconscious they were, most of them, of the great, great cost at which only it could be procured. I have seen the children of my brother officers sucking the pieces of old water bags, putting scraps of canvas and leather straps into the mouth to try and get a single drop of moisture upon their parched lips.' The heat – between 120 and 138 degrees – was relentless. 'It was often quite impossible to touch the barrel of a gun, and once or twice muskets went off at midday, either from the sun exploding their caps or from the fiery heat of the metal. Across the plain, the mirage, which only makes its appearance in extremely hot seasons, painted its fantastic scenes, sometimes of forest scenery, sometimes of water, but always extending to a vast distance, and presenting a strange contrast in its unbroken stillness to the perturbed life within our mud walls.'

While the garrison inside the entrenchment held out, Europeans in the surrounding countryside were being rooted out of hiding and brought before the Nana Sahib on whose orders, and often in whose presence, they were killed – after their severed noses and ears had been strung around their necks. On 12 June the Nana Sahib was informed that a boatload of Europeans was approaching Cawnpore. Guns were brought to bear on the boats and their surrender was called for. Some Europeans refused, slipped ashore and managed to escape, but the majority, feeling they had no choice, came ashore. These – some 126 fugitives from an uprising at Fatehgarh, mostly women and children – were brought before the Nana Sahib and murdered. The women and children were killed with swords and bamboo spears, and the men, after hours of torture and torment, were despatched with pistol shots to the head. The Nana seems to have adopted a policy of terror, using atrocities such as these to ensure his followers' total commitment to his cause. With such deeds to their name, there could be no question of accommodation with the British.

The following day rebel gunners succeeded in setting fire to the roof of the barracks – forty of the inmates were killed, and nearly all the medicines and surgical instruments destroyed. Thinking this was the end some four thousand of the besiegers advanced to the attack, but were driven off by the fire of Wheeler's guns. On the night of 15/16 June Captain John Moore of HM 32nd – who, like his wife in her sphere, was a stalwart of the defence – led a sortie against the natives' nearest battery. With twenty-five men Moore captured the battery, bayoneted the gunners and spiked three guns. They then went on to storm a second battery, killing the gunners there, spiking two more guns and blowing up a 24-pounder, all for the loss of one man killed and four wounded. The next day, however, fresh guns were mounted and the rebel cannonade continued as before.

Several more times between then and 21 June the rebels made similar attempts to storm the defences, only to be driven back. Captain Moore wrote to Sir Henry Lawrence at Lucknow on 18 June: 'Our troops, officers, and volunteers, have acted most nobly and on several occasions a handful of men have driven hundreds before them. Our loss has been chiefly from the sun and their heavy guns. Our rations will last a fortnight, and we are well supplied with ammunition. Report says that troops are advancing from Allahabad, and that any assistance might save our garrison. We are, of course, prepared to hold out to the last.'

On 23 June, it being the anniversary of Plassey, the rebels – as at Delhi – launched an all-out assault. Reinforced with large numbers of volunteers from Oude, they occupied the outlying barrack buildings and attempted to dislodge the defenders from a small foothold they had in the remainder. Captain Moore of the 32nd led a counter-attack with twenty-five men who, covered by grape from the entrenchment's guns, expelled the rebels. Elsewhere on the perimeter, men of the 1st NI, led by their senior Native officer, advanced behind large bales of cotton to within 150 yards of the entrenchment; but when they attempted to charge, they were driven back by grape and volley-firing – with the women of the garrison loading rifles for the men – leaving two hundred dead or wounded behind them, including their commander.

By 24 June, with no sign of relief from Allahabad, the situation of the defenders was desperate. The rains were coming, and the expected deluge would in all likelihood bring down the barracks and sweep away the entrenchment. They were on half rations – even dog soup and old horse were becoming rarities. Thomson described their physical state at this stage: 'Tattered in clothing, begrimed with dirt, emaciated in countenance, were all without exception; faces that had been beautiful were now chiselled with deep furrows; haggard despair seated itself where there had been a month before only smiles. Some were sinking into the settled vacancy of look which marked insanity. The old babbling with confirmed imbecility, and the young raving in not a few cases with wild mania; while only the strongest retained the calmness demanded by the occasion.' The guns were wearing out and the ammunition supply was failing. There was wild talk of a sortie in force – a course that would surely have ended in the deaths of all involved. As Wheeler pondered his options there came into the camp a white woman – an emissary of the Nana. There is some disagreement as to the identity of the woman. Some say she was a Mrs Greenway, wife of a Cawnpore merchant, whose family had been spared on the promise of a ransom of a lakh (10,000) of rupees, though Amelia Horne claims she was a Mrs Henry Jacobi, wife of a Cawnpore watchmaker. Whatever her identity, this white woman bore a letter from Azimullah Khan, writing on the Nana's behalf, offering terms.

Although the prospect of surrender was repellent to the soldiers of the garrison, the likely fate of the women and children was uppermost in men's minds. The Nana's terms seemed reasonable. 'All those who are in no way connected with the acts of Lord Dalhousie, and are willing to lay down their arms, shall receive a safe passage to Allahabad.' Ignorant of the fate of the Fatehgarh fugitives, Sir Hugh Wheeler authorized Captain Moore to negotiate. The following day a treaty was drawn up. On the part of the British Government Sir Hugh agreed to give up all money, stores and guns within the entrenchment; the Nana, on his part, swore on the waters of the Ganges – the most sacred oath a Hindu could swear – 'not only to allow all the inmates of the garrison to retire unmolested, but to provide means of conveyance for the wounded, and for the ladies and children.' All firing ceased and preparations were set in hand for the garrison's removal by river to Allahabad. That night the garrison slept better than they had for a month. Many a man slept that night – according to Thomson, who reckoned he had only had two hours' continuous sleep since the siege began – 'with a pillow of brickbats, made comfortable by extreme fatigue and prolonged suspense, and with a comfortable sense of having done all that he could, or that his country could require.' Before they slept they drank deep. 'Though the *debris* of bricks and mortar had made the water cloudy, it was more delicious than nectar. It was not given out by thimblefuls that night.' Although a number of women gave way to anxiety with the question, 'Do you think it will be all right tomorrow?' the children, wrote Thomson, were most cheerful, having had their wants more liberally supplied than for a long time past. In the unaccustomed silence of the night scavengers came to the camp: 'The jackal took the opportunity offered to him to prowl amongst the animal remains around the intrenchment,' wrote Thomson, 'without alarm from the guns; and day-break disclosed to view hosts of adjutant birds and vultures gloating over their carnivorous breakfast. These are the only parties who have to thank the sepoys for the rebellion of 1857.'

On the morning of 27 June the garrison left the entrenchment for the one-mile journey to the Satichaura Ghat on the Ganges, where forty thatch-roofed boats were waiting to transport them to safety. 'It was about seven o'clock when we left for the Ghat,' wrote Amelia Horne,

> mounted on elephants ... The elephants provided for our conveyance were not allowed by their *mahouts* [the men who managed the elephants] to sit down so that we might mount in comfort. We were therefore obliged to climb up by their tails, and you can imagine the brutality of such a proceeding (instigated by the Nana), when the wounded and sick had to adopt this mode of ascent and fell to the ground. This nearly cost my poor mother her life, for, hampered as she was by her *enceinte* condition, and weakened by hunger and privation, the task was a most Herculean one for her to perform, and she fell heavily.

'Never, surely was there such an emaciated, ghostly party of human beings as we,' wrote Thomson. 'There were women who had been beautiful, now stripped of every personal charm, some with, some without gowns; fragments of finery were made available no longer for decoration, but decorum; officers in tarnished uniforms, rent and wretched, and with nondescript mixtures of apparel, more or less insufficient in all. There were few shoes, fewer stockings, and scarcely any shirts; these had all gone for bandages to the wounded.' Officers from Native regiments like Thomson saw among the sepoys who accompanied them many men of their own former regiments. These men did not help, but neither did they hinder the Europeans. 'The sepoys were loud in their expression of astonishment that we had withstood them so long,' wrote Thomson, 'and

The last of the Mogul Emperors, Bahadur Shah II. (Private Collection/Dinodia/Bridgeman Art Library)

In the Punjab the authorities reacted swiftly – with disaffected units disarmed and ringleaders hanged (*above*) or blown from guns (*below*). (Corbis/Bettmann)

The Kashmir Gate, Delhi.
(Hulton-Deutsch
Collection/Corbis)

The superiority of the
'point'. Lieutenant
William Alexander Kerr
earns the VC at Kolapore,
unusually against mutinous
Bombay sepoys. Apart
from this outbreak, the
sepoys of the Bombay and
Madras armies remained
loyal. (By Louis
Desanges/Courtesy of the
Council, National Army
Museum, London/
Bridgeman Art Library)

John Nicholson. (Dannenberg Album/British
Library)

Sir Archdale Wilson. (Art Archive/John Meek)

*'The Slaughter Ghat on the banks of the Ganges.'* Satichaura Ghat – scene of the first massacre.
(Dannenberg Album/British Library)

The interior of the Bibighar, Cawnpore – a contemporary sketch. (British Library/Bridgeman Art Library)

'The "Well" where the women and children were thrown, dead and living. Enclosed by General Neill.' Cawnpore. (Dannenberg Album/British Library)

To

# The Glory of God

AND

# In Memory of

MORE THAN A THOUSAND
CHRISTIAN PEOPLE
WHO MET THEIR DEATHS HARD BY
BETWEEN 6TH JUNE, AND 15TH JULY,
1857.

## These Tablets

ARE PLACED, IN THIS THE
MEMORIAL CHURCH,
ALL SOULS,
CAWNPORE,
BY THE
GOVERNMENT, N. W. P.

### Staff:

MAJOR-GEN. SIR H. WHEELER, K. C. B.
LADY WHEELER AND DAUGHTERS.
LIEUT. G. R. WHEELER, 1ST N. I., A.-D.-C.
LIEUT.-COL. E. WIGGENS, 52ND N. I., D. J. A. G.
MRS. WIGGENS.
MAJOR W. LINDSAY, A. A. C.
MRS. LINDSAY, AND DAUGHTERS.
ENSIGN C. AND MRS. LINDSAY.
BRIGADIER GENERAL JACK, C. B.
MR. JACK.
CAPT. SIR G. PARKER, 74TH N. I., CANT. MAGISTR.
CAPT. WILLIAMSON, 71ST N. I., D. A. C. G.
MRS. WILLIAMSON AND CHILD.

TABLET NO. 1.

IN MEMORIAL CHURCH, CAWNPORE.

### Bengal Artillery.

MAJOR C. LARKINS, WIFE AND CHILDREN.
LIEUT. C. DEMPSTER, WIFE AND CHILDREN.
  ,,    B. ASHBURNER.
  ,,    J. MARTIN.
  ,,    ST. G. ASHE.
  ,,    J. A. H. AND MRS. ECKFORD.
2ND LIEUT. C. M. W. SOTHEBY.
  ,,    F. W. BURNEY.
ASST. SURG. D. MCAULEY, M. D.
HOSPITAL-STEWARD W. HEFFERAN.
ASST-APOT. W. SLANEY.
63 NON-COMMISSIONED OFFICERS AND MEN.
BESIDES WOMEN AND CHILDREN.

### Bengal Engineers.

CAPT. F. WHITING.
LIEUT. S. C. JERVIS.

### 32nd Light Infantry.

CAPT. J. MOORE, WIFE AND CHILDREN.
LIEUT. F. MRS. AND MISS WAINWRIGHT.
ENSIGN E. C. AND MRS. HILL.
ASST.-APOT. I. THOMPSON.
HOSPT.-APPT. W. A. EMMOR AND WIFE.
82 NON-COMMISSIONED OFFICERS AND MEN.
41 WOMEN AND 61 CHILDREN.

### 84th Foot.

LIEUT. F. J. G. SAUNDERS.
47 NON-COMMISSIONED-OFFICERS AND MEN.

### 1st E. M. Fusiliers.

15 NON-COMMISSIONED OFFICERS AND MEN.

LIEUT. C. J. GLANVILLE, 2ND E. B. F.

\*

TABLET NO. 3.

IN MEMORIAL CHURCH, CAWNPORE.

Four of the many memorial tablets in All Souls church, Cawnpore, built at the site of Wheeler's entrenchment, Cawnpore. (Dannenberg Album/British Library)

## 2nd Light Cavalry.

[MA]JOR E. VIBART, WIFE AND CHILDREN.
[CAP]TAIN E. C. VIBART.
  ,,    E. J. SEPPINGS, WIFE AND CHILDREN.
  ,,    R. U. AND MRS. JENKINS.
[LIE]UTENANT R. O. QUIN.
  ,,       C. W. QUIN.
  ,,       J. H. HARRISON.
  ,,       W. J. MANDERSON.
  ,,       F. S. M. WREN.
  ,,       M. G. DANIEL.
  ,,       M. BALFOUR.
[COR]NET W. A. STIRLING.
[SU]RGEON W. R. AND MRS. BOYES.
[ASS]T. SURG. E. C. CHALWIN, AND WIFE.
[VET.] MR. D. WALSH, WIFE AND CHILDREN.
[SE]RGT. MAJOR H. CLADWELL.
[SUB-]MR.-SERGT. F. AND MRS. TRESS.
[COR]NET C. MAINWARING, 6TH L. C.
[LIE]UTENANT A. J. BOULTON, 7TH L. C.

## 1st Native Infantry.

[LIE]UT.-COL. JOHN EWART, WIFE AND CHILD.
[LIE]UT. J. H. C. EWART, 12TH N. I.
[CAP]TAIN A. TURNER, WIFE AND CHILD.
  ,,    E. J. ELMS.
[LIE]UTENANT H. S. SMITH.
  ,,      R. M. SATCHWELL.
  ,,      F. REDMAN.
[EN]SIGN J. C. SUPPLE.
[SUR]GEON A. W. R. NEWENHAM, WIFE AND CHILDREN.
[SER]GEANT MAJOR C. HILLING, WIFE AND CHILD.
[SUB-]MR.-SERGT. T. ANDREW AND FAMILY.
[MU]SICIANS, 5 WOMEN AND 9 CHILDREN.

✳

## 53rd Native Infantry.

MAJOR W. R. HILLERSDON.
CAPT. J. H. REYNOLDS, WIFE AND CHILD.
  ,,   H. MRS. AND MISS BELSON.
LIEUT. F. G. JELLICOE, WIFE AND CHILDREN.
  ,,   H. H. ARMSTRONG.
  ,,   G. A. MASTER.
  ,,   O. S. BRIDGES.
  ,,   W. G. PROLE.
  ,,   F. H. TOMKINSON.
ENSIGN A. DAWSON.
  ,,   T. W. FORMAN.
SURGEON N. COLLYER.
SERGEANT-MAJOR T. MCMAHON, WIFE & CHILDREN
QR.-MR. SERGT. W. GORDON, WIFE AND CHILDREN.
10 MUSICIANS, WOMEN AND CHILDREN.

## 56th Native Infantry.

COL. S. WILLIAMS, WIFE AND DAUGHTERS.
MAJOR W. R. AND MRS. PROUT.
CAPTAIN W. L. HALLIDAY, WIFE AND CHILD.
  ,,    G. KEMPLAND, WIFE AND CHILDREN.
MISS KEMPLAND.
LIEUT. T. A. RAIKES.
  ,,   G. R. GOAD.
  ,,   W. A. CHALMERS.
  ,,   H. FAGAN.
  ,,   W. L. G. MORRIS.
  ,,   H. J. G. WARDE.
  ,,   J. W. HENDERSON.
  ,,   R. A. STEEVENS.

✳

General James Neill. (Dannenberg Album/British Library)

Sir Henry Havelock. (Art Archive/John Meek)

The Residency building, Lucknow. (Hulton-Deutsch Collection/Corbis)

said that it was utterly unaccountable to them. We told them that had it not been for the failure of our food we should have held the place to the last man.' A sepoy of Thomson's regiment – the 53rd BNI – told him the rebels had lost between 800 and 1,000 men. Officers who had been popular were asked after: 'Inquiries were made by men after their old officers whom they had missed, and they appeared much distressed at hearing of their death. Such discrepancies of character will possibly mystify the northern mind, but they are indigenous to the East.' Some officers, such as Major Vibart – father of the Edward Vibart who jumped from the walls of Delhi – had their property carried for them by sepoys who had served under them. 'They loaded a bullock cart with boxes, and escorted the Major's wife and family down to the boats, with the most profuse demonstrations of respect.'

The embarkation was to be supervised by Tantia Topi, deputizing for the Nana Sahib. Crowds of natives from the city also thronged the banks to witness the – presumably final – departure of the *Gora Log*. The boats waiting at the Ghat were 30 feet long by 12 feet wide, and moored in shallow water. Amelia Horne wrote:

Reaching the Ghat, we found that the boats were not very close to the shore, and the task of getting on board was a most difficult one. We had to wade knee-deep through the water, and it was pitiful to witness the difficulty of the aged, the sick, and the wounded in clambering up the boat's sides. Under the awning of our boat were seated my step-father, two brothers and two sisters and an Indian nurse; while on the deck or forepart were two soldiers, my little sister, and myself. In the hopeless scramble and confusion that ensued, and also on account of the want of room in our boat, my poor mother was conveyed to another boat a short distance away ... After all had embarked – which took about two hours to accomplish – the word was given to proceed. Instead of the crew obeying these orders, a signal was given from the shore and they all leaped into the water and waded to the bank, after having first secured burning charcoal in the thatch of most of the boats. Immediately a volley of bullets assailed us, followed by a hail of shot and grape which struck the boats. The two soldiers seated alongside me were wounded, and crept into the shelter of the awning to escape being made further targets of. In a few minutes pandemonium reigned. Several of the boats were seen to be wrapped in flames, and the sick and wounded were burnt to death. Some jumped overboard and tried to swim to the opposite shore, but were picked off by the bullets of the sepoys. Others were drowned, while a few jumped into the water and hid behind their boats to escape the pitiless fire. But the guns continued their vile work, and grape and musketry were poured into the last-mentioned people from the opposite bank which soon became alive with rebels who had been placed there to intercept refugees to that shore. A few succeeded in pushing their boats to the further side of the river, and were mercilessly slaughtered.

Thomson – on Major Vibart's boat – saw 'the identical troopers who had escorted Major Vibart to the ghaut [open] upon us with their carbines. As well as the confusion, caused by the burning of our boats, would allow, we returned the fire of these horsemen, who were about fifteen or sixteen in number, but they retired immediately after the volley they had given us.' Among the first men Thomson saw struck by enemy fire was the cowardly senior officer who had lain concealed throughout the siege 'his cowardice was unavailing; a bullet through the boat's side that despatched him caused the only death that we regarded with complacency'. Thomson and a number of others now jumped out of the boats to try to push them into deeper water, but the boats were mostly too heavy to push. 'It seemed that thousands of men fired upon us,' he wrote, 'besides four nine-pounders, carefully masked and pointed to the boats, every bush was filled with sepoys ... Some of the boats presented a broadside to the guns, others were raked from stem to stern by the shot. Volumes of smoke from the thatch veiled the full extent of the horrors of that morning. All who could move were speedily expelled from the boats by the heat of the flames. Alas! The wounded were burnt to death ... Wretched multitudes of women and children crouched behind the boats, or waded out into deeper water and stood up to their chins in the river to lessen the probability of being shot.' Seeing Major Vibart's boat floating down-stream, Thomson threw into the Ganges his father's Ghuznee medal and his mother's portrait ' ... all the property I had left, determined that they should have only my life for a prey', and struck out for the boat.

Meanwhile, closer to shore, wrote Amelia Horne,

the cavalry waded into the river with drawn swords and cut down those who were still alive, while the infantry boarded the boats to loot. One unfortunate, a Mr Kirkpatrick, in trying to ward off the blows from a sabre with his arms, had both arms chopped off. I saw him about half an hour later lying in the water still alive! The air resounded with the shrieks of the women and children and agonised prayers to God for mercy. The water was red with blood, and the smoke from the heavy firing of the cannon and muskets and the fire from the burning boats lay like dense clouds over and around us. Several men were mutilated in the presence of their wives, while babies and children were torn from their mothers' arms and hacked to pieces, the mothers being compelled to look on at the carnage! Many children were deliberately set fire to and burned, while the sepoys laughed and cheered, inciting each other to greater acts of brutality! My poor little sister, the one who had had her leg fractured in the entrenchment, moaned piteously, crying all the while 'Oh, Amy, don't leave me!' A few yards away I saw the boat containing my poor mother slowly burning, and I cowered on the deck overwhelmed with grief, not knowing what horrible fate the next moment had in store for me. My heart beat like a sledge hammer, and my temples throbbed with pain; but there I sat, gripping my little sister's hand, while the bullets fell like hail around me, praying fervently to God for mercy, and every second expecting to be in the presence of my Maker! The sepoys quickly boarded our boat, and a few trinkets I had with me were forcibly taken possession of by one of them. These not being sufficient to satisfy his avarice, he had the barbarity to fetch me a blow on the head with his musket. Shortly after I was beckoned by a sowar who was on his horse riding alongside of our boat, the water reaching up to his saddle. I turned sick with fear, but paid no heed, pretending I had not seen him. He then levelled his carbine at me, but finding that it had not the effect of frightening me into submission to his wishes, and unable to approach near enough to the boat, he shouted out to another sepoy who was in the boat to throw me into the water. I was thereupon brutally seized round the waist, and though I struggled and fought wildly, I was quickly overcome and tossed into the river. The cries of my poor little sister, imploring me wildly not to leave her, still ring in my ears; and her last look of anguish ... has haunted me ever since. That was the last I ever saw or heard of my family.

Meanwhile, Mowbray Thomson was still swimming towards Vibart's boat: 'There were a dozen of us beating the water for life; close by my side there were two brothers Ensign Henderson (56th Native Infantry) and his brother, who had but recently come out to India. They both swam well for some distance, when the younger became weak, and though we encouraged him to the utmost he went down in our sight, though not within our reach; presently his survivor, JW Henderson, was struck on the hand by a grapeshot. He put the disabled arm over my shoulder, and with one arm each we swam to the boat.' The boat – alternately drifting and running aground – bumped down the Oude bank of the river under constant fire. 'Just after I had been pulled into the boat,' wrote Thomson, 'Mrs Swinton, who was a relative of Lieutenant Jervis of the Engineers, was standing up in the stern, and having been struck by a roundshot, fell overboard and sank immediately. Her poor little boy, six years old, came up to me and said, "Mamma has fallen overboard." I endeavoured to comfort him, and told him mamma would not suffer any more pain. The little babe cried out, "Oh why are they firing upon us? did they not promise to leave off?" I never saw the child after that, and suspect that he soon shared his mother's fate.' Most of the occupants of Thomson's boat died over the next few days – including Edward Vibart's father. Forced, at last, to abandon it, Thomson and just three companions – two Irish privates and Lieutenant Delafosse, who went temporarily mad and believed he had inherited an estate in Scotland – survived to find safety under the protection of the Rajah of Moorar Mhow, Dirgbijah Singh. Amelia Horne, who had been thrown into the water by a sepoy, was dragged on shore by the sowar of the 3rd Light Cavalry who had beckoned to her – Mahomed Ismail Khan – who carried her off, disguised her in native costume and brought her before two Maulvies who forcibly converted her to Islam. Her captor married her – and eventually allowed her to escape to Allahabad, on condition she sign a paper exonerating him. Her fate seems to have been similar to that of Ulrica Wheeler – daughter of Sir Hugh Wheeler. Sir Hugh himself was cut down by a sowar, as witnessed by Eliza Bradshaw and Elisabeth Letts, whose husbands had been drummers in the 5th BNI. The two women saw General Wheeler killed by a sword cut across the neck. 'My son was killed near him,' said Mrs Bradshaw, when interviewed months later.

I saw it ... Some were stabbed with bayonets others were cut down ... Children were stabbed and thrown in the river. The schoolgirls were burnt to death. I saw their clothes and hair catch fire. In the water, a few paces off, by the next boat we saw the youngest daughter of Colonel Williams. A sepoy was going to kill her with his bayonet. She said, 'My father was always kind to sepoys.' He turned away, and just then a villager struck her on the head with a club and she fell into the water

... A sepoy killed a child with his bayonet, it was about four years old;
another sepoy took a young child by the leg and threw it into the water.

These two women saw the death of General Wheeler – and his older
daughter Eliza was known to have died at the river – but nobody knew
what had become of Ulrica.

Ulrica Wheeler, Amelia Horne and the two drummers' wives, Mrs
Bradshaw and Mrs Letts, came from widely differing social backgrounds
but had one thing in common – they were all half-castes, products of
European fathers and Indian mothers. It was this that in all likelihood
made Amelia appealing to the sowar who carried her off, and it easier to
pose – as did the drummers' wives – as a Muslim. In Ulrica's case, in the
absence of facts, myth took over. Ulrica was supposed to have been
abducted by a sowar of the 2nd Light Cavalry – a number of witnesses
claimed to have seen this – and later to have killed him with his own
sword. Alternatively, she shot her captor with a pistol, but both versions
agree that she then killed herself by jumping down a well to escape
'dishonour'. Dishonour – a Victorian euphemism for rape – featured
largely, if only by implication, in contemporary British accounts of the
horrors of Delhi, Cawnpore and elsewhere, and did much to justify – to
the British – their own savage reprisals. Later extensive investigations by
British officials, however, turned up very little evidence of this ever taking
place. For many years, though, the 'death before dishonour' version of
Ulrica's fate remained the accepted story. What seems to be the truth,
however, if less heroic in Victorian terms, is no less remarkable.

In 1907 Florence Leach, a missionary doctor in Cawnpore, was called
to the bedside of an old, dying, native woman, who told her in perfect
English that she was the daughter of Sir Hugh Massey Wheeler. She
had been rescued – not abducted – from the Satichaura Ghat by a sowar,
whom she had married and lived with thereafter. All she requested from
Miss Leach was the presence of a priest to comfort her during her last
hours.

One hundred and twenty-five other women and children were pulled
from the river alive – all the men were killed – and taken on the Nana
Sahib's orders to the Savada House in Cawnpore, where they joined the
few refugees from Fatehgarh that had not been murdered. That same
afternoon the Nana Sahib ordered a series of artillery salutes fired in his
honour as Peshwa. A salute of nineteen rounds was ordered for his
brother Bala Sahib, who was appointed his Governor General. A third

salute was fired for Jowalla Pershaud – a rebel Brahmin – who was appointed commander-in-chief. On that same day the first news reached London of the outbreak of the Mutiny at Meerut. Beside the site of Wheeler's entrenchment there now stands a fine Anglican church with a thriving Indian congregation. Behind the altar, tablets record the names of the more than one thousand men, women and children who died in the siege and massacres of Cawnpore. Many of them are buried in the surrounding churchyard. Around the wall of one mass grave, commemorating among others Major Vibart, Edward's father, are inscribed words that might stand as a memorial to them all: 'In the world ye shall have tribulation, but be of good cheer, I have overcome the world.'

# 7

# HAVELOCK'S MARCH

Among the first of the reinforcements that had been ordered up from Madras by Lord Canning on hearing the news of the Mutiny was the 1st Madras Fusiliers – 'Neill's Blue Caps'. This regiment was immediately sent north-west, arriving at Benares on 4 June. Benares, lying on the Ganges nearly halfway between Calcutta and Delhi, is Hinduism's holiest city and the centre of its learning and mythology. Its population of 188,000 was, at the time, notoriously volatile – and the presence there of the 37th NI, the Ludhiana Sikhs and the 13th Bengal Irregular Cavalry, all of questionable loyalty, gave its civilian administrators cause for concern. Foremost among these was the district judge, Mr Frederick Gubbins who, in the absence of the Commissioner, assumed authority. The only European troops in the garrison were the gunners of Captain Olpherts' battery and 150 'brave Irishmen' of HM 10th Foot. With the arrival of Neill, however, and sixty of his Madras Fusiliers, it was decided to pre-empt any attempt at mutiny by disarming the 37th NI. There was no question that the 37th were intent on mutiny as soon as opportunity presented itself. It was assumed that the Sikhs would remain true to their salt, and its officers assured Gubbins and his advisers of the fidelity of the Irregular cavalry.

Colonel James Neill, the commander of the Madras Fusiliers – 47 years old, thirty years a soldier – was a Scotsman who would not have been out of place in the armies of the Covenant. If the British had looked to the New Testament in their drive to 'improve' India, they embarked on its reconquest in the spirit of the Old. For such a task Neill was the ideal man – he was in no doubt that God had called him personally to the task of restoring order in Upper India. Already, on his way up country, in Ranigunj, he had arrested a native stationmaster, a stoker and an engineer who had proved too slow-moving for his liking, called them traitors and loudly regretted that it was out of his power to hang them. His arrival in Calcutta had put new spirit into the civilians there, and he had had the same effect in Benares. At the meeting on the morning of 4 June, as Gubbins tried to convince his colleagues of the necessity for firm action, it was Neill who brusquely announced that any delay would be fatal. Accordingly, at five o'clock that evening, the 37th were paraded – against the protests of their commander Major Barrett – and ordered to place their muskets in the bells of arms. Some had already done so when the European troops were seen wheeling into line. The sepoy guard fired on them, at which all of the 37th NI except the Light Company regained their weapons and began firing at the British and their own officers. These at once fled to the safety of the European guns, with the exception of Major Barrett, who tried to reason with his men until a few of the less disaffected carried him forcibly to one side. There followed a firefight in which seven men of HM 10th were killed before the sepoys dispersed, leaving a hundred of their own dead behind them. As the British infantry pursued the sepoys to their lines, the Sikhs and the cavalry arrived on the scene. Confusion reigned – the 13th Irregular Cavalry cut their own commanding officer, Major Guise, out of the saddle after he was fired on by sepoys. The Sikhs opened fire, some on the mutinous cavalry, some on their own commanding officer. Captain Olpherts, limbering up his guns to return to camp, heard the cry 'The Sikhs have mutinied!', unlimbered them and opened fire with canister. The Sikhs charged three times – but failed to reach the guns and they and their cavalry dispersed. That the city did not erupt at this point was due in large measure to the conduct of Surat Singh – a prisoner in Benares since the Second Sikh War, who steadied the Sikhs then guarding the European population at the Mint; Frederick Gubbins, who showed himself about the city in a public show of confidence; and the Rajah of Benares, who opted to throw in his lot with the British.

The next day many of the Sikhs returned to their duty, claiming that they had acted out of fear of the sepoys, or out of confusion. Certainly there were many witnesses who believed that in running towards the guns the Sikhs had intended to pass through the battery – where their officers had taken refuge – and defend it. Meanwhile Neill, who had assumed the military command from the ailing Brigadier Ponsonby, had been scouring the countryside – beginning that process which was to earn him the nickname 'Neill the Avenger'. Gallows were set up near the Mint – natives in the city or surrounding countryside who were suspected of treason were flogged, shot or hanged. Captured sepoys and sowars were brought back into the city to be blown from guns. Under Neill's influence, informal hanging parties of civilian volunteers continued the work – one gentleman boasting not only of the number of natives he had strung up from trees, but of the artistic way it had been done, with the victims arranged in figure-of-eight patterns. So energetic was Neill's pursuit of rebels and rooting out of sedition – and it should be noted that many, who later deplored his methods, cheered him on at the time – that when Lord Canning sent him a telegram urging him to push on to Allahabad he wired back, 'Can't do it, wanted here.'

It wasn't until 9 June that Neill was satisfied that Benares was secure enough to allow him to move on to Allahabad. His journey was not an easy one, the whole country along the banks of the Ganges being in a state of anarchy. It was not until 11 June that he and his men – travelling in post-carts – appeared on the banks of the Ganges opposite the fort at Allahabad. Here, the 6th NI – one of the most trusted sepoy regiments – had mutinied five days earlier, killing seven of its officers on the parade-ground and eight young ensigns fresh out from England. The city rose too – the gaol was opened up and thousands of prisoners freed. European houses were burned and fifty Europeans killed. The railway station was burned, the rails torn up and the locomotives, which the natives regarded with superstitious awe, were – in an act that is almost emblematic of the Mutiny – peppered with round shot from a safe distance. The European population in the fort was guarded by a company of the 6th NI and a company of the Ferozepore Sikhs. These last, having heard of the deaths of their comrades in Benares, were inclined to mutiny too, but were restrained by their commander Lieutenant Brayser (or Brazier), who pointed out to them how rich they could become if they did not mutiny and, at the same time, that he had laid a trail of powder to the magazine and would take himself with them to the next world if they did. It worked, and the company of the 6th was disarmed by the Sikhs and some European invalid artillerymen. As in the Punjab, securing the loyalty of the Sikhs proved crucial. Captain Maude – at this time still in Calcutta – later learned from the Sikhs at Allahabad how close-run it had been: 'With their usual engaging frankness, they afterwards told our force that they had seriously debated among themselves as to whether they should remain loyal or not. But the preponderance of opinion among them was that the British would eventually succeed in the campaign, and so they very prudently resolved to back the winners.' Maude was full of praise for the Sikhs' commanding officer, who had so dramatically offered them the choice between riches or death. 'In several instances the personal attachment of the Sepoys to their officers undoubtedly went far towards keeping the men staunch. In this way the courage and noble presence of Brazier certainly exercised a powerful influence over the "Regiment of Ferozepore". He had risen from the ranks, and was every inch a soldier. Throughout our marching and fighting his turban and flowing white beard were always to be seen in front of his gaunt and sinewy "Singh log" (Lion people) as they proudly named themselves.' Pondering further the decision of the Sikhs to side with the British, Maude concluded:

> Few things were more remarkable than the extraordinary loyalty, and even devotion, of some of our native regiments, and notably of the Sikhs, who, having been but lately conquered and their country annexed by us, might have been supposed to have still some wrongs to avenge. With few exceptions, however, the Sikhs remained faithful to our 'Raj.' It is true that the delicate question of caste was not of the all-absorbing interest to them that it was to the Brahmins, or perhaps the Mussulmans. Nor do they possess the fanatical and proselytising spirit of the latter. But perhaps the best reason was that they hated them both very cordially.

Neill crossed the river to the fort in a small boat procured from the far bank by a party of his men – two died of sunstroke during the crossing. The walk to the fort almost prostrated Neill himself, but he did not sleep until he had prepared his plans for the following day. In the morning he opened fire from the fort on the suburb of Daryaganj – held by an insurgent mob – as a prelude to the reconquest of the city. Now Allahabad – which had already suffered from the rapine and score-settling that attended the Mutiny everywhere – was subjected to the vengeful return of British rule. In Neill's pacification of Allahabad thousands died. Hundreds fell to the bullets and bayonets of Brayser's Sikhs and Neill's Blue Caps, enthusiastically aided by European Volunteers. Hundreds more swung from trees and from gallows erected in public places – at signposts, crossroads and in public squares. As at Delhi guilt was largely assumed, and most victims were executed with only the barest semblance, if any, of a judicial process. Eight dead-carts toured the city cutting down the hanged – who were soon replaced – and taking the bodies to be thrown in the Ganges. Outside the city whole villages were ringed by cordons of troops and put to the torch. 'God grant I may have acted with justice,' wrote Neill on the 17th, as if even he had his doubts. 'I know I have acted with severity.' By now he was satisfied that the city and the surrounding countryside was cowed and he could proceed with his next task – the relief of Cawnpore. On 24 June, however, as he was planning his advance, Neill learned that he had been superseded.

With the troops that Lord Canning had summoned from Persia was 62-year-old Brigadier General Henry Havelock. A soldier since 1815 – the year of Waterloo – promotion had been slow for Havelock. It had taken him until 1846 to make brevet lieutenant colonel, despite seeing service in Afghanistan, Burma, the Punjab and, most recently, Persia. Austere in manner – he was nicknamed 'Mr Pomposity' by members of his staff, and 'the Gravedigger' by others – he was a deeply religious Baptist. Like Neill, he felt personally called by God to the duty of restoring British rule.

En route to India, on board the *Erin*, Havelock had drawn up a memorandum recommending the formation of a Movable Column to restore British authority in the revolted districts above Allahabad. Arriving in Calcutta on 17 June he learned three days later from Sir Patrick Grant – now, with the death of Anson, commander-in-chief – that he was to command this column. His instructions were that 'after quelling all disturbances at Allahabad, he should not lose a moment in supporting Sir Henry Lawrence at Lucknow and Sir Hugh Wheeler at Cawnpore; and that he should take prompt measures for dispersing and utterly destroying all mutineers and insurgents'.

Havelock felt that if he had one thousand each of European troops, Sikhs and Gurkhas he could beat everything the rebels could bring against him, but in the event he only had some two thousand men of all arms. The good news was that his force would be based around HM 64th Foot and the 78th Highlanders – two regiments that had served under him on the Euphrates and in whom he placed great confidence. The rest of the news was bad. He was being required to begin his march at a time of year when received wisdom in India indicated that campaigning should cease – a season of overpowering heat, varied only by occasional torrential rain. His main problem was lack of transport –

the 1,600 Commissariat bullocks that had been assembled at Allahabad had vanished during the sack of the cantonment, and those that remained to draw his six guns were undersized and unused to the work. He was deficient in trained gunners; Captain Maude had brought only thirty with him from Ceylon, and numbers had to be made up from invalids and thirty-one men of the 64th, who had some prior knowledge of gun drill. If his British infantry was of high quality, only a quarter were armed with the new Enfield rifle; the remainder still carried the old musket. He had no cavalry that he could rely on, without which reconnaissance was all but impossible.

Undeterred, and confident of Divine aid, Havelock set to work. As the rains had begun he decided that the troops and their camp equipment should go up river by steamer, leaving the carts and bullocks to bring the ammunition and stores up the Grand Trunk road. Before leaving Calcutta, he obtained orders to make a generous use of secret service money, hoping by the use of well-paid spies to stay one step ahead of the enemy. The heat claimed victims from Havelock's force almost as soon as it left Calcutta. F. C. Maude of the Royal Artillery recorded the fate of his friend Captain Clutterbuck of HM 37th Foot (Hampshire): 'Clutterbuck marched his men to Barrackpore ... a distance of only sixteen miles, but which was largely increased by their having actually mistaken the road, no guide having been sent with them! Poor fellow! on his arrival at his journey's end, thoroughly exhausted, he drank off a glass of water, and fell down dead. Several of his men also died that day from the same cause – heat apoplexy.' Maude's gunners started on Waterloo Day – 18 June. 'Our marches were "forced", but they never exceeded thirty-miles a-day, three miles an hour being very good going for oxen, even on a "kunka" metalled road. We always halted during the extreme heat of the day, when the bullocks were watered and fed. We had scarcely been a day on the road when the cholera broke out among us, and no less than six out of our fifty-eight splendid men died before we reached Benares. We buried them by the roadside, marking the spot by a short inscription on a piece of tin.' They were travelling through country that was hostile or at best indifferent. 'Somewhat as did the soldiers of Cortez, in Mexico,' wrote Maude,

> we felt that our boats, so to speak, were burnt, and that we had only to go straight on ahead as best we might. In fact throughout our experiences with Havelock's 'Flying Column,' which, as its name

implies had no regular base of communication, there was an all-pervading sense that we were, humanly speaking, carrying our lives in our hands, and that there was nearly as much danger in the rear as in the front of the day's work, marching or fighting as the case might be ... this feeling was not without influence upon our actions, and may somewhat account for the fact that instances of breach of discipline, or misbehaviour before the enemy, were of the very rarest occurrence. This may be said of the whole of our force, whether private soldiers, non-commissioned officers, or officers.

Starting from Calcutta himself on 25 June Havelock arrived at Benares on 28 June. The massacre of the Cawnpore garrison had taken place the previous day, but as he took over the command of the intended relief expedition, Havelock was unaware of this. His first act in Benares was to set about raising a force of Volunteer cavalry formed of 'officers of regiments which had mutinied, or had been disbanded; of indigo planters, of patrols, of burnt-out shopkeepers; in short of all who were willing to join'. This was placed under the command of Captain Lusada Barrow of the 5th Madras Light Cavalry. The column arrived at Allahabad on 30 June to find that Neill – on orders from Calcutta – had already despatched Major Renaud with a small force to attempt the relief of Cawnpore and mete out summary justice to any who were suspected of disloyalty. Renaud's force – 400 European infantry, 300 Sikhs, 100 Irregular cavalry and two 9-pounder guns – was too small and too late to aid the doomed garrison at Cawnpore, but set about the second part of its orders with enthusiasm.

On 3 July – the same day that Havelock sent a hundred men up the Ganges in a steamer to join Renaud – a galloper came in from Renaud informing him of the disaster at Cawnpore. Later in the day two spies sent by Sir Henry Lawrence from Lucknow – who had passed through Cawnpore and observed events there – confirmed the terrible news. Havelock immediately telegraphed the news to Sir Patrick Grant at Calcutta saying: 'My duty is therefore to endeavour to retake Cawnpore, to the accomplishment of which I will bend every effort. I advance along the trunk road as soon as I can unite 1400 British infantry to a battery of six well-equipped guns. Lieut.-Col Neill, whose high qualities I cannot sufficiently praise, will follow with another column as soon as it can be organised.' Organizing the battery fell to Maude, who soon found that compromises had to be made: 'It was soon evident that it would cause considerable delay before we could equip a Horse Battery. So, rather reluctantly at first, but, as we afterwards considered, most fortunately, we were persuaded to adopt the serviceable Indian system of bullocks for drawing our guns ... We soon got together a very complete little six-gun battery, consisting of two 6-prs., two 9-prs., and two 12-pr. howitzers; together with the requisite ammunition wagons, forge cart, etc., etc. The different kinds of ammunition were rather confusing to the men at first, but, as will be seen, that difficulty was very speedily surmounted.' The shortage of trained gunners was soon made up from the infantry: 'Being terribly short-handed, having only 51 men left, we asked for, and at once obtained, 31 volunteers, from among the regiments of our Brigade who had been instructed in gunnery. The 64th (North Staffordshire) supplied most of these. Afterwards some came from the 84th (York and Lancaster). They had all been very well taught, and after a few days' drill with our gunners, took a great liking to the work, to say nothing of the (small) extra pay.' The column's equipment was not of the best. 'Our guns and muskets were for the most part of antiquated patterns,' wrote Maude.

> The 1st Madras Fusiliers were the only regiment in our force which had Enfield rifles. The 'flank companies,' as they were then called, of some others had been supplied with them. But this arm at that date was very far from being perfect, and the ammunition used often to 'jam' in a dreadful and disappointing manner. The others used 'Brown Bess,' which was not a bad weapon with its very effective bayonet at close quarters. We, of the Artillery, used nothing but port fires, priming powder, and smooth bore-guns, Armstrong's breech-loaders not having yet reached India. In fact, even the rudimentary quill tubes were not procurable, until the smart troops from England joined us, and brought friction or percussion tubes, lanyards, and similar luxuries.

Other stores, however, were of the finest quality:

> During the looting of the merchants' stores at Allahabad, the Sikhs had secured many dozens of excellent champagne and moselle. The Commissariat Department, very wisely, bought these up at trifling price, and then, in order to make room in their 'godowns' [warehouses] for sterner munitions of war, they retailed the wine at the liberal rate of one shilling (eight annas) a bottle. At this moderate figure we felt justified in piling a few dozen on a couple of our spare ammunition

waggons. It is a pleasure now to remember that nearly the whole of it was consumed by our sick or wounded officers. A few bottles, it is true, we drank ourselves, and some were *re-annexed* by Messrs. T. Atkins and Co, of the —— Regiment.

The column when assembled bore little relation to any British soldiers seen in the military paintings of the time: 'The wardrobes of our poor gunners were of the scantiest; so much so, indeed that when the forces united, early in the following Spring ... only one man had a vestige of uniform, he being the proud possessor of a jacket, which had belonged to the kit of a deceased Bengal Artilleryman. The other regiments of our force were dressed in white, or the nearest approach to it procurable, the Madras Fusiliers alone wearing blue covers to their caps (*nil topees*), pronounced "Neil." The Highlanders did not wear kilts. The Sikh had turbans, tight-fitting white pantaloons, and sandals.'

Havelock's force left Allahabad on 7 July, passing through a sullen Muslim population who, remembering Neill, confined itself to scowls and grimaces. Maude gives us a good portrait of the General at this time:

His figure was slight and small, but neat and erect. He was always well-mounted, and a good rider, quick of speech too, and ready of retort, grandiloquent and Napoleonic in his style both in writing and in conversation. He knew infantry and brigade movements thoroughly well. Everybody knows that he was God-fearing and blameless in his life, yet he was sterner and more severe than seems to have been generally understood. His face was older than his years, and much tanned by the Indian sun; his moustache, whiskers, and beard being rather long and perfectly white. The omission of these in his statue in Trafalgar Square deprives an otherwise good likeness of some of his characteristics as we knew him.

Havelock's intention was to recapture Cawnpore, retrieve any survivors and then proceed to the relief of Lucknow. J. W. Sherer, the Magistrate of Futtehpore – from which he had been forced to flee and to which the column was now marching – described the mood of the column: 'Uniform was at a discount, and appearances could not be kept up; but hearts were in the right places – spirits were high, and the desire to meet the foe was intense ... The Sikhs burned to avenge old scores on the Brahmin tribes.' The force consisted of 600 men of HM 64th Foot, 600 of HM 78th

Highlanders and 500 Madras Fusiliers, Maude's company of the Royal Artillery, Brayser's Sikhs and twenty mounted European Volunteers. 'Although the number of fighting men was small,' wrote Maude,

> the cavalcade made an imposing appearance ... we took the field with an equipment, in regard to tents and some other matters, according to a stately fashion which is still *de rigueur* for an Indian Army on the march. The transport of these required a goodly number of admirably-trained 'tusker' elephants, which, for the most part, were laden with our tents. There were also long strings of cross-looking camels, whose guttural protests against the putting-on of their burdens in the middle of the night used to make those hours, to us, hideous indeed. Then there were bullock hackeries almost without number, besides the peri-patetic meal for the morrow, which consisted of minute and skinny sheep. Lastly there were the suggestive 'dhoolies,' or covered stretchers, each carried by four bearers; empty that afternoon, but very soon to be filled to repletion with their ghastly load of sick, wounded and dying.

Within three hours they were engulfed in a deluge of rain and forced to camp for the night. Sherer was sharing a *pal* (tent) with his friend Bews (a railway engineer also attached to the column), which was, in his own words, little better than 'a large curtain hung over an exaggerated clothes horse'. After riding through the ferocious rain they had reached the camp to find it 'a sea of mud ... as evening was coming on we struggled into our tent, where we were very uncomfortable indeed. There was nothing to eat or drink; the earth was steamed up, and we sat on our beds, drenched as if in a vapour bath. Insects of all sorts were attracted by our light, and either dashed into the flame or singed their wings and fell on the table. All the noises of the rains were present – frogs and earth-crickets, with at intervals, the splashing of showers and bubbling of water courses.' 'The steam from the wet ground and our sodden tents,' wrote Maude, 'together with the myriad of insects, put both our valises and our patience to the severest tests. On the first night a colony of white ants, also probably on the march or the war path, bored a large hole clean through the lower part of my portmanteau, traversing *en route* a pair of gold-laced overalls, which of course were completely ruined. *Sic transit gloria mundi!*' The morning march, noted Sherer, soon restored good spirits: 'By the time the bugle sounded for a halt for "little breakfast" we were all in high spirits. The camp, when reached, was in a garden of trees, and it was bright and dry; and the soldiers seemed very happy, though they would go out without any covering on their heads, and chose to look on the sunshine as indicative of agreeable haymaking weather in England.' Despite the rains the temperature during the day was above 100 degrees Fahrenheit. 'We marched as much as possible during the night,' wrote Maude, 'so as to avoid the intense heat of the sun, the *reveille* usually sounding about 1.a.m., and the camp being pitched shortly before noon.'

As they marched they passed through country that had been pacified by Major Renaud and his advance guard. Renaud was Neill's second-in-command in the Madras Fusiliers, and very much of his commander's frame of mind. 'In the first two days of our march towards Cawnpore,' wrote Maude, 'we passed several dead bodies hanging from trees near the road. These had been executed by Renaud's men, presumably for complicity in the Mutiny; but I am afraid some innocent men suffered, for a comrade who ought to know says that "Renaud was rather inclined to hang *all black creation*". In every case, where the feet were near the ground, pigs (either wild or belonging to the villagers) had eaten the lower part of the bodies; the stench from the latter, in the moist still air, being intolerable.' Perhaps unsurprisingly, Havelock's column saw very few natives en route. Even loyal natives, however, were routinely subject to casual brutality as Sherer recorded: 'One morning a *syce* [native grass-cutter] distinguished himself by outrage and disobedience. He would not listen to me ... or anybody else, so I had to make an example of him; and I had him tied to a tree, and gave him a dozen rattans. He said something about telling the General, but I would not listen. Meeting the younger Havelock the same day, he said, "I must thank you for punishing my *syce*; it has done him a world of good."' The younger Havelock was the General's son, also Henry, who was serving on his father's staff.

Renaud's force – 400 Europeans, 300 Ferozepore Sikhs, 120 Native Irregular cavalry and two 9-pounder guns – had been pushed forward on Neill's orders to attempt a relief of Cawnpore. Since Havelock had arrived at Allahabad Renaud had been halted, under orders from Havelock, to 'Keep a good look-out to rear, front, and flanks ... Burn no more villages, unless actually occupied by insurgents, and spare your European troops as much as possible'. By liberal use of secret service money Havelock was well informed of the enemy's intentions. The Nana Sahib, after the massacre of Wheeler's force at the Satichaura Ghat, had now determined on marching the 45 miles from Cawnpore to Futtehpore and attacking

Renaud's small force with an army estimated at 3,500 regular sepoys, together with a mass of fresh native levies and twelve brass and iron guns looted from the Cawnpore arsenal. Thus, in spite of the protests of the medical officers – both the 78th, having been cooped up in steamers for weeks, and the Madras Fusiliers, with a high proportion of recruits, had suffered on the march – Havelock pushed his force forward to a junction with Renaud. This was accomplished shortly after midnight on 11 July. Sherer described the scene: 'The men were drawn up along the side of the road. I remember being struck, in the moonlight, by the yellow colours of the Sikhs. Then we all marched on together, and at last halted a little short of Futtehpore.'

The combined force began making camp at about 8 p.m. Sherer had made friends with the captain commanding Havelock's small cavalry force: 'Barrow had a wonderful Madras servant, who was a good rider and stayed near him on a good horse. This man kept a small kettle and teapot slung near him, and sugar and milk in bottles in his *cummerbund*, or waist-band, and was game to make tea in no time. He dismounted and made a fire ... I think we had got the tea, when bang went a gun, and certainly not far off.' Seconds later, Colonel Fraser-Tytler, Havelock's assistant quartermaster general, came galloping into the camp with the news that the enemy was close at hand. Fraser-Tytler had ridden 2 miles forward of the camp to reconnoitre and had met two spies sent down from Lucknow by Sir Henry Lawrence. They informed him that the rebels were themselves encamping at Futtehpore. Fraser-Tytler sent them back to the General and rode forward himself to get a closer look. No sooner had Fraser-Tytler and his small escort been spotted by the rebels, than they – imagining that they had only Renaud's force to deal with – began a general advance. It was just as Lawrence's spies were reporting to Havelock that the first round, a 24-pounder – which had disturbed Mr Sherer's tea – landed in the camp, 200 yards from where the General was standing. 'There was a complete transformation scene in a moment,' wrote Sherer, 'Barrow hurried off to the head of his Cavalry, and we saw the Infantry being collected and led straight ahead, and the guns, eight in number, pushed forward.' In his despatch after the battle, Havelock described the enemy's onrush and his reaction: 'They insolently pushed forward two guns, and a force of infantry and cavalry cannonaded our front, and threatened our flank.' Havelock's force had marched all day and had not eaten: 'I wished earnestly to give our harassed soldiers rest, and so waited until this ebullition should expend itself, making no counter-disposition beyond posting a hundred Enfield riflemen of the 64th in an advanced copse. But the enemy maintained his attack with the audacity which his first supposition had inspired, and my inertness fostered. It would have injured the *morale* of my troops to permit them thus to be bearded; so I determined at once to bring on an action.' Futtehpore was a strong position – the Grand Trunk road ran through the centre of the village and was the only means of access as the ground on either side was flooded. The village consisted of walled gardens surrounding strongly built houses. In front of the village were hillocks and mango groves that were occupied by the rebels.

Havelock placed his guns – now, as Sherer had noted, eight in number, with the addition of Renaud's two 9-pounders – on either side of the road, guarded by one hundred Enfield men of the 64th Foot. The rest of the infantry were formed into quarter columns and advanced on either side of the road, covered by skirmishers. The Volunteer and Irregular cavalry advanced by the harder ground on either flank. 'We advanced in line,' wrote Maude, referring to his guns.

I took the two guns on the road myself while each of the three subalterns had a sub-division of two and conformed with the movements of the infantry. We opened fire at 800 yards; our second round disabled their leading guns; so perceiving that their fire was silenced, and that they were falling back in confusion, we limbered up on the road, and advanced to the enemy's guns. But as we did so, the infantry of the latter halted, and appeared inclined to re-form; while at the same moment, a large body of cavalry advanced down the road towards us. So we came into action again at 650 yards; and at the first shot, the cavalry turned about and bolted, leaving in view two elephants, two heavy guns, and a large body of infantry. We peppered into these so smartly that they could not stand to their guns; which latter, by the way, when we came to them, we found to be loaded, and turned them upon the retreating masses.

Soon, two staff officers came up to Maude and offered him a tempting target.

Stuart Beatson (our D.A.A.G.) and Fraser-Tytler (D.Q.M.G.) were at this time close beside me on the road, and urged me to 'knock over that chap on the elephant.' Accordingly I dismounted, and laid the gun myself, a 9-pr., at 'line of metal' (700 yards) range; and, as luck would have it, my first shot went in under the beast's tail, and came out at its chest, of course rolling it over, and giving its rider a bad fall. This was the thirteenth and last elephant I ever shot; but in subsequent actions we lost several of our own. It was said at the time that the man on the elephant was Tantia Topee, who afterwards showed some courage and military aptitude, giving us a lot of trouble. But his fall that day certainly completed the panic of the enemy, who, it should be remarked, were at the time being well-pounded on the flanks.

Maude then took his guns through the swamps to almost point-blank range. Renaud's men took a hillock on the right and pushed on through the swamp – the 78th Highlanders extended from Renaud towards the centre, the 64th in the centre and the 84th on the left, together with Brayser's Sikhs, drove the enemy back towards the village itself. Approaching Futtehpore, Havelock decided he needed the benefit of local knowledge and sent back for Sherer, who had been Magistrate there. Sherer had been waiting with the baggage train when he was summoned forward:

> So I rode up and told him what the town was like inside, and as he passed into a field near the garden walls skirting the suburbs, I went too, and with me my bearded sowar, Azim Ali. The General was apparently recognised, for some people behind the walls were plainly taking shots at him. Azim, who was close to me, said in an undertone; '*Yih achacha jagah nahin!*' (This is not a suitable place!) The remembrance of this afterwards made one laugh, and in subsequent adventures, when matters occasionally got awkward, the phrase recurred, – '*Yih achacha jagah nahin!*'

In the streets and houses of Futtehpore, the rebels could have made quite a fight of it, but they had had enough. 'Notwithstanding the barricades,' wrote Sherer, 'the Sepoys all cleared out of the streets, our troops marched right through, and the camp was set up on the Cawnpore side. I rode through my own little town, and laughed at some pottering improvements which had been thought of, and which seemed such rubbish now.' In Havelock's estimation the whole battle had lasted little more than ten minutes. The fire of the Enfield rifle – knocking men over at extreme ranges – had clearly demoralized the sepoys and, as Maude had it: 'The rebels were completely taken by surprise. They were moving down, in very fair style, to attack, as they thought, Renaud's little force, which would have fallen an easy prey to them, the more especially as nearly half his men were Sepoys, whose loyalty was not too surely to be relied upon.'

Three of the enemy's guns were abandoned on the road in front of the village: 'Stuart Beatson, Fraser-Tytler, and myself raced up to the guns,' wrote Maude,

and the former was, I think the first to touch one of them with the point of his sword. Some of the skirmishers of the Madras Fusiliers, and our two guns, came up a very few seconds later. The elephant was still alive, but groaning. By its side lay a handsome silver-mounted 'chowree,' which one of the Fusiliers picked up, and sold to Major Renaud, at whose auction I bought it three or four days afterwards. The chowree is the bushy tail of a 'yak' or Thibet ox. It is the emblem of Royalty in India. On grand occasions, such as State dinners and the like, the Viceroy always has two native servants standing behind his chair, each holding a chowree. Near the elephant a wounded Sepoy was lying, with a thigh badly smashed. As we passed I saw a Fusilier go up to him with his rifle cocked. The poor creature joined his hands together, crying piteously 'Aman! Aman!' (pardon!) 'In the name of the Company' (E.I.C.) I added an entreaty that a wounded man should not be shot. But Beatson over-ruled me, saying sternly that there would be 'no mercy shown in that campaign'. Accordingly the Fusilier promptly blew the man's brains out. Although a good deal shocked at the time, I confess that subsequent events very much deadened our susceptibilities. And most people will probably agree with Beatson in thinking that, at all events during the actual hostilities, a mutineer, taken in arms against his comrades, should be put to death without mercy.

Due to exhaustion, the heat and the lack of an adequate cavalry force – the Irregular cavalry were considered not to have distinguished themselves and were disbanded two days later – there was no pursuit.

The following day Havelock wrote to his wife: 'One of the prayers oft repeated throughout my life since my school days has been answered, and I have lived to command in a successful action . . .' before noting that his victory had been won on the anniversary of the Battle of the Boyne. In one of his Napoleonic addresses to his troops, penned the same day,

Havelock attributed the victory to: 'The fire of British artillery, exceeding in rapidity and precision all that the Brigadier has ever witnessed in his not short career; to the power of the Enfield rifle in British hands; to British pluck, that great quality which has survived the vicissitudes of the hour, and gained intensity from the crisis; and to the blessing of Almighty God on a most righteous cause, the cause of justice, humanity, truth, and good government in India.' A halt having been ordered for the 13th, the troops set about looting the town. 'We captured an immense quantity of guns, ammunition, stores, uniform, and baggage, on the 12th and 13th,' wrote Maude, 'besides some large sums in rupees, which were intended for the payment of the rebel troops ... On the 13th while riding through the town to collect and classify the captured ordnance, I came upon Sibley and another distinguished member of Havelock's Staff, the former being the Paymaster of the Forces, who were sitting by the side of the road hastily stuffing their pockets, holsters, and handkerchiefs with as much coin as they could carry. I called out to them, "All right! I'll go shares", to which they agreed, though ruefully; but I never claimed my portion.' Sibley was described by Sherer as 'an old officer of the 64th, who had grown grey in long regimental service ... perhaps of West Indian extraction, and may be called, *par excellence*, "*the* Old Campaigner"'. If he was not above stuffing his pockets with rebel gold he was by no means alone and he was, according to Maude's account, scrupulously honest with the money committed to his care. 'I am happy to say ... that our gunners picked up several hundreds of rupees that day. These they tied up roughly in gunny bags, and deposited in Sibley's Field Treasure Chest. Twelve months afterwards the bags were all identified and claimed; and although several of them had completely rotted, the exact value of their contents had been noted, and was either handed to the survivors or paid to the next of kin. At that time Prize Agents had not been appointed.' The now usual summary executions were meted out – Sherer saw: 'One young fellow, a *jogee* or mendicant devotee ... under the preposterous idea that our soldiers would be interested in his religious freedom from partisanship. I tried to get him away, but he was obstinate, and met his fate, receiving two or three balls into him before he succumbed.' No doubt in anticipation of such treatment, most of the natives had fled the town.

A store of wine and beer was found in a merchant's *godown*, and what could not be commandeered by the Commissariat went down the throats of the soldiers. The effect of large quantities of drink on exhausted men under a burning sun caused more casualties than the action had. 'As frequently happened afterwards,' wrote Maude, 'the excitement carried us on; but the moment it was over the re-action was very great, and many collapsed from its effects. I had a near shave from sun-stroke, and it was thought I was down with it. No less than twelve men dropped dead from heat-apoplexy, although we did not lose one from the enemy's fire.' J. W. Sherer had retired to the camp to sleep during the afternoon heat. Near by were laid out some dead from the Irregular cavalry: 'Three black-bearded men, olive-coloured in death, with their rigid boots sticking up, were festering in the sun.' When he awoke later, Sherer had acquire a new neighbour:

> I observed a large strong man, with a red beard, lying near, with his head on his arm, and a blue handkerchief with white spots propped on two sticks to make a little shelter for his face. He was a man of the 78th Highlanders, and some of his mates came presently to look after him. They tried to rouse him, but, alas! he was beyond all appeals. He had been, it appeared, indulging rather freely in the stores which had been found in the town, and lying down to sleep, had passed away in apoplexy. His name was Campbell.

Soon the man's brother was found – he, too, had been drinking. 'The second Campbell, a younger and slighter man, was distracted with the loss that had befallen him. He sat on the ground, and wrung his hands. "Oh brother dear!" he cried, "shall I never see to you more? Speak to me. Speak to me. Will you never speak to me again? What have you left me alone for? Brother, brother, come back to me."' As his comrades tried to carry the body away on a *charpoy* 'the younger Campbell threw himself on his brother, clasped him in his arms, and in this way, wrapped in a last embrace, they were both carried away together. I heard the bagpipes soon after, droning in the distance, as the body was taken to the grave.'

As Captain Maude noted, the Sikhs (known to the European soldiers as the 'Sykeses', and Havelock as the 'Six') showed a taste for drink to compare with that of the British soldier: 'When a halt was called, and no fighting was imminent, squads of the tall, upright, Hebraic-visaged Sikhs used to march into their Commanding Officer's tent, where they stood to attention in silence, with one hand raised in the orthodox salute. "What do you want, my men?" was the question in Hindustani. "May it please the protector of the poor, we want two days' leave." "What for?" "To get drunk, Sahib!" And their request being considered reasonable was usually granted.' As with the British soldier, the fault was overlooked in the light of their fighting qualities. 'It is hard to conceive of anything more gallant than the behaviour of the Sikhs before the enemy,' wrote Maude. 'In common with the "Seaforth Highlanders" or "Ross-shire Buffs," they permitted themselves a certain rough familiarity with their officers, somewhat that of clansmen with their chiefs. That they were ruthless and even now and then a trifle unspeakable, is not altogether to be denied. *Sic tempora, sic mores*. And it must be admitted that, generally speaking, it was a rough-and-ready time.'

Their unspeakable qualities were called upon now. A party had been out to look for the remains of the Futtehpore judge, Robert Tucker. Tucker, who had refused to leave the town with Sherer and his colleagues, was one of those Europeans who had almost invited his fate, loudly proclaiming his Christian faith and even having a pillar bearing the Ten Commandments erected on the roadside. Tucker had died on the roof of his house, pistol in one hand, Bible in the other, having killed a dozen of his assailants. Havelock decided that an example should be made of the town, and as the column continued its advance on 14 July, the Sikhs were left behind for what Sherer described as 'the not unwelcome task of looting and burning the place'.

With the rebel guns captured in Futtehpore, Maude was able to augment the column's artillery: 'From the ordnance captured that day I made up a complete 9-pounder battery, five of the guns being of that calibre, with one 24-pounder brass howitzer, together with ammunition-waggons and stores sufficient for several weeks' campaign.' Although he claimed never to have helped himself to any loot, Maude later discovered he could have made a tidy profit: 'At a subsequent period I was advised by an officer in the Bengal Artillery conversant with the customs of those days, that I had a whole field-battery of equipment lying to my credit at the Paymaster-Generals, and that I had only to prosecute my claims to receive its value in cash! Whether this was so or not I never ascertained, for just at that time I was ordered to England on promotion, and the matter dropped.' Another acquisition at Futtehpore, as Maude recorded, proved of incalculable value.

One of the regiments engaged against us was the 1st B.N.L.I. (Gillis-ka-Pultan) or Gillis's regiment. It was then frequently the custom to name the regiment after some officer of distinction who had been for some time associated with it ... Anjoor Tewaree belonged to it, and instantly after this day's action he came and surrendered himself, explaining that he was a comparatively young soldier (although a 'Naik' or Corporal) and had been led away by the others. He admitted having been a witness of the disasters of General Sir Hugh Wheeler at Cawnpore; also of the surrender, massacre in the boats, and other incidents.

In due course Tewaree became 'the very bravest and most useful, because the most intrepid and intelligent spy we employed ... he was with us all through, and proved to be of the very greatest service on several occasions. It may be well to notice that he ... was handsomely rewarded, receiving both pension and honours, besides a comfortable "jaghir" or grant of land.'

On 14 June the march resumed. One of Havelock's first acts, once clear of the now-burning Futtehpore, was to disband his Irregular cavalry – in the battle of 12 June they had been ordered to charge the mutinous 2nd Light Cavalry. Their commander, Lieutenant Palliser, had galloped off towards the enemy, never once looking back to see if his men were following – it wasn't done; British cavalry officers always assumed that they were – and had found himself almost alone in the midst of the enemy's sabres. He would have died but for the bravery of his Native rissaldar, Najab Khan, who saved Palliser's life at the cost of his own. The remainder of the Irregulars had either deserted to the enemy or ridden to the rear. The men were dismounted and disarmed. Sherer watched the disarming. 'Everybody felt sorry for their commander, Palliser. If weakness it is, the weakness is more creditable than some strength – to believe that those who have often gallantly followed you will follow you to the last. One or two of the native officers, handsome fellows with that Jewish type of face so common in the extreme North, who looked sorrowful with a haughty, wounded sorrow, refused altogether to avail themselves of the opportunity of going away, and rarely allowed Palliser ... out of their sight.' The Irregulars' horses were made over to Captain Barrow for his European Volunteer cavalry. This force – largely made up of officers from revolted Indian regiments – would have double the workload from now on, particularly when it came to the cavalry's bread-and-butter work of scouting and screening. One of its officers described the Volunteer cavalry's composition:

New to the country, new to the service, unaccustomed to roughing it,
brought up in every luxury, and led to believe that on their arrival in
India they would have the same, these young officers (deprived of
employment by the mutiny of their regiments) willingly threw themselves into the thick of the work, often without a tent or cover of any
sort to shelter them from the rain or sun, with bad provisions and hard
work. Side by side with the privates they took their turn of duty, and
side by side with them they fought, were wounded, and some of them
died.

The column advanced, constantly scanning the horizon ahead expecting
to see – through the heat haze – the enemy's cavalry observing their
movements. Sherer described a halt to observe 'enemy cavalry', which
turned out to be cattle on the edge of a grove:

Before the halt there had been the tramp of feet, the rattle of gun-
carriages, the creaking of cart wheels, the hum of human voices, and
the sudden pause was very striking. For as the guns were unlimbered,
and field-glasses sedulously applied to the distant trees, expectation
arrested speech, and there was a dead silence. At this rather interesting
moment, there sounded from a neighbouring copse the cry of 'Cuckoo!'
It was Wordsworth's 'wandering voice,' the companion of the spring-
time of our youth ... the veritable *cuculus canorus* not often heard, in
my experience, so far south in the Provinces of India. Visions of village
greens, shady dingles and dells, and the faces of pretty girls were,
doubtless, brought into many minds by the familiar note. At any rate,
a soldier close to me called out to his mate, in a tone about whose
heartiness there was no mistake, and in words whose frankness need
not be modified: 'I say, Bill, who'd ha' thought o' the likes o' that?
Blest – if it was not a damned old cuckoo!'

On the morning of 15 June the column arrived shortly before daybreak at
the village of Aong, where – 200 yards behind the village – the rebels
were discovered to have entrenched themselves across the road with two
9-pounder guns, supported by regular mutineer infantry with cavalry on
both flanks. Taking command of the main body himself, Havelock sent
Colonel Fraser-Tytler forward with approximately one-third of his force
to attack the village. The delay in disposing the column was interpreted
by the rebels as hesitation, and they at once advanced to the village and

lined the gardens and walls. The Madras Fusiliers under Renaud were ordered to dislodge them and this they did, but not until Major Renaud was hit in the left leg by a bullet that drove part of his scabbard into the wound. One of his officers stopped to help him but was told, 'Go – go on with your men.' As Fraser-Tytler pushed on through the village driving the sepoys before him, the enemy's cavalry swooped down from both flanks to attack the main body, but were repeatedly driven off. 'We were … threatened on both flanks by the Cavalry,' wrote Maude, 'and twice loaded with canister to receive them; but they could not make up their minds to charge "home." … The enemy's skirmishers came out from the village in excellent order, and were hotly engaged with ours on the left. It was by them that Major Renaud was mortally wounded.' Maude's own gunners suffered too: 'We lost a very fine young soldier, Bombardier Harding, who was wounded while laying his gun. A round-shot shattered his arm from the fingers to the elbow. "If you please, sir, may I fall out?' he said to me, saluting as if on parade, and pointing to the mangled arm. He died that evening from loss of blood … In addition to Harding we lost an Invalid (Bengal) Artilleryman, killed, and a N.C.O. wounded, four gun-bullocks killed, and one native driver terribly wounded; one of our guns being struck in two places but not rendered unserviceable.' At last, seeing their infantry in full retreat, the rebel cavalry fell back and followed them down the road towards Cawnpore. Here again the lack of cavalry – to turn the enemy's retreat into a rout – was felt.

In the village Maude's men found welcome refreshment:

In almost the first store my gunners found several casks full of commissariat porter. They asked leave to tap one of them, to which I had not the least objection; but the barrels seemed to have been left so suspiciously handy that I was suspicious of poison. Consequently I called for two 'volunteer tasters' to step forward, to each of whom we handed a foaming beaker of about a quart. After waiting fifteen minutes, and finding that no ill-effects followed, we all partook of the excellent tipple, pushed on through the village and halted on the other side, in the sun, while our wounded were looked to, and we cleaned our guns, shifted ammunition etc., etc., for the duties of artillerymen are very far from being completed when an action is over.

The column settled down to cook breakfast, but Havelock's thoughts were on the road ahead – in particular, the bridge over the river Pandu

Nudee only 2 miles distant. Guessing from the presence of the sepoys at Aong – presumably a delaying force – that the bridge was still intact, Havelock was keen to press on and seize it. The Pandu Nudee, although only a stream 60 or 70 yards wide was, at this season, swelled by the rains and therefore unfordable. Worse, it ran through a steep ravine. The column had no pontoon train, and in hostile country procuring boats would be well nigh impossible; it was vital to capture the bridge intact. Havelock was in no doubt that the enemy – with Cawnpore only 23 miles beyond the bridge – would be taking measures to destroy the bridge. It was with this in mind that he rushed his column on. After a two-hour march the column reached the river to find the enemy – under the Nana Sahib's brother – ready to dispute the passage of the river and making preparations to destroy the bridge. For some days previously they had been entrenching themselves on the far side of the stream, and on a salient in their entrenchments had placed a 24-pounder and a 24-pound carronade so as to sweep the bridge itself and the road leading up to it. The effect of this heavy weight of shot was felt early: 'We ... moved on, in the usual column formation ...', wrote Maude. 'We soon found ourselves in a tope of mango trees, among which there suddenly came crashing several 24lb shot, which were very well aimed, killing and wounding two or three of the infantry.'

If a salient – a forward 'bulge' in a defensive line – can direct fire in three directions, it is also vulnerable from those three directions. It was at Captain Maude's suggestion that the British guns were divided into three detachments – three in front of the salient, two to the right and two to the left – to bring the enemy's heavy artillery under a three-way crossfire.

> I at once deployed the battery into line, and advanced in this order; taking the guns on the road myself, assisted by Lieutenant Crump of the Madras Artillery. Maitland (R.A.) and Harward (Bengal Artillery) each commanded a sub-division on the respective flanks. But on both sides of the road, this being the rainy season, the ground was very heavy and uneven; so that, as we advanced smartly along to try con-clusions with the enemy's 24-prs, we were very nearly alone, and presented a fair mark for their guns. But one of the points which they scarcely ever seized, fortunately for us, was to depress their guns so as to meet advancing troops. Consequently, although some of their shots aimed at us did a little damage to our right and left rear, we only lost

two gun-bullocks and one native driver, killed in that advance. Then, coming into action at 600 yards range, we commenced our usual duel.

While Maude's guns traded shots with the enemy's battery, a white cloud arose above the bridge followed by the sound of an explosion. The rebels had tried to blow the bridge, but their train had been laid in haste and its only effect had been to damage the parapets and one of the bridge's masonry arches. Now the fire of the rebel heavy guns began to slacken. Maude's crossfire had been taking its toll. 'By a wonderful Providence,' he wrote, 'in three rounds of spherical case-shell, we broke the sponge-staves of their heavy guns.' Whether, in fact, the rebel gunners' sponge staves were broken by Maude's shrapnel or whether, as some observers thought, the men themselves – seeing their position was hopeless – broke the staves and spiked their guns, the fire from the rebel salient slackened and died. The men of the Madras Fusiliers, who had been dropping gunners with their Enfields from the edge of the ravine, now – under Major Stephenson, who had taken over command from Renaud – dashed across the bridge in the teeth of enemy musketry and seized the guns.

The Nana Sahib's brother fled with his command to report to the Nana that the British were across the river and only 23 miles from Cawnpore. 'They retired in good order,' wrote Maude, 'and at once made excellent preparations for meeting us on the morrow.' That night Havelock wrote to Neill, still at Allahabad, calling for the despatch of at least two hundred, preferably three hundred, European troops, as well as quantities of artillery and Enfield ammunition. Exhaustion, exposure and battle casualties had reduced his small force, and he feared that unless reinforced he would not be strong enough – after leaving a garrison in Cawnpore – to push on into Oude and relieve Lucknow. Havelock had another worry that night. News had reached him that 210 women and children who had survived the 'boat massacre' at the Satichaura Ghat were still alive in Cawnpore. The advance on Cawnpore would be a race against time to save them from sharing the fate of their countrymen and women.

In Cawnpore that night the Nana Sahib and his civil and military advisers were reviewing their options, with the British over the river. Some were for a retreat to Bithur, others for a move towards Fatehgarh. The Nana, though, eventually opted for a further stand before Cawnpore, before

turning to the question of the prisoners. Since 1 July these had been held
in a small bungalow known as 'the Bibighar' (the ladies' house) – the
former home of the Indian mistress of a British officer. Here, in two
rooms 20 feet by 10, without furniture or straw for bedding, they had
awaited their fate. Responsible for their captivity was a member of
the Nana's household, Hosainee Khanum – a former prostitute's maid
nicknamed 'the Begum'. It was she who had supervised their inadequate
diet of chapattis and *dhal* (lentil soup). After twenty-eight had died in
the first fortnight, better food was provided and they were allowed out
on to the verandah for an occasional breath of fresh air. Apart from this
the prisoners were rarely seen, except once or twice when locals saw
English women grinding corn or washing clothes – menial tasks no
memsahib would normally have performed.

Among the Nana Sahib's entourage there had been divided counsels
as to the military measures to be adopted, but as regards the prisoners
there was unanimity. They were useless as hostages, his advisers declared,
and dangerous, as witnesses of the first massacre at the river's edge. The
British were pushing on with the intention of rescuing them – if they
were killed, it was argued, the British would be discouraged and turn
back, unwilling to risk further depleting their meagre forces in an already
lost cause. There may too, have been a spirit of revenge abroad – fuelled
by tales of British reprisals. Possibly there was a belief that killing the
prisoners would involve one and all so deeply in the Mutiny that there
could be no possibility of defection or negotiation. The execution of the
prisoners in the Bibighar was agreed upon.

First the male hostages – three refugees from Fatehgarh, an English
merchant, Mr Greenaway and his son, and a 14-year-old boy – were
brought out of the house to the front of the Nana's headquarters, a hotel
just 50 yards away. They were shot by a sepoy firing squad, while the
Nana Sahib looked on. An hour later the sepoys were ordered to proceed
to the Bibighar and shoot the women and children. They refused – the
women of the Nana's household had also protested at the order, refusing
food and threatening to throw themselves off the rooftops. The guard,
threatened with being blown away from guns, marched down to the
house and, pointing their muskets through windows, fired into the ceiling.
It was then that the Begum took a hand. Summoning a member of the
Nana's Maratha guard – reputedly her lover – two Muslim butchers and
two other townsmen, she brought them to the house to do what the
sepoys had refused to do. What followed, after they entered the house,

was witnessed by an Eurasian drummer named Fitchett, of the 6th NI, who was interviewed by British officials some months later.

I heard fearful shrieks. This lasted half an hour or more. I did not see any of the women or children try to escape. A Velatiee [foreigner – in this case Afghan], a stout, short man, and fair, soon came out with his sword broken. I saw him go into the Nana's house and bring back another sword. This he also broke in a few minutes, and got a third from the Nana . . . the groans lasted all night . . . At about 8 o'clock the next morning the sweepers living in the compound, I think there were three or four, were ordered to throw the bodies into a dry well, near the house. The bodies were dragged out, most of them by the hair of the head, those whose clothes were worth taking were stripped. Some of the women were alive, I cannot say how many, but three could speak; they prayed for the sake of God that an end might be put to their sufferings. I remarked one very stout woman, a half-caste, who was severely wounded in both arms, who entreated to be killed. She and two or three others were placed against the bank of the cut by which bullocks go down in drawing water from the well. The dead bodies were first thrown down. Application was made to the Nana about those who were alive. Three children were also alive. I do not know what order came, but I saw one of the children thrown in alive. I believe the other children and women, who were alive, were thrown in . . . There was a great crowd looking on; they were standing along the walls of the compound. They were principally city people and villagers. Yes, there were also sepoys . . . They were fair children, the eldest I think must have been six or seven, and the youngest five years; it was the youngest who was thrown in by one of the sweepers. The children were running round the well, where else could they go to? and there was none to save them. No, none said a word.

Even as the women and children in the Bibighar were being murdered, the men who hoped on the morrow to be their rescuers were settling down to a brief and fitful sleep. The cattle were slow in coming up to camp – by the time they were slaughtered most men had made do with biscuit and porter and turned in. By early morning, as the column moved off, the discarded meat was already rotting. A 16-mile forced march brought the column to Maharajpore, just 7 miles from Cawnpore. Scouting ahead, the Volunteer cavalry met two natives – who turned out to be the spy Anjoor Tewaree, who had joined the column after Futtehpore, and a colleague. The two men had spent the previous night in the rebel camp. While the column ate a hasty meal – biscuit and porter again – Havelock learned from Tewaree the enemy's dispositions. The Nana Sahib had taken up a strong position at the village, Aherwa, where a road leading into the Cawnpore cantonment diverges from the Grand Trunk road that leads into Cawnpore itself (see map 5 on page xix). His left flank was anchored on the Ganges, a mile to his left down a steep slope. His front consisted of five entrenched strongpoints based on five villages, each with walled enclosures providing cover for his infantry. His 8,000 men were distributed among these villages with eight guns – equal in number to the British artillery, but throwing a much heavier weight of shot – four 24-pounders on his left, a 24-pounder and a 6-pounder in the centre and two 9-pounders on his right. The whole rebel force formed a crescent with the horns forward. Any force attacking it frontally up the Grand Trunk road – seemingly the only approach – would walk into a murderous crossfire from heavy artillery. Massed behind the rebel left was their cavalry. Having closely questioned what locals his cavalry could round up, Havelock established that the ground to the enemy's left and the river was firmer than that of the swampy ground on his right, and decided to attempt an envelopment of the rebel left flank. It was a gamble – one that involved risking his communications with Allahabad, to his rear, and – once he had taken his force round the enemy's flank – fighting with his back to the Ganges. The alternative, however, was 'another Ferozeshah' – a Sikh War battle at which Havelock had been present, where the British had frontally attacked a similar position, only capturing it after taking horrific casualties. With only 1,100 Europeans and 300 Sikhs such a butcher's bill was unthinkable.

Havelock summoned his commanding officers, among them his artillery commander Captain Maude:

Havelock ... explained to us his proposed plan of attack, the spies at the same time drawing in the dust of the road a clever sketch of the enemy's position. He invited any suggestions or improvements we might have to offer, but his dispositions appeared to us to be admirable. Turning to young Captain Currie, who had just come up with us and taken command of the detachments of the gallant 84th Regiment, he said to him: 'Young as you are, sir, if you come out of today's affair with credit I promise you your promotion to Major.' Currie bowed, and smilingly thanked the General.

Leaving the baggage in the rear at Maharajpore, therefore, Havelock marched his whole force in columns of subdivisions up the Grand Trunk road, the cavalry leading – for all the world as if he was about to make the frontal attack for which the Nana Sahib was hoping. The men were exhausted, the sun the hottest they had yet encountered. 'We had not gone five hundred yards,' wrote Maude, 'before the men began to fall out, lying down on the right and left of the road. Several of them died from sun-stroke; others, who were not able to stagger back to the baggage, were cut to pieces by the enemy's Cavalry, who came down between us and it when we made our flank movement.' The flank movement began just short of the point where the road divided – the main road going on into Cawnpore, the smaller road forking to the right to lead to the cantonment. Havelock wheeled the whole force, including Maude's guns, to the right. The cavalry continued to advance straight at the enemy's line to screen this right hook for as long as possible. The ground on the British right consisted of a number of mango groves, which served Havelock's manoeuvre for about 1,000 yards. At this point a break in the line of trees allowed the rebels a view of the British force moving across their front. At once the guns on the enemy left opened up. Among the first casualties, as Maude noted, was the young officer to whom Havelock had promised promotion: 'By a strange chance, one of the first round-shots fired by the enemy (a 24-pounder) carried away nearly the whole of the lower part of poor Currie's body, inflicting a most ghastly wound. Yet he lingered for nearly three days, mainly, as we were told, owing to the support he received from my champagne.'

Seeing the British turning movement, the Nana's troops tried to redeploy to meet it, covered by an advance of their cavalry. Although the mutinous sepoy regulars had on numerous occasions proved formidable in defence they were generally – perhaps in the absence of their British officers – slow in manoeuvre. Before they had re-formed their line to meet this new threat, the British had passed round their left, wheeled into line and were advancing upon them – at right angles to their defensive line. The 78th were on the right of the line, next to them came HM 64th Foot, then the 84th and the Sikhs on the left – the Madras Fusiliers were out in front along the whole line in skirmishing order. Maude's guns were in three detachments down the line. 'We ... lost several men in the column by the fire of their heavy guns,' wrote Maude,

> yet we succeeded in turning their left flank, and as soon as we had done so we came into action, at 900 yards range, and commenced to engage the guns on their left. These, however, were so well protected by the 'moorcha' as well as by being hidden in a tope of trees, that it was some time before we could silence them. Besides which their plan was always to run away from the gun, as long as we were firing at them; then, when they saw us limbering up, they would usually, unless they had lost several of their gunners, return to their guns and blaze away again.

These artillery duels were a severe test of nerve as Maude noted:

> While speaking to Maitland, one of the enemy's round-shots passed between his face and my own. We were distant about six feet from one another. Maitland, who was certainly one of the coolest of the men in our force, only smiled. He had his nerves so well under control that he had brought himself to be able to hear, and actually sometimes to see, a shot pass close to him without even winking. I confess I never arrived at that point, though I do not believe more than two or three men in our battery ever even bobbed their heads. *That* was considered 'bad form' among 'the Royal Gunners.'

In such situations it was perhaps easier for the officers and NCOs, who had a position to maintain, than for the gunners. Maude described a drastic remedy for one case of nerves.

> In the middle of the action one of the sergeants reported to me that a certain gunner, whose name we will suppress, had lost his nerve, and was confusing the ammunition which it was his duty to serve out. It was difficult to find a suitable remedy; but it occurred to the writer to threaten, in a solemn manner, that if a similar complaint was again made, the delinquent should be tied on to one of the waggon-limbers and brought into action seated in this conspicuous manner. The poor young fellow managed to overcome his nervousness, and did excellent work from that hour.

Seeing that the enemy's heavy guns could not be silenced by artillery alone, Havelock turned to the 78th: 'The opportunity had arrived for which I have long anxiously waited,' Havelock wrote in his despatch, 'of developing the powers of the 78th Highlanders. Three guns of the enemy were already posted behind a lofty hamlet well entrenched. I directed this regiment to advance, and never have I beheld conduct more admirable! They were led by Colonel Hamilton, and followed him with surprising steadiness and gallantry under a heavy fire. As they approached the village they cheered and charged with the bayonet, their pipes sounding a pibroch. Need I say that the enemy fled, the village was taken, and the guns were captured?' As they fled the scene, the rebels spilt into two groups – one moved off down the cantonment road, the other rallied in the centre round the heavy howitzer. This gun, which had been unable to fire before for fear of hitting their own troops on the left, now became the rallying point for a new rebel front – at right angles to the old. Havelock, however, had no intention of letting them rally. Quickly re-forming his troops, he pointed to the howitzer and the enemy infantry massing round it crying: 'Now, Highlanders, another charge like that wins the day!' With a cheer the 78th issued out from behind a causeway where it had re-formed and – with the 64th and 84th on its left – stormed the new rebel position.

The rebel centre had collapsed, but the guns on the right were still untouched. 'The enemy's guns on the left being at length completely silenced, we advanced again, to engage those which they had on their extreme right, and which were also in a tope of trees. After three or four rounds these were entirely deserted, one of them having had a piece taken clean out of its muzzle, like a scoop of cheese, by a shot from one of my guns.' Another village still offered resistance. 'Who'll take this village,' cried Havelock, spurring his horse to the front, '64th or 78th?' The answer was another shout as both regiments raced towards it. Maude's gun-bullocks were too exhausted, now, to pull the guns much further, but their commander went in with the 64th. 'I rode up with the 64th Regiment into the tope of trees where the enemy had made their stand. As we did so we came under a hot musketry fire from the railway embankment, which faced us, and behind which the rebels had retired, there being a very deep "jheel" or ditch, between us and the railway. With the assistance of the 64th I turned the enemy's guns upon their Infantry and dispersed them. A gunner named Batley then came up, and at my desire, spiked the guns.' It was at this point that the Volunteer cavalry, who had been steadily advancing up the Grand Trunk road, arrived, just in time to pursue the enemy's retreating infantry. A regiment of enemy cavalry – acting as a rearguard – blocked its way. Mustering only eighteen sabres, the Volunteers charged at once – urged on by a staff officer, Captain Beatson, who, stricken with cholera, had had himself carried to the front in a cart. With Captain Barrow in the lead shouting, 'Point, point, no cuts!' they plunged into the rebels' ranks, scattering them at once to the cheers of the watching infantry.

Meanwhile Maude's guns and the Sikhs – left behind in the speed of the advance – were now in danger from the enemy's cavalry, who having swept round and cut up the British wounded now attacked them. 'We then returned to the main road,' wrote Maude,

> and halted upon it. Here Fraser-Tytler (D.A.Q.M.G.) rode up, and told me to form my Battery in line upon the road, and halt there, as that would be the centre of our camp. Also that the Infantry were going to advance a short distance and clear a village in front of us, but that they would return, and form the camp where we then were. He then rode off and left us, while we proceeded to carry out his orders. But, while we were doing so, we were at once threatened by Cavalry on both sides of us, who came so near that we had to bring our flank guns into action 'right' and 'left' respectively, while, at the same time, a dropping, but gradually increasing, fire commenced in our rear, from the enemy's Infantry on the railway embankment, so we had to keep a sharp look-out with a couple of guns in this direction also. After about half-an-hour of this work two of their guns opened out on our left front, to which we also turned our attention, with three of our guns, at about 1,500 yards range. So that we were actually facing towards all four points of the compass at the same time, all the while being *utterly without support.*

Also without support were the men of the 78th, 64th and 84th. Whatever his other personal qualities – and his memory is revered in modern India – the Nana Sahib was not lacking in courage. Rallying his troops once more around a reserve 24-pounder on the Cawnpore road and with fresh troops from the city, he rode among them, and with bands and bugles playing led them forward in one last all-or-nothing counter-attack. The fire of the 24-pounder forced the British infantry to take cover in the village it had just captured as the Nana's whole force advanced in a crescent formation with cavalry on the flanks. Havelock's horse was shot under him but, mounting a pony, he rode to the front. 'The Madras Fusiliers,' he wrote in his despatch, 'the 64th, 84th, and 78th detachments, formed in line were exposed to a heavy fire from the 24-pounder on the road. I was resolved that this state of affairs should not last; so calling upon my men, who were lying down in line to leap on their feet, I directed another steady advance. It was irresistible. The enemy sent round shot into our ranks until we were within three hundred yards, and then poured in grape with such precision and determination, as I have seldom witnessed.' Thirty or forty men of the 64th fell as they advanced straight towards the muzzle of the enemy's gun. 'The 64th, led by Major Stirling and my aid-de-camp [*sic*],' wrote Havelock, 'who had placed himself in their front, were not to be denied. Their rear showed the ground strewed with the wounded; but on they steadily and silently came, then with a cheer charged and captured the unwieldy trophy of their valour. The enemy lost all heart, and after a hurried fire of musketry gave way in total rout.'

Moments later four of Maude's guns came up, having been summoned from a mile to the rear by a staff officer. 'Hargood came up with a pressing order to advance to the succour of the Infantry, saying that he thought he could pick out a fairly good bit of road. So we limbered up and plunged into the sodden ground ... On our again coming up with the force we were loudly cheered by the latter, and the whole line advanced just at that moment. When we got clear through the plantation, under cover of which the rebels had rallied, we fired a few shots at their retreating Cavalry, and emptied several saddles. Thus ended the Battle of Cawnpore.' At Havelock's side throughout the day had ridden a drummer of the 78th, who had been given charge of the General's watch. At the first enemy shot he had been told to note the time. As Maude sent his last round off after the retreating rebels the boy produced the watch and announced to the General, 'Two hours and forty-five minutes, Sir!'

The 'aide-de-camp' whom Havelock refers to as having ridden ahead of the 64th towards the enemy 24-pounder was his own son, Henry Havelock (later Havelock-Allen). While there was no dispute about his having performed this feat of gallantry, there was anger in some quarters when Havelock recommended his son for the Victoria Cross. Although he praised the 64th warmly in his General Order the day after the battle ('Your fire was reserved till you saw the colour of your enemies' moustaches – this gave us the victory'), the officers of the 64th decided that the wording of the younger Havelock's citation reflected badly on their regiment and their commander, Major Stirling. In it, Havelock senior had written 'the lieutenant continued to move steadily on in front of the regiment at a foot pace on his horse ... In went the corps, led by the lieutenant.' Although Stirling was mentioned as being 'in front, dismounted,' the officers felt that the citation reflected on the courage and ability of Major Stirling, and implied that his regiment would not follow him. This complaint went via the commander-in-chief in India – by then Sir Colin Campbell – to the desk of the Duke of Cambridge at Horse Guards. Campbell took the regiment's part, writing 'This instance is one of many, in which, since the institution of the Victoria Cross, advantage has been taken by young aids-de-camp [sic] and other staff officers to place themselves in prominent situations for the purpose of attracting attention. To them life is of little value, as compared with the gain of public honour, but they do not reflect, and the generals to whom they belong do not reflect, on the cruel injustice thus done to gallant officers, who, beside the excitement of the moment of action, have all the responsibility attendant on this situation.' Eventually ruffled feathers were smoothed and young Havelock got his VC, but the resentment remained.

As the rebels fell back the Nana Sahib galloped off to Bithur, and many thousands fled Cawnpore in anticipation of the terrible revenge that would surely follow the arrival of the British. Havelock made his camp 2 miles outside the city: 'As it grew dark,' he wrote, 'the roofless barracks of our artillery were dimly descried in advance, and it was evident that Cawnpore was once more in our possession.' The General slept with his arm through his horse's bridle, which stood saddled beside him. In only eight days his small force had marched 126 miles in the heat of an Indian summer and fought four actions against overwhelming odds. They had killed countless numbers of mutineers and captured twenty-four pieces of artillery. They would discover in the morning that they had arrived too late. One of the first men into the city in the morning was J. W. Sherer. Riding in with his friend Bews (whose sister, Nora, was later to marry Frederick Roberts), Sherer suddenly saw 'far in the distance, a great tongue of fire flung up towards the sky, and immediately afterwards, what looked like a vast black balloon ascended, as if in pursuit of it, showing us, in its dispersion, that it was smoke. Then after a perceptible pause there was the noise of a violent explosion, and at that moment I felt a pluck at my knees that made me involuntarily sit tighter.

This compression was the passage of the great air-wave, for the Cawnpore battery had just been blown up.' Havelock's army entered a city almost deserted – many had no doubt heard of the events at the Bibighar – and feared, with good reason, the reaction of the British to what they would find. Those few who remained seemed eager to ingratiate themselves. 'As Bews and I entered the city,' wrote Sherer, 'we were met by a man with a small kettle-drum; and, without orders, he put himself just before us, and proclaimed the restoration of the former rule. Whether he had in a similar manner proclaimed the Nana cannot be well known; but he diligently rattled away, sonorously shouting an intimation, framed on the same lines as the one mentioned to have been used by the rebels in Banda, but worded as follows:

> *Khalki-i-Khuda*
> *Mulk-i-Kampani Bahadur*
> *Hukmi-Sahiban alishan.*

Sherer and his party were met by a large group of Bengalis who 'professed themselves delighted with our return; but were rather afraid of the soldiers'. Having arrived at Mahomed's hotel, which had been the Nana's headquarters, the two men were escorted to the Bibighar.

It was of one storey, with a court in the middle, and a tree grew in the court. Bews and I were certainly among the first who saw it; but Colonel Fraser-Tytler had been there, and one or two others. But there is no question that the aspect of the place, when we entered was entirely unchanged ... The attack had evidently been made from the front entrance, and there is reason to suppose that it commenced by muskets being pushed through the venetians and discharged. There had been a rush across the court to the opposite side, and a mass of human beings were collected in the arched chamber facing the entrance. And thither, doubtless, they were pursued by the assassins with swords. For the whole of the pavement was thickly caked with blood ... There is no question in my mind that when the bodies were taken away, the place had been tidied a little and painful objects had been removed. There were certainly a few odds and ends of clothing, some locks of hair, some little shoes, straw hats, and so on. Of mutilation, in that house at least, there were no signs, nor at that time was there any writing on the walls.

Sherer, who was soon to be Magistrate of Cawnpore – was more level-headed than many who saw the evidence of the massacre. The truth, he felt, was bad enough and in no need of embellishment. The Bibighar was to become a place of pilgrimage for all the many drafts of officers and men who passed through Cawnpore – and a place for the swearing of terrible oaths of vengeance. According to Private Metcalfe of the 32nd, the Highlanders knelt when they entered the building and took an oath to kill a hundred for every one of the victims 'and I need not add that they kept their vow'. Metcalfe was not there at the time, but the story rings true, and not just of the Highlanders. Officers and men took mementos – locks of hair or scraps of clothing, and kept them as talismans for the coming battles, and to keep their anger warm. The writing on the walls Sherer refers to was graffiti – such as 'Countrymen Avenge!' – written by soldiers but believed, by those who came later, to have been written by the women just before or even during the massacre. One genuine item was a scrap of paper in which a Miss Caroline Lindsay – one of the victims – chronicled the destruction of her family: 'Mamma died, July 12th; Alice died, July 9th; George died June 27th. Entered the barracks May 21st. Cavalry left, June 5th. First shot fired June 6th. Uncle Willy died, June 18th; Aunt Lily, June 17th. Left barracks, June 27th. Made prisoners as soon as we were at the river.'

'From this dreadful place,' wrote Sherer,

we passed down the garden to the narrow well into which many of the bodies of the victims of the assassination were thrown. I say many, because the receptacle was far too small for all, and there can be little doubt that bodies were dragged across the open space to the river, which was at no great distance ... When we got to the coping of the well, and looked over, we saw, at no great depth, a ghastly tangle of naked limbs ... I heard a low cry of pain, and saw Bews almost crouching with a sickening anguish. There is no object in saying more.

A little later in the day Sherer approached the General – already preoccupied with his advance into Oude – about the well.

I found him sitting on a chair, in a field by himself, with an umbrella over him. I asked him about the well, and said that for one thing, of course, it would soon become very pestilential if something were not done; and he replied; 'Please at once procure some coolies, and have it filled up with earth.' So getting hold again of Bews, and the Commissariat Baboo ... we visited the horrible spot once more, and had the well filled up in a rough manner, and not a moment too soon, for the effluvia was becoming excessively bad.

The soldiers had already started drinking and taking indiscriminate revenge on the local population, but it was not until Brigadier General Neill arrived a few days later that the retribution was organized and – in Neill's eyes – refined. By this time Havelock had left the city – it was just as well, as relations between the two men had started badly and were getting worse. Havelock had forbidden Neill to issue any orders while he was there. Neill, for his part, had assumed that Havelock had summoned him to assist on the advance into Oude and was disappointed to be left behind to defend Cawnpore. In fact, Havelock badly needed somebody on whom he could rely to secure his rear area and communications – if he didn't care for Neill he respected his ability. Confined to a 'police' action, Neill clearly felt the need to do something spectacular. It came in the form of a notorious order of 25 July. 'Whenever a rebel is caught,' wrote Neill, describing the results of his order,

he is immediately tried, and unless he can prove a defence, he is sentenced to be hanged at once; but the chief rebels or ringleaders I make first clean up a certain portion of the pool of blood, still two inches deep, in the shed where the fearful murder and mutilation of the women and children took place. To touch blood is most abhorrent to the high-caste natives; they think by doing so they damn their souls to perdition. Let them think so. My object is to inflict a fearful punishment for a revolting, cowardly, barbarous deed, and to strike terror into these rebels. The first I caught was a soubhadar [*sic*], or native officer, a high-caste Brahmin, who tried to resist my order to clean up the very blood he had helped to shed; but I made the provost-marshal do his duty, and a few lashes compelled the miscreant to accomplish his task. When done he was taken out, immediately hanged, and after death buried at a ditch at the roadside. No one who has witnessed the scenes of murder, mutilation and massacre can ever listen to the word 'mercy', as applied to these fiends.

What Neill did not mention in this letter – to a newspaper in his native Ayr – was that the 'cleaning' was to be done with the tongue – a patch of the congealed blood having been specially wetted for the purpose by Untouchables of the Native Police. Victims were also force-fed on pork or beef before execution. How many times the order was put into practice is still a matter of debate, but there were few at the time – certainly among the officers and men – who would have dissented from Neill's methods. The order remained in place until November, when the new commander-in-chief, Sir Colin Campbell, banned it as unbecoming a Christian nation. Nor can there be any doubt that many thousands died in Cawnpore and the surrounding districts with only the slightest pretence of legal process. The Governor General – mockingly nicknamed 'Clemency Canning' – and Lady Canning, the not-usually-squeamish Sir John Lawrence, even the Queen herself, all might be expressing doubts about such harsh measures, but in Cawnpore Neill had free rein. The one person who might, possibly, have called a halt – General Havelock – had put Cawnpore behind him. Having failed to save the garrison of Wheeler's entrenchment, or even the survivors of the massacre, all his thoughts were now centred on another garrison, larger, but threatened with a similar fate – in the Residency at Lucknow.

# 8

## LUCKNOW

Lucknow, on the west bank of the river Gumti, 42 miles east of Cawnpore and 610 from Calcutta, was the capital of the province of Oude, whose annexation, in 1856, was the root of so much discontent in the sepoy army. If British rule had been more just – in Western terms – and more efficient than the somewhat chaotic rule of the exiled Nawab, Wajid Ali, it had materially damaged the interests of many. Lucknow that May was swarming with people who had reason to resent the arrival of British rule. L. E. R. Rees, who came to Lucknow on business in May 1857, described the mood of the population as he saw it:

> We had done very little to deserve their love and much to merit their detestation. Thousands of nobles, gentlemen, and officials, who during the king's time had held lucrative appointments, and who were too idle to work, were now in penury and want, and their myriads of retainers and servants thrown out of employ of course. Then the innumerable vagabonds, bravos, and beggars, who, under the native rule infested the city and found bread in it, were starving during our administration. The native merchants, shopkeepers, and bankers, who while Wajid Ali was on the throne, made large profits from supplying the luxurious wants of the king, his courtiers, and the wealthy ladies of the thronged harems, found no sale for their goods; and the people in general, and especially the poor, were dissatisfied because they were taxed directly and indirectly in every way. We had been so very anxious to show a large balance-sheet in

our favour, that we were less careful to make the people happy than
to make them fill our treasuries.

Good government costs money – there were new duties on food, houses,
ferries, petitions – even opium. Rees wrote that: 'Opium was an article
as extensively used in Lucknow as in China, and the sudden deprivation
of this drug was most severe upon the poorer opium-eaters. Many who
could not obtain it at the increased rates actually cut their own throats in
desperation.'

To borrow an old pun, Oude had been the nursery of the Company's
infantry. Its population was armed and militarized – and provided soldiers
for more than just the British. Along with the Nawab's extensive Court,
his army had been disbanded – some 200,000 men plus all the supporting
services, the armourers alone numbering 12,000. As well as dispossessing
many of the landowners – the *talukdars* – of their rights and powers, the
British had disbanded their private armies, throwing still more armed
men out of employment.

The arrival of Sir Henry Lawrence as Chief Commissioner of Oude
might, in time, have served to reconcile the natives to British rule.
While in the Punjab he had strongly disagreed with the policies of Lord
Dalhousie – and of his brother Sir John Lawrence – and had been forced
to resign. His mild and judicious rule in the Punjab, however, had won
the British friends there who were even now proving friends in need.
With his natural understanding of, and sympathy for, native sensibilities –
and of the need for change, when it must take place, to do so slowly – he
might, in due course, have proved to be the one man capable of pacifying
Oude. As it was, by the time he arrived, in March 1857, much of the
damage was done. By early May Sir Henry had for some time been
watching with growing alarm the three Native regiments that consititued
the bulk of the Lucknow garrison – the 13th, 58th and 71st NI. Men of
the disbanded 19th NI from Barrackpore had been returning to their
home state spreading disaffection with British rule and the rumours that
had inflamed sepoys elsewhere. At the first symptom of unrest Sir Henry
had been quick to act. On 3 May, on rumours of disaffection among the
7th Irregular Cavalry, he had marched – with men of HM 32nd Foot, his
only British regiment, a force of sepoys and a battery of eight guns – to
the camp of that regiment and disbanded it. Private Henry Metcalfe of
the 32nd was with Lawrence's force. 'We dropped on them at midnight
and had the Assemble sounded for them. We formed three sides of a

square, the Artillery forming the head part of it. The guns were loaded with grape and canister. Of course we were loaded with Ball cartridge. When these fellows were ordered to pile arms they refused, but when the Gunners were ordered to prepare and our lads to present, the gallant mutineers altered their tactics and quietly laid down their arms and scattered to their homes.' Following this, on 12 May, Lawrence held a great *durbar* in Lucknow, which British residents, European and Native officers of the sepoy regiments and native officials all attended. After reminding those present of the religious persecutions of the past – of the Hindus under the Moguls and Muslims in the Punjab under Ranjit Singh – and contrasting this with the toleration now prevailing under British rule, he went on publicly to reward certain Native NCOs who had shown loyalty in the recent crisis.

News of Meerut and Delhi reached Lucknow on 16 May, after which Sir Henry applied to Canning for, and received, the rank of brigadier general, with the powers that this implied to take what steps he saw fit. Sir Henry at once set about creating a fortified position based around the Chief Commissioner's house – 'the Residency' – close to the banks of the Gumti, and the Machi Bhawan, an old fortress used for storing supplies, from which it was possible to dominate the Iron Bridge – one of two bridges that linked the city with its suburbs on the eastern bank of the Gumti (see maps 6 and 7, on pages xx and xxi).

The Residency compound – an area 2,150 feet long from north-west to south-east and 1,200 feet broad from east to west – he enclosed with a series of entrenchments, incorporating buildings into the defences as strongpoints, strengthening walls and blocking windows where necessary, and demolishing outlying buildings so as to clear fields of fire. Into this compound he moved the families and sick of the 32nd Foot and all Europeans and Eurasians and their families. Rees described the scene inside the Residency at this time:

> The Residency was crowded with ladies, women and children, and every house and outhouse was occupied. Preparations for defence were continued, and thousands of coolies were employed at the batteries, stockades and trenches that we were everywhere completing. We buried the treasure and ammunition, of which fortunately we had a large supply, and brought together as many guns as we could collect. The Residency and Muchee Bhawn presented most animated scenes. There were soldiers, sepoys, prisoners in irons, men, women, and children,

hundreds of servants, respectable natives in their carriages, coolies carrying weights, heavy cannons, field-pieces, carts, elephants, camels, bullocks, horses, all moving about hither and thither, and continual bustle and noise were kept up from morning to night. Tents were pitched; and in fact there was scarcely a corner which was not in some way occupied and turned to account.

By 24 May he had gathered all the troops, women and children, and civilian men inside the Residency compound. These latter were soon formed into a Volunteer corps, which was armed and drilled. Inevitably these amateur soldiers attracted a certain amount of scorn, initially at least, from the professionals. Henry Kavanagh – one of the Volunteers – was in no doubt about their value in defence.

> The whole body afterwards distinguished themselves by their courage and endurance, and their superior intelligence made them as good, if not better than regular troops, for the kind of warfare they were engaged in. Precise military instruction is not so essential for fighting behind defences as it is on the open plain, where the drilled soldier would, for a time, be superior to volunteers. No troops go into action with the precision of a parade, although great efforts are made to do it; and those who argue for the superiority of regular troops, should remember that the common soldier's share in an engagement is very simple.

All magazine stores were concentrated in the Machi Bhawan, guarded by one company of the 32nd with thirty guns. By 27 May Sir Henry felt able to inform Lord Canning by letter that the Residency and Machi Bhawan was 'safe against all comers'.

Even so, by then all of Oude apart from Lucknow was in enemy hands. At Sitapore the 41st NI and the 9th Irregular Cavalry had mutinied. At Maulaun, 44 miles north of Lucknow, the natives had taken matters into their own hands and massacred the European civilians there, and the same happened at Mohamdi on the Rohilkhand frontier. Faizabad, Sikrora, Gondah, Bahraich, Malapur, Sultanpur, Saloni, Dryabad, Purwa ... the list goes on. At each administrative centre in the former Kingdom of Oude there were sepoy risings, supported by the local population and native landowners. By the end of the second week in June only Lucknow, in the whole province, remained under British control. It did not remain so for long.

On the night of 30 May the sepoys of the 71st NI mutinied and burned their bungalows. 'The screams of the mutineers in their lines,' wrote Henry Kavanagh, ' − their figures gliding across the streets, firing the empty thatched bungalows around us − the lurid glare of the fierce flames − the crackling of the burning bamboos − and the noise of the falling roofs, resembling distant guns − aroused serious thoughts of the appalling trial foreboded.' The 32nd were quickly turned out and Brigadier Hanscombe was soon on the spot. Private Metcalfe witnessed what followed:

> General Anscombe [*sic*] asked our Colonel to let him have half the light Company of my regiment so that he, the General, might go into the Sepoy lines and pacify these wretches, but the Colonel tried to dissuade him from going near them in their excited state, but he was not to be dissuaded from his object. The General thought that if he only showed himself among them it was sufficient to quieten them, as he formerly commanded one of the Regiments, and thought his men would do anything he told them. But he reckoned without his host. No sooner had he showed himself than they rushed at him. He then saw his mistake and thought to rectify it, but it was too late. As soon as he turned about to return they fired at him and killed him, so that a General Officer was the first I saw killed in the Great Mutiny.

Also killed were Lieutenant Grant and Cornet Raleigh. The mutineers then headed off for Mudkipore. Sir Henry pursued them with the 48th NI and the 7th Light Cavalry, but the latter regiment, and a good part of the former, deserted en route. Even so, with what remained, Sir Henry succeeded in driving the rebels from their positions. By the time he returned to Lucknow, however, all of the 7th Light Cavalry, most of the 48th NI and a few of the 13th NI had shown their hands as mutineers.

The exertions of the previous few weeks took their toll on Sir Henry, who took to his bed, but was soon raised from it once more by the action of his temporary successor − Mr Gubbins − in sending away all those Oude sepoys who had so far proved loyal. Lawrence was convinced that the perimeter he had established could not be held without their help, and as well as recalling them he also called in some five hundred pensioners − veteran sepoys − of whom 170 were judged fit for service. On the night of 11/12 June the cavalry and infantry of the Native Police broke out in open rebellion.

Despite the defection of the majority of the native soldiers and police, up until 28 June it was by no means certain that the Residency would be besieged. Hopes were high of relief from Allahabad, via Cawnpore. On that day, however, came the news that Cawnpore had fallen. 'The heads of our women reeled,' wrote Kavanagh, 'and their hearts sickened, as the harrowing story was told amidst the curses and the fierce resolves of the men. Many a savage vow was made then, which was awfully fulfilled on the bodies of our enemies, and CAWNPOOR was afterwards the war-whoop for atrocities which the British soldier will disown in the next generation.' In the wake of this dispiriting news, Sir Henry decided that what was needed was an effective military demonstration against the natives.

At six in the morning of 30 June Sir Henry led his force out $4\frac{1}{2}$ miles up the Chinhut road, against an enemy reported by his spies to be an advance guard approximately five thousand strong. His force consisted of 300 men of HM 32nd, about the same number of loyal sepoys, mostly from the 13th NI, thirty-six mounted volunteers and 120 Native troopers, mostly Sikhs. In addition, he had ten guns, six field pieces manned by Natives, four more manned by European gunners and a European-manned 8-inch howitzer – nicknamed the 'Turk' by the troops. Unknown to Lawrence the rebels were in far greater strength – possibly as many as 15,000 with twelve guns.

Lawrence found the rebels drawn up in a strongly entrenched camp to the left of Chinhut – a large village on the banks of a lake, close to which was an old royal hunting lodge. Near by was a small hamlet of seven or eight huts. Further to the left was the village of Ismailganj. Sir Henry sent HM 32nd forward to skirmish in front of this village, with those sepoys of the 13th, 48th and 71st NI who had not mutinied, extending to their right. The 'Turk' was placed on the road, with the European-manned guns to its right. The Native guns were deployed on either side of the road further back. The Volunteer, and some Sikh, cavalry were behind the British guns on the right. In the ravine running north to south through the British position were placed the Native Police, armed with firelocks and bayonets, swords and pistols. The action began with the British opening fire with the 8-inch howitzer, directed by its commander Lieutenant Bonham. One of its first shells exploded over the head of the enemy's main column, and this, together with the fire of the European-manned guns to the right of the road, after about twenty minutes forced the enemy to move off the road. Whether this move was a feigned retreat by the rebels designed to draw the British on, or whether it was genuine, its effect was to convince the British that the battle was all but won. Captain Wilson, the deputy assistant adjutant general cried, 'That's it! There they go! Keep it up!' It was clearly expected that confronted with an attack by British troops the rebels would simply melt away. In fact, the rebel commander, Barkat Ahmed, was already feeling his way round the British right flank, pushing masses of cavalry that way – a move that the inexperienced British Volunteer cavalry failed to notice.

It was at this point that some of the natives in the British force showed their hand, as L. E. R. Rees recorded:

> The whole of the Police Force, as soon as the first shot was fired, went at once over to the enemy, as if by a preconcerted arrangement, and commenced firing at us. At the same time, our native gunners, without firing a shot, cut the traces of the artillery horses and escaped, some deserting to the rebels, others galloping off in the direction of Lucknow … the large howitzer, which the men had christened 'Turk' continued to play on the enemy, and was working splendidly, tearing great gaps in the enemy's ranks with each shell thrown from it by our European artillerymen. The native drivers of the elephants that had been yoked in it had, however, also escaped, and our position was now anything but comfortable.

Meanwhile, in front of Ismailganj, the 32nd found themselves under heavy fire from enemy sharpshooters who occupied in strength the loop-holed walls of the village. The first man hit was the commanding officer, Colonel Case, 'as nice an officer, and as good as ever drew a sword', according to Private Metcalfe. 'He belonged to my regiment and was only after coming back from England where he had been to get married, so that his wife very soon became a widow, as did a good many more before the struggle was over.' Captain Bassano, seeing the Colonel fall, ran over to assist him. 'Captain Bassano,' the Colonel exclaimed, 'leave me to die here. Your place is at the head of your company. I have no need of assistance.' With the death of their commander the heart went out of the 32nd's attack and they were soon taking cover behind a small rise in front of the village. Shortly afterwards, Bassano himself was hit – he was carried to safety by a loyal sepoy – and the 32nd fell back in confusion.

As they did so, the rebels emerged from the village in quarter columns, preceded by skirmishers, many of whom now began working round the British left. On the British right, the loyal sepoys of the 13th and 48th NI and the Sikhs of the 71st NI stood and traded volleys with their erstwhile comrades until the British withdrawal in the centre became general.

Withdrawal soon turned to all-out retreat. The Sikh cavalry, who had not so far distinguished themselves, were among the first to leave the field. They charged at the rebel cavalry on their right, who – not caring to tangle with them – let them gallop off in the direction of Lucknow. The artillery were ordered to withdraw, and all the European and two of the Native guns were limbered up and drawn off – the remaining guns falling into the hands of the rebels. The heavy howitzer was a problem – a sergeant had tried, and failed, to bring up the elephants to drag it off. 'Seeing the enemy's cavalry approach the howitzer,' wrote Rees, 'Lieutenant Bonham called out to Captain Ratcliffe to protect it. Four men accordingly fell out . . . They came in time to disperse four of the enemy's cavalry, who were riding up to the very muzzle of the gun. One of them fired his carbine at Lieutenant Bonham, and wounded him in the arm. That officer determined to spike the gun, since there was no chance of yoking the elephants again by drag-ropes.' 'Spiking' a gun meant driving a thick nail into the vent by which it was fired, rendering it useless until the spike could be blown out by an armourer. 'Unfortunately,' wrote Rees, 'there was no spike at hand. Sergeant Suttle, who was there, accordingly broke off the priming wire in the touch-hole, and abandoned it.' The 'Turk' then fell into rebel hands, and in less than forty-eight hours was turned on its former owners with terrible effect. Another gun was saved by a cavalryman. He was a former comrade of Private Metcalfe of the 32nd: 'There was one man by the name of Johnson who was a transfer from the 9th Lancers to ours. This man was one of the Volunteer cavalry. He saw that one of our guns was in danger of falling into the hands of the enemy as all the drivers were killed. He immediately jumped off his horse and jumped on the battery horse which was leading and in the face of the enemy galloped off with the gun to Lucknow. This man was recommended for the Victoria Cross, which he richly deserved, but Fate ordained it otherwise.' Johnson died of cholera a few weeks later.

In the rear all was confusion. The enemy's cavalry – launched on its right-flanking movement early in the battle – had blocked the road between the bridge and the retreating British, thus cutting off their only escape route. With rebel skirmishers creeping round the British left, and the cavalry all around their right and across their road home, the destruction of Lawrence's entire force was at hand. The rebel cavalry was commanded, wrote Rees, by a European, who was seen waving his sword and urging his men to charge. 'He was a handsome-looking man, well-built, fair, about twenty-five years of age, with light mustachios, and wearing the undress uniform of a European cavalry officer, with a blue and gold-laced cap on his head. Whether he was a Russian – one suspected to be such had been seized by the authorities, confined, and then released – or, what is more likely, one of the renegade Christians who had changed their religion and adopted the native habits, manners and costume, I cannot tell.' If the Volunteer cavalrymen had shown their rawness by missing the enemy's outflanking manoeuvre, they now saved the day. This force, numbering at that moment only twenty-five to thirty men, was ordered to charge and clear the road. 'The Volunteers – though few of them had ever seen a shot fired,' wrote Rees, 'obeyed their order right gallantly. They charged; but the enemy never waited for their approach, flying as they advanced, to what was then our right.' As Rees points out, what had been the British left, was now their right since they had turned about and were now fleeing towards Lucknow. As the rebel cavalry had been cleared from the road, the British force began to flee across the Kokrail Bridge. The British were covered on their right by loyal sepoys who, as if determined to prove their loyalty and wipe out the disgrace of their comrades' treachery, held back the enemy's skirmishers with volley fire. It was noted, too, that these sepoys carried European wounded many miles in the retreat that followed, often at the expense of their own. In the bitterness of defeat, however, some British were not inclined to give any native the benefit of the doubt. 'While the guns were galloping back . . .' wrote Rees, 'the musket of a sepoy of the 13th, running beside one of them, accidentally went off, and slightly wounded a gunner. Immediately suspecting it to be done intentionally, he drew his pistol, and shot the man dead.'

As the British poured across the Kokrail Bridge, the remaining guns were drawn across the road in an attempt to deter the rebels who were pressing them close. Deter was all they could do – all the ammunition had been fired off – but the sight of the guns, with gunners standing at their posts with port-fires smoking, was sufficient to cause the whole rebel force to halt. After the event the British were quick to blame treachery on the part of the Natives for this humiliating reverse, but there is no escaping the fact that Sir Henry Lawrence was out-generalled at Chinhut by Barkat Ahmed. Sir Henry knew it. 'My God, my God,' he was heard to say. 'And I brought them to this.' Handing over command to Colonel Inglis, son of the Bishop of Nova Scotia and former commanding officer of the 32nd, Lawrence rode back to Lucknow to prepare the Residency for the force's reception. As the British fled, the rebels pressed them close. 'Many poor fellows,' wrote Rees, 'desperately wounded and unable to rise, whom none could or would assist, were seen fighting like bull-dogs held at bay, till at last they fell dead. Parched with thirst, and weak from exertion and fatigue, under the intense heat of a June sun, numbers fell down exhausted, and were cut up by the enemy's cavalry. Others fell struck by apoplexy.' The retreat was little more than a rout, with each Volunteer cavalryman carrying two or three exhausted infantrymen; the gun limbers were similarly loaded. The *dhoolie*-bearers (stretcher-bearers) had fled, too, early in the battle, so the wounded were either left to their fate or carried on men's backs. The heat of the sun, which had punished the European troops during the advance, prostrated many now. 'I saw on that retreat some of our finest soldiers drop down with sunstroke never to rise again,' wrote Private Metcalfe. 'I saw one fine young fellow who was wounded in the leg. He coolly sat down on the road, faced the enemy, and all we could do or say to him would not urge him to try and come with us. He said – "No, you fellows push on, leave me here to blaze away at these fellows. I shan't last long, and I would never be able to reach Lucknow." He remained, and was very soon disposed of poor fellow.' Later Metcalfe saw a wounded soldier of his regiment, who was being carried on a limber: 'A bonny young man, by name Jones . . . saw his brother being struck down with a bullet from the enemy, and without the least warning he jumped off the limber on which he was riding and joined his brother to be killed with him. Another man, maddened by the heat and fatigue, charged in single-handed into the ranks of the enemy and was soon put to rest.'

By the time the British limped across the Iron Bridge into Lucknow they had lost 118 European officers and men killed and fifty-four wounded, 128 Native officers and men killed and eleven wounded. The bridge was defended by Lieutenant Edmondstone of the 32nd, with thirty-eight men. 'They defended the bridge most gallantly,' wrote Private Metcalfe, 'and covered our further retreat to the Residency and Muchee Bhaun. The latter place was where I was stationed, and on our arrival I saw several men drop down with apoplexy and fatigue. Indeed, I am afraid if the enemy were not checked at the Iron Bridge, we would be able to show them a very feeble resistance indeed.'

Mrs Inglis agreed with him. 'We heard dreadful shouting and screaming in the city,' she wrote, 'we afterwards learnt they had been plundering and committing the most dreadful atrocities. Their being employed in this way the first few nights of the siege doubtless saved our garrison. Though they came boldly forward and invested us on all sides, they could not resist the temptation to plunder which the defenceless city afforded; and this gave us time to settle down ... had they at once assaulted our entrenchments, so great was the confusion, that the garrison would most likely have been put to the sword. The plunder of the city saved us, our first night.'

Henry Kavanagh had been too ill to march out to Chinhut, but he saw the force return. 'It entered angry, fatigued and disheartened, through the residue of the garrison, who looked on alarmed and astonished. The spirit of the defenders instantly sank, and the prowess of the victorious mutineers assumed unmerited importance in their eyes.' After such a defeat – with rebel forces now flooding into the town – it seemed, to many, only a matter of time before they, too, suffered the fate of the Europeans at Cawnpore. 'I rose from my sick bed,' wrote Kavanagh, 'and went out to help in the defence, with a vague idea of the extent of the disaster. I found every one in motion, and confused by a feeling which looked like fear. Gates were rapidly being shut – doors closed – barricades constructed – walls loopholed – guns rolled into position. Surprise and wonder were depicted on almost every face. The suddenness of the assault, and the disgrace it followed bewildered all. I sat on a cot (near what was always called our defences, but was only a thin wall five feet high), with my face buried in my hands.'

It was after the disaster at Chinhut that the siege of Lucknow can properly be said to have begun. On 1 July all British forces were concentrated in the Residency. That night the Machi Bhawan was evacuated. The rebels – having an exaggerated idea of the strength of that post – could not believe that such a withdrawal was planned and had only lightly guarded the roads. The post's garrison with its guns was able to pass the enemy's pickets without a shot being fired. Private Metcalfe was among them: 'I happened to be with the last party who left the Fort, as a portion of my Company acted as a covering party to cover the retreat of the others, and so well was the whole affair arranged that the enemy kept pounding away at the old place till long after the place was vacated and we safely landed at the Residency.' Whatever military stores they could not carry with them they had prepared for demolition. L. E. R. Rees saw them arrive at the Residency: 'The last cannon had reached with the last man when a tremendous report shook the earth. The port-fires had burnt down, and the Fort Muchee Bhawn was no more! All our ammunition, which we had not had time to remove, and about 250 barrels of gun-powder, and several millions of ball-cartridges, were destroyed, along with all the buildings and their contents. An immense black cloud enveloped even us in the Residency – darkness covering a bright starry firmament.' At first the rebels thought it was their doing. 'When the magazine, which contained all the powder, shot and shell etc. was blown up by our men,' wrote Private Metcalfe, 'the enemy thought they had done it by their incessant firing of shot and shell, and they gave such a yell of triumph that you would have thought, with Shakespeare, that Hell had become uninhabited, and that all the Demons were transferred to Lucknow.' Metcalfe and his comrades arrived in a Residency com-pound still in shock from the disaster at Chinhut: 'After we got into the Residency, I shall never forget the heartrending scenes. Mothers and relatives, who clung as a last hope that their lost ones might be with the survivors of the Muchee Bhaun party, but poor things, in most cases they were doomed to disappointment. Mothers asking for their sons, wives for their husbands, it was heartbreaking.'

As it turned out, the garrison had not all been evacuated – the following morning sentries were astonished to see a British soldier standing outside the fortifications shouting, 'Arrah, by Jasus, open your gates.' The man, in a drunken sleep, had been left behind in the Machi Bhawan and was still there when the explosion took place. 'He had been blown in the air,' wrote Rees, 'had returned unhurt to mother earth, continued his drunken sleep again, had awoke next morning, found the fort to his surprise a mass of deserted ruins, and quietly walked back to the Residency without being molested by a soul; and even bringing with him a pair of bullocks attached to a cart of ammunition.'

In the city anarchy reigned, with mutinous sepoys, the private armies of the *talukdars*, former soldiers of the ex-King and *badmashes* roaming the streets plundering and settling old scores. With the ex-King under lock and key in Calcutta, leadership fell to one of his wives, Hazrat Mahal, via her 10-year-old son, Birjis Qadr who – his father still being alive – took the title of Wali (Governor). Hazrat Mahal, who had been sold into the King's household as a child and progressed via dancing girl to concubine and, after the birth of her son, to *mahal* (queen), was a woman of strong character and quickly asserted her dominance in rebel counsels. Her lover was made Minister of Justice, while other posts were shared out between Hindus and Muslims. Perhaps crucially, Barkat Ahmed, who had beaten the British at Chinhut, was bypassed for command of the rebel forces for having backed a rival candidate for Wali. Military command was passed to men of lesser – or no – experience. Failures of leadership – disunity, competition between rival interests and religious groups, the practice among mutinied regiments of electing leaders or governing through soldiers' councils – was a consistent feature of the rebellion, and not just in Oude. Also active and influential in Lucknow at this time was the Maulvi of Faizabad, who calling himself the *khalifat-ullah*, supported the young prince, and soon acquired his own armed following.

By the morning of 2 July the garrison of the Lucknow Residency consisted of 535 men of HM 32nd Foot, 50 men of HM 84th Foot, 89 European gunners, 100 British officers mostly from mutinied sepoy units, 153 civilians and 765 natives, including loyal sepoys and servants. The fortifications basically consisted of a number of domestic dwellings and public buildings – none of them built for military purposes or designed to withstand cannon fire – linked by earthworks. Where possible the buildings were strengthened and windows filled in. L. E. R. Rees described some of the efforts to make such buildings more defensible:

> The splendid library of Captain Hayes, consisting of priceless Oriental manuscripts, and the standard literary and scientific works of every nation of Europe, and dictionaries of every language spoken on earth, from the patois of Bretagne down to the Cingalese, Malay, and ancient Egyptian, were for the nonce converted into barricades. Mahogany tables, valuable pieces of furniture, carriages and carts, were everywhere within our entrenchments taken possession of for the same purpose. The records of the offices, in large boxes, chests of stationery, and whatever else could be laid hold of, were made use of to serve as a cover from the enemy's fire.

Among the non-combatants, wrote Kavanagh, there was great confusion:

> Clothes and furniture were being dragged from room to room – women squabbled for the safest places, distracted by screaming children – loud

orders seemed to come from everyone, and masters and mistresses screamed for servants, who were fast deserting them. Before the fighting began, accommodation was apportioned to families according to their respective positions in life; that is to say, the greatest lady had the most airy and comfortable room; but, when the enemy's artillery and musketry poured in their shot and shell, those places did not always prove the safest, and nearly all changed their residences without distinction – for danger is a great leveller.

From the opening day of the siege the rebels' cannonade was almost continuous. As usual, the rebel artillery was well handled. 'It must be confessed,' wrote Rees, 'that the enemy's artillerists, taught by ourselves, were excellent marksmen. With incredible rapidity, with remarkable ingenuity, and with indomitable perseverance, they had in the very first week, made batteries in positions where one would have fancied their erection impossible – some having actually been moved to the tops of houses, and others placed most cleverly in places where our own batteries could not effectively open on them, and which were well protected from musketry fire.' It was generally believed that some of the artillery commanders were renegade Europeans – one was seen several times laying a gun. Rees thought he knew who they were. 'From the description given me, it is not unlikely that it was either Captain —— or Captain Rotton, who had both remained in the city, and during the disturbances never came near the Residency ... Rotton was a man born in Lucknow, whose daughters were married to Mussulmans, and whose sons served as native officers or troopers in the late king's army. He himself commanded a portion of the ex-king's artillery. Both these persons were said to have adopted the Mohamedan faith.'

The rebel gunners gave early warning of their prowess. On 2 July Henry Lawrence, worn down by the exertions of previous weeks and shattered by the debacle at Chinhut, for which he blamed himself, was resting in his room at Dr Fayrer's House. The previous day the rebels had lobbed a shell into the room, and his aides had urged him to move into the main Residency building. Sir Henry had demurred – quoting the sailors' belief that the safest place on a ship was where the enemy's shot had made the last hole – but finally agreed to move on the following day. At eight o'clock on the morning of the 2nd, while Sir Henry lay on his bed conducting business with his adjutant general, Captain Wilson, an 8-inch shell – fired from the howitzer abandoned at Chinhut – crashed into the room and exploded.

George Lawrence, who was lying near by, was uninjured. Wilson had the shirt torn from his back, but was otherwise unharmed. When he whispered, 'Sir Henry are you hurt?' there was at first no reply. When the enquiry was repeated, Wilson heard Sir Henry whisper – 'I am killed.' Sir Henry was wounded in the thigh and abdomen; amputation was impossible and the doctors saw at once that his wound was mortal. They carried him to a verandah on the north side of the building – the rebels, knowing where the wounded man lay, concentrated their fire there. Despite enemy round shot, and although in great pain, Sir Henry remained lucid for most of the forty-eight hours left him. He appointed Major Banks as his successor, with Brigadier Inglis of the 32nd as military commander. He left his final instructions to the garrison – to conserve ammunition, check all wall firing, spare the Europeans as far as possible from shot and sun, continue to entrench, maintain an inventory of all supplies and food, enrol as many natives as possible for work parties and expel the rest, and turn all horses out of the entrenchment except his own, which was a gift for his nephew. He talked at length of the mistakes that had been made in Oude in alienating the landowners, and of the causes of the Mutiny. At last he took Holy Communion and asked for the following words to be written on his tomb: 'Here Lies Henry Lawrence, who tried to do his duty. May God have mercy on him.' Sir Henry Lawrence died at sunrise on 4 July. Four men of the 32nd were called in to carry his body away – one man lifted the coverlet and all four kissed the dead man's forehead.

The death of Lawrence was yet another blow to the morale of the garrison. As Rees wrote:

> It had not generally been known that our brave old general was dead, for even after he had been buried for some days, the report was circulated that he was getting better. At last, no doubt remained on the minds of any that Sir Henry was indeed no more, and the grief with which the news was received was universal . . . No military honours marked our last acts to his corpse. The times were too stern for idle demonstrations of respect. A hurried prayer, amidst the booming of the enemy's cannon and the fire of their musketry was read over his remains, and he was lowered in the pit with several other, though lowlier, companions of arms.

As well as the constant bombardment of shot and shell, the garrison was subjected to a continuing fusillade as rebel sepoys, landowners and their retinues, town *badmashes* – anyone, in short, who owned a firearm – would wander down to the siege lines to take potshots at the hated 'Fheringees'. 'The mutinous troops,' wrote Lieutenant Birch of the 71st NI, Inglis's ADC, ' – most of whom were Oude men – were living in free quarters in the city, or had gone on short excursions to their homes. They were supplemented by large numbers of the martial population of Oude, matchlock men, and men armed with bows and arrows. Many of their arrows were found in the entrenchment; some had oiled wicks attached to the end, with the intention of setting fire to our grain-stacks, on which the commissariat cattle depended for food.' Under the almost continuous fusillade, casualties mounted. Rees recorded one or two of his lucky escapes: 'At one time a bullet passed through my hat; at another I escaped being shot dead by one of the enemy's best riflemen, by an unfortunate soldier passing unexpectedly before me, and receiving the wound through the temples instead; at another I moved off from a place where in less than the twinkling of an eye afterwards a musket-ball stuck in the wall.' One of the most notorious of the enemy's snipers was an African, nicknamed by the garrison 'Bob the Nailer'. From his post in a chair high up in Johannes's House, outside the walls, this eunuch from the ex-King's harem claimed a victim with every shot he fired from his double-barrelled rifle. Ever-present death made men by turns callous and emotional, as Private Metcalfe saw:

> We had a man by the name of Tomlinson who, when he had his allowance of grog no one could stop his tongue from wagging. So much so that he got the soubriquet of 'Chatter-box'. Well, one day after he had his allowance he must have a look over the parapet to see how his friends the rebels were getting on, and to show your head was to get a bullet through it. Well, this poor individual shewed himself and of course received the usual pill through the head, which of course put an end to his career. Upon this his comrade remarked, 'It serves you jolly well right, you confounded ass. I often told you you would be served like that before you were done and my words have come true.' After considering a while and contemplating the corpse of his comrade he burst out crying and said, 'Well, I am sorry poor Jack. You were as good a comrade as ever a soldier had,' and it was hard to see this generous hearted soldier shed tears. But so it was, from recklessness to tears and from tears to recklessness again, and so on.

The defence was not all passive. On 4 July three Irish soldiers of the 32nd – Privates William Cooney, William Dowling and Michael Smith – accompanied by a number of Volunteers, sallied out from Innes's post and attacked a 9-pounder that the rebels had placed behind a small mosque. It being early afternoon, the rebel gunners were asleep and only the sentries were armed. Rushing the position, bandsman Cooney drove a spike into the gun's vent, Dowling bayoneted an Indian officer and Smith shot and bayoneted two more, before all three ran back unscathed through enemy musket fire. Four days later another sortie – an official one this time – was launched against Johannes's House, again at noon. Fifty men of the 32nd and twenty Sikhs – commanded by Captain Mansfield of the 32nd, with Lieutenant Lawrence and Ensign Studdy – dashed out from the Martinière post under cover of artillery fire from the ramparts and rifle fire from the roof of the Brigade Mess. The house was soon occupied – the plan had been to blow it up, but seeing the enemy gathering beyond, Brigadier Inglis called the men back. They had time before they left, though, to surprise 'Bob the Nailer' – engrossed in his duel with the officers on the Brigade Mess roof – and put him to the bayonet. Fifteen to twenty rebels were killed – one Sikh and one of the 32nd were slightly wounded. Lieutenant Lawrence had one of his trouser legs blown off. Private Cooney was there too, wounded in two places and rewarded by the Brigadier with a tot of brandy. Cooney was to distinguish himself during the siege. Birch wrote of him:

His exploits were marvellous; he was backed by a Sepoy named Kandial, who simply adored him. Single-handed and without any orders, Cuney [*sic*] would go outside our position, and he knew more of the enemy's movements than anyone else. It was impossible to be really angry with him. Over and over again he was put into the guard-room for disobedience of orders, and as often as not let out when there was fighting to be done. On occasion he surprised one of the enemy's batteries, into which he crawled, followed by his faithful Sepoy, bayoneting four men, and spiking the guns. If ever there was a man deserving the V.C. it was Cuney. He seemed to bear a charmed life. He was often wounded, and several times left his bed to volunteer for a sortie. He loved fighting for its own sake.

The fighting was not solely above ground – the mutineers included numbers of British-trained sappers and miners who soon got to work digging tunnels under the Residency. This was a standard practice in siege warfare – the purpose being to dig a tunnel leading to a 'chamber' under an enemy strongpoint, which would be filled with explosives and then blown up as the prelude to an assault. The advent of the rains provided the first evidence, washing away the roofs of several mines, as Lieutenant Birch recorded: 'We had been sure from the sounds heard, and this exposure verified it, that the enemy were undermining us from several directions, especially about the Sikh square, which lay between the brigade mess and Mr Gubbins' house. Our mines were worked so as to meet theirs, and we succeeded on several occasions in breaking into their gallery which we made use of.' The aim of countermining was to destroy the enemy's mines and kill the miners, and some small but brutal fights took place underground. The 32nd, nominally a Cornish regiment, actually contained some Cornishmen – this was by no means always the case with regiments that bore a county name. A number of these men had experience of mining and eight of them, selected by Captain Fulton, the garrison engineer, were soon instructing the men at the various outposts or 'garrisons'. Listening shafts were soon dug at all the most vulnerable outposts – four new enemy galleries were detected and countermining was begun. When enemy miners were detected, Captain Fulton would sit with his revolver waiting for them to break through. One European, enquiring if Fulton was in a particular mine, was told by a sergeant: 'Yes, sir. There he has been for the last two hours, like a terrier at a rat hole, and not likely to leave it either all day.' Most rebel mines were started from nearby buildings, outside the defences, and a number of night raids were organized to clear, and then destroy, these houses. As soon as a house was cleared by the infantry, wrote Birch, 'Captain Fulton appeared on the scene accompanied by a muscular Sikh, Hookum Singh, who could carry a barrel of powder on his back. On several occasions I and my Sikhs formed his escort.' Powder was laid at the columns and corners of the building. 'As soon as the train was laid the order was given to "withdraw the escort." I generally sent it away with the native officer, leaving only sentries to warn us of a rush of the enemy. Then came the second order, "Withdraw the sentries," and with them I used to rush in, leaving Captain Fulton all alone in the enemy's country to fire the train. He returned at full speed and simultaneously came the blow up. I never knew him fail.'

On 20 July the rebels launched their first major assault on the Residency. Wrote L. E. R. Rees,

I was cleaning my musket and whistling a merry air when the cry of 'To arms', and the doubling of men past my little room made me come to a dead halt. In runs a friend, and tells me that the rebels had been seen, assembling in large bodies towards the church side and across the river, and that I had better be off to my post. My preparations were quickly made, but I scarcely had time to put on my belt when a loud explosion shook the earth. I at first imagined that one of our powder-magazines had been blown up, but I soon after learnt that a mine had been sprung by the enemy, near the Redan.

When a mine was blown, infantry waiting in columns of attack would dash through the smoke and storm the wreckage of the enemy's position. If the initial assault was successful, supports would be pushed through to exploit the success. Having exploded their mine, the rebels attacked the Residency at a number of points – to prevent the garrison from rushing men to the threatened sector, in this case the Redan. In Rees's words 'every garrison was now a separate field of battle'. To the British this must have seemed to be the final assault – the all-out, overwhelming, attack that would consign them to the fate of the garrison at Cawnpore. Every able-bodied man now ran to the walls. 'Even of the wounded and the sick many had left their couches, seized any musket they could lay hold of, and fired as often as their strength enabled them to do so. It was indeed heart-rending to see these poor fellows staggering along to the scenes of action, pale, trembling with weakness, and several of them bleeding from their wounds, which reopened by the exertions they had made.'

As Rees rushed to his point of duty, Fayrer's House, the enemy opened up with volley after volley of musketry and a fierce cannonade. The guns of the garrison were not slow in replying. By the time Rees reached Fayrer's House, the rebels were attempting to assault: 'They were mowed down by our grape in scores; and as their leaders advanced, shouting and encouraging their men, they were picked off by our rifles and muskets ... This tremendous fire of musketry and cannon, both from out and in, rendered our position one mass of sulphurous smoke, so that we could scarcely see.' Rees admitted that at first he was almost paralysed with fear: 'I was certain, and I think most of our little handful of men too, that this was our last day upon earth.' Like many soldiers before and since, however, he found that once having arrived at that decision his fear passed. 'As the fire became more and more infernal, and as we saw their men boldly advancing, my fear gave place to a nervous excitement, and at last the desire to kill and to be revenged predominated over every other feeling.' After a while he moved across to the Water Gate battery to see what had happened at the Redan. 'I saw the men still advancing, but evidently not so boldly as before. I picked off a few of them, and then a strange feeling of joy came over me. I no longer thought of myself, but only of the numbers I could kill.'

If the mine had exploded under the Redan, the rebels might indeed have been able to enter the Residency compound and begin their slaughter of the Europeans; but mining was an exact science. If the mine was not in the right place, the resulting smoke and wreckage could prove an obstacle, even a death trap for the assaulting troops. So it proved here – the Redan wasn't damaged. 'Fortunately,' wrote Rees, 'they had miscalculated the distance, and therefore their mine did no damage to us. They were ignorant, however, of this, and fancied they had made a breach, for, owing to the smoke caused by the mine and the fire of our guns and theirs, they could not see before them.' Private Metcalfe was posted at the Redan that morning: 'They miscalculated the distance and a good job for us, for their intention, to use a nautical phrase, was to board us in the smoke. Well, on they came like so many demons in human forms – all round the position with their bands playing all our National airs, their bugles sounding, flags flying, etc. Scores of times they advanced to the charge and of course on each occasion they were beaten back.' 'They doubled up the glacis with bayonets fixed,' wrote Rees, 'covered by the musketry of a regiment or two stationed on the house opposite ... The obstacles in the way, however, checked their advance, and whilst in this plight hundreds were shot down. Still they were unwilling to retreat; one of their leaders waving his sword, on the point of which he had placed his cap, shouted "Come on, my braves". Again they advanced, but again terrible gaps were made in their ranks by our grape, and one of our musket balls killed their leader.'

At Innes's battery the sepoys advanced ahead of their ladder parties, not realizing their mistake until they reached the walls. 'Then only they shouted, "siree layou", "bring the ladders",' wrote Rees. 'The ladders were accordingly brought, but the men who carried them could scarcely make a few paces, when our volunteers and soldiers shot them down. This happened several times, and each shot told and removed three of the number at the same time. For no sooner did one fall than two of his companions, only too glad of an excuse to escape from our well-aimed and murderous fire, carried the body off, and did not return.' Rees's last comment explains the seemingly hard-hearted order given before British assaults that there should be no stopping for the wounded. At another part of Innes's compound was a Volunteer named Bailey, the son of an Indian Christian captain formerly in the King of Oude's service, and two loyal sepoys. The mutineers assumed that Bailey was a Hindu or Muslim and offered him his life if he would desert his post. Rees records the Homeric exchange of insults between Bailey and the rebels as they traded shots:

> 'Come,' cried one of the rebels, who had found shelter in one of a large number of huts, not five yards away from the palisade which Bailey defended, 'come over to us, and leave those cursed Feringhees, whose mothers and sisters we have defiled, and whom we shall kill this day. Come over to us; what have you to do with them? Will you be made a Christian too? (pop) or have you already lost your caste?' 'Take that,' firing his piece, cried Bailey; 'do you think that I have eaten pig's flesh like yourselves. Do you think that I too shall disgrace myself, by proving unfaithful to my salt? Take that thou son of a dog! (pop) Thou whose grandfather's grave I have dishonoured!' (pop) 'Wait, you offspring of a dishonoured mother,' cried another, 'we are coming. I shall just be with you and jump over your wall. My sword is sharp.' 'Is it,' cried Bailey, 'but thy heart is craven. Come along then boaster. My bayonet is ready, scale the wall. We are all prepared, and as for you, I shall catch you on the point of my bayonet. But first here's for you.'

Bailey's post was covered by the guns of the Redan and although he was badly – though not mortally – wounded, his post held.

At the Cawnpore battery the rebels managed to get under the British guns, but were beaten off after about half an hour by improvised hand grenades thrown down on them from above. All around the perimeter – at Sago's House, the Financial, the Brigade Mess and Gubbins' garrison – repeated rebel attacks pressed with great spirit were at length driven off. By four o'clock it was over – British casualties were fifteen Europeans and ten Natives killed – the rebels lost at least a thousand.

The defeat of the rebels on 20 July served in great measure to wipe out from men's minds the memory of Chinhut. Henry Kavanagh noticed the difference at once: 'When I retired to my sick chamber, at the beginning of the month, all was confusion, and success was doubtful: when I issued from it, after the severe fight of the 20th July, in which the defenders fought all day with signal valour, all was cheerfulness and confidence. It pleased me to look on their gallant faces, as they passed to and fro in their clay-stained dresses, with hopeful greetings for each other.' Among the rebels – across Upper India – there were many for whom the current state of anarchy represented an opportunity. The same was true for some on the British side. Henry Kavanagh cheerfully admits to having been glad that the siege had not ended before he was able to win a name for himself:

> The period had, I thought arrived when I might earn a character for devotion to duty equal to that of others. I had always striven to be a good servant, but my assiduity and impetuosity were attributed to selfish ambition, and I gained no credit for my exertions. After more than twenty years of toil my spirits sank at the miserable prospect of a life of drudgery, under the eye of a service that slowly, very slowly recognised any merit not its own. Reader, you may blame the spirit that rejoiced at a revolution which opened a broad field for fair play, if you have never laboured under a despotic rule; but I could not, and did not, attempt to conceal the pleasure which the contemplation of the future now afforded; and I resolved to die in the struggle rather than survive it with no better fame than I took into it.

Others contemplated their mortality in more sombre mood. 'I met with Mrs Martin today,' wrote Julia Inglis in her diary, 'when sitting with Mrs Cowper. She asked me the question which, I fancy, had been much discussed, whether in the event of the enemy getting in, I thought self-destruction would be justifiable. I said what I feel now, that it could not be right, and that I thought, if the time of trial came, our God who sent it would put it into our hearts how to act. They told me several of the ladies had poison at hand.'

'After it had quite terminated,' wrote Rees of the battle on the 20th, 'the rebels sent a flag of truce and begged permission to remove the slain and wounded whom they had not been able to carry away. This permission was readily granted, for their stench might have created a pestilence.' For the British this was a matter of urgency. The compound was rapidly filling with filth, which the occasional rainstorms only partially alleviated. Disease, Rees wrote, was already starting to become a problem: 'The stench from dead horses and bullocks and other animals killed by the enemy's fire, was worse than disagreeable, it was pestilential, and laid the seeds of many diseases from which we afterwards suffered.' It was the children who suffered most. The British cemeteries in India are filled with the graves of babies and infants who died in times of peace. The conditions in Lucknow merely accelerated the process. Henry Kavanagh's family was not untouched by this continuing tragedy:

> Besides the calamities of war, cholera, fever, and small-pox, about the end of July, began to lessen our ranks, and to destroy our children. At one time, there was three young ones lying near me suffering from the latter infectious disease ... Four days' illness killed our youngest daughter, and we were in great anxiety for the others, whom it was impossible to keep away from diseased children. We encouraged our children to play in the open air, exposed to the fire of the enemy, rather than remain in our pestilential quarters; and by the mercy of Providence, they enjoyed better health, in consequence, than most of the youngsters in the garrison.

Rebel cannon, small arms fire, exhaustion, hunger and disease all contributed to a relentless drip-feed of casualties, as revealed in the pages of Mrs Inglis's diary:

> *July 1st* ... Poor Miss Palmer had her leg taken off by a round shot today, she, with some other ladies having remained in the second storey of the Residency house ... *Friday 3rd.* – Miss Palmer died ... *8th* – Mr Polehampton, one of our chaplains, was shot through the body to-day whilst shaving ... *Sunday, 19th* – Mr Arthur, 7th Cavalry, was killed today at the Cawnpore battery. Mr Harmer, 32nd, had his leg fractured by the splint of a table struck by a round shot, which came into the mess-room whilst the officers were at breakfast. I was much shocked this morning at hearing from John that Mr Polehampton the chaplain had been attacked with cholera; he had only just recovered from his wound ... *July 20th* ... Poor Mr Polehampton died today ... *21st* – Major Banks was killed today on the top of the roof of Mr Gubbins' house ... Mrs. Dorrin was killed today at the Gubbins' house ... a very small bullet struck her in the forehead ... *Sunday 26th* – Mr. Lewin, of the artillery, was shot dead at the Cawnpore battery to-day. He left a young widow; their only little girl, one of the prettiest children I have ever seen, had died from cholera at the commencement of the

siege ... *30th* ... Dr Scott told us today that Captain Grant had died from a wound in his hand caused by the bursting of a hand grenade that he was throwing. His wife died from cholera almost the same time; two orphans were left.

On the death of Major Banks – Sir Henry Lawrence's successor as Chief Commissioner – Brigadier Inglis declared military authority to be paramount and took upon himself the chief command, increasing his already heavy load.

'The brigadier ... took measures to render our position, in a sanitary point of view more endurable,' wrote Birch. 'Fatigue parties were told off under cover of the night to bury the dead horses and bullocks that lay strewed about, and which it was impossible to approach by daylight. Many loose animals, maddened by hunger or thirst, had to be secured, or, if wounded, shot down. It was a work of some danger. Officers and volunteers were told off for these duties, as the trained soldiers were mostly kept to their arms.' Conditions within the Residency compound were a shock to those unaccustomed to fending for themselves. 'Many of our servants ... decamped,' wrote Rees,

and left us without food, without clothes, without attendance. The greater portion of them deserted during the first week; and for gentlemen, ladies and children accustomed to all the luxuries and comforts of an Indian life to be thus suddenly thrown upon their own resources, and gradually to be deprived of all conveniences and attendance, was very hard indeed. Many, less fortunate than others, who had been able to retain at least some of their servants, were afterwards obliged to sweep their own rooms, to draw water themselves from the well, to wash their own clothes, to cook their own food, and to perform all the menial duties of a household ... Many were huddled into a large room in common with dozens of other families. All privacy was destroyed, and the houses within the Residency compound resembled small barrack rooms rather than the apartments of respectable families.

Fuel was at a premium. Lieutenant Birch recalled, 'I have seen ladies going out, at the risk of being shot, to pick up sticks.' Clean clothes became a distant memory: 'It was fortunate,' wrote Birch, 'that just before the siege commenced, the whole of the white clothing of the troops had been dyed kharkee, or mud colour, as washermen were conspicuous by their absence. Some of the refugees from the neighbouring stations presented a most ragged appearance. One officer, whose clothes had been torn in the jungle, cut the cloth of the Residency billiard-table, and donned a suit of Lincoln green.'

Flies added to the discomfort and the danger: 'In the day flies,' wrote L. E. R. Rees,

> at night mosquitoes. But the latter were bearable, the former intoler-able. Lucknow had always been noted for its flies, but at no time had they been known to be so troublesome. The mass of putrid matter that was allowed to accumulate, the rains, the stores, the hospital, had attracted these insects in intolerable numbers ... We could not sleep in the day on account of them. We could scarcely eat. Our beef, of which we get a tolerably small quantity every other day is studded with them; and while I eat my miserable dall and roti (boiled lentil soup and unleavened bread), a number of scamps fly into my mouth, or tumble into the plate, *impromptu* peppercorns.

The hospital replicated the worst horrors of the Crimea. 'The upper galleries of the hospital were almost deserted,' wrote Henry Kavanagh, 'being exposed to the shot of the enemy. The rooms on the ground floor were low, dark, narrow, ill-ventilated, and unbearable from the stench of sloughing wounds and other causes, and could not be cleaned as often as necessary. The servants had deserted and no one could be spared from duty.' There were one or two *dhobi-wallahs* who, working without soap and for an exorbitant wage, made an effort at washing sheets and linen, but they were overwhelmed with work. Boys from the Martinière (the local British public school) were employed in the losing battle to keep the flies off the sick. Rees was horrified at what he saw when visiting sick comrades:

> Everywhere wounded officers and men were lying on couches, covered with blood, and often with vermin. The apothecaries, hospital attend-ants, and servants, were too few in number, and with all their activity could not attend to everybody; and as for a change of linen, where was that to come from? ... Many of the wounded were lying groaning upon mattresses and cloaks only. Everywhere cries of agony were heard, piteous exclamations for water or assistance. The fumigations to which recourse was had were not sufficient to remove the disagreeable, fetid

smell which pervaded the long hall of the sick, and the air in it was pestilential and oppressive.

Few places within the Residency were entirely safe from the enemy's almost constant fire, and the hospital was no exception. Shells and round shot claimed victims among the wounded and their attendants. The presence near by of some high-profile prisoners, wrote Birch, did eventually improve matters. 'The native prisoners that we had, princes of the royal houses of Delhi and Oude, were confined in the banqueting hall, a part of which was also used as a hospital, and their presence, as soon as it was known, saved our sick and wounded from being fired on.' The hospital windows were barricaded and only the doors at the extreme ends – facing the Residency building itself and the Baillie Guard – could be opened to admit light and what passed for fresh air.

A foul miasma hung over the whole compound. Birch recalled that: 'The bad smells from imperfectly buried bodies was horrible; the want of change of diet was beginning to be felt, and in addition to other diseases cholera, small-pox, and especially scurvy, began to be fearfully prevalent. We lost several fine fellows from these diseases, who had escaped the enemy's fire. Scurvy took the form of loose teeth, swollen heads, and boils, and gained the name of garrison disease.'

'Dysentery and diarrhoea,' wrote Rees, 'swelled the numbers in hospital almost as much as the balls of the enemy. The exposure we all had at last affected the majority of all of us. Though all did not go into the hospital, many were ailing at their posts, or in the apartments, and the bad food we had to swallow did little towards invigorating us.'

'All had to undergo the hardships of bad cooking and coarse food,' wrote Birch. 'The boys of the Martiniere College, and such servants as were left, helped to grind the corn with the hand-mills used in India for this purpose, and an officer was detailed to overlook the labour and prevent waste and peculation. Nothing was thrown away. The full rations at first starting were a pound of meat and a pound of flour per man; this was reduced to twelve ounces, then to six.'

Under the pressure of rationing, loyalties became strained. Quite early in the siege Private Henry Metcalfe of the 32nd was seated on the verandah of the house where he was stationed.

A gentleman came out of the house and held a beautiful white terrier dog by a chain. He asked one of our men if he would shoot the dog as he had not the wherewithal to feed the dog . . . This man (I mean the soldier) said he would shoot the dog as he wanted to empty his piece for the purpose of cleaning it, and he would have done it had I not interposed and asked the gentleman if he would let me have the dog to keep, and he said I would not be able to keep him as my allowance was too little for myself. I replied it did not matter, I would share my little allowance if he would let me have it. He consented, and the dog's life was spared, and a valuable one it proved to me.

The dog belonged to Reverend Harris and his wife, who, delighted at the offer to save its life, promised to Metcalfe that 'anything he could do for me he would'. The clergyman, clearly expecting to be asked for help gaining a position in civilian life after the siege, was amused when Metcalfe asked him for a pipe. This proving unobtainable he procured instead a box of cigars. 'After this,' wrote Metcalfe, 'the dog accompanied me wherever I went, both day and night, and indeed, it was a good job on some occasions, for when on sentry at night and when the least sign of drowsiness came over me, the dog was sure to notice it and catch my trousers between his teeth and shake me to keep me awake, for it was very hard indeed to keep from getting drowsy considering being belted and under arms day and night.'

'Members of the different garrisons rarely left their posts,' wrote Birch, 'and then only at night when they could not see. The cook-boys had to take the men's dinners to the various garrisons, and many were shot.' Only the cook-boys and the staff, he added, really knew their way around the entrenchments. 'Once by day and once by night the brigadier went his rounds. Captain Wilson, adjutant-general, went round also, and I had to go at daylight every morning to collect the reports of the casualties of the previous night, so that the garrison was always kept on the alert. Had it been otherwise, a moment's carelessness might have been our ruin.' The aim of Inglis's defensive plan was to keep the trained soldiers under cover in positions they knew well. 'The constant brigade order was to keep under cover, always be on the alert, and never to fire unless you could see your man. This saved a great deal of ammunition, and on occasions of attack enabled us to give the enemy a warm reception.'

Duty in the outposts and batteries seemed preferable to many who, under normal circumstances, would have been deemed too sick for work. Fit at last, Henry Kavanagh threw himself into his duties, eager for the recognition he felt had, so far in life, eluded him: 'I hoped to secure the management of the mortars on a vacancy occurring, but there were others, with more right to that honour, and quite as much zeal as myself, who coveted that distinguished duty, and it consequently never fell to me. In all sieges, excepting in making and resisting assaults, musketry does little execution, and our extraordinary success against the hordes who surrounded us, is attributable to the perfection of the artillery, and the zeal of the officers, soldiers, and volunteers of that arm.' Because of their exposed positions, casualties in the batteries were heavy.

> Every officer was either killed or wounded, and to supply their places, several officers of the native infantry, whose men had mutinied, some civil engineers, and some gentlemen of independent means, who had come to visit the country, were trained in artillery drill and so proficient did they become that each in turn came to be trusted with a command. Two or three – Lieutenant Ward, Mr Macrae, Mr Lucas, and Mr Cameron – especially distinguished themselves. The first two were skilled in throwing shells, a difficult task, as the enemy being so close to us, it required great care to prevent the shell exploding in our own lines. Bits constantly came singing back to us.

Among the infantrymen-turned-gunners was Henry Metcalfe, who during one engagement learned of the Royal Artillery's prejudice against 'bobbing':

> On this occasion we had only ... one man of the Artillery. His name was Barry, which bespeaks his nationality. The bullets were whizzing both thick and fast and the men were ducking from them, although when the whizz of a bullet is passed that bullet is passed also, but indeed he must be a very self-possessed man who will not duck his head occasionally. However, this old Artillery man rebuked the lads for ducking so to musket shots. He said you should never duck to anything under a 9 pound shot. While he was going on at this rate a fine young Grenadier was shot through the head with a musket ball. This hardened old gunner made remark – 'Ha, that fellow has ducked to a musket ball at all events,' and he said, if ever I am killed in action, I hope it will be from a cannon ball and right in the head. I need not say his death was soon and sudden.

When not at his battery, Henry Kavanagh spent long hours on the rooftop of his dwelling watching – like many others around the perimeter – the activities of the enemy, and recording their movements in a book. It was hazardous duty, exposed to enemy artillery and sharpshooters, but the reports compiled often gave advance warning of an attack. Kavanagh's example of a typical report gives a good picture of the variety of forces arrayed against the British at Lucknow:

> A large body of infantry, with six standards, gone from left to right. – A long line of matchlock-men, with numerous green and red colours, gone in the same direction, – in all about six thousand. – About five hundred cavalry, regular and irregular, preceded by drums, apparently escorting men of rank mounted on elephants; swordsmen mixed with bowmen following for about ten minutes. – Two brass guns, seemingly twelve-pounders, drawn by bullocks, and escorted by infantry and cavalry went by at a trot – two small horse artillery guns, and wagons, pulled by bullocks. – A small party of regular cavalry, some in grey uniform, escorting a man of consequence, preceded by drums and two standards. – Several dhoolies. – More infantry and matchlock men in irregular order, and a long line of running swordsmen and archers.

Camraderie helped to pass the time: 'We spent some of the time there in reading, composing satirical rhymes reflecting on the idle and selfish, and scratching caricatures of each other upon the walls at the top of the staircase: where we took shelter from rain and sun, when nothing remarkable was happening … We bore the twits and fancies of each other with temper, and many a joyous moment have we passed together amidst the patter of bullets, the bursting of shells, and the accompaniments of noise, dust and smoke.'

During this opening month of the siege, the garrison was not entirely cut off from the outside world. A number of native messengers had been sent out with despatches for Allahabad, but none returned and their fate is unknown. Some of the Sikh troopers seemed to be in constant touch with the besieging rebels and via them some news filtered back to the British officers – but it was mostly gossip and rumour, much of it merely local. Far more reliable was one of the pensioned sepoys that Lawrence had recalled. This man – Angad, or Ungud – proved able to slip through the rebel lines at will. On 29 June he had been sent out in the direction of Cawnpore – he returned thirteen days later with the news that the

Nana Sahib had been defeated, and that he had, with his own eyes, seen British troops at Cawnpore. This, the first good news the garrison had heard, prompted a series of communications – in a mixture of English, Latin and French, written in the ancient Greek alphabet – between Brigadier Inglis and General Havelock. On 22 July Angad was sent to Havelock bearing a letter from Inglis giving the current strength of the garrison and concluding, 'Aid is what we want, and that quickly. Our defences are straggling, and our numerical strength quite inadequate to man them. Our artillery is weak, and the casualties heavy.' Late at night on the 25th Angad reappeared – bearing a letter from Colonel Fraser-Tytler, Havelock's deputy assistant quartermaster general. While Angad gave to a waiting crowd the mixed news of the Nana's defeat, and the massacre of the women and children at the Bibighar, Inglis read Fraser-Tytler's letter. In it he promised that 'in five or six days we shall meet'. So relief was on the way, and soon. Morale in the garrison revived, but the five or six days passed without sight or sound of a relieving column. On everyone's lips was now the question – Where is Havelock?

Victorious over the Nana, possessed, though too late, of Cawnpore, Havelock had found himself out on a limb. At Bithur was the still dangerous Nana Sahib with forces more numerous than his own. In front of him – across the Ganges – was the wholly hostile province of Oude, with the beleaguered garrison of Lucknow, 45 miles away, the sole remaining British presence. To his left rear, at Kalpi – also 45 miles away – the Gwalior contingent was concentrating. This force – part of the personal army of the young Maharajah Scindia of Gwalior – was a British-officered force of four field batteries, a siege train, two regiments of cavalry and seven of infantry. The contingent – considered among the best Native troops in India – had mutinied on 14 June, and although the Maharajah had remained loyal to the British, it had remained under arms and was now marching with the aim of joining the Nana Sahib.

Even with Neill's reinforcements Havelock's force was now reduced to 1,500 effectives, of whom only 1,200 were Europeans. It was barely strong enough to consider holding Cawnpore – let alone advancing on Lucknow. Nevertheless, no doubt driven on by what he had seen in the Bibighar, Havelock determined to attempt a relief of the garrison there. If certain precautions were taken, he reasoned, such an attempt – backed by the reinforcements that were coming into Calcutta – might yet succeed.

His first precaution was to send Major Stephenson to destroy the Nana

Sahib's capital at Bithur. Stephenson burned the Nana's palace, blew up the magazine and brought back twenty guns that the Nana had abandoned. In the meantime, Havelock completed work on a fortification near the banks of the river for the three hundred men he intended leaving as a garrison under Neill. On 21 August he sent his guns across the Ganges, his infantry followed over the next few days and on the 25th Havelock himself moved with the force to Mangalwar, 5 miles on the road to Lucknow, where he spent the next three days organizing transport for his force. On the 28th his column began its first advance – sixty Volunteer cavalry and ten guns, and an infantry force of about 1,100 drawn from HM 64th, HM 84th, the 78th Highlanders, the Madras Fusiliers and Brayser's Sikhs. The following day – after a 3-mile march – the column found the enemy in force at Unao, and dislodged them, killing five hundred and capturing fifteen guns. Six miles further on they found a larger rebel force in a stronger position in the town of Bashiratganj.

Bashiratganj was a walled town through which the main road to Lucknow ran via its turreted gateway. It had strong walled defences fronted by a water-filled ditch. In front of that was a large *jhil*, with another behind the town along which the road to Lucknow continued over a narrow causeway. Havelock determined to send the 64th on a wide flanking movement to block the causeway in the enemy's rear, while he attacked frontally with the rest of his force. In the event the turning movement took longer than anticipated, with the result that the enemy, defeated in front, were able to escape across the causeway.

Taking stock of the situation after the action at Bashiratganj, Havelock found that the two actions fought so far had cost him eighty-eight men killed or wounded. He now had the same number of sick – he had insufficient transport to carry them forward with him, and insufficient men to guard them if he left them behind. Moreover, he had used up one-third of his artillery ammunition, had advanced only 15 of the 45 miles to Lucknow, and disturbing news had come in of a rising of sepoys at Dinapore. With unknown numbers of rebels operating in his rear, Havelock decided to fall back – on 31 July – to Mangalwar, from where he wrote to Neill informing him of the move and stating his opinion that relief of Lucknow would not be possible without reinforcements of at least one thousand men and another battery of artillery.

In spite of – or perhaps because of – a similarity of temperament, Neill and Havelock had never got on. Neill's reply to this letter brought their relations to crisis point. 'I deeply regret that you have fallen back one foot,' he wrote. 'The effect on our prestige is very bad indeed.' Neill went on to say that the natives would believe he had been forced back and added that once some iron guns and the men escorting them arrived, 'you ought to advance again and not halt until you have rescued, if possible, the garrison at Lucknow'. Havelock wrote a blistering reply: 'I do not want and will not receive any advice from an officer under my command, be his experience what it may. Understand this distinctly; and that a consideration of the obstruction that would arise to the public service at this moment alone prevents me from taking the stronger step of placing you under arrest.'

Even so, perhaps stung by Neill's reply, Havelock marched – without reinforcements – on 4 August. By the 5th he was once more in Bashiratganj – once more the town was taken and once more the rebels escaped, only to take up an even stronger position further down the road. After this second battle, F. C. Maude was called to Havelock's tent: 'Havelock asked me if I "knew how to blow a man from a gun?" Naturally this had not formed part of our *curriculum* at Woolwich; but I had no hesitation at once in answering in the affirmative.' Havelock told him that he would send him a man that evening – Maude thought the man had been taken as a spy. Blowing from guns was not a method of execution normally favoured by Havelock – probably on the Nicholsonian principle of economy of powder – so perhaps he felt the need to make an example. A large crowd of officers and men gathered to watch the execution that evening. As Maude recorded:

> The first man led out was a fine-looking Sepoy, with good features, and bold resolute expression. He begged that he might not be bound, but this could not be allowed, and I had his wrists tied tightly, each to the upper part of a wheel of the gun. Then I depressed the muzzle, until it pointed to the pit of his stomach, just below the *sternum*. We put no shot in, and I only kept one gunner (besides the 'firing No.') near the gun, standing myself about ten feet to the left rear. The young Sepoy looked undauntedly at us during the whole process of pinioning: indeed he never flinched for a moment. Then I ordered the port-fire to be lighted, and gave the word 'Fire!' There was a considerable recoil from the gun, and a thick cloud of smoke hung over us. As this cleared away, we saw two legs lying in front of the gun; but no other sign of what had, just before, been a human being and a brave man. At this

moment perhaps from six to eight seconds after the explosion . . . down fell the man's head among us, slightly blackened, but otherwise scarcely changed. It must have gone straight up into the air, probably about 200 feet. The pent-up feelings of the bystanders found vent in a loud gasp, like ah-h! Then many of them came across the ditch to inspect the remains of the legs, and the horrible affair was over.

Later, wrote Maude,

> I became aware that I was covered, from head to foot, at least in front, with minute blackened particles of the man's flesh, some of it sticking in my ears and hair. My white silk coat, puggree, belt, etc., were also spotted in this sickening manner. As I announced the execution to Havelock, I called his attention to the state I was in. He came through his tent door, and, striking a sort of tragic attitude of horror, said, in a stage voice, 'Improving' Shakespeare: – 'E'en such a man, in such a plight, Drew Priam's curtains in the dead of night, And told him that a man was slain!' Always ready-witted was the old General!

By now it had become clear to Havelock that the force that had been inadequate to effect a relief only days earlier was no better able to do so now. Advised by his staff – foremost among them Fraser-Tytler, Crommelin and his own son, Henry – he fell back once more, reaching Mangalwar on the 10th. Hearing of a large gathering at Bashiratganj he marched there once more – keen to inflict a telling blow before retreating – and captured the town a third time, killing two hundred rebels and capturing two guns. There was no escaping the fact, however, that the column had failed in its intended purpose. Recrossing the Ganges on 13 August Havelock learned, on entering Cawnpore, that the reinforcements he had been relying on were to be denied him.

Five days later, in Lucknow, Mrs Inglis was awakened by 'an explosion, which our now practised ears knew at once to be a mine blowing up'. No doubt encouraged by Havelock's withdrawal across the Ganges, the rebels had determined on an all-out assault on the Residency. Hearing the mine go up, wrote Lieutenant Birch, 'We hastily buckled on our arms, which lay by our side; our boots we never took off. The reserve of the 84th was immediately called to arms, and as their officer, Lieutenant O' Brien, was wounded, the brigadier sent me in command.' A breach had been blown in the entrenchments by Sikh Square: 'It is believed that the tramping of the horses of the Sikh cavalry, who suffered dreadfully from the flies, had prevented the underground operations of the enemy being heard. On previous occasions our countermines had been successfully worked, and danger averted, and it seemed strange that in spite of all our precautions a gallery should have been pushed so far.' Lieutenants Mecham and Soppitt and Captain Orr were blown up as well as Band Sergeant Curtain who was blown outside the entrenchments and killed by the advancing enemy. Six drummers and a sepoy were buried in the remains. The remaining drummers and the Sikh cavalrymen abandoned the outer wall, leaving their weapons, and fell back to an inner wall parallel to it. The rebels were running into Sikh Square as Birch arrived with the men of the 84th. 'The outer square had been abandoned, some of the enemy had come in over the breach, and a fine native officer of the irregular cavalry was seen leading them on. A short and well-sustained fire from the brigade-mess took them in front, and considerably dampened their ardour. The native officer was shot within our defences, and this was the first and only time that the foot of the foe ever came within our crumbling but well-contested fortifications. There is no doubt this was the best chance the enemy ever had of getting in.' The breach was large with good cover close by and offered the rebels a way into the heart of the British position. Brigadier Inglis was soon on the spot, bringing up two guns to cover the outer square. 'I think these arrangements, which could plainly be seen by them, deterred the enemy from making any further advance,' wrote Birch. The Sikhs' horses in the centre of the square suffered badly from the fire of both sides, 'What was more harrowing to our feelings,' continued Birch,

> was the sight of the struggles made by the unfortunate drummers entangled in the debris of the morning's explosion. It was useless to send any party forward as they would instantly have been shot; but one man, a comrade, was allowed to steal forward and see what could be done. He came back and said that one drummer was alive with a beam across his chest, and he wanted a saw to release him ... As soon as the drummer returned with the saw, another attempt was made; but by this time the enemy observed our movements, and a shot turned the drummer back.

The fighting was at close range. 'We found holes dug through the outer walls that remained standing, and hands intruded trying to pick out the muskets and swords abandoned in the morning. I had five shots with revolver at one of these holes, through which protruded a man's hand, and I think I hit him, as he gave up his attempt.' In the evening shutters were procured from the windows of the Residency house and under cover of these, men of the 84th and a group of officers, including Birch, advanced down both sides of the square. 'Only one shot was fired as we advanced. I put my shutter down into the hole where we had seen the poor drummer struggling: he was quite dead, and his body, with those of the other poor fellows, formed the foundation of the barricade which we hastily constructed across the breach. It was soon fairly strong, and we then regained the ground we had lost in the morning.' Later that evening, wrote Julia Inglis, her husband led a small party out against a rebel outpost: 'Calling on Mr McCabe, 32nd to follow him with a hand-grenade, he advanced beyond our position to that occupied by the enemy. Suddenly they came to a door leading into a house; a sentry was posted there with a *tulwar* (sword) in his hand. John fired; his pistol snapped. Mr McCabe threw his hand-grenade, and the man fled; then John called out, "32nd follow me!" The men ... quickly obeyed the summons. The enemy fled without attempting opposition, and two barrels of gunpowder being sent for, the place was blown up.'

On 28 August Inglis received another letter from Havelock – brought in by the tireless Angad, who was earning £500 a trip – informing them that he was expecting reinforcements within twenty to twenty-five days, and that at that point he would make Lucknow his priority. He ended on the ominous note: 'Do not negotiate, but rather perish sword in hand.'

'My first thoughts were, "All is over with us, we can't hold out till then." But John seemed more hopeful, and said our provisions would last; still it was a gloomy prospect, and we hardly dared look forward.' The strain was taking its toll on her husband, as his ADC Lieutenant Birch noted: 'The prolonged suspense and terrible heat had their effect upon the brigadier, who was far from well; his hair turned quite grey during the siege and therein no doubt the responsibility was awful. His words and presence were most encouraging, and his example had the best effect in keeping good heart in all.' Good heart was needed now – on the 28th came a further communication from the relieving force holding out the prospect of relief within another twenty-five days. Hope deferred made some hearts sicken – on 5 September Mrs Inglis wrote in her diary: 'Captain Graham committed suicide today by shooting himself in bed; he left a young widow.' On that same day the rebels made another assault in which the loyal sepoys of the 13th NI, led by Lieutenant Aitken – fighting against their own regimental comrades – distinguished themselves. For the rest of the month the rebels contented themselves with maintaining their fire with cannon and small arms against the compound.

Among the wives of the men of the 32nd – as every schoolboy once knew – was a young corporal's wife by the name of Jessie Brown. One night in late September Jessie lay consumed with fever wrapped in a plaid, asking those round her to be awakened when 'her father returned from the ploughing'. As her companions listened to the sound of rebel cannonading, Jessie suddenly awoke, stood, and appeared to be listening intently. 'Dinna ye hear it? Dinna ye hear it?' she cried. 'Ay I'm no dreamin', it's the slogan of the Highlanders! We're saved, we're saved.' Her companions listened too, but heard only musketry and cannon. Jessie was insistent, 'Hark to the slogan – to the McGregor, the grandest o' them a'. Here's help at last!' Her companions strained to hear anything above the noise, but to no avail, while Jessie raved on 'Will ye no believe it noo? ... the Campbells are comin'. D'ye hear, d'ye hear?' At last, however, ears that had listened for weeks in vain for the sound of the relieving force heard from within the city the unmistakable sound of bagpipes. It is one of the great symbolic moments in the history of the British Empire, commemorated in the painting 'Jessie's Dream' by Fredrick Goodall. Sadly the story of Jessie Brown is now generally agreed to be a myth – but like most myths it contained an essential truth. They were coming.

Back in Cawnpore, Havelock rested his troops for two days before marching to Bithur on 16 August, where some four thousand sepoys had gathered in his absence. After a hard day's fighting this force was dispersed with the loss of two guns, but Havelock's own losses were sixty, including twelve from sunstroke. The following day Havelock learned, via the *Calcutta Gazette*, that Sir James Outram had been given the command at Cawnpore. Returned to Cawnpore once more Havelock, having reviewed his position there, wrote to the Commander-in-Chief at Calcutta that he could not be confident of holding Cawnpore unless he was substantially reinforced. Sir Colin Campbell – who had become commander-in-chief on 17 August – wrote to Havelock telling him to stay.

Since 3 August reinforcements had, in fact, been arriving. Sent ahead of him by Sir James Outram were HM 5th Fusiliers and Eyre's battery of

18-pounder guns. Outram himself arrived at Cawnpore on 16 September, bringing with him HM 90th Light Infantry. Major General Sir James Outram GCB, of the Madras Army, had been recalled by Lord Canning from Persia, where he had been in command of the expeditionary force. He had distinguished himself in Afghanistan, among the savage Bhils in Khandesh, and in Scinde, where his commander, General Sir Charles Napier, described him – in a reference to the chivalric French hero – as 'The Bayard of India'. There was no question that Havelock had been removed from command through official dissatisfaction – Outram had been appointed to command the Cawnpore and Dinapore divisions, which posts Havelock had never held. If he harboured any resentment at being denied the prize for which he had laboured so hard, the pill was sweetened by an extraordinary – even, Bayard-like – gesture on Outram's part. Recognizing that Havelock had made a noble attempt at relieving Lucknow and that, had he then had the fresh troops now in Cawnpore, he would have been able to accomplish it, Outram resolved to allow Havelock the honour of completing the task. To this end he announced that he would 'waive' his military rank until Lucknow was relieved, would accompany Havelock's column as Chief Commissioner of Oude, and in the meantime serve Havelock as a Volunteer.

When Sir Colin Campbell described Outram's act as one of 'disinterested generosity' he knew what he was saying. As well as the glory of relieving Lucknow, Havelock stood to gain the lion's share of the £250,000 of public money in the Residency – which would then become prize money – that would otherwise have fallen to Outram. Such an action was not entirely unprecedented – in the First Sikh War Sir Henry Hardinge, the Governor General, had placed himself as second-in-command to Sir Hugh Gough. It had not worked then, and it did not now. It was not long before Outram was disagreeing with Havelock over whether to divide the force into 'wings' or 'brigades', countermanding his orders to cross the Ganges, and generally interfering to such an extent that the younger Havelock described it as 'anarchy' and threatened to quit the staff and join the Volunteer cavalry. It was young Havelock's opinion that Sir James had only offered to serve as a Volunteer in order to get the Victoria Cross – no doubt by placing himself in a prominent position at the head of somebody else's regiment, as he had done. The elder Havelock, however, refused to bring the issue to a head, and it continued to add to his difficulties.

The force now at Havelock's disposal amounted to 3,179 men of all arms, divided into two infantry brigades, an artillery brigade and a small cavalry force. The 1st Brigade, commanded by Brigadier Neill, consisted of the Madras Fusiliers, HM 5th Foot, HM 84th and two companies of HM 64th; the 2nd Brigade, commanded by Colonel Hamilton of the 78th with the rank of brigadier, was made up of the 78th Highlanders, HM 90th and Brayser's Sikhs. There were three batteries of artillery – Maude's, Olpherts' and Eyre's 18-pounders, a total of eighteen guns – and the cavalry, understrength as usual, amounted to 109 Volunteers and fifty-nine Native horsemen of the 12th Irregulars.

Leaving Colonel Wilson and the headquarters of the 64th, together with small parties of convalescents, to hold Cawnpore, the force crossed the Ganges on 19 September. It found the enemy entrenched with six guns at Mangalwar, with their right anchored on a village. Havelock threw the bulk of his force against the enemy left while the guns pounded their centre. The 90th cleared the village, upon which the rebel centre – menaced by the advancing Fusiliers – retreated down the Lucknow road, pursued by Barrow's cavalry. Foremost in this pursuit was Havelock himself, and the 'volunteer' Sir James Outram, laying about him with his malacca cane. Plunging into a formed body of sepoys beyond the village, they chased them as far as Bashiratganj – the scene of three previous fights, killing over a hundred. Here, confronted by an earthwork armed with two guns, they charged. Barrow and his men rode over the earthwork, sabring the gunners and capturing the regimental colour of the 1st BNI – the principal actors in the Cawnpore massacres. At last Havelock had something approaching a cavalry force to exploit the victories won by his guns and infantry, but, as Maude pointed out, pursuing flying sepoys was a hazardous business.

> The Infantry Sepoys, who were as lithe and active as cats, especially the Oude men, when pursued by our Cavalry, used to fling themselves on the ground, and then, as the horse jumped over or passed close to them, they would make an upward cut with their razor-edged scimitars, which seldom failed to take effect, either upon the horse or its rider. 'Peter' Wilkin, who had previously taken part in the Balaklava Charge while serving in the 11th Hussars, was lamed for life ... in this manner; the sword slicing clean through his boot and deep into the ball of his foot.

The General himself could testify to this. 'The moment the charge was over,' wrote Maude, 'Havelock rode straight up to my guns, his horse bleeding copiously from four or five tulwar cuts. As the poor beast commenced to stagger, the General quickly dismounted saying to me, with a proud but melancholy intonation: "That makes the sixth horse I have had killed under me!" and, sure enough, the animal died in a few minutes.' Meanwhile, the column had been delayed by a single casualty. 'One of the fine elephants with Eyre's battery,' wrote Maude, 'had the lower part of its trunk carried clean away by a round-shot, and the poor, wounded, terrified beast came charging amongst the battery in a very uncomfortable and dangerous manner.' Its screams so disconcerted the other elephants that they refused to budge an inch further – the column trudged on, pulled by the less sensitive bullocks. 'It afterwards completely recovered,' wrote Maude, 'although the dimensions of its trunk had been reduced, so to speak to those of a Gladstone bag.'

The next day they reached the bridge over the Sai at Bani that – no doubt deeming the city of Lucknow itself eminently defensible – the rebels had neglected to destroy, and now failed to defend. Crossing the bridge and camping for the night on the far bank the column fired a royal salute with the guns to indicate to the defenders that help was near at hand. On the morning of 23 September the force awoke with Lucknow just 16 miles away and the prospect of a hard day's fighting ahead of it. The fact that there came from Lucknow no sound of guns cannonading the Residency indicated that all the rebels' efforts would now be directed to the defence of the city. For the first 10 miles of the advance – splashing down the water-logged road – there was no sign of the enemy, but as Neill's brigade approached the walled garden of the Alam Bagh (Garden of the World), 5 miles south-east of the Residency (see map 6 on page xx) enemy infantry were spotted on their flanks. Soon a defence line extending over 2 miles, manned by 10,000 sepoys, was discerned. Its right and centre were behind mounds, and its left was anchored on the Alam Bagh itself – a royal summerhouse and mosque, standing in a 500-yard square garden surrounded by high walls. The enemy's batteries were observed in a tope of trees in front of the enemy centre and left – and from the accuracy of their opening salvo it was clear that they had certain ranges marked out on the ground. Eyre's heavy guns were soon directing their fire upon this battery, while Olpherts' battery – making its way over very rough ground – moved to a flank and opened up on the enemy from their right. Under this crossfire the enemy's centre-left soon gave way – Lieutenant Johnson and some Native horsemen capturing a 9-pounder and sabring its gunners – but the

Alam Bagh held firm, with two guns firing from embrasures in the wall.

To storm this position Neill sent in a wing of the 5th Fusiliers. The men dashed forward into the teeth of the enemy fire and were soon fighting around the guns. As they did so, the 78th Highlanders stormed the main gate and came to their aid, attacking the enemy from the rear. The Madras Fusiliers were close behind, and within ten minutes the Alam Bagh was cleared. The rebels – fleeing down the road into the city – were pursued by Barrow's cavalry and Sir James Outram as far as the Yellow House, close to the Char Bagh (Four Gardens) Bridge (see map 6 on page xx), which they found to be strongly defended. Riding back with the cavalry Outram was handed a despatch informing him that Delhi had fallen. Riding over to Havelock he informed him and then – bareheaded – announced the good news to the cheering troops.

The next day – the 24th – the men rested and dried their clothes, while Havelock made plans for a final assault on the 25th. The rebels kept up a constant artillery fire, but Havelock drew his line back so as to be out of range. Two and a half miles south of the Residency a canal runs east–west that, with the river Gumti, virtually encircles the city. It is curious that the rebels – as at the Sai – had neglected to destroy the canal bridges, preferring to trust in firepower and entrenchment. The road from Cawnpore – on which Havelock's army now rested – crosses it at the Char Bagh Bridge. On the direct route from the bridge to the Residency, the streets had been entrenched and the houses loopholed – any direct advance could expect to meet strong resistance. Havelock's plan, therefore, was to force the bridge, then follow the line of the canal round to the right until within striking distance of the Residency, before turning left and fighting through the palaces and bazaars to link up with the garrison. Accordingly at half past eight on the morning of the 25th, the advance was sounded and the 1st Brigade advanced towards the Yellow House with Maude's battery leading. The original plan had been for the 2nd Brigade to lead the way, giving the task of heading the advance to Olpherts' Bengal Horse Artillery. 'As I knew very well that the rebels had been trying the range during a great part of the day, I looked forward with no little curiosity to see what sort of practice the Bengal gunners would make of it in the morning and entertained a very sincere hope that they would take the edge off it, so to speak, before we, with the first Brigade, appeared on the scene. It was, therefore, much to our disgust that, at day-dawn on the 25th September, the orders were suddenly changed, and the post of honour was given to the Royal gunners.' As

Maude rode down the road his superior, Major Cooper – commanding all the artillery in Havelock's force – gave him a disconcerting send-off: 'He called out to me: Good-bye, old fellow! A somewhat uncomfortable salutation, which I can only explain as the result of a foreboding of his coming death. A few hours later he was shot through the head.' It may have been a premonition – such things are common enough before battle – but it may have been an unconscious reflection on what awaited Maude and his men. The bridge was well defended on both banks of the canal. As they moved down towards the bridge, wrote Maude, 'For a few seconds the enemy reserved their fire, and then they let us have it, hot and heavy. A battery on each flank managed to pop a round-shot in among us now and then; but the heaviest fire came from two guns, which were loaded in the lane behind the Yellow House, and then run out on the main road, carefully laid, and admirably served. Meantime, there were large bodies of Infantry on both sides of the road, in the cornfields, and among the gardens, from behind the walls of which they kept up a well-directed fire.' Notwithstanding a bullet-wound to the arm, Outram led the 5th Fusiliers to try and clear the Char Bagh garden with a view to opening a flanking fire on the defenders of the bridge. Maude's gunners engaged the enemy on the bridge, while to their left twenty-five men of the Madras Fusiliers, under Lieutenant Arnold, attempted with their Enfields to suppress the musketry from the houses on the far bank. The remainder of the Madras Fusiliers were held 300 yards to the rear, lying down behind a bend in the road, until the moment came to charge.

The Char Bagh Bridge was blocked by an earth rampart 7 feet high with a gap in the middle wide enough for only one man to pass. On the parapet of the earthwork were six guns, two of them 24-pounders. In the initial artillery duel, then, the advantage – both in weight of shot and position – lay with the rebels and Maude's gunners were soon dropping fast.

The finest soldier in our Battery, and the best Artilleryman I have ever known, Sergeant-Major Alexander Lamont, had the whole of his stomach carried away by a round-shot. He looked up to me for a moment with a piteous expression, but had only strength to utter two words, 'Oh God!' when he sank to the ground. Just then another round-shot took off the leg, high up on the thigh, of the next senior Sergeant, John Kiernan; he was afterwards carried back to the Alam Bagh, but soon died from the shock. Kiernan was an excellent specimen of a Roman Catholic, North of Ireland soldier. He was true as steel.

Moments later a young gunner had his head taken off and 'for about a second the body stood straight up, surmounted by the red collar, and then fell flat on the ground'. Maude asked repeatedly for permission to advance – at closer range Maude's guns could at last do some damage – if they survived. Watching Maude's guns deploy was Captain Frederick Willis of the 84th:

I never shall forget seeing the two leading guns unlimber, and come into action on the road at very close range (150 yards) opposite the Char Bagh (Bridge) under a murderous fire from the enemy's guns in position on the further side of the bridge ... The first discharge from one of the enemy's guns disabled one of Maude's guns, the greater part of the detachment serving it being either killed or wounded. It was then I offered to assist him, by calling for volunteers from the Regiment, many men of which, for some time, whilst lying inactive at Cawnpore, had, by order, been instructed in gun-drill. Private Jack Holmes was the first man of the Regiment to respond, and his example was followed by others ... the gun was again served and the men remained with it the remainder of the day.

Sitting his horse calmly amid the storm, Maude continued to direct the fire of his guns, while his lieutenant, Maitland, worked a gun himself, acting the role of a bombardier.

We held our own for half an hour against those tremendous odds, and although the range was only 150 yards, we really lost comparatively few men, keeping the enemy's fire down, if we did not exactly silence all their guns ... Our guns were of the old pattern, dating probably from the days of Clive; and the only means provided for priming the vents was a large leathern pouch carried on the right side, full of loose powder. The gun number, whose duty it was to prime, simply took a handful out of his pouch and poured in on the vent. As the lane was very narrow, the two guns were exceedingly close to one another, and when they recoiled past each other, amid a shower of sparks and smoke, they frequently set fire to the loose powder in the priming pouch, and blew the poor gunners up. In this way four or five gunners were injured that morning.

At last, Maude called out to a staff officer – the younger Havelock later claimed it was him – who stood mounted near by, begging him to 'do something'. Havelock rode to Neill suggesting that he charge the bridge – Neill, however, was unwilling to attack the bridgehead until Outram and the Fusiliers had occupied the Char Bagh and could fire on the bridgehead from a flank. Colonel Fraser-Tytler, too, attempted to persuade Neill to action but with the General close at hand, the Brigadier felt unable to attack on his own responsibility. The young Havelock, seeing that nothing would shift the Brigadier, galloped off down the road, waited and then galloped back, shouting to Neill, 'You are to charge over the bridge, Sir.' Assuming the order to have come from Havelock senior, Neill gave the word, and Lieutenant Arnold (Madras Fusiliers) and Willis of the 84th, with a dozen men each of their respective regiments, together with Fraser-Tytler and young Havelock dashed forward across the bridge into a hail of fire. In seconds Arnold was shot through both thighs and Fraser-Tytler – with his horse shot under him – was wounded in the groin. Of the twenty-eight men who ran forward, only Havelock and a Corporal Jakes reached the earthwork unwounded. There they stood – Havelock sitting his horse, calling on the main body, while Jakes calmly fired and reloaded. The gap in the earthwork was closed overhead, so that Havelock could not pass through while mounted. A sepoy standing on the parapet fired a shot at Havelock and the ball passed through his helmet. Havelock dropped the man with his revolver, as the men of the main body closed up and stormed the entrenchment, bayoneting the gunners. 'I well remember,' wrote Willis, 'during this charge, the leading officer of the Madras Fusiliers (Lieutenant Groom) had his foot shot off at the ankle, at my side, and I myself was wounded by the last discharge from the guns in position at the Char Bagh Bridge. When these guns were captured ... I recall with pride that General Outram, when he came up, complimented the 84th and Madras Fusiliers for the dash and gallantry they had displayed in the capture of these guns.' Beyond the bridge two rebel guns still maintained their fire until Colonel Campbell of the 90th – who had won a CB in the Crimea – led a charge that captured them; he was mortally wounded later in the day. Captain Olpherts – 'Hell-Fire Jack' to his men – dragged them away under fire with spare gun teams. For their conduct at the Char Bagh Bridge, Captain

Maude and Private Holmes received the Victoria Cross. Of the first two men across the bridge, Havelock had already been gazetted for his action on 16 July and Corporal Jakes, who was killed later in the day, was ineligible (posthumous awards not having been instituted at that time).

It seems that the younger Havelock (or Havelock-Allen as he was called in later life) had put backs up among more than just the 64th Foot, as is reflected in Maude's last comments on the fight at the Char Bagh Bridge: 'As for the actual storming of the bridge, the *ruse* which Havelock-Allen says he practised on Neill to force the latter to advance, and his own conduct in leading a charge of twenty-five Fusiliers, accompanied by Fraser-Tytler and the two officers of the "Blue Caps" . . . some of this may have happened as he has told it, although I have not been able to find anyone to corroborate his story.'

Once the 1st Brigade was across, the 2nd followed and the whole force turned right and set off along the line of the canal in the direction of the Dilkusha Bridge. Only the 78th Highlanders remained, ordered to cover the advance of Eyre's heavy guns, and then to act as rearguard to the column. Making for the required point on the Cawnpore road, the 78th was awaiting the arrival of the heavy guns when it was attacked by large numbers of natives. For three hours the Highlanders beat off every attack until – as rebel numbers steadily increased – they stormed a nearby temple and held it against every assault. When the rebels brought up three brass cannon, the Highlanders issued out, captured the guns and threw them into the canal. It took another charge before the rebels drew off and the 78th was able to move on. Having given up all hope of uniting with the heavy guns, the Highlanders set off in search of the main body.

The main body, meanwhile, having followed the canal bank for 3,000 muddy yards, approached the Dilkusha Bridge. Here its progress was barred by a bridge over a small *nullah*, guarded by two guns and dominated by fire from the nearby Kaisar Bagh (Imperial Gardens). The bridge was only wide enough to be crossed by two men abreast, but a small party charged across and commenced firing on the enemy on the far bank. At this moment help arrived from an unexpected quarter – in the form of the missing 78th who, having taken a shorter route, arrived close to the Kaisar Bagh just as the small party of fusiliers were coming under a heavy fire. The Highlanders had suffered terribly battling their way through narrow streets – the Queen's colour had passed from the ensign (shot) to a bandsman, to a sergeant (also shot) to the assistant surgeon, who was still holding it aloft when they arrived before the Kaisar Bagh. In front of them was a rebel battery, firing on the handful of men at the head of the bridge – at once the Highlanders charged and carried it, killing the gunners. With the fire from the Kaisar Bagh slackening, the main body was able to cross, though not without heavy casualties. The crossing effected, the force rallied in the area of the Chattar Manzil (Umbrella) and Farid Bakhsh (Heart's Delight) palaces – not 1,300 yards from the Residency.

Inside the Residency all eyes and ears were turned towards the city. The previous night Julia Inglis had noted in her diary: 'Distant guns were heard during the day ... I could not sleep from excitement and anxiety.' All through the day the sounds of heavy firing marked the approach of the relieving column, and during the afternoon, wrote Mrs Inglis, 'The enemy ... could be seen leaving the city in large numbers, swimming the river and crossing the bridges. We shelled them severely to expedite their departure.' It would seem that Rees was right in his judgement that 'Natives expect defeat' for the battle was far from over. The column had all but disappeared in the streets of the city. 'They were outnumbered a hundred to one,' wrote Captain Birch,

> and had to make their way through narrow streets and dense parts of the city. Indeed, so dense were the suburbs, that they completely swallowed up the force, preventing our seeing them. The first sign of their approach was the evident panic among the citizens. Crowds streamed out of the city in headlong flight. Horsemen rode to the banks of the river and, cutting the tight martingales of their horses, plunged into the stream. Our irregular cavalry, of which we used to think so much, behaved the worst, in a fighting point of view, of all our ancient army. They were the first to leave the city; whilst the gunners and small-arm men still opposed the advance of the relieving force.

They were still massed between the Residency and the Chattar Manzil, where the relief column had paused. Outram, having been delayed by the clearing of the Char Bagh garden, now proposed to Havelock that – as darkness was falling – the force should hold firm where it was until morning. The Chattar Manzil could easily be held, and a halt would allow the rearguard, the heavy guns and the wounded to close up with the main column. There was much to commend the plan – not least the fact that the way ahead to the Residency lay through the Khas bazaar, which was now filled with rebels. Havelock, however, was insistent that joining the garrison overrode all other considerations and, since Outram had agreed to subordinate himself to Havelock until the Residency was relieved, the force began its final push – the Highlanders and Sikhs leading. The rebels were numerous, still full of fight and occupied most of the city – as the column moved off, Olpherts had to bring a gun into action against a battery in the Kaisar Bagh that was firing on its rear. All the streets were entrenched – obstacles designed to halt the advancing British so that they could be fired on from the adjoining houses and rooftops. Volleys met them at every corner and showers of missiles rained down from every rooftop. As Brigadier Neill halted to give an order to an ADC he was shot through the head from above – by one of a party of sepoys who had lain concealed as the British passed. Through a gauntlet of fire the Sikhs and Highlanders pushed on until, battling their way clear of the bazaar, they heard the sound of cheering from the Residency – probing forward in the dark they found themselves in front of the defences of the Baillie Guard.

Among those cheering on the ramparts of the Baillie Guard was Captain Birch: 'The enthusiasm in the garrison was tremendous, and only equalled by that of our relievers. H.M.'s 78th Highlanders and the 14th Sikhs raced up to our gate, which was earthed up, and which we did not dare to open, as the enemy kept up their fire till the last moment.' At last the relievers effected an entry. 'It was a sight never to be forgotten,' wrote Birch, 'to see the hand-shaking between relievers and relieved. Hirsute Sikhs and brawny Highlanders were seen taking up the children in their arms and kissing them.' Henry Kavanagh had watched the column arrive from his isolated place on top of the Post Office: 'I cheered and waved my hat till tired, and sobbed as I rushed down to welcome our deliverers at the gateway. I ran from one to another, pressing the exhausted men and officers to drink my last three bottles of liquor; which they readily did, overpowering me with profuse thanks and blessings.' 'Oh what welcome, what joy,' wrote Private Metcalfe. 'Comrades shaking hands, rough soldiers embracing and kissing little ones. Women asking for absent friends.' Moments later the Generals arrived. 'Generals Outram and Havelock came in at an embrasure which had been pretty well knocked about and admitted them,' wrote Captain Birch. 'General Havelock was an old friend of my father, Sir Richard Birch, and they had been in several campaigns together. I was able to introduce him to the brigadier; he was buttoned up to the chin in a blue coat. We of the old garrison had long deserted red and blue, and, with flannel shirts, white clothing dyed dust-colour and soiled with gunpowder, we looked more like buccaneers than officers of the British army. I sent Ellicock, the brigadier's orderly for his sword, for he had only pistols in his waist belt, and I tried to make him look a little more like the generals who had invaded us.'

Mrs Inglis knew from the noise that the long-awaited moment had at last arrived.

At 6 p.m. tremendous cheering was heard, and it was known our relief had reached us. I was standing outside our door when Ellicock rushed in for John's sword; he had not worn it since Chinhut, and a few moments afterwards he came to us accompanied by a short, quiet-looking, gray-haired man, who I knew at once was General Havelock. He shook hands with me, and said he feared we had suffered a great deal. I could hardly answer him; I longed to be with John alone, and he shared my feelings, for erelong he returned to me, and never shall I forget his heartfelt kiss as he said, 'Thank God for this!' Yes, we were safe, and my darling husband spared to me. It was a moment of unmixed happiness, but not lasting. I felt how different my lot was to others.

Many of the defenders of Lucknow were from HM 32nd, a company of which had been at Cawnpore, and with the relief column came bad news for some. 'A little later,' wrote Mrs Inglis, 'Mrs. Roberts, a sergeant's wife in the 32nd, came to tell us that the account of the Nana's treachery and the Cawnpore massacre was but too true. One of the survivors had come in and his accounts were most fearful. This alone was enough to cloud our joy at being relieved and to remind us of what might have been our fate.'

The relief was not without its accidents either. Rees recorded an incident at a battery guarded by sepoys of the 13th NI, who had distinguished themselves during the siege. 'The 78th Highlanders coming upon the Bailey Guard Battery, guarded by our sepoys, and not knowing it to be within the Residency, stormed it, and bayoneted three of our men, whom they mistook for insurgents. They never resisted, and one of them waved his hand, and crying "*Kootch purwanni* (never mind); it is all for the good cause; welcome friends!" fell and expired.'

Outside the Residency the heavy guns, which had been left to their own devices, had a difficult passage over ground much cut by trenches, but directed by Lieutenant Moorsom – who had been sent back by Havelock to guide them – they arrived, miraculously unopposed, at the Baillie Guard. Not all the relief column entered the Residency that night, some lay out in the open between the Baillie Guard and the Farhatbaksh Palace, and came into the compound the following morning. The rear-guard, with two heavy guns unaccounted for, were found the following morning – by a force despatched for that purpose by Colonel Robert Napier – holding the area of the Moti Mahal. The search for the wounded, however, did not end so happily – their escorts having lost their way, the wounded fell into the hands of the enemy and were murdered – some stabbed, some burnt alive in their *dhoolies*.

Havelock's column had at last reached the Residency, but at a great cost – 196 killed and 535 wounded. It had been, in truth, a messy affair – only one-third of the column actually reached the Residency on the night of the 25th. Another third came in the following morning; the remainder were dead or *hors de combat*. 'It is difficult to resist the conclusion that the affair was a muddle,' wrote Maude, 'however gloriously conducted, from beginning to end ... The officers led their men right well; but of generalship *proprement dit*, that day there was little if any at all.' It had been Outram's intention – now that he was in command – to withdraw with the garrison, the women and children to Cawnpore, there to place his forces under the command of the commander-in-chief, Sir Colin Campbell. Having lost five hundred men in the advance, however, it seemed to him to attempt a retreat, while still surrounded by a numerous and aggressive enemy and encumbered by women and children, would be to court disaster. The only course was to stay put – enlarge the perimeter, occupy some of the adjacent palaces and await Sir Colin Campbell. Lucknow, it seemed, was not so much relieved, as reinforced.

# 9

# The Storm of Delhi

The news from Delhi that had reached Havelock and Outram on 24 September – and which had so cheered the men of the Lucknow relief column on the eve of their biggest battle – was ten days old. The build-up to those events, however, had begun in August. 'What a sight our camp would be,' wrote an officer on the Delhi Ridge at that time,

> even to those who visited Sebastopol; the long lines of tents, the thatched hovels of the native servants, the rows of horses, the parks of artillery, the British soldier in his grey linen coat and trousers; the Sikhs, in their red and blue turbans; the Afghans, with their wild air and gay head-dresses; and the little Ghoorkas, dressed up like demons of ugliness, in black Kilmarnock caps and woollen coats ... If we go to the summit of the ridge which separates us from the city, we see the river winding along to the left, the bridge of boats, the towers of the palace, the high roof and minarets of the great mosque, the roofs and garden of the doomed city, and the elegant walls, with batteries here and there, the white smoke of which rises slowly among the green foliage that clusters round the ramparts.

Few among the British officers on the Ridge now doubted that the city was doomed. Nemesis was coming from the north, in the form of a siege train of heavy guns and a Movable Column led by a figure as terrifying as anything out of Greek mythology – John Nicholson.

According to Frederick Roberts, this feeling was growing among the rebels too. Both sides seem to have been well informed of the others' plans, strength and morale. There was a free-flow of civilians in and out of the city and the British camp, which by now had its own thriving bazaar. Spies were everywhere – many of them no doubt drawing an income from both sides. William Hodson, it was said, knew what the rebels had for dinner. 'The enemy were much depressed by the failure of the Bakhra Id attack from which they had expected great things,' wrote Roberts.

> They began to despair of being able to drive us from our position on the Ridge, which for seven weeks had been so hotly contested. They heard that Nicholson with his Moveable Column was hastening to our assistance, and they felt, unless they could gain some signal victory before reinforcements reached us, we should take our place as the besiegers instead of being, as hitherto, the besieged. Disaffection within the city walls was on the increase; only the semblance of authority remained to the old and well-nigh impotent King, while some of his sons, recognizing their perilous position, endeavoured to open negotiations with us. Many of the sepoys were reported to be going off to their homes, sick and weary of a struggle the hopelessness of which they had begun to realize.

It was known in the city that reinforcements were arriving at Calcutta from across the 'black water' (the ocean) including, one native wrote to a friend, 'A Regiment of women [who] have arrived and play Old Harry with everybody, and have an awful savage appearance, and no chance for anyone seems left!' The 'women' – in their tartan skirts – were believed to be the ghosts of memsahibs slaughtered at Meerut, Delhi and Cawnpore.

On 7 August Nicholson arrived on the Ridge, ahead of his troops. Nicholson's arrival was regarded as little less than an epiphany by some. It was 'like a King coming into his own', according to Daly of the Guides. Hodson regarded him as 'a host in himself', adding the proviso 'if he does not go and get knocked over as Chamberlain did'. Others took exception to his manner – which was considered sneering and so 'imperial' that soldiers at Headquarters presented arms to him, despite his being, as he pointed out to them, only truly a captain. There was little doubt among anyone, however, that Nicholson's arrival heralded great events. Almost at once he assumed the mantle of command, touring the defences with Alexander Taylor, Engineer second-in-command and 'Director of the Trenches' – Baird-Smith was incapacitated by a wound – and poring over plans for an assault. It was not long before he, with the Engineers, was hectoring poor, sick, anxious Wilson – his superior officer – on the need for an assault as soon as the siege train arrived.

On 12 August, in what Frederick Roberts described as 'a very brilliant little affair', a small column under Brigadier Showers expelled the mutineers from Ludlow Castle, from which their guns and skirmishers had kept up a constant harassing fire on the British outposts. Moving up before dawn Showers' men approached the position in silence until the cry of a sepoy was heard – 'Ho come dar?' ('Who comes there?') He was immediately shot dead, and after a volley the British infantry, Sikhs and Gurkhas stormed the position. The sepoy gunners managed to fire off two rounds from their four guns, but an Irishman by the name of Reegan bayoneted the gun commander of the third before he could apply the port-fire to the vent. The gunners fought to the death round their guns – the remainder fled, leaving 250 dead behind them. 'The return to camp was a stirring sight,' wrote Roberts, 'the captured guns brought home in triumph, pushed along by the soldiers, all madly cheering, and the horses ridden by men carrying their muskets with bayonets fixed.'

Two days later the Movable Column marched into the camp on Delhi Ridge. Watching it arrive was Edward Vibart – the Delhi fugitive, now serving with the 1st Bengal Fusiliers.

On August 14, the Punjab movable column, numbering some four thousand men, amongst them being that splendid regiment, the 52nd Light Infantry, marched into camp under the command of the famous General John Nicholson. How well I remember seeing his tall commanding figure riding along at the head of his men, and as we stood by the roadside and cheered each regiment as with confident demeanour, and a long swinging stride, it filed into camp, the predominant feeling in our minds was one of supreme elation at the thought that with the arrival of this additional reinforcement and its masterful leader, a victorious issue of the long protracted struggle was at length assured for the British arms, and the fate of Delhi irrevocably sealed!

The arrival of the Movable Column brought the Delhi force up to 8,000 rank and file of all arms – everything now depended on keeping the Ferozepore road clear for the arrival of the siege train. On 16 August William Hodson rode out at the head of 230 of Hodson's Horse, plus a hundred Guides and twenty-five Jhind horse – a mixed force of Sikhs, Punjabis, Muslims and Afridis – in the direction of Rohtuk. In and around Rohtuk and Panipat a warlike tribe known as the Rhaugurs – emboldened by the presence of mutineers – was threatening British communications with the north. Among Hodson's six European officers was Hugh Gough. Gough was glad to have two troops of the Guides present: 'We were fortunate in having these two troops of this famous corps to serve as a backbone to our somewhat undisciplined and irregular men in "Hodson's Horse," who, brave and dashing as they were, would be none the worse for the steadier example of the more experienced "Guides."' An added bonus to Gough's mind was that the Guides were commanded by his brother, Charles. The first place the force arrived at was the fortified village of Khurkoda, where – Hodson's intelligence told him – there were a number of sowars of the 1st Irregular Cavalry who had been on furlough when the Mutiny broke out. Since they had not returned to duty they were assumed to be mutinous. By the time Hodson had surrounded the village Bashrat Ali – a rissaldar of the 1st Irregular Cavalry – had come out of the village bearing a *nuzzur* (peace offering) of fruit as a tribute to the British Government. Hodson was unimpressed and placed the man under arrest.

Entering the village Hodson learned from the villagers that a party of mutinous sowars had taken refuge in a large house in the centre of the village. The only entrance to this house was via a long low tunnel, which had to be entered on hands and knees. Hugh Gough – unwilling to crawl head first in the dark towards cornered and armed sowars – elected, with the help of his Muslim rissaldar, Kanon Khan, to negotiate: 'Kanon Khan even took out his Koran, which he always carried about with him; and he held it out, and offered to swear to them on the holy book – for they also were Mohammedans – that their lives should be spared if they gave themselves up. I remonstrated with him, saying I could not guarantee their lives; but he quite ridiculed the idea of our keeping faith with such *mufsids* (or rebels), saying that an oath to such scoundrels was not a binding one.' Unable to persuade the rebels to surrender, Gough procured a ladder and scaled the house wall – as he did so the sowars ran on to the roof, where there was a two-roomed building in which they barricaded themselves. A number of Gough's men now entered the house and joined him on the roof in front of the building: 'A rush was attempted; but one or two men were cut down, and Hodson, who had come up, ordered further attempts by direct attack to cease.' There was a hole in the roof of the building and Hodson ordered a party to climb up and push burning straw inside. In a few moments they had smoked the rebels out. 'They rushed out sword in hand,' wrote Gough. 'There were not more than ten or a dozen of them; but they were fighting for their lives, and their charge was a most gallant one, against great odds. A furious *melee* ensued.'

Gough now had more reason than ever to be thankful for his brother's presence:

> When the enemy made their desperate rush I was rather in the forefront of the party awaiting them, and in the *melee* which took place I was forced backwards, and suddenly making a false step from the roof on to a lower roof about a foot down, fell or was forced on my knees. While thus half falling, one man made a cut at me with his heavy sword, which cut right down my riding-boot. Another was aiming a better-directed blow, when my brother, seeing my danger, rushed forward and attacked the two, killing both, and thus undoubtedly saved my life. As it was the hilt of my sword was forced into my wrist by a sword-cut, inflicting a slight wound.

The rebels were soon finished off. 'Having disposed of our enemy in this short but rather smart little skirmish on the top of a house,' wrote Gough, 'a type of fighting I have since carefully avoided – we returned to our bivouac.'

The next day Hodson's force arrived outside Rohtuk. 'On reaching Rohtak [*sic*],' Hodson wrote to his wife, 'we found the Mussulman portion of the people and a crowd of Irregulars drawn up on the walls, while a considerable party were on a mound outside. I had ridden forward with Captain Ward and a few orderlies to see how the land lay, when the rascals fired and ran towards us. I sent word for my cavalry to come up and rode slowly back myself in order to tempt them out, which had partly the desired effect, and as soon as my leading troops came up, we dashed at them and drove them helter-skelter into the town, killing all we overtook.' Hodson camped outside the town, and the villagers supplied his force with food and fodder for the horses, but the next morning the men had a rude awakening. One Babar Khan had arrived with three hundred Rhaugur horse, backed by nine hundred footmen armed with swords and matchlocks. Hodson, who had kept his horses saddled, lost no time in turning out his men, while his Jhind horsemen bore the brunt of the enemy's initial attack. 'Directly the whole detachment was ready and formed up,' he wrote, 'I sent what little baggage and followers we had to the rear under a sufficient escort, and prepared for a further attack.' Hodson drew his force up in three lines in the open ground in front of the village – with a troop to the left under Lieutenant McDowell and one on the right under Lieutenant Wise – to attack the enemy on both flanks, should the rebels come on. They did not come on, but contented themselves with lining the village buildings and firing with their match-locks, a fire which Hodson's Jhind horsemen returned 'exceedingly well, and most cheerfully'. For an all-cavalry force attacking a fortified village presents difficulties – seeing that there was nothing his cavalry could do but stand and take casualties, Hodson, in his own words, 'determined to draw them out into the open country behind our position, and endeavour to bring on a fight there'.

The feigned retreat is a dangerous and sometimes controversial military stratagem. Many of the 'feigned retreats' in history – notably that of the Norman cavalry at Hastings – were probably actual retreats, which by a combination of luck and fresh reserves turned into victory. There was no question about Hodson's, but with untried Irregular troops there was a real danger of it turning into a stampede – or in Victorian military parlance, a 'Donnybrook' (after the Irish race meeting). Nevertheless, he ordered his force to fall back. 'This we did,' wrote Hugh Gough, 'retiring by alternate troops – a movement, in the face of the enemy, requiring great steadiness and nerve, and especially difficult to a young corps like Hodson's Horse, but the tried steadiness of the Guides was our backbone and safeguard.' Gough had his trusted rissaldar Kanon Khan at his side: 'As we were retiring, I saw him take out his small Koran, already alluded to and begin to mutter his prayers. In my youthful arrogance and ignorance, I rather chaffed him, asking if he was afraid. He answered, "No sahib, but a man should always be prepared," a quiet rebuke which I felt I deserved.' The sight of the 'British' (although this force was, but for six officers, entirely Indian) retreating was too much for the Rhaugurs. 'The enemy moved out the instant we withdrew,' wrote Hodson, 'following us in great numbers, yelling and shouting and keeping up a heavy fire of matchlocks. Their horsemen were principally on their right, and a party galloping up the main road threatened our left flank. I continued to retire until we got into the open and comparatively dry ground, and then turned and charged.'

'Hodson ordered the "About and charge," which was most promptly obeyed,' wrote Gough, 'and we went with a will and a dash into the masses of the enemy, who, from their superior numbers, ought to have annihilated us; but our attack was irresistible, their pluck failed them, and they broke and fled! Still we got well home into them in grand style.' This was Gough's first charge: 'How well I can recall the moment of intense enthusiasm, and feeling of victory in anticipation, which pervaded my very soul as we dashed into the fight! Somehow, that curious feeling of victory already won seems to be the prevailing sentiment in a good home charge.' The enemy fled, leaving fifty horsemen dead on the ground, and dispersed to the surrounding villages. The following morning, reinforced by a further eighty well-equipped horsemen sent by his friend the Rajah of Jhind, Hodson rode home in triumph.

News had reached Delhi of Hodson's predicament at Rohtuk, news that rumour had inflated into a disaster. Hodson's friend, Charles Thomason, was patrolling the Grant Trunk road 'very, very down at the sad news'. Ahead of him he saw some Native cavalry. 'I was not at all sure who they were, but went on my way, when to my delight, I recognised Hodson and McDowell chatting jovially together at the head of "Hodson's Horse." Mutual salutations followed, something in this fashion: "Hullo, William, is that you? I just heard before leaving camp that you and all your men had been annihilated at Rohtak." "Not a bit of it, Charlie," was the reply: "you don't catch a weasel asleep, and here, as you see, we are, as merry as grigs. Fact is, Mac and I have been playing at William the Conqueror and the battle of Hastings."'

Perhaps predictably, controversy soon followed Hodson's exploit. Bashrat Ali, the rissaldar whom Hodson had arrested at Khurkoda, was shot out of hand as a mutineer. This was normal practice at the time and no one would have batted an eyelid but for the fact that Bashrat Ali was known personally to Hodson. In fact, Bashrat Ali had once stood surety for Hodson for a loan from his regimental bank. Hostile rumour soon had it that Ali had been a witness to Hodson's former financial misdeeds and had been shot to silence him. There seems little doubt that Bashrat Ali was genuinely committed to the rebel cause and that Hodson's execution of him was, by the standards then prevailing, entirely justified. Nor – according to the inquiry – had their been any misdeeds for Ali to be a witness to, but the murmurings proved once more that if Hodson had a gift for disposing of enemies he also had a gift for making them.

The other threat to the siege train came from within Delhi itself. The rebel commander-in-chief, Bakht Khan, swore he would capture the siege train or die in the attempt. On 24 August, therefore, he set out with a force of 6,000 of all arms – men from the garrison of Neemuch, in Rajputana, considered the elite of the sepoy army – and eighteen guns, and marched towards the Najafgarh *jhil* (see map 8, on page xxii). The following day Nicholson set out himself with 1,600 infantry – including HM 61st Foot and the 1st Bengal Fusiliers – sixteen horse artillery guns and 450 cavalry, intending to overtake Bakht Khan's force and bring it to battle. The rain fell in torrents and the ground became a quagmire – in the first seven hours Nicholson's force only covered 10 miles. Two miles further on the force encountered two large swamps through which the gunners had to manhandle their guns. After a further 12 miles' hard marching the force halted and Sir Theophilus Metcalfe – acting as a scout – rode forward to look for the enemy. He found the rebels – at about 4 p.m. – in a strong defensive position with thirteen guns, based around an old serai (rest house) with villages on either side and behind. The whole position was $1\frac{3}{4}$ miles in length, with a large drainage canal to its right and rear. The rebels' route back to Delhi lay via a bridge over the canal to their rear.

Nicholson's advance brought him on the enemy's right – with water between him and them. It was 5.30 in the afternoon and there was little time for reconnaissance. Nicholson decided to attack through the water into the rebels' left centre, then wheel his force to the left and roll up their line. Before the attack he addressed his European troops: 'Men of the 61st,' he cried, 'remember what Sir Colin Campbell said at Chili-anwala, and you have heard that he said the same to his gallant Highland Brigade at the Alma. I have the same request to make of you and the 1st Bengal Fusiliers. Hold your fire until within twenty or thirty yards, then fire and charge, and the serai is yours.' Nicholson led the advance in person, plunging into the water on horseback and heading straight for the serai. With the Bengal Fusiliers was Edward Vibart:

> The troops had to wade across a broad sheet of water, which in some places nearly reached up to our waists; after negotiating which obstacle we came upon a large serai, or walled enclosure, strongly held by the rebels with infantry and guns. A column composed of ourselves, a wing of Her Majesty's 61st Foot and the 2nd Punjab Infantry, was then told off to attack it, and, having advanced to a point about three hundred yards from the building, we were directed to deploy, halt, and lie down, while the General and his staff rode out to the front to reconnoitre the position. Immediately afterwards a Battery of Horse Artillery galloped up, and, unlimbering at close range, poured in a heavy fire of round

shot for a few minutes on that face of the serai that fronted us. The order was then given to the attacking column to stand up, and having fixed bayonets, the three regiments, led by General Nicholson in person, steadily advanced in an almost unbroken line to within about one hundred yards of the enclosure, when the word of command rang out from our commanding officer, Major Jacob, 'Prepare to charge!' 'Charge!' and in less time than it takes to relate it, we had scaled the walls, carried the serai, and captured all the guns by which it was defended. Only a few of the rebels fought with any pluck, and these were seen standing on the walls, loading and firing with the greatest deliberation until we were close upon them. But few of these escaped, as they were nearly all bayoneted within the enclosure. During the advance I had a narrow escape from being hit, a bullet striking the blade of my sword a few inches above the hilt, the impact creating a jar which nearly knocked it out of my hand. At the same instant I heard a soldier in the ranks just behind me shout out, 'Thank you, sir, that saved me;' and possibly, had the course of the bullet not been diverted, it might, as he seemed to think, have pierced his body.

The serai captured, Lieutenant Lumsden led his Punjabis forward – Coke having been wounded at Ludlow Castle – and attacked the villages with the bayonet. There was hard fighting, in which Lumsden and several of his men were killed, before the villages were cleared of the enemy, who finally fled leaving eight hundred dead behind. The few cavalry Nicholson had with him were employed guarding his own baggage and guns and those that had been captured, so pursuit was impossible, but the Neemuch Brigade was finished as a fighting force. Large quantities of enemy ammunition had been destroyed, ten or twelve wagons had been blown up and large sums of money were recovered – one private pocketed 900 rupees. To prevent any further attacks up this road from the direction of Delhi, Captain Geneste of the Engineers blew up the bridge. Nicholson's force – having suffered two officers and twenty-three men killed and three officers and thirty-eight men wounded (two of the officers mortally) – returned to the camp at Delhi the following evening, exhausted but triumphant.

On 4 September the siege train arrived before Delhi, having covered 268 miles in twenty-five days. For 8 miles the Grand Trunk road was crammed with thirty-two pieces of ordnance, 18- and 24-pounder guns, 10- and 8-inch howitzers and mortars, mostly drawn by elephants. Behind them came seven hundred bullock carts and tumbrils carrying ammunition. Now at last the besieged could become the besiegers, and Wilson found himself hard pressed by Nicholson and the Engineers. Worn down by a near-fatal attack of cholera – in Baird-Smith's opinion he was 'off his head' – Wilson was still reluctant to commit his force to assaulting a city that, as he believed, contained 40,000 soldiers, 144 heavy guns, sixty field guns and unlimited ammunition. He now knew that there was no immediate prospect of reinforcement either from the south or from the Punjab. Wilson's fears – of the assaulting forces being bogged down in street-fighting, surrounded and overwhelmed by the enemy's superior numbers – were not groundless. For Nicholson, Baird-Smith and Taylor, however, the risks of inaction to the whole British position in India were even greater. As John Lawrence had written to Wilson only days earlier, 'Every day's delay is fraught with danger. Every day disaffection and mutiny spread. Every day adds to the danger of the Native Princes taking part against us.' Lawrence knew whereof he wrote – his province was far from secure. There had been conspiracies among the Muslim tribes in the Muree Hills and an insurrection in the Gogaira district; among the Sikhs, recruiting in the land between the Sutlej and Ravi River was sluggish – many were still looking south to see what would happen. 'Fortunately for the continuance of our rule in India,' Roberts wrote,

> Wilson had about him men who understood, as he was unable to do, the impossibility of our remaining any longer as we were. They knew Delhi must either be taken or the army before it withdrawn. The man to whom the Commander first looked for counsel under these circumstances – Baird-Smith of the Bengal Engineers – proved himself worthy of the high and responsible position in which he was placed. He too was ill. Naturally of a delicate constitution, the climate and exposure had told upon him severely, and the diseases from which he was suffering were aggravated by a wound he had received soon after his arrival in camp. He fully appreciated the tremendous risks which an assault involved, but in his opinion, they were less than those of delay.

For his part, Nicholson was convinced that the mutineers would break once the British were inside the walls, that they would flee the city, and should be allowed – even encouraged – to do so.

At a council of war on 7 September, Baird-Smith presented General

Wilson with his 'scheme' for the assault. This involved breaching the enemy's northern walls between the Water bastion and the Kashmir Gate. This sector was chosen because the ground offered good cover for assaulting troops, the Jumna would cover their left flank, and once inside the walls the troops could regroup in the open spaces behind the Kashmir Gate (see map 4 on page xviii). To make practicable breaches east of the Kashmir Gate batteries would have to be established close to the walls at great speed and with the element of surprise. The first step was to establish control of the ground to the north of the walls where the breaching batteries were to be erected. To this end – and to deceive the enemy into expecting an attack further to the west – a powerful battery, Number One Battery, was to be established north of, and 700 yards from, the Mori bastion. To cover the building of this battery it would be necessary to seize and hold Ludlow Castle. Wilson's anxieties about the feasibility of this having been allayed by a reconnaissance by Nicholson and Taylor the night before, which had found it to be empty, he finally gave the plan his approval – but in such a way, it was generally felt, as to leave all responsibility in the event of failure on the shoulders of Baird-Smith.

For Wilson personally, the stakes at this meeting had been higher than he knew. One of many anxiously awaiting the results of this council of war was Frederick Roberts:

Nicholson was not a man of many intimacies, but as his staff officer I had been fortunate enough to gain his friendship. I was constantly with him, and on this occasion I was sitting in his tent before he set out to attend the council. He had been talking to me in confidential terms of personal matters, and ended by telling me of his intention to take a very unusual step should the council fail to arrive at any fixed determination regarding the assault. 'Delhi must be taken,' he said, 'and it is absolutely essential that this should be done at once; and if Wilson hesitates any longer, I intend to propose at to-day's meeting that he should be superseded.' I was greatly startled, and ventured to remark that, as Chamberlain was *hors de combat* from his wound, Wilson's removal would leave him, Nicholson, senior officer with the force. He smiled as he answered: 'I have not overlooked that fact. I shall make it perfectly clear that, under the circumstances, I could not possibly accept the command myself, and I shall propose that it be given to Campbell, of the 52nd; I am prepared to serve under him for the time being, so no one can ever accuse me of being influenced by personal motives.'

There seems little doubt that Nicholson would have carried out this extraordinary step, nor that if he had done so it would have been with the backing of the majority of the officers in the force. Many years later Roberts, by now a field marshal, wrote: 'That Nicholson would have carried out his intention if the council had come to a different conclusion I have not the slightest doubt, and I quite believe that his masterful spirit would have effected its purpose and borne down all opposition. Whether his action would have been right or wrong is another question, and one on which there is always sure to be great difference of opinion. At the time it seemed to me that he was right.'

Work on the Number One Battery began on the night of the 7th. To erect such a work overnight was a formidable task – Lieutenant Julius 'Jules' Medley, second-in-command of the engineering party, described the work:

The moon rose on a busy scene, hundreds of camels arriving, dropping their loads and returning; and hundreds of men, busy as bees, raising up a formidable work which was to be finished and ready to fire in the morning. The night was hot, but the excitement prevented anyone feeling fatigued. I went up to Hindu Rao's house, and on returning found we had at length got rid of the camels; but now commenced arriving the long strings of artillery carts, laden with shot and shell. Then came the huge guns, drawn by twenty pairs of bullocks each. At three o'clock the place presented a scene of awful confusion. Sappers, pioneers, artillerymen and infantry, all mixed up together with an inert mass of carts, guns and bullocks. Scarcely another hour remained before daylight, and then we knew what to expect from the irate enemy. Men and officers worked like horses. Nevertheless with all our exertions, we had only one gun ready for the Moree when day began to dawn; the other five platforms being still incomplete ... With the first break of day the enemy saw what we had been at, and then we caught it.

For the next few hours, under a heavy fire of round shot and grape from the Mori bastion, Maunsell, the 'Directing Engineer of the Right Attack', Medley and their sappers worked on, supported by a single howitzer brought out into the open by Major James Brind. Within a few hours, at a cost of seventy men killed, all the guns were mounted – four 24-pounders facing the Kashmir Gate and five 18-pounders and an 8-inch mortar facing the Mori bastion. From the Ridge, Richard Barter and his comrades watched the artillery duel that followed: 'Our fellows continued to fire salvos, that is, all the guns fired together like an Infantry volley, and the effect of such a weight of metal striking the wall at once soon became apparent for the Moree began to look like a large heap of earth, and gun after gun was disabled in front of it.' Frederick Roberts watched as the British guns established their dominance over the Mori: 'The enemy ... poured in round after round of shot and grape causing many casualties. Their fire slackened as our guns were gradually able to make themselves felt, and by the afternoon it was silenced. Nothing remained of the Mori bastion but a heap of ruins.'

Number One Battery was commanded by Major Brind, who had stood out in the open all morning with the crew of his howitzer. Roberts described him as 'the bravest of the brave. It was said of him, "he never slept." It was Brind's practice to lie reading his Bible – at the lookout's cry "Shot from the Moree" or, "Shell from the Kashmir," he would carefully mark the passage he had been reading, place the Bible under his pillow and jump up on to the parapet. He would then pace up and down in full view of the enemy asking calmly "No 1 gun are you ready?" On receiving the answer, "All ready sir," he would give the order to fire and raise his glass to watch the fall of shot.'

As well as destroying the Mori bastion and harassing the Kashmir, Number One Battery was able to provide some protection to the men erecting the breaching batteries nearer the river. On the same night that Number One Battery was being erected, the lines of the principal breaching battery, Number Two, were being traced on the ground in front of Ludlow Castle, 500 yards from the Kashmir Gate. This battery was also to comprise two 'wings' – the left half, of nine 24-pounders, was to breach the curtain wall to the east of the Kashmir bastion, the right, of two 18-pounders and seven 8-inch howitzers, was to breach the bastion itself or the curtain close to it. By 11 September this battery, too, was completed, armed and 'unmasked' – that is to say, the boughs and foliage that had disguised the work were removed, prior to firing. Having been deceived by the erection of Number One Battery the rebels were not slow to respond to this new threat to their north wall, directing a heavy fire of shot, shell, grape and musketry against Number Two Battery and the

working parties preparing Numbers Three and Four Batteries. Number
Three, initially intended for the Kudsia Bagh, had been resited – the
ground proving unsuitable – inside the Customs House, only 160 yards
from the wall. Work on this battery proved costly – a high proportion of
the casualties being Indians. Roberts recalled: 'During the first night of
its construction 39 men were killed and wounded; but with rare courage
the workmen continued their task. They were merely unarmed pioneers;
and with that passive bravery so characteristic of Natives, as man after
man was knocked over, they would stop a moment, weep a little over a
fallen friend, place his body in a row along with the rest, and then work
on as before.' By the morning of the 10th the platforms were ready, but
falling masonry, heavy casualties and the task of dragging six 24-pounders
and twelve 5.5-inch mortars from the rear meant that this battery was
not finished until the morning of the 12th. When it opened fire, however,
it did so with devastating effect. Medley recorded: 'The enemy's guns
were dismounted or smashed almost immediately, the face of the bastion
was beaten into a shapeless mass, and the parapet sent flying about
in fragments. In a few hours the breach seemed almost practicable.'
Meanwhile, Number Four Battery – four 10-inch and six 8-inch mortars,
targeting the Kashmir and Water bastions and the Kashmir Gate – had
been established on the night of the 10th between numbers Two and
Three, 550 yards from the wall.

From the morning of the 11th the north wall of Delhi was subjected to
a sustained bombardment. Richard Barter described the scene: 'The roar
of the heavy guns and those from the city was now most incessant, never
ceasing day nor night . . . The city guns were not idle, giving gun for gun
with interest. While the rattle of musketry kept filling up the pauses, I
can give some idea of the part the Infantry played in the trenches from
having one night to send ammunition down in the absence of the Quarter
Master, and that night, which was nothing out of the common, two
hundred men fired thirty thousand rounds between one and three o'clock
in the morning.' Soon, wrote Barter, the parapets and the bastions
looked like so many earthworks. 'The round shot striking the wall always
reminded me of a pack of hounds taking a high fence into a covert
together.' The sound of the guns could be heard 30 miles away in Meerut
where Mrs Muter discovered that: 'By putting my ear to the ground I
could hear the guns, and by dint of practice I could detect any difference
in sound. I at once perceived the opening of the siege guns and flew into
the house to tell Miss Custance that the assault had begun. I looked at

the clock and afterwards found that I had been correct.'

The bombardment went on day and night – the only pauses coming when the guns grew too hot to fire and the artillerymen stopped to let them cool. Frederick Roberts was in Number Two Battery in command of the two right-hand guns of the left wing.

> At eight o'clock on the morning of the 11th September we opened fire on the Kashmir bastion and the adjoining curtain and as the shots told and the stones flew into the air and rattled down, a loud cheer burst from our Artillerymen and some of the men of the Carabiniers and 9th Lancers who had volunteered to work in the batteries. The enemy had got our range with wonderful accuracy, and immediately on the screen in front of the right gun being removed, a round shot came through the embrasure, knocking two or three of us over. On regaining my feet, I found that the young Horse Artilleryman who was serving the vent while I was laying the gun had had his right arm taken off . . . Night and day the overwhelming fire was continued, and the incessant boom and roar of guns and mortars, with the ceaseless rain of shot and shell on the city, warned the mutineers that their punishment was at hand. We were not, however, allowed to have it all our own way. Unable to fire a gun from any of the three bastions we were breaching, the enemy brought guns into the open and enfiladed our batteries. They sent rockets from their martello towers, and they maintained a perfect storm of musketry from their advanced trench and from the city walls. No part of the attack was left unsearched by their fire, and though three months' incessant practice had made our men skilful in using any cover they had, our losses were numerous, 327 officers and men being killed and wounded between the 7th and 14th September.

By the evening of the 13th two breaches could be seen in the enemy's walls – one on the east side of the Kashmir bastion and another near the Water bastion. Earlier that day a council of war was held at which Wilson read out the orders for an assault, to be made at dawn on the 14th. The meeting was held in conditions of great secrecy, as Wilberforce of the 52nd observed: 'It was held in a tent pitched for the purpose and was guarded from spies by sentries posted at a distance of 100 yards. The sentries kept meeting each other as they paced backwards and forwards. As the tent in which the Council was held had no sides, we, who stood beyond the sentries, could see the legs of those seated at the Council-table, and could also see through the tent. I mention this to show how impossible it was for any one to have been concealed in the tent. This Council, we afterwards knew, settled the final plan of assault for the next day.'

The plan was for almost the entire Delhi force to attack the city in five columns, under the command of John Nicholson. No. 1 Column, which Nicholson would lead in person, would take the breach near the Kashmir bastion by assault and escalade, No. 2 Column would storm the Water bastion breach – both of these columns would then swing right and attack down the line of the walls via the Mori bastion, the Kabul Gate and the Burn bastion as far as the Lahore Gate, with the eventual aim of advancing up the Chandni Chowk towards the King's Palace. Meanwhile, No. 3 Column would attack the Kashmir Gate – which would be blown in by an engineer party – and advance straight into the heart of the city and the Jama Masjid. These three columns would ultimately unite to complete the capture of the city. No. 4 Column was intended more as a diversion – to 'pin' the enemy on the walls further east and prevent the rebels reinforcing the troops defending the breaches. Its role was to clear the suburbs of Paharipur as far as the Lahore Gate. No. 5 Column was to act as a reserve and, eventually, follow No. 1 Column into the city. It was an audacious plan; fatigue, fighting and disease had reduced the force severely – the 52nd had only 200 effectives out of the 600 who had arrived with Nicholson three weeks earlier, while the 75th were down to 361 out of the 928 with which it had started the campaign. In all some 6,500 men were to assault a fortified city manned by 30,000 sepoys.

In the afternoon Nicholson went down to visit the breaching batteries to see for himself the state of the breaches. In Roberts' wing of No. 2 Battery, he said 'I must shake hands with you fellows; you have done your best to make my work easy tomorrow.' Once the British artillery had ceased fire A. M. Lang of the Bengal Engineers ran forward under a heavy fire and lay down at the edge of the ditch in front of the Kashmir bastion. That night he returned with 'Jules' Medley, descended into the ditch and examined the breach at close quarters. At the same time two other Engineer officers, Greathed and Hovenden, inspected the breach at the Water bastion. Both breaches being declared practicable the assault was confirmed for the following day. At 3 p.m. Nicholson assembled in his tent the column commanders and three officers from each regiment to hear their orders. Richard Barter of the 75th was there with Lieutenant Herbert and Captain Brookes of his regiment: 'On a table before him

[Nicholson] was a map of the city, and he stood up, his right foot on a chair, and explained what we were expected to do in a clear and lucid manner.'

Three officers from each regiment were present so that in the case of one or two being killed, the third would know the plan. Nicholson would – they were told – be easily distinguishable in the confusion of battle by his green flag borne by one of his faithful Afghans. His orders given, Nicholson took the adjutants down to the trenches to show them their regiments' forming-up positions. That evening the order was published for the storming of Delhi before dawn the following morning. It will not have been lost on the officers and men of the Delhi force – many of whom had been there – that this was the third anniversary of the allied landings in the Crimea.

'Of course, after the announcement we had received, sleep was out of the question,' remembered Wilberforce of the 52nd.

So when all our arrangements were completed we started out to find our friends and see what they were doing. Gradually, however, we gravitated towards the mess-tent, where we filled up our bottles and whiled away the time before parade as cheerily as we could. The 'bottles' were due to the forethought of our Colonel; they were soda-water bottles covered with leather and slung round the neck with a strap which passed under the sword-belt. Not only had all the officers one of these bottles, but all the men had one as well. When therefore the allowance of rum was served out – that morning the allowance of rum was doubled – our men put the rum in their bottles, and did not, like some others, drink it off sooner than leave it.

With the 75th Highlanders, Richard Barter and his mess-mates

looked carefully to the reloading of our pistols, filling our flasks, and getting as good protection as possible for our heads, which would be exposed so much going up the ladders. I wound two puggarees round my old forage cap with the last letter from the hills in the top and committed myself to the care of Providence. There was not much sleep that night in our Camp. I dropped off now and then but never for long and whenever I awoke I could see that there was a light in more than one of the officers' tents and talking was going on in a low tone amongst the men, the snapping of a lock or the springing of a ramrod sounding far in the still air telling of preparation for the approaching strife.

A little after midnight the 75th fell in near their tents – by lamplight, General Wilson's general order for the assault was read out to the men. There was to be no stopping for the wounded – whether officers or men they were to be left where they fell, and picked up by the *dhoolies*; in the event that the attack failed they must expect the worst. There was to be no looting – all plunder would be placed in a common stock to be divided later by the prize agents. Wilson's order concluded:

> The Major-General feels assured that British pluck and determination will carry everything before them, and that the bloodthirsty and mur-derous mutineers against whom they are fighting will be driven head-long out of their stronghold, and exterminated ... Major-General Wilson need hardly remind the troops of the cruel murders committed on their officers and comrades, their wives and children, to move them in the deadly struggle. No quarter should be given to the mutineers! At the same time, for the sake of humanity, and the honour of the country they belong to, he calls upon them to spare all women and children that may come in their way.

To this last the men muttered, 'No fear, Sir.' The officers pledged their honours on their swords to abide by these orders, and the men promised to follow their example.

'It has often struck me as very singular,' wrote Hope Grant, 'that officers and men should apparently feel so little, and be so cool, on the eve of a battle, when so many fearful scenes are about to take place, and when no-one can tell whether he will be carried safely through them or not. Such was the case on the eve of the storming of Delhi. Men seemed to regard the coming struggle as if it were a cricket match, in which every one felt confident that his side would win.' Man Singh – one of Hodson's Horse – was fond of recalling in later years, when he was a guard at the Golden Temple at Amritsar, a conversation he had with Hugh Gough on the eve of battle: 'Gough Sahib came to me on the day before the assault and said, "Man Singh, there is going to be a great battle tomorrow, and we are going to take Delhi. Hodson says he will ride to Jehannum [hell] after the Pandies. I wonder how it will end." I said to Gough Sahib, "Well, Sahib, wherever Hodson goes we'll all go." Whereupon Gough

Sahib said "Well, Man Singh, salaam; then we'll all go to Jehannum together."'

It had been intended to assault the breaches at daybreak, but some of the men detailed for the storming parties had been on picket duty all night and took some time to rejoin their units. Overnight the enemy had effected some repairs to the breaches so a further delay was imposed as the breaching batteries commenced firing once more to destroy the new works. While this final bombardment was taking place, Frederick Roberts watched John Nicholson at the head of his column:

I ... wondered what was going through his mind. Was he thinking of the future, or of the wonderful part he had played during the past four months? At Peshawar he had been Edwardes' right hand. At the head of the Moveable Column he had been mainly instrumental in keeping the Punjab quiet, and at Delhi everyone felt that during the short time he had been with us he was our guiding star, and that but for his presence in the camp the assault which he was about to lead would probably never have come off ... Any reluctance to serve under a Captain of the Company's army, which had at first been felt by some, had been completely overcome by his wonderful personality. Each man in the force, from the General in command to the last-joined private soldier, recognised that the man whom the wild people on the frontier had deified – the man of whom a little time before Edwardes had said to Lord Canning, 'You may rely upon this, that if ever there is a desperate deed to be done in India, John Nicholson is the man to do it' – was the one who had proved himself beyond all doubt capable of grappling with the crisis through which we were passing – one to follow to the death.

Waiting with No. 3 Column was Reginald Wilberforce:

We stopped for an hour and a half, losing the precious darkness, and watching the daylight creep up into the sky. Many of our men fell out here, some indeed had fallen out at the start – men whose bodies had been weakened by fever, but whose courage induced them to try to be sharers in the assault on the city we had been outside of so long. While we halted, Nicholson passed by us; his last words were, 'Good-bye! I wish I was going with you.' At last we drew close to Ludlow Castle; it was daylight now ... While we waited, the 60th Rifles passed by us in skirmishing order; they were going to try and clear the walls, which we could see were densely covered with mutineers; they could not do much, for they were exposed, whilst their opponents were shielded by the battlements. Soon we saw their wounded being carried by us, not much of an encouragement to our men, who well knew what lay before them. Here we were joined by the Engineer party who were to blow open the Cashmere Gate; one of these, Salkeld, was an old schoolfellow of mine. We had not seen each other since we had left school, and were mutually surprised to meet where we did.

One officer with No. 1 Column, a Major Cobbe of the 87th Royal Irish Fusiliers, who was that morning attached to the staff, was ordered to go up to the Flagstaff Tower and, when he heard the force advancing, to come down and take up his position beside his general. Cobbe went up to the Flagstaff as ordered, sat down, lay down and by the time the sun was rising was fast asleep. He was still sleeping peacefully in the early morning sunshine as the British batteries fell silent, Nicholson finally gave the long awaited signal and Nos 1 and 2 Columns emerged from the Kudsia Bagh and marched towards the walls of Delhi.

Richard Barter and his men ran straight towards the Kashmir bastion:

In column of fours right in front we rushed at the double through a high archway into a garden of roses and through this to the foot of the glacis. Small birds were twittering amongst the trees as we rushed on and the perfume of the roses was quite apparent in spite of the sulphury smell of powder. Like magic the dark forms of the 60th Rifles seemed to spring out of the earth as they lined the bank at each end of the garden, keeping up a galling fire on the walls and breach; day had broken and the sun was showing like a great red ball in the East as passing through the lines of the 60th, who cheered us loudly, we emerged on the glacis, and there straight before us was the breach: a huge gap in the wall full of men whose heads showed just over the edges of it, while along the walls they swarmed thick like bees. The sun shone full on the white turbans and black faces, sparkling brightly on their swords and bayonets, and our men cheered madly as they rushed towards the breach ... round shot came screaming from the guns far on our right, while grape and shells whistled from those nearer, and the walls seemed a line of fire along our front. Bullets whistled in the air, and tore up the ground about our feet and men fell fast, among the first Lieutenant Colonel Herbert with a ball through his leg.

From his vantage point at Ludlow Castle Roberts watched as 'a storm of bullets met them from every side, and officers and men fell thick on the crest of the glacis. Then for a few seconds, amidst a blaze of musketry, the soldiers stood at the edge of the ditch, for only one or two of the ladders had come up.' 'Three times the ladder party was swept away,' wrote Barter, 'and three times were the ladders snatched from the shoulders of the dead and wounded. The only man with them who escaped untouched, as if by a miracle, being the officer Lieutenant Faithfull.' Together with Captain Brookes – who had now assumed command – Lieutenants Fitzgerald and Briscoe and a handful of officers and men of the Grenadier Company, Barter 'slid down into the ditch and calling for the ladders, had two thrown down to us. Fitzgerald quickly got his up and was placing it against the wall, but I was still lame and weak from my wound and had it not been for Briscoe, who slid down to help me, I'd have made a slow job of it. We put the two ladders then together according to rule. Briscoe was in the act of mounting before me when I caught him by the arm and claiming my right as senior officer soon stood side by side with Fitzgerald in the breach, up the face of which we now scrambled.'

Over to Barter's right, A. M. Lang – who had examined the breach the afternoon before – was at the head of the 1st Bengal Fusiliers: 'I had to lead two hundred and fifty of the 1st Fusiliers up the face of the Kashmere bastion ... it was most gloriously exciting; the bullets seemed to pass like a hissing sheet of lead over us, and the noise of the cheering was so great that I nearly lost my men, who doubled too far down the road before I could turn them, so they got more fire on the glacis than they needed: the edge of the ditch reached, down we slipped; just as I slid down, on my left I saw Medley and the 75th beginning to swarm their breach.' Over to the left, Barter was finding it hard work, 'the breach ... was like a sloping beach of sea sand from the pounding of our shot, and behind it were some gabions between which the enemy kept up a smart fire, so close that I could feel the flash of each discharge hot on my cheek. To spoil their aim I kept firing my revolver with my right hand while I scrambled up with my left, holding my sword under my arm as best I could for we carried no scabbards. They kept heaving great blocks of masonry at us, and tried to roll some down, but they stuck in the bed of the breach, and hurt no one.'

Close behind Barter were men of his own regiment and the Punjabis who, unable to get on to the crowded ladders, climbed up on each other's shoulders in their eagerness. 'The sight was too much for the defenders of the breach,' wrote Barter, 'and they retreated into the city leaving Fitzgerald and myself standing close up to the gabions. We shook hands and parted, he down the proper right of the breach as it faced us, and I along the parapet to the left towards the Kashmir gate. I never saw him again, he was killed by a discharge of grape inside the walls immediately after I parted from him. A braver man never lived, but it was patent to us all that he expected to be killed for he was silent and gloomy all the night instead of, as he always used to be, full of fun and cheery.'

Meanwhile, on the other side of the breach, Lang and his men were climbing too: 'Up went our little ladder, but once on the berm we instantly saw that there was no place for placing our long ladders, so up we scrambled just a steep crumbling wall of masonry. I have seen it since in cold blood, and wondered how we got up at all. I was just falling backwards on our own bayonets when a Gurkha pushed me up luckily, and presently over we were.' Also with the Bengal Fusiliers were John Nicholson and Alex Taylor, as well as a number of Volunteers – men, mostly NCOs, who had been serving in departments in Delhi and had lost their families in the massacres of 11–16 May.

As Highlanders, Sikhs and Bengal Fusiliers were gathering on the ramparts of the Kashmir bastion, the men of No. 2 Column were crowning the breach at the Water bastion (see map 4 on page xviii). Led by Brigadier Jones, and guided by the Bengal Engineer officers Greathed and Hovenden, the storming party, like that of No. 1 Column, was met by a withering fire. Both officers and twenty-nine out of thirty-nine men of the ladder parties were shot down within minutes. After two failed attempts, however, the men of HM 8th Foot raised their ladders and held them while Captain Baines, two lieutenants and seventy men ascended. Joining with a second party of the same regiment, they quickly cleared the rampart and, as at the Kashmir bastion, no quarter was asked or given. The whole of the north wall between the Kashmir and Water bastions was now in British hands.

At the Kashmir bastion Richard Barter, who was to claim the honour of being second man in Delhi – a pace behind the now-dead Fitzgerald – turned west towards the Mori bastion:

I ran along the parapet for some thirty or forty yards and to this day I cannot make out how I did it for the depth into this ditch must be I fancy at least forty feet, while to make matters worse the parapet was knocked away in several places. At any other time I couldn't even stand on the parapet, for my head won't permit my going about at any height, but now it didn't seem to trouble me in the least and I could look from my elevated position over to our batteries and see them crowded with the Artillery officers and men watching our movements. While running along, followed by a bugler, I heard a loud explosion in my front and saw the Kashmir gate blown in.

This gate had been the objective of No. 3 Column – commanded by Colonel Campbell of HM 52nd Foot, and composed of that regiment, the Kumaon Battalion and the 1st Punjabis. When the signal to advance had been given Reginald Wilberforce – part of the 52nd's storming party – advanced beside his old school fellow, Salkeld of the Bengal Engineers. 'He and I walked together till within about twenty yards of the glacis, when he went on to do his duty,' The engineer contingent, termed the 'Explosion Party' was to blow down the gate, after which, on a signal from the bugle, the 52nd were to dash forward and enter the city. As the Engineers ran forward the whole force came under fire from the walls. Wilberforce recalled:

A storm of fire rained round us and the order was given to lie down; this was promptly obeyed – indeed one of ours obeyed the order so promptly that not looking for his resting place, he threw himself into some cactus-bushes that grew just the other side of the road, the sharp thorns of which made their existence suddenly and painfully perceptible. Most of us took refuge in a wide but shallow ditch that ran alongside of the road. From this partially sheltered position we saw a storm of bullets pour down upon the road on which we had just been standing, and tear up the dust in all directions. One of the ladder party, who immediately followed us, finding that his comrade had dropped his end of the ladder and sought safety in the ditch, remained on the road with the end of the ladder still on his shoulder. His Captain called out to him, 'Come under cover!' He lustily shouted for some one to come and help him with the ladder, but this idea of duty cost him his life, for he fell dead almost immediately, pierced by many bullets. So heavy was this fire, directed at us from a distance of only about fifty yards, that a Crimean veteran who was present said that even in the Crimea he had never seen anything to exceed it.

The Explosion Party – Lieutenants D. C. Home and P. Salkeld of the Bengal Engineers, three British NCOs, fourteen Indian soldiers of the Bengal Sappers and Miners, ten men of the Punjab Sappers and a British bugler – now ran forward to blast a way into the city for Campbell's waiting infantry. The plan was simple. Split into two groups they would run to the ditch, cross it and approach the gate itself. Home's party carried 25lb bags of powder, which they would place at the foot of the gate. Once under the gateway it was assumed they would be safer owing to the difficulty the sepoys above would have in firing their muskets directly downwards – although they could also fire through a wicket gate in the main gate that had been left open for the purpose. Salkeld's party would then come up, lay more bags, light the fuses and jump into the ditch before the gate exploded. All this had to be done in the teeth of the fire from which the 52nd were sheltering 50 yards to the rear, and under the noses of the enemy.

Home's party dashed forward into a hail of fire. Home described what followed: 'Sergeants John Smith and Carmichael, Mahdo Havildar, all the Sappers and myself arrived at the Cashmere Gate untouched a short time in advance of the remainder of the party under Lieutenant Salkeld, having found the palisade gate on the outside of the ditch and the wicket of the Cashmere Gate open and three planks of the bridge across the ditch removed.' Running across the plank bridge – under fire from above and through the wicket gate – Home's men laid their bags at the foot of the gate. 'As Sergeant Carmichael was laying his bag,' wrote Home, 'he was killed by a shot from the wicket. Havildar Mahdo was, I believe, also wounded about the same time. Lieutenant Salkeld, carrying the slow match to light the charge, now came up with a portion of the remainder of the party.' It was crowded by the gate so Home and his men, their job done, dropped into the ditch. With Salkeld was Sergeant John Smith:

I placed my bags and then Carmichael's bag, arranged the fuse and reported 'All ready' to Lieutenant Salkeld who held the slow match. In stooping down to light the match Lieutenant Salkeld was shot through the thigh and, in falling, held out the 'slow' and told me to fire the charge. Burgess was next to him and took it. He turned round and said, 'It won't go off, sir; it has gone out, sir,' not knowing that the officer had fallen into the ditch. I gave him a box of lucifers, and as he took them he let them fall into my hand – he being shot through the body – and fell over after Lieutenant Salkeld into the ditch. I was left alone. Keeping close to the charge I struck a light when the port-fire in the fuse went off in my hand, the light not having gone out as we had thought. I took up my gun and jumped into the ditch, but before I had reached the ground the charge went off. As soon as the dust cleared I saw Lieutenant Salkeld and Burgess covered in dust. Lieutenant Salkeld's arms were broken. Lieutenant Home got out of the ditch leaving me in charge of the wounded.

Climbing out of the ditch with Bugler Hawthorne of the 52nd, Home ordered him to sound the 52nd's 'Regimental Call' and the 'Advance'. If Richard Barter up above on the Kashmir bastion had heard the gate being blown, it was not audible above the roar of the guns and the rattle of musketry to the men of the 52nd waiting in the ditch. There was, therefore, a pause until Colonel Campbell and others with him saw the plume of smoke caused by the explosion. He at once ordered the storming party under Captain Bayley forward. Within seconds Bayley had fallen, shot through the leg. Close behind him was Lieutenant Wilberforce: 'I saw Captain Bayley on the ground. For a moment I stopped – "Shall I pull you under cover?" "No, go on." I saw my Captain, Crosse, go in through the hole in the gate, it was only large enough to admit one at a time. I was going next when Corporal Taylor pushed me on one side and got second.' Inside the gate Crosse found an 18-pounder gun loaded to the muzzle with nails and bits of iron. Its crew – the men who had shot Salkeld – lay dead around it, killed by the explosion. One sepoy was still on his feet and Crosse fired his revolver at him and missed. The man raised his musket but before he could fire Corporal Taylor ducked under the barrel of the gun and bayoneted him. Wilberforce was the third man in: 'Through the gateway we saw an open square, the sunlight pouring into it – empty . . . The gate was soon thrown open, and our men, Coke's Rifles and the Kumaon Battalion, who formed our assaulting column, poured in after us.'

As they crossed the plank bridge over the ditch the stormers passed above the dead and wounded bodies of the Explosion Party. Sergeant Carmichael and Corporal Burgess were dead, and Lieutenant Salkeld and Havildars Tullok Singh and Mahdo wounded. Salkeld and Tullok Singh both died of their wounds. Salkeld lived on for two days, just long enough to receive the ribbon of the Victoria Cross. 'It will be gratifying to send it home,' he whispered – almost his last words. Lieutenant Home, Bugler Hawthorne and Sergeant Smith were also awarded the VC – Carmichael and Burgess would probably have received it, too, had posthumous awards been allowed at the time. All of the Indian soldiers were rewarded with the Indian Order of Merit, promotion or grants of land. The blowing of the Kashmir Gate was ever after remembered as the most daring feat performed by engineers, sappers and miners in India.

Inside the gate, wrote Wilberforce:

> The whole column formed up in the large open space inside the gateway, and while there we saw the column which had been told off to storm the Cashmere breach, come over the walls. Our Sikhs had fired a *feu de joie* in the air just before the arrival of the stormers. While waiting in the square, one of my brother officers addressed me with – 'Halloa! you are wounded; blood is running down your leg.' It was not the case, but I found I had had a very narrow escape; the soda-water bottle covered with leather, which in common with the rest I carried, and which my sword-belt held down over the hip, was broken by a bullet which, tearing my trouser, passed between my hip and the bottle.

Wilberforce's company, part of Campbell's column, was about to move off into the heart of the city – aiming for the city's main mosque, the Jama Masjid. This was to be one part of a two-pronged thrust into the heart of the city. The other two columns, led by Nicholson, were to swing right and – via the ramparts and a road that ran along the foot of the walls – push down towards the Mori bastion and the Lahore Gate, then, swinging left, advance up the Chandni Chowk. The plan was that the two forces would reunite in the area of the Bank and assault the King's Palace. As soon his men were assembled, Campbell led them off. As Wilberforce recalled, their guide was a man who knew every inch of the city: 'We ... moved on guided by Sir Theophilus Metcalfe, and came to the entrance of the Water bastion; as this was one of the places assaulted it did not seem worth while stopping to enter; however, we went in and found it full of the enemy. They were so astonished by our appearing in their rear, that they hardly showed fight, but fled panic stricken to the walls to scramble or jump down. One of ours, a big fellow he was, cut at one of the mutineers as he was escaping, and with his sword – only a tailor's one – all but cut his head clean off.' The owner of that sword was lucky, as Wilberforce and a brother officer discovered: 'We attacked a man not both together but one at a time. I had the first try, and my sword bent almost double against the man's chest without inflicting any wound. My companion fared but little better, for his sword glanced along a rib, inflicting a long, shallow, skin wound, and had not the revolver been handy, it might have been awkward for one or both of us.'

The presence of mutineers in the Water bastion after No. 2 Column had stormed it and moved on down the walls testifies to the confusion that reigned inside the walls of Delhi in the first few minutes of the assault, as does the account of A. M. Lang, also with No. 1 Column: 'Here was a little confusion: no one was exactly sure of the way; Nicholson and Taylor ran up towards Skinner's house – wrong way – Pemberton and I under Captain Hay and a few more took the proper turning, under the ramparts along narrow lanes, ramparts on our right, and mud walls on our left.' In fact, Nicholson knew exactly what he was doing. With some men of the 75th and the 1st Fusiliers he advanced to clear the area around St James's Church about 150 yards south of the breaches. This with some adjoining buildings was quickly captured and a defensive base established, to guard against a possible counter-attack. His orders were that the bulk of the 75th and the 1st Bengal Fusiliers should assemble in the open ground by the Kashmir Gate before pushing on to the Kabul Gate. Here they would link up with No. 4 Column – still outside the walls – admit them to the city, and then both columns would capture the Lahore Gate before turning left and pushing into the heart of the city (see map 4 on page xviii).

On arriving at the blown-in Kashmir Gate with the 75th, Richard Barter found about eight or ten of the enemy lying around, injured by the explosion: 'I polished off a gunner on the way with a back stroke of my sword as I passed him.' Realizing that in the chaos round the gate – with groups from No. 1 Column assembling in order to push on down the line of the walls, and men of No. 3 Column pouring in through the gate for their push into the city – it was impossible to form his men into quarter-distance columns:

I called on the men to follow me and with Wadeson made off up through an archway on the road to the Church, looking out for the passage along the wall, of which Brigadier Nicholson had told us the day before in his tent. Up the road a little way, a Sepoy suddenly dashed out sword in hand, I fancy from some doorway for I didn't see him before, and seizing one of our men's firelocks close to the muzzle and thereby preventing him from using it in any way, attempted to cut him down. He was bayoneted by another of our men to whom I shouted and at the same moment I took the top of his head with a sweep of my sword. A little further on and the churchyard came in view, the wall round it lined with Sepoys, while to our right up a lane about three or four hundred yards off some more fellows were making off with a couple of Field pieces. We fired at these hoping to disable the horses but they were too far off. I was then running round the corner towards the Church when one of the men catching me by the back of the collar pulled me down calling out, 'Don't go there Mr Barter sir, you'll be killed.' As he spoke a rattling volley of musketry was poured into us, the bullets flattening against the wall behind us, and Wadeson fell into my arms shot through both blade bones of the back. Drawing him into better shelter I gave him a nip out of my flask and looking about me, saw that we had come too far, for a few yards behind me was the dark passage of which we had been told, so I harked the men to it, and holding up Wadeson who kept his legs wonderfully, we darted down it. To my great joy I discovered that we were right, as the walls were reached in less than twenty paces and we were joined by Brookes, Drew, Justice, and the other fellows with the remainder of the Regiment and the 2nd Punjabis, one of whom, a tall Sikh, jumped from the wall on to my shoulders with a shout of 'Bravo Sahib!'

Also driving down the foot of the walls were men of the 1st Bengal Fusiliers, and with them the engineer A. M. Lang. They ran a gauntlet of enemy fire: 'On we rushed,' wrote Lang, 'shouting and cheering, while grape and musketry from each bend, and from every street leading from our left, and from rampart and housetop, knocked down men and officers. It was exciting to madness and I felt no feeling except to rush on and hit: I only wondered how much longer I could possibly go on unhit, when the whole air seemed full of bullets. We took tower after tower, gun after gun, never stopping.' Close by were Richard Barter and his men:

On we went, fighting every inch of the way, but never coming to close quarters, the Enemy firing at us from the windows of the high houses or from behind the walls of gardens etc. from our left, which ran parallel to those of the city, from which they were separated by the roadway up which we advanced. The insides of the walls of Delhi have arched recesses about four or five feet deep into the walls, and into these we used to rush when we saw the port fires being put to the guns, which we came upon now and again raking down the road. When the storm of grape had flown past, and before they could be reloaded, we used to take them with a rush and bayonet and shoot the gunners.

The very threat of cold steel, Lang remembered, seemed to be enough to drive the mutineers along before them: 'We seemed hardly to shoot any, but occasionally in some bend or in some tower caught fellows who were late in flying.' In his own hands, however, he found it had its limitations: 'I found that I was no hand at using a sword; I cut at several, but never gave a death blow; to my surprise I didn't seem able to cut hard, but it was of no consequence, as Gurkhas' kukri and Europeans' bayonet instantly did the business.'

On the ramparts above, men of the 1st Bengal Fusiliers under Lieutenant G. Money were also pushing on down the ramparts in the direction of the Kabul Gate. Halfway there they came upon an enemy 12-pounder whose gunners were firing at men of No. 4 Column, outside the city walls. Seeing Money and his men, the mutineers turned the gun towards them. As the gunners loaded with grapeshot, Money and his men charged. It was a race with high stakes – if the gunners failed to load and fire in time they would be bayoneted; if the infantry didn't reach the gun in time they would be blown away by a blast of grape. When Money and his men were still yards from the gun's muzzle they saw the gunners jump aside as the port-fire was applied to the vent. The expected blast, however, never came – in his haste, the gun's number two had failed to prick the cartridge – the gun failed to fire and in seconds Money and his men had bayoneted the crew. Pushing on, they approached the Mori bastion, where a battery, apparently unaware that the British were within the walls, was still firing at the siege batteries. Again the Fusiliers charged – some of the gunners taken by surprise jumped through the embrasures down into the ditch below, others drew swords and fought around their guns. A sepoy cut at Money, who was saved by the arrival of Private Patrick Flynn. Grabbing Flynn's muzzle, the sepoy cut at Flynn's head, half stunning him with the hilt and wresting the rifle from his hands. Flynn took a step back and then punched the sepoy between the eyes. As the man fell, Money finished him off.

Money and his men had gained a lodgement in a corner of the bastion, but the sepoys soon counter-attacked. Outnumbered, the Fusiliers found themselves hard pressed. First help came in the form of a party of 9th Lancers. Some of the troopers who had been serving in the siege batteries rode up to the walls and asked if they could be of assistance. Minutes later, having scrambled up the breach, they were manning one of the captured guns. If the Lancers' intervention didn't turn the tide, it stemmed it – and relief was at hand. A. M. Lang and his party were already at the Mori Gate, short of the bastion, where: 'I shouted out to line the parapet and give three cheers; bad advice! for we were fired on from our own batteries: we tore strips of white, red, and blue from dead Pandies' clothes, and put up an impromptu flag and then rushed on again.' In the streets below Richard Barter and his men were also approaching the bastion:

> Not far from the Moree gate we passed a large house on our left, the venetians of which being closed we took to be deserted, but a volley of musketry from it soon showed us we were mistaken; the venetians were torn aside and we then found it was occupied by some two or three hundred men of an Irregular Cavalry Regiment, who had treated us to a salute from their carbines as we passed; firing through the windows our men quickly made a lodgement on the ground floor, and hunting the sowars from storey to storey at last bayonet met sword on the broad flat roof on which in a few moments not a trooper remained alive; all were hurled over the low balustrade which ran round the top, and it was a strange sight to see them come tumbling down in their jackboots and plated head pieces, which had a spike through the centre and were bound round with a crimson velvet put on like a small turban.

On his arrival at the foot of the Mori bastion, Barter found that it had a large mound of earth thrown up over it, to stop British shot from entering the city. The only way into the bastion was up a flagged causeway, at the top of which in the gap was a 24-pounder and, close by, a sentry who was looking across at a corner of the bastion to where Money and his band of fusiliers and lancers were fighting off a series of counter-attacks. The Highlanders' attack from below took them by surprise: 'They never expected us,' wrote Barter, 'and only had time to deliver a straggling fire when we were on them; Knighton, the Colonel's orderly was shot through the arm here and as he was falling I caught him, and he got covered with his blood which gushed out freely, an artery I fancy having been cut. I had already got a benefit from Wadeson and others but this finished me.'

On top of the bastion Money's men were soon reinforced by men of the 8th, more of the 75th, the 2nd Bengal Fusiliers and the 2nd Punjabis, under Brigadier Jones, and after a few minutes hard fighting – bayonet and *kukri* against *tulwar* – the Mori bastion was in British hands. 'After a smart tussle,' wrote Barter, 'the Moree was ours and as I was by this time pretty well done up I was left in charge of it with about thirty or forty of our fellows. We at once pitched the dead Sepoys over the parapet into the ditch, and crammed the 24-pounder with grape of which, as well as shells, cartridges etc. there was a goodly supply.' One man who should have been on the ramparts of Delhi by now, was not – Major Cobbe, it will be remembered, had sat down by the Flagstaff Tower to await the passing of his column and had fallen asleep. A few hours later he woke up and seeing all about him quiet and the columns all gone, assumed that the attack had, like others before it, been cancelled. He rode back to the camp, enjoyed a leisurely bath and strolled into the mess tent for his breakfast. After a while, seeing that he was the only officer present, he asked the Mess Sergeant where everybody was – 'Why sir,' said the Sergeant, 'they are in Delhi. They stormed the city last night.' How Cobbe explained himself to his general is unrecorded, but the mishap doesn't seem to have affected his career – he died a major general.

So far – within the walls of Delhi – the assault had gone according to plan; outside it had been a different story. No. 4 Column was composed of whatever European troops could be spared from the pickets, as well as some invalids, Major Reid's Gurkhas of the Sirmoor Battalion – Reid was to command the column – the Guides infantry and 1,200 men of the Kashmir contingent, who had arrived with much panache and blood-thirsty promises on the 4th, along with the siege guns. The column's task was to advance through the Kishenganj and Paharipur suburbs – shadowing the main British advance along the ramparts – and effect an entrance through the Kabul Gate. From the start things went wrong. Four guns that were to accompany the column were late arriving – when they did arrive there were only enough gunners to man one of them. The signal for the column to advance was the blowing of the Kashmir Gate, but before the main assault started, Reid pushed out four hundred men of the Kashmir contingent towards the Idgah, to create a diversion. The Kashmir contingent – commanded by another of the Lawrence brothers, Richard – was a colourful unit. Richard Barter had seen its arrival on the 4th. 'They had some very pretty Field pieces of small calibre and many were armed with a curious kind of flint-lock brass-barrelled weapon with a bell muzzle like a blunderbuss; this was called a shere butcha, literally a lion's whelp; it was fired with the stock under the right arm, by which it was kept close to the side, and the man when firing it slewed himself about under the impression that by that means he distributed the slugs and pieces of old iron with which it was crammed, in the same way that water can be thrown round with a sweep of a garden water pot.' These men soon found themselves under attack from a strong mutineer force that had issued out from the Lahore Gate.

Seeing that his force was already engaged, Reid decided to advance at once ahead of the main assaulting columns. Leading the advance – as with the other columns – were the 60th Rifles, and this detachment was led by Douglas Muter, whose wife was even now anxiously listening in Meerut to the sound of the guns: 'My company (60th Rifles) led; [one] subdivision advanced in skirmishing order; the other in support at the head of the column. The move delayed for guns, which did not come, was then so rapid that the skirmishers could do little to cover. A bridge had to be crossed over a canal (dry) right under the walls of Kissengunje, held by the enemy in great strength, and the fire was heavy. Here Major Reid was wounded and his fall checked the advance of his Ghoorkas he was leading.' As Reid, wounded in the head, was carried off on the back of one of his Gurkhas, Lawrence's Kashmiris broke, abandoning their four guns. This earned them the contempt of many British officers, but in fairness to the Kashmiris, even a hardened campaigner like Chamberlain – watching from the roof of Hindu Rao's House – had been impressed by the order in which the sepoys attacked 'and could not fail to admire the conduct of the mutineer native officers as they rode along in front of their regiments endeavouring to incite their men to press home their advantage'.

Meanwhile, by the canal, the casualties of the main column were mounting: 'The 1st Bengal Fusiliers passed through at "the double,"' wrote Muter, 'and continued the rush in front or along the wall, suffering from the fire as they made for the street which opened to the left and where the Sepoys were gathered in force. Here, in front of the Fusiliers, McBarnett was killed. Then the 1st came up, but the confusion had become great as detachment after detachment got mingled on the other side of the bridge, with the enemy all the time firing from loopholes some fifty yards away ... We could neither give orders nor get them executed, and we were fighting with this deep canal (for it was deep and difficult ) in our rear.' A low, stone wall ran along the canal and this was soon lined with officers and men of the different units – in some confusion – all firing towards the Kishenganj. The wounding of Reid, the column commander, at the outset added to the confusion. Richard Lawrence attempted to assume command, but Douglas Muter – as the senior officer in command of European troops – felt it should be his. Other officers present clearly agreed:

> The Guides under Shebbeare had come up ... Shebbeare said, 'You had better assume the command. We must make a desperate effort to break away from this cover.' The 'assembly' was sounded, and soon a group of officers was assembled. Then the 'advance' and, waving our swords we went over the wall calling on the men to follow. The bugle notes aroused the enemy, and the fire became furious – so withering that it was almost impossible to live for a few minutes exposed to it. The Adjutant of the Guides was killed as he mounted the wall. Shebbeare was shot through the cheek, and the number who fell on the instant effectually checked the movement.

Muter then consulted with an Engineer officer about the possibility of working round to the right. The two men concluded that such a move might expose the Ridge itself to attack, denuded as it was of troops. 'While speaking to the Engineer officer he was, as we all supposed, mortally wounded. Then I returned to see how we could best withdraw, and heard that Shebbeare had been again hit.'

With the whole column stalled and taking heavy casualties and many officers killed or wounded, Muter concluded that the position was hopeless. With the enemy who had routed the Kashmiris still coming on strongly, however, even a withdrawal was going to be hazardous:

> It was under these circumstances I decided to send a message to the Crow's Nest Battery to open on the enemy regardless of us. A young officer carried that message with great rapidity, and while awaiting the opening of the big guns I encouraged the withdrawal of the wounded, and by this time, for we had long been under fire, the force had considerably dwindled. Lieutenant Evans, the young Artillery officer in charge of the Crow's Nest Battery, had fortunately prepared for the emergency, and he could see from his commanding height that our attack had failed. With the utmost precision, he pitched his shrapnel

over our heads and enabled us to withdraw with an ease otherwise impossible. But for this the retreat might have been disastrous.

The repulse of No. 4 Column was to have repercussions inside and outside the city. This column was supposed to effect an entry at the Lahore Gate and then join with Nos. 1 and 2 Columns on their drive into the city; now Nos. 1 and 2 Columns would have to go it alone. The more immediate danger, however – as Douglas Muter had foreseen – was to the Ridge itself. Just about every able-bodied man in the Delhi force had been committed to the assault, leaving the camp only lightly defended. If the rebel force now driving No. 4 Column back was to push on to the Ridge, the men storming Delhi might, on looking over their shoulders, see the enemy storming their own camp. If this was the worst-case scenario, scarcely better was the possibility of this same force turning back, re-entering the city via the Lahore Gate and joining the stiffening resistance to the advance of Nos. 1 and 2 Columns. It was in these circumstances that Hope Grant led forward his Cavalry Brigade – consisting of his own 9th Lancers, a part of the 6th Carabiniers, and various Sikh and Punjabi cavalry – of six hundred horsemen, only a third of whom were British. Having until now simply guarded the Ridge, the brigade's new task was to prevent any further advance of the mutineers who had defeated No. 4 Column, and 'pin' them and prevent them re-entering the city.

As the cavalry moved forward, Hope Grant saw on the ramparts above him the lean figure of John Nicholson stalking across the Mori bastion. Nicholson shouted down to him that the assault was going well and he was about to attack the Lahore Gate. Grant's immediate concern was with the heavy guns at Hindu Rao's House. These had already – with blasts of grape – slowed the advance of the rebels and assisted the withdrawal of No. 4 Column, but their own position was now under threat. It fell to the cavalry to support them. As the ground was unsuitable for the cavalry to charge, they were reduced to doing that for which cavalry was never designed – holding ground. While his horse artillery, under Major Tombs, galloped forward and opened up on the rebels with grape, Grant's troopers were obliged to sit their horses under a heavy fire from the houses and gardens of the Kishenganj. William Hodson's men were part of the force. 'For more than two hours,' he wrote, 'we had to sit on our horses under the heaviest fire troops are often exposed to, and that, too, without the chance of doing anything but preventing the enemy coming on ... My young regiment behaved admirably as did all hands. The loss of the party was, of course, very severe.' Another officer watched Hodson as he sat 'like a man carved in stone, and as calm and apparently unconcerned as the sentries at the Horse Guards, and only by his eyes and his ready hand, whenever occasion offered, could you have told that he was in deadly peril, and the balls flying among us as thick as hail'. Hope Grant and his staff had four horses shot under them; Tombs's troop of horse artillery had twenty-five men out of fifty wounded and seventeen horses. The 9th Lancers had thirty-eight men and seventy-one horses hit. 'Nothing daunted,' wrote Hope Grant in his dispatch, 'those gallant soldiers held their trying position with patient endurance; and on my praising them for their good behaviour they declared their readiness to stand the fire as long as I chose. The behaviour of the Native Cavalry was also admirable. Nothing could be steadier; nothing could be more soldierlike than their bearing.' Under the cover of the front formed by the cavalry, No. 4 Column and the Kashmiris who had been expelled from the Idgah were able to withdraw to positions of safety behind Hindu Rao's House, but the cavalry's ordeal was not over. The enemy's fire intensified as sepoys who had manned the walls to oppose No. 4 Column were now free to turn their attention to the Cavalry Brigade. Soon showers of grape from a 24-pounder on the Lahore bastion showed that British pressure on that sector, too, had ceased. If the defenders of the Lahore bastion now felt free to turn their attention to the cavalry outside the walls, then something had gone wrong within them.

To find out what, we need to retrace our steps to the Mori bastion where Grant last saw Nicholson. Shortly after it had fallen, Major Jacob of the 1st Bengal Fusiliers came up with 250 men and pushed on through to attack the next bastion, the Burn, which overlooked the Lahore Gate. Here, a hollow lane 10 feet wide ran along the base of the walls – every 30 yards, the walls' buttresses narrowed it to 4 or 5 feet. It was down this lane, which was covered by two guns on the ramparts and one in the lane, that Jacob and his men now tried to advance. At the first attempt Jacob was mortally wounded. Shot through the thigh, he refused to be carried to the rear calling out, 'Let me lie; go on and capture the guns.' Under the command of Captain Greville, who had come to the assault straight from hospital, the Fusiliers charged and captured two of the guns – one in the lane and one above. The third, however, was sited 100 yards further back on the ramparts, its crew protected by a corrugated iron screen. While the Fusiliers spiked the two guns they had taken, this third maintained a fire of grape that pinned the men behind what cover they could find. Not long after, Nicholson arrived on the scene, determined on the capture of the Lahore Gate. By now the flat roofs of the houses on the left of the British were occupied by large numbers of enemy sharpshooters who added their fire to that of the screened gun on the ramparts. Seeing that the men were exhausted by the pace of the advance, Captain Greville suggested to Nicholson that they should out-flank the screened gun by breaking through the walls of the houses, which were made of poor quality unbaked bricks. Nicholson, though, impatient of delay, ordered '1st Fusiliers charge down the lane – 75th charge along the ramparts and carry the position above'. Both regiments charged. The Highlanders above were met by a hail of grape and musket balls and were driven back. In the lane Lieutenants Butler and Speke (brother of the explorer John Hanning Speke), with a dozen fusiliers, reached the rear of the Burn bastion, but were unable to break through the bricked and loopholed entrance. Butler managed to climb a little way up, but was forced off by sepoys' bayonets thrust at him through the loopholes. Nicholson arrived at the entrance to the lane to find the 1st Fusiliers tired and demoralized – having lost fifty men and eight officers – and most of the regiment now taking cover behind the buttresses. Decid-ing once again to lead from the front, Nicholson dashed into the lane waving his sword over his head and cheering. Almost at once he fell, shot through the chest by a sepoy on one of the rooftops. Dragged to the shelter of a buttress, he refused to be evacuated, saying that he would stay where he was until Delhi was taken. Shortly afterwards, as the attempt on the Lahore Gate was abandoned and the troops fell back to the Kabul Gate, Nicholson was placed in a *dhoolie*, still alive, and carried away.

Frederick Roberts, who had watched the opening of the assault at General Wilson's side, had, as it progressed, ridden with him down through the Kashmir Gate to St James's Church. Wilson was ill, tired and far from confident in the outcome of the battle. Hearing of No. 4 Column's defeat, the wounding of Nicholson and a false report that both Hope Grant and Major Tombs of the Horse Artillery were killed, Wilson sent Roberts forward to assess the situation and report back.

Just after starting on my errand, while riding through the Kashmir gate, I observed by the side of the road a dhoolie, without bearers, and with evidently a wounded man inside. I dismounted to see if I could

be of any use to the occupant, when I found, to my grief and con-
sternation, that it was John Nicholson, with death written on his face.
He told me that the bearers had put the dhoolie down and gone off to
plunder; that he was in great pain and wished to be taken to the
hospital. He was lying on his back, no wound was visible, and but for
the pallour of his face, always colourless, there was no sign of the agony
he must have been enduring. On my expressing a hope that he was not
seriously wounded, he said, 'I am dying, there is no chance for me.'
The sight of that great man lying helpless and on the point of death
was more than I could bear. Other men had daily died around me,
friends and comrades had been killed beside me, but I never felt as I
felt then – to lose Nicholson seemed at that moment to lose everything.

Roberts searched for the dhoolie-bearers without success – like many of
the Delhi force camp followers they were already searching the nearby
houses for whatever they could carry off. Eventually rounding up four
men, he placed them under the command of a sergeant of the 61st and
ordered him to carry Nicholson to the field hospital.

While Nos. 1 and 2 Columns had been clearing the ramparts as far as
the Kabul Gate, Reid's No. 4 Column was being repulsed and the Cavalry
Brigade was undergoing its ordeal by fire in front of the Lahore Gate,
No. 3 Column, under Colonel Campbell, had been pushing on into the
heart of the city. These were the men who had stormed through the
Kashmir Gate after it had been blown by Salkeld and Home's Explosion
Party, and their destination was the Jama Masjid, the city's main mosque.
After a hard fight at the back of the Water bastion, where Reginald
Wilberforce of the 52nd and a brother officer had bent their swords
uselessly against the chest of a mutineer, the column's advance was at first
only lightly opposed. There were other dangers, though, as Wilberforce
wrote: 'As we passed along the streets we noticed large basins full of
different sorts of liquor, put out by the natives, who had full knowledge
of the British soldier's drinking propensities. We heard afterwards that
this liquor was all poisoned. As we went along we broke these basins and
spilt the liquor.'

Campbell's column advanced unopposed through the Begum Bagh
(Queen's Garden) towards the Delhi Bank. 'When close up to the Bank,'
wrote Wilberforce, 'we met the first sign of opposition, a howitzer with
some men around it. Unwilling to lose men, our Colonel ordered us to
halt, and, taking a few men, he made a detour so as to get behind the gun

and its guardians. Unfortunately, our Major, who was left in command, mistook the Colonel's orders, and before the latter could get round ordered a charge. The gun was taken, but we lost one of our officers, who was shot dead, and several men.' The column's further advance was unopposed, Wilberforce recalled, until it reached the Jama Masjid 'only to find its great gate closed and the houses round it filled with numbers of the enemy who kept up a hot fire upon us. We drew a little way back, so as not to be exposed to a direct fire and then waited for the other columns, which never came.'

With the failure at the Lahore Gate, Nos. 1 and 2 Columns were not able to enter the Chandni Chowk and advance up it to link with Campbell's column, which had been the plan for what we would nowadays call the 'Second Phase' of the assault on Delhi. Campbell's column was now exposed and isolated in the heart of the city, without support and without orders. Wilberforce recorded his Colonel's reaction. 'Our Colonel ... would not retire; he said, "The 52nd have never retired without orders yet, and as long as I live they never shall," a speech loudly cheered by the men who heard it. Meanwhile, as we waited, the Ghazis made some desperate charges upon us. They came galloping down the street, their linen clothes flying in the wind, their tulwars waving around their heads, shouting *"Deen, Deen, Allah Deen!"* None ever went back, they came to die and die they did, but every time they came, some one of us was killed or wounded.' After about half an hour, along with news of the failure at the Lahore Gate and the wounding of Nicholson, came the order to retire.

By this time, however, we were surrounded, and to get back appeared hopeless. All the officers shook hands with one another and said 'Good bye.' Our dead we had to leave, our wounded we took with us; we got some native beds and some shutters to carry them on, and putting them in the middle we started. Very different was that retreat to the advance. As we came up hardly a shot was fired, now the houses on each side seemed alive with men, and cavalry kept charging down the street as we retired. A brother ensign and myself were the rearguard; we used to halt some of our men, make them kneel down in the street, fire, and then we ran on to overtake the rest of the rearguard.

On their advance, the 52nd had crossed at right angles the wide street of the Chandni Chowk – up which the other columns had been expected

An attack on the Redan battery, Lucknow. (Bettmann/Corbis)

Evacuating the wounded in 'dhoolies', Lucknow. Surgeon Anthony Dickson and Assistant Surgeon William Bradshaw (centre) were both awarded VCs after this action. (By Louis Desanges/Courtesy of the Council, National Army Museum, London/Bridgeman Art Library)

'*Baillie Guard Gate, with the opening on the extreme right, through which Sir H. Havelock and his brave army entered the Residency.*' Lucknow. (Dannenberg Album/British Library)

'*The Clock Tower and Ruins of the Residency Building, North, in the tower of which "Bob the Nailer" secreted himself, keeping up a deadly fire against the defenders of the Residency.*' Lucknow. (Dannenberg Album/British Library)

General Sir Robert Napier, with his ADC
Major Greathed, at Lucknow. (Courtesy
of the Council, National Army Museum,
London/Bridgeman Art Library)

Sir Colin Campbell. (Art Archive/John Meek)

The storming of Delhi – British and Sikh infantry attack a rebel earthwork. On the left an officer
'spikes' a captured gun. (After George Atkinson/British Library/Bridgeman Art Library)

The King of Delhi surrenders
to William Hodson at
Humayun's Tomb. (Hulton-
Deutsch Collection/Corbis)

LYING IN WAIT. 'Like a terrier
at a rat hole' – tunnel warfare at
Lucknow. (British Library/
Bridgeman Art Library)

*'Bridge-of-boats thrown over the Goomti by Sir Colin Campbell, near and below La Martinière on the
2nd day of the assault, troops passed over it at dawn.'* Lucknow. (Dannenberg Album/British
Library)

'*Enclosure of Secundra Bagh, where over 2,000 rebels were stationed to oppose our army, and where General Peel, Blunt, and others brought the seige guns to bear against the wall and battered it, to enable our troops to enter. The hole in the wall is where the figure is standing, to the right "Young Richard Cooper of 93rd Regiment outrun the remainder of his comrades, flying through the hole and landed unscathed, he was followed by Col. Ewart of the 93rd Regiment and by three Privates of his Regiment and then by Sikhs and Highlanders."*' The word 'General' has been corrected in pencil to read 'Captn' in the original caption. (Dannenberg Album/British Library)

The released garrison of the Lucknow Residency crossing the Ganges. (By J. Needham/Cragside House/National Trust/Derrick E. Witty/Bridgeman Art Library)

'Loot' – a Hindi word. British and Sikh infantry plundering the Kaisar Bagh, Lucknow. (By Egron Lundgren/British Library/Bridgeman Art Library)

*'The Residency, East, as it was found by the victorious army under the leadership of General Sir Colin Campbell.'* Lucknow. (Dannenberg Album/British Library)

The massacre at Jhansi. (Hulton-Deutsch Collection/Corbis)

Soldiers of Her Majesty's 95th Foot, as they appeared during the Central India campaign.
(By John Crealock/Art Archive/Sherwood Foresters Museum/Eileen Tweedy)

A new Indian Army. Officers and NCOs of the 2nd Cavalry, Punjab Frontier Force, 1863. All of the men wear the Indian Order of Merit, awarded during the mutiny. The decision of the Sikhs to stick with the British proved crucial. (By Gordon Hayward/Courtesy of the Council, National Army Museum, London/Bridgeman Art Library)

to advance to join them. By the time they reached the street leading back to St James's Church numbers of enemy horse and foot had worked round their flanks and were now trying to block their escape route. Most of the regiment made it across the street and the walled canal that ran down its centre, but Wilberforce and his fellow ensign found themselves lost in the smoke and confusion: 'We, who were the last to go, discussed whether we should go straight across, climbing the low wall of the canal, or whether we should run up the street until we came to a bridge crossing. We did not know that there was a bridge immediately in front of us, and we could not see for the smoke that was hanging about; we decided on going up the street, and accordingly we started to run as hard as we could.' By now more mutineers were arriving moment by moment – freed by the stalling of the British attack on the Lahore Gate – and soon they had deployed guns in the street.

As we two boys ran up the street searching for the bridge, we ran straight towards a large body of men who were in the street, and our men who had got over were astounded at the sight they saw. They saw us running headlong at a large number of men; suddenly they saw these men turn round and run also. They evidently thought that we were the *avant couriers* of a charge of infantry. The clouds of smoke which had hidden the bridge crossing from our view hid what was behind us; for all they knew hundreds might have been following – at any rate they were not going to wait and see, and bolted incontinently and so saved us.

The two men's luck almost ran out, however: 'Some of the rebel cavalry saw that there were only two of us, and made a dash to cut us off. Just as they were on us, we swerved close to the canal, where some small trees were growing, and as we came opposite to where our men were, they came out into the street, and we crawled in somehow under the horses of the enemy, unharmed and unscathed.' The 52nd, having arrived in the Begum Bagh, were joined by various missing men and the Kumaon Battalion. Still under heavy fire to which they could not retaliate, the troops held the Begum Bagh for another hour and a half – losing more men there than at any other place – before retiring, at 11.30 a.m., back to St James's Church.

Meanwhile, Roberts had continued his tour of the British front line, found Hope Grant to be still alive and the cavalry now able to fall back.

'It had shortly before been relieved from its perilous and unpleasant position as a target for the enemy by the timely arrival of the Guides Infantry and a detachment of the Baluch battalion. I was rejoiced to find Tombs still alive and unhurt and from him and other members of my regiment I learnt the tremendous peppering they had undergone.' Roberts galloped back to try and assuage Wilson's anxieties. Despite the setbacks at the Lahore Gate morale among the stormers was still high. Up on the Mori bastion at noon, Richard Barter and his men

> had the satisfaction of seeing the Union Jack, which during the entire siege had been regularly displayed from the Flagstaff Tower, hoisted on the Kashmir bastion, announcing to all that the British Force had succeeded in the assault. Its appearance was the signal for cheers from all round the walls from the Water bastion to the Kabul gate, which rang out again as the breeze unfolded it, and in spite of the smoke. When the different Regiments caught sight of it, men cheered and laughed and capered with delight and to a calm looker-on the whole thing would, I am sure, have seemed rather absurd, but to men who had fought so long in front of these walls, and who had borne with patience the terrible heat and hardships of the Siege, it was a most exciting moment, and the thoughts of most, indeed I may say of all were, 'what will they say at home?'

General Wilson was not cheering. Frederick Roberts had arrived at Headquarters. 'The news I was able to give for the moment somewhat cheered the General, but did not altogether dispel his gloomy fore-bodings; and the failure of Campbell's column (which had just at that juncture returned to the church), the hopelessness of Nicholson's con-dition, and above all, the heavy list of casualties he received later, all appeared to crush all the spirit and energy out of him. His dejection increased, and he became more than ever convinced that his wisest course was to withdraw from the city.' Never an optimist at the best of times, Wilson's fears about the assault seemed to him confirmed. Certainly, casualties had been heavy. Richard Barter, by 2 p.m. the senior officer still standing and therefore in command of his regiment, went to Head-quarters for orders: 'There was a goodly tiffin spread out on tables ... and inside we could see General Wilson pacing up and down a large room in a troubled manner and looking a strange contrast to the beaming faces of the men we had lately parted from. We heard that he was horrified at the toll of killed and wounded.' He had good reason – about 3,300 men of all ranks who were actually engaged in the storming of Delhi were dead or wounded by two o'clock.

J. E. W. Rotton, chaplain to the Delhi Field Force, was at the hospital – half a mile distant from the walls of Delhi, where surgeons and chaplains worked from sunrise to sunset: 'Soon after the assault commenced the dhoolies, freighted with European and native wounded and dead, hastening along the various avenues from the city towards the hospital. No sooner were one set of dhoolies emptied of their contents and discharged for fresh patients, than the same sad duty had to be repeated again and again, moment after moment and hour after hour, in long succession.' As casualties mounted, Rotton wrote, the hospital was soon filled to capacity:

> Every apartment is crowded with charpoys (common native bedsteads), and every charpoy is occupied; some have been not only twice but a score of times, even before the sun had reached the meridian. Indeed the wounded were so many that a little straw strewn on the ground served many a brave English and native soldier for a bed. We could not give them more. In the verandah around the house, here and there, were to be seen tables of wood roughly put together, and lying prostrate thereon, with head slightly raised, now a wounded officer, and now a common soldier. Around them were assembled surgeons and apothecaries, all busily engaged in operating. Almost every kind of amputation was performed: legs and arms, even fingers, bloodless and shrivelled, no longer members of their respective bodies, laid carelessly on the ground, were common sights of horror.

Mounting casualties, confused street-fighting, setbacks to two of the columns, the continuing threat of an outflanking attack on the British right outside the walls – all these played on the mind of Wilson. Yet there were some grounds for optimism. The whole of the north wall of Delhi from the Water bastion to the Kabul Gate was now in British hands – if the situation of the Delhi force as afternoon turned to night was precarious, a withdrawal would have been certainly disastrous for the force, and possibly for the whole British position in India. As Wilson contemplated withdrawing from Delhi – an order that Richard Barter was sure 'would not have been obeyed' – the mood of his staff was very different. Roberts remembered that 'every officer on his staff was utterly opposed to any retrograde movement'. For Roberts, the hero of the moment was the senior engineer: 'Baird-Smith's indomitable courage and determined perseverance were never more conspicuous than at that critical moment, when, though suffering intense pain from his wound, and weakened by a wasting disease, he refused to be put on the sick list; and on Wilson appealing to him for advice as to whether he should or should not hold on to the position we had gained, the short but decisive answer, "We *must* hold on," was given in … a determined and uncompromising tone.' Baird-Smith's advice was backed by a note from the gunner Colonel Brind, which read 'God has given you a great victory, see that you don't throw it away.' Clearly Wilson's subordinates had the measure of him. Neville Chamberlain, consulted by note on the same subject, wrote from the roof of Hindu Rao's House stressing the advantages already gained and the demoralization of the enemy. Even the dying Nicholson, hearing of Wilson's proposal to withdraw was able to gasp 'Thank God I have strength yet to shoot him if necessary.'

Borne down by such a weight of opinion Wilson abandoned all plans to withdraw – the force would consolidate its gains, establish communication between the various columns and prepare for further advances the next day. It is perhaps too easy to write off Wilson as a hopeless ditherer, but his fears both before the assault and now were not irrational. In his note to Chamberlain he had stated: 'We have lost so many men that the troops are not under proper control.' This opinion seems borne out by the experience of Richard Barter and his friend Coghill, when returning to the Mori bastion.

> We heard voices in anger and proceeding evidently from Europeans engaged in some scuffle; quickening our steps we came upon two soldiers of the 2nd Bengal Fusiliers holding a pony by the bridle and threatening the rider with their fixed bayonets. He was evidently an officer and was holding a bottle high above his head. We shouted to the men to stay their hands and on running up found that the officer was Captain Burnside of the 61st, and Brigade Major to the 3rd Infantry Brigade. He was passing by near the place and seeing the bottle with the two men asked them to show it to him and was then proceeding to ride away with it when they seized his bridle and had not Coghill and I come up I fully expect that there would have been bad work.

Instead of being grateful, however: 'He was rude and offensive to us for remonstrating with him for doing such a foolish thing as to attempt to take a bottle away from two men of a strange Regiment, and knowing as I supposed he must, that the men of the Company's Regiment were not the best disciplined in the world or obedient to strange officers.' Roberts, visiting the positions inside the walls at Wilson's request, found:

> Great confusion – men without their officers, and officers without their men – all without instructions, and not knowing what was going on in their immediate neighbourhood, the inevitable result of the rapid advance . . . The fact is too much had been attempted on that eventful morning. We should have been satisfied with gaining possession of the Kashmir and Water bastions, and getting a lodgement within the city walls. This was as much as three such weak columns should have tried, or been asked to accomplish. No one who was present on that occasion, and experienced the difficulty, indeed impossibility, of keeping soldiers in hand while engaged in fighting along narrow streets and tortuous lanes, would ever again attempt what was expected of the assaulting columns.

As afternoon turned to evening there were counter-attacks. At sunset the rebels attacked the Mori bastion in some strength but contented themselves with firing from a distance. At length the men on the bastion brought the captured 24-pounder into action and after a few rounds of grapeshot the enemy drew off. Another rebel attack, according to Frederick Roberts, was driven off without a shot being fired: 'Early in the evening the enemy appeared from their movements to be preparing to attack us, but just at that moment the band of the 4th Punjab Infantry struck up, "Cheer, Boys, Cheer!" upon which the men of the regiment did cheer most lustily, and other regiments caught up and continued the inspiriting hurrahs, which apparently had the effect of disconcerting the mutineers and keeping them quiet.'

That night officers and men exhausted by weeks of preparation and thirteen hours of hard fighting, slept where they could. General Wilson and his staff in Skinner's House passed a relatively quiet night. Near by, in St James's Church, Reginald Wilberforce was not so lucky: 'I searched for and found some empty sand-bags, and carrying them into the church made up a bed, and went to sleep for some two hours. I was awakened by some one rudely shaking me; I opened my eyes, and saw a live shell blazing away on the floor of the church. The mutineers were shelling the church; all the other occupants had been aroused by the bursting of the shells and had got out, and our Adjutant came in to get me out also. I was soon sound asleep again outside.' Before they could settle down to rest, Richard Barter and his men – on the Mori bastion – had to tidy up:

> The wind, as is usual in India, failed and only came in occasional puffs. The stench from the dead bodies, with which the ditch which surrounded the bastion was pretty well filled, became abominable, so much so that many of us got very ill and were taken with cholera symptoms. There was one whiff most particularly disagreeable, and the cause of it was for a long time to puzzle us. At length about 9 or 10 p.m. the sentry on lookout at the centre embrasure seemed struck with a strange idea. I noticed him carefully turning over with his bayonet a coarse heap of cloth for sandbags called tat on which he had been standing to enable him to look clear of the parapet. Presently desisting from this he looked in my direction and proclaimed in triumph, 'Here's the beggar that was stinkin' sir.' I went over and found a dead Sepoy, who had I suppose been placed there by his comrades until he could be removed. We at once shot him over into the ditch below, finding his absence a great relief.

Barter was not destined to sleep for long – at midnight he was roused by the challenge of a Sikh sentry at the centre embrasure, and went over to join the man:

> He was actually shaking from excitement as he pointed out to me a dark mass of men moving slowly down from the Lahore Gate and it was by the greatest difficulty that I prevented him from firing at them. He whispered in Hindustani, 'They are the Enemy, they are the Enemy certainly sir.' I told him to keep quiet and challenge again, for I was in great doubt, not believing that the enemy would place himself in such a position. The reply undeceived me. To the challenge 'Who goes there?' came back in Hindustani 'Don't fire, brother, don't fire, we are the Bareilly Force, General Bakht Khan is going his rounds.' Again I made him challenge, to gain time for us to receive our visitors with all due respect and affection, and again the same answer was returned, with an enquiry as to where the Feringhee dogs were, as up to that time, though they had come a long distance they had not seen anything of them. This was a finisher for the Sikh, he could stand it no longer,

but shouting, 'Here they are you pigs,' he fired slap into the party. There was at once a howl of 'Don't fire brother, don't fire,' but feeling there was no information to be got now, the word was given to the Artillery and they at once commenced with grape shot from the 18-pounder which bore immediately on the Bareilly lot. This was followed by groans and shrieks with the trampling of horses and the roll of guns all tearing away to get out of danger, and we were undisturbed for the rest of the night.

The following day, the 15th, was a day of consolidation. Guns and mortars were mounted inside the city to fire on the palace and on houses containing sharpshooters. 'Order was restored among the troops,' wrote Roberts, 'who . . . had become somewhat demoralised by the street fighting. Regiments and brigades were got together; raids were made on all the store shops within reach, and every bottle of beers and spirits was broken. Some of the liquor would doubtless have been of great use in the hospitals, but there was no means of removing it, and the General wisely determined that it was best to put temptation out of the men's way.' The bottles and basins of liquor – as encountered by Wilberforce on the way to the Begum Bagh the day before – have entered the mythology of the siege. It was widely believed at the time that the mutineers had put these out to encourage the British soldiers to drink themselves into a stupor. If it was a deliberate trap, however, the mutineers failed to take advantage of it. In the district where the British made their assault were concentrated the wine merchants of the city, and it seems unlikely that the British soldiery – or the Sikhs for that matter – needed any help in ferreting out supplies. Certainly there were some scenes of disorder – as Barter and Coghill witnessed on their return from Headquarters – but Roberts was adamant that 'I did not see a single drunken man throughout the day of the assault, although . . . I visited every position held by our troops within the walls of the city.'

The seeming reluctance on the part of the mutineers to press home their counter-attacks the previous afternoon, and the absence of any concerted attempt to drive the British from their lodgement in the city – a narrow strip of ground only a few hundred yards deep and a mile wide – the following day, testifies to the demoralization in the enemy camp. Chamberlain had been right, it seems, to emphasize this in his note to Wilson. Indeed, Wilberforce believed that large numbers of the enemy had decamped before the assault began. 'Our loss would have been much heavier if we had had to encounter the full force of Sepoys who had flocked to Delhi, but numbers, which have been variously computed at 10,000 up to 40,000, like the Assyrians of old, "heard a rumour," and marched out of the city on Sunday night – some never to return again.' It had always been Nicholson's belief that if offered a Golden Bridge to escape, many of the mutineers would take it once the British were within the walls of Delhi. In Meerut Mrs Muter, who had listened with her ear to the ground the previous day to the intensifying bombardment, now received confirmation that Nicholson had been right.

> On the morning following that great day when the columns advanced to the storm of Delhi, a native runner arrived with the news. He said he had been borne across the bridge of boats in a throng so great that his feet could scarcely touch the ground, and the country around was covered with the fugitive army and denizens of the imperial city.
>
> As rumours to this effect had often been received the man was secured, with the promise of reward if the account proved true, and if false of a punishment which would have left him nothing more to hope for in this world. On receipt of further news our joy was considerably modified. An entrance had, indeed, been effected, though with immense loss of life, and the force was still fighting for its existence in the streets of Delhi. The deep, low sound which had spoken such volumes to my heart had indeed, ceased; yet I knew the warfare then going on to be more deadly, though less loud, and my anxiety was rather increased than diminished.

On the 16th Neville Chamberlain took command of the troops in the city – Wilson having declared himself 'getting weaker and weaker every day, mind and body being quite worn out'. There followed five days of vicious house-to-house fighting. The headlong advances of the first day having proved costly – two out of nine men in the force were now casualties, and there were few reserves and no immediate prospect of reinforcement – it was decided that further advances would be made by 'sapping' from house to house. Edward Vibart, at last back in Delhi from whose walls he had jumped on 11 May, described the process: 'We frequently found ourselves on one side of a brick wall with the enemy facing us on the other. The *modus operandi* was as follows. The engineers would first break through the wall of a house, which we at once proceeded to occupy, and then carrying sand-bags to the top of the roof would construct a parapet, from behind which a covering fire was kept up on the house next to be taken.' Not all of the houses were unoccupied. Reginald Wilberforce of the 52nd wrote: 'Sometimes we got into the basement of the houses before the Sepoys had time to escape. Generally they were in some large room on the first floor. Up we used to go, batter in the door, throw ourselves flat on our faces for the volley which always came when the door was open, and then rush in, and make short work of those inside. One time as soon as the door fell in, no volley came. I looked up, and saw instead of armed mutineers a quantity of beds ranged along the wall like a hospital. A rapid inspection showed that they were tenanted by women.' Wilberforce ordered his men to go upstairs, where the sepoys must be. As he was leaving the room he saw one of his men raise his musket and bring it down on the occupants of the bed:

> I ran to the man threatening him with dire punishment for being such a coward as to hurt a woman when the man, an Irishman, said – 'Och yer honour did ye iver see a woman with such a prutty moustache as this?' and raised from the bed the unmistakable face of a Sepoy ... ordering the girls to get up – it was during the daytime and they were all dressed – we found the firing party we were in search of, who having heard us come in through the wall, sought for safety under the bodies of the women. The man who made the discovery explained afterwards, that although the order had been given not to hurt the women, no order had been given against kissing them, and he had merely placed his arm round the girl's neck to give her a kiss, when he became aware that his hand had in its passage round the neck of this girl come into contact with the face underneath.

A day or two later one of his soldiers caught a sepoy trying to escape disguised as a veiled woman: 'After this the other officer who was present and I, posted ourselves at the end of the street and compelled each woman to lift her veil before we allowed her to go by. By adopting this course we stopped a considerable number of Sepoys from escaping, as all who were discovered were immediately executed.'

Immediate execution was the order of the day. Richard Barter and his men, while filling their water bottles at a well, were accosted by an old woman claiming to be a Christian. She told them she was the wife of a musician in a sepoy regiment and had three sons who were drummers. Musicians and drummers in Native regiments were usually Christian

Eurasians – to whom the leather of drumskins was not offensive. She told them they had all been forced to march with the regiment to Delhi when it mutinied, but that on arrival her husband and sons had all been slaughtered and she had been kept as a slave. On Barter's men capturing a naik (corporal) in a nearby house, the woman pointed him out as having shot her son – the man was immediately hanged from the tree by the well.

The excuse that they had been forced to participate in the mutinies – which was in many cases no doubt true – was offered by many captured sepoys, and they had their supporters among the British, as Wilberforce recalled: 'A considerable number of officers from native regiments that had been disarmed or mutinied, hung about head-quarters; and some of these men, in spite of all that had happened, were still so infatuated with the idea that their adored Sepoy had only been led astray by a few evil men, and that the mass were still loyal and only wanted an opportunity to return to their allegiance, that they were very indignant with my fellow commander and myself that we immediately executed all the male prisoners we got. There really was nothing else to be done, except to let them go free, and this, with the Cawnpore massacre fresh in our minds, was out of the question.'

Inevitably, civilians caught up in the fighting suffered the worst of all, subject to casual insult and even violence from an army in vengeful mood. Richard Barter and his men occupied the house of a wealthy Indian, who came to Barter lamenting that his honour was gone as the men had entered his *zenana*. Entering the room Barter found a group of veiled women and one bewildered grenadier. With the treatment of the British women in mind – and all the citizens of Delhi were considered to be complicit in these crimes – Barter decided to take a look at the women. Lifting their veils he declared 'I . . . never saw a more abominably ugly or dirty-looking set of females anywhere.' Placing a sentry on the room, Barter told the husband not to worry. The man stuck to him like glue for the remainder of the day until, panicking – Barter later thought it was because of threatening gestures made by his men when he wasn't looking – he jumped out of a upper window into a tree. Trying to drop to the ground, he was impaled on the bayonet of a waiting Sikh, whose comrades finished the man off amid ferocious laughter.

If the pace of the British advance into Delhi was depressing General Wilson – 'dreadfully slow work', he called it – its pace was having an even worse effect upon the King of Delhi. Yet, it was still felt by the King and his general, Bakht Khan, that if the Lahore Gate, the Magazine and the King's Palace could be held, the British might be confined to the northern part of the city and, ultimately, compelled to withdraw. On the 16th the British captured the Magazine with small loss and beat off a counter-attack by the rebels. That same day the mutineers withdrew from the Kishenganj suburb and thus ended the threat to the British right, but the effect of this inside the walls was to thicken up their resistance to the British advance inside the city, the more so as their line contracted. This and their use of field artillery firing point-blank made the British advance necessarily slow. If it was slow, however, it was also relentless. On the 19th the British turned their attention to the Burn bastion. The advance was directed by Captain Alex Taylor of the Engineers, who had been shot in the chest two days earlier but had now returned to duty. Frederick Roberts was with him: 'We worked through houses, courtyards and lanes, until on the afternoon of the 19th we found ourselves in rear of the Burn bastion, the attempt to take which on the 14th had cost the life of the gallant Nicholson and so many other brave men. We had with us fifty European and fifty Native soldiers, the senior officer of the party being Captain Gordon of the 75th Foot. A single door separated us from the lane which led to the Burn bastion. Lang, of the Engineers, burst this door open, and out dashed the party. Rushing across the lane and up the ramp, the guard was completely surprised, and the bastion was seized without our losing a man.'

The capture of the Burn bastion, which overlooked the Lahore Gate – the principal entrance to Delhi and the main objective on the 14th – seems finally to have convinced the King of Delhi that all was lost. Having decided to evacuate the city, Bakht Khan urged the King to accompany the sepoy army out into open country and there continue the war, but timid counsels prevailed. The King's civilian advisers, Hakim Ahsanullah Khan and Mirza Ilahi Baksh, convinced him that his best hope lay in flight and negotiation. If he led the army in person, they said, and fought in front of his palace – as had been his intention at one point – there would no longer be any doubt about his involvement in the rebellion. The same would be true if he accompanied the army out of the city. His only hope, they argued, was to distance himself from the rebellion – retire to a safe distance, submit to the British and present himself as a victim of circumstances. That same day the King, accompanied by the Begum Zenat Mahal and his sons, left the city and retired to Humayun's tomb, $3\frac{1}{2}$ miles south of the city. If the rebels were preparing to leave the city, the British were in no mood to hinder them. Reginald Wilberforce, at the Magazine, had persuaded an artillery officer to let him fire one of the mortars there:

> My great desire was to get a shell inside the Jumma Musjid [*sic*], that great Mosque outside of which we were stopped on the day of the assault. At last, some one found the right elevation and the correct charge, then we sent shell after shell into the great Mosque, but we were soon stopped. A messenger from Col. Baird Smith came galloping up with 'What are you doing? stop that instantly!' We were then told that we were not to fire on the Mosque or on the bridge of boats which we could see on our left. At the time we could not comprehend the latter part of this order, but next day, when we saw the bridge crowded for hours together with people leaving the city, we realised the full significance of the command.

By the following morning, then, as the British prepared to capture the Lahore Gate and begin the advance up the Chandni Chowk, the sepoy army was already marching out, over the bridge by which the first Meerut mutineers had arrived on the morning of 11 May. The bloodless capture of the Burn bastion had encouraged a belief that the Lahore Gate might be taken in a similar way. Sapping towards the Lahore Gate in the approved fashion, Frederick Roberts and his party came across some *banias* who, he noted, seemed as afraid of the sepoys as of the British: 'The men of our party nearly made an end of these unfortunates before their officers could interfere, for to the troops (Native and European alike) every man inside the walls of Delhi was looked upon as a rebel, worthy of death.' Although it was clear that these men were inoffensive, it was decided to pretend that they were suspected, but offer them their lives if they guided the British to a place from which the Lahore Gate could be overlooked. Led by their unwilling guides, Roberts and his men soon found themselves in a room within 50 yards of the gate: 'From the window of this room we could see beneath us the sepoys lounging about, engaged in cleaning their muskets and other occupations, while some, in a lazy sort of fashion, were acting as sentries over the gateway and two guns, one of which pointed in the direction of the Sabzi Mandi, the other down the lane behind the ramparts leading to the Burn bastion and Kabul gate. I could see from the number on their caps that these sepoys belonged to the 5th Native Infantry.' From this position it was possible to take the Lahore Gate from the rear. Roberts and his men returned and rejoined the main party: 'It was decided to repeat the manoeuvre which had been so successful at the Burn bastion. The troops were brought by the route we had just traversed, and drawn up behind a gateway next to the house in which we had been concealed. The gate was burst open, and rushing into the street, we captured the guns, and killed or put to flight the sepoys whom we had watched from our upper chamber a short time before, without losing a man ourselves.' With the capture of the Lahore Gate, the way into the Chandni Chowk – and therefore the heart of the city – was wide open. The advance thereafter was rapid: 'I got Wiles,' wrote A. M. Lang, who was with Roberts, 'and his twenty-five of the 2nd Europeans, and what Sikhs I could rescue from looting the big last house I had occupied, and we descended into the street and marched our gallant little army up the Grand but deserted Chandni Chowk, finding none but dead and wounded Pandies, and wondering at finding our way all clear before us. We marched straight to the Lahore Gate of the Palace; there I spied through chinks in the great big doors and saw four great guns, crammed to the muzzle with grape, pointing, within ten feet of the door. I went back for powder.' As he did so his colleague Lieutenant Home arrived on the scene, and Frederick Roberts saw what followed:

Home of the Engineers, the hero of the Kashmir gate exploit … advanced with some Sappers and blew in the gate. At this, the last struggle for the capture of Delhi, I wished to be present, so attached myself to a party of the 60th Rifles, under the command of Ensign Alfred Heathcote. As soon as the smoke of the explosion cleared away, the 60th, supported by the 4th Punjab Infantry, sprang through the gateway; but we did not get far, for there was a second door beyond, chained and barred, which was with difficulty forced open, when the whole party rushed in. The recesses in the long passage which led to the palace buildings were crowded with wounded men, but there was little opposition, for only a few fanatics still held out. One of these – a Mohammedan sepoy in the uniform of a Grenadier of the 37th Native Infantry – stood quietly about thirty yards up the passage with his musket on his hip. As we approached he slowly raised his weapon and fired, sending the bullet through McQueen's helmet. The brave fellow then advanced at the charge, and was, of course, shot down. So ended the 20th September, a day I am never likely to forget.

The King of Delhi having opted for self-preservation over a martyr's death at the head of his army, members of his extended family made the same choice. Mirza Ilahi Baksh, the father-in-law of the King's eldest son – in return for his life and a pension – soon betrayed to the British the King's refuge. William Hodson at once approached General Wilson, pointing out that the British victory was incomplete as long as the King and his family were at large, and requesting permission to ride after him and bring him back a prisoner. Wilson was at first reluctant to commit men to what he considered a risky venture, but pressed by Neville Chamberlain among others, he finally agreed to let Hodson take a party of his own sowars and offer the King terms – his life and the life of Zenat Mahal and his favourite son, Jawan Bakht. With a hundred men Hodson rode out to Humayun's tomb, down a road that was still thronged with the King's armed followers. Again, it is difficult not to feel sympathy for the aged King as he awaited his fate in the splendid marble tomb of his ancestor, surrounded by reminders of the glory of the Moguls. His brief time as restored Emperor – an honour he had not sought – had been unhappy and inglorious, and now surely the dynasty was at an end. On arriving at the gate of the complex of buildings that comprise the tomb, Hodson concealed his men near by. The whole of the compound was filled with the King's retainers, armed and willing to fight, but looking to the King for leadership which was not forthcoming. Unknown to them, the King had already decided on surrender. Sending in two emissaries to negotiate the terms of surrender, Hodson waited for two hours before a messenger came out of the building to announce that the King would surrender if 'Hodson Bahadur' himself would guarantee the King's safety. Walking into the compound, sword in hand, Hodson declared that if the King would come out he would repeat the Government's promise to spare his life, but that any attempt at a rescue would mean instant death for the King. A few moments later a train of palkis emerged bearing, first, the Begum Zenat Mahal, and close behind, the King and his son. Hodson would later describe the ride back to Delhi as the longest 5 miles of his life. For most of the way he and his party were followed by a host of the King's retainers, armed and angry, restrained only by the presence of Hodson himself at the King's side. The British troops at the Lahore Gate were about to raise a cheer at the sight of the captive King, until Hodson informed them that the old man would take it as an honour intended for himself. Processing up the Chandni Chowk to the palace, the King and his family were handed over to Charles Saunders, the new

Commissioner, whose words to Hodson: 'By Jove! Hodson, they ought to make you commander-in-chief for this,' contrast sharply with the greeting of General Wilson: 'Well, I am glad you have got him, but I never expected to see either him or you again!' That night the King slept – a prisoner – in the Begum's quarters of the palace.

His success at Humayun's tomb raised Hodson's reputation still higher in the army. What followed was to plunge him – not for the first time – into controversy. Early the following day Hodson again approached Wilson, this time for permission to return to Humayun's tomb and arrest the Shahzadas. These three princes – Mirza Mogul and Mirza Khizr Sultan, the King's two sons, and his grandson Mirza Abu Bakr – were believed to have been implicated in the May massacres. Wilson agreed, adding Pilate-like: 'But don't let me be bothered with them.' Hodson replied, ominously, that it was only by Wilson's own orders that he had been 'bothered' by the King 'as I would much rather have brought him into Delhi dead than living'. Accompanied by his subaltern Charles McDowell and a hundred men, Hodson rode out again to Humayun's tomb. 'I laid my plans,' wrote Hodson, 'so as to cut off access to the tomb or escape from it, and then sent in one of the inferior scions of the royal family (purchased for the purpose by the promise of his life) and my one-eyed *maulvi*, Rajab Ali, to say that I had come to seize the Shazadas for punishment, and intended to do so dead or alive. After two hours of wordy strife and very anxious suspense they appeared and asked if their lives had been promised by the Government, to which I answered, "Most certainly not," and sent them away from the tomb towards the city under a guard.'

As the prisoners made their way to the city, Hodson went on up to the tomb and demanded of the armed retainers there that they surrender their arms and baggage. Leaderless and demoralized the crowd complied and soon Hodson had piled five hundred swords and as many firearms on to carts, and collected numbers of horse and bullocks. Spurring down the road to join his prisoners and their escort, Hodson found them hard pressed by the increasingly hostile crowd: 'I came up *just in time*, as a large mob had collected and were turning on the guard. I rode in among them at a gallop, and in a few words appealed to the crowd, saying that these were the butchers who had murdered and brutally used helpless women and children, and that the Government had now sent their punishment.'

'The increasing crowd', wrote McDowell,

pressed close on the horses of the sowars, and assumed every moment a more hostile appearance. 'What shall we do with them?' said Hodson to me. 'I think we had better shoot them here; we shall never get them in.' ... There was no time to be lost ... We halted the troop, put five troopers across the road behind and in front. Hodson ordered the princes to strip and get again into the cart. He then shot them with his own hand. So ended the career of the chiefs of the revolt, and of the greatest villains that ever shamed humanity. Before they were shot, Hodson addressed our men, explaining who they were and why they were to suffer death. The effect was marvellous: the Mussulmans seemed struck with the wholesome idea of retribution, and the Sikhs shouted with delight, while the mass moved off slowly and silently.

As with nearly everything else Hodson did, there was controversy. Hodson's making the prisoners strip was done – some said – in order to plunder them of their jewellery. Others felt that the shooting was unnecessary, in fact a crime. 'Strange,' Hodson wrote, 'that some of those who are loudest against me for sparing the King are also crying out at me for destroying his sons.' Even Hodson's admirer, Hugh Gough, regretted that Hodson should have placed himself in 'a position unworthy of so brave a man ... I have always held that Hodson was right in all he did, only excepting that false step'. Gough's own horsemen, however, had no such worries. 'It is said there was an ancient prophecy among the Sikhs that Delhi should fall by their arms, and that her royal princes should be exposed in her public streets; and the men of "Hodson's Horse," when they saw the bodies of these men exposed on the Kotwali [main square] of the city, fully believed the prophecy had been fulfilled.' Hodson's supporters argued that the escape of the descendants of Timur might have prolonged the rebellion and further endangered the British position in Upper India. Frederick Roberts – who emerging from a visit to the King 'was surprised to see the three lifeless bodies of the King's two sons and grandson lying exposed on the stone platform in front of the *Kotwali*' – pointed out that no breach of faith had been involved, as Hodson had not promised them their lives. He too, though, regretted that Hodson had carried out the act in person and in a summary manner: 'He did ... undoubtedly by this act give colour to the accusations of blood-thirstiness which his detractors were not slow to make.' His detractors, however, were in a minority. Sir Robert 'Pickwick' Montgomery writing from the Punjab doubtless spoke for the majority: 'My Dear Hodson, – All honour to you (and to your

"Horse") for *catching* the king and slaying his sons! I hope you will bag many more! – In haste, ever yours, R. Montgomery.'

John Nicholson was dying. James Hope Grant had visited him in his tent the night after he was wounded. 'Everything was now changed for him – ambition, the hopes of rising to greatness – all was vanishing from him before his eyes. He was like a noble oak riven asunder by a thunderbolt.' Messages of sympathy and support came from the Punjab – from his friend Edwardes and Sir John Lawrence. Told on 20 September that the city was now entirely in British hands, he said, 'My desire was that Delhi should be taken before I die and it has been granted.' He died on the morning of the 23rd, his death in the hour of victory, in the Empire's most desperate struggle, securing his place in the Pantheon of Imperial heroes. He was extravagantly mourned, not least by the Punjabis and Pathans of his Multani Horse. R. G. Wilberforce was present at his funeral on the 24th.

> Throwing themselves on the ground, they sobbed and wept as if their very hearts were breaking; and be it remembered that these men held the creed that a man who shed tears was only fit to be whipped out of his village by the women. Probably not one of these men had ever shed a tear; but for them Nicholson was everything. For him they left their Frontier homes, for him they had forsaken their beloved hills to come down to the detested plains; they acknowledged none but him, they served none but him. They believed as others, that the bullet was not cast, the sword not ground, that could hurt him; over and over again in the frontier skirmishes they had seen Nicholson pass unharmed where others must have been killed; and now that the earth was placed on his coffin, they threw their tradition of manhood to the wind.

A few days later, wrote Wilberforce, 'An order was received by them from headquarters to march somewhere – they returned for answer that they owed no allegiance to the English Government; that they had come down to protect and save Nicholson, and to loot Delhi ... And when they had collected as much plunder as they could, they marched back again, up-country, to their own homes, carrying their plunder with them.'

They were not the only ones plundering. Long before the prize agents could get to work officers and men engaged in wholesale looting. One surgeon wrote that every officer who was at the siege would be able to retire at once. Captain Griffiths of HM 61st Foot noted that when his regiment returned to England unusual numbers of NCOs and enlisted men bought their discharges from the army, and the windows of many jewellers' shops in the town where they were quartered displayed items of Eastern manufacture.

The British had to act fast – for the Sikhs the plunder had been the object of the exercise, the reason they had marched, fought and suffered on the Ridge. The prophecy that the Khalsa would one day loot Delhi – a prophecy the British had reminded them of at difficult times during the siege – was now fulfilled with a vengeance. They proved adept at rooting money and jewels out of the most unlikely places – behind false walls and buried in secret caches, which they discovered by pouring water over floors and observing where it sank. If that failed, sheer terror induced householders to surrender their valuables. Like the violence, the looting barely discriminated between friend and foe. Even the prize agents operated on the principle that 'all must be considered enemies who cannot satisfactorily prove they are friends'.

'The prize agents employed a number of officers in the search,' wrote Mrs Muter.

> For a short time it became the most exciting pursuit, and my husband was actively and successfully engaged. After an early breakfast, he would start, with a troop of coolies armed with picks, crowbars, and measuring lines. A house said to contain treasure would be allotted for the day's proceedings, and the business would commence by a careful survey of the premises. The houses enclosed a large extent of ground, generally containing two or three courts. The rooms faced on the courts, which were usually planted with grass, and shaded with shrubs. The houses seldom rose above one storey, with flat roofs, and staircases leading up to them, greatly facilitating the survey. By a careful meas-urement of the roofs above and of the rooms below, any concealed space could be detected. Then the walls were broken through, and if there was a secret room or a built-up niche or recess, it would be discovered, and some large prizes rewarded their search.

The prize agents alone amassed between half and three-quarters of a million pounds sterling – which was distributed among the officers and men of the Delhi force. Private looters had already taken the lion's share. Plundering a city taken by storm was standard practice at the time, and there were few among the British to shed tears for a city whose name –

like 'Cawnpore' – had become a battle-cry. The only objection voiced by Mrs Muter, for example, was 'the way the city was plundered by those not working for the army. Days were spent in ascertaining where a treasure had been hid, only to learn that the prize was gone, most probably to some of the ruffians who aided in the plunder of the cantonment, and who had imbrued their hands in the blood of the victims of Delhi.'

Delhi had new victims now – by the thousand. Sir Theophilus Metcalfe alone hanged them by the dozen in the ruins of his father's mansion. Multiple gallows were erected in the squares of the city, where British officers and soldiers watched – officers puffing cigars, soldiers their pipes – while the victims danced the 'Pandies' hornpipe'. Martial law proved no better than the anarchy it replaced. From the Punjab, Sir John Lawrence wrote to Lord Canning deploring the state of affairs in the city: 'I am a strong advocate of prompt and severe punishment when such has been deserved. But the systematic spoliation which I understand goes on at Delhi cannot fail to exasperate the natives, and render more wide and lasting the breach which has taken place between them and us.' Canning, too, had his doubts – for which he had already been contemptuously nicknamed 'Clemency Canning' – but it was to be December before the administration of Delhi was placed in the hands of the Punjab Government and Sir John Lawrence took personal control of affairs.

The fall of Delhi broke the back of the rebellion, but there was much still to do. The garrison of the Residency had yet to be relieved and Oude to be reconquered. Central India was almost entirely in rebel hands. On the morning of Nicholson's funeral a column marched out of the city under Brigadier Edward Greathed. Frederick Roberts marched with it:

That march through Delhi in the early morning light was a gruesome proceeding. Our way from the Lahore Gate by the Chandni Chauk led through a veritable city of the dead; not a sound was to be heard but the falling of our own footsteps; not a living creature was to be seen. Dead bodies were strewn about in all directions, in every attitude that the death struggle had caused them to assume, and in every stage of decomposition. We marched in silence, or involuntarily spoke in whispers, as though fearing to disturb those ghastly remains of humanity. Here a dog gnawed at an uncovered limb; there a vulture, disturbed by our approach from its loathsome meal, but too gorged to fly, fluttered away to a safe distance. In many instances the positions of the bodies were appallingly life-like. Some lay with their arms uplifted as if beckoning, and indeed the whole scene was weird and terrible beyond description. Our horses seemed to feel the horror of it as much as we did; for they shook and snorted in evident terror. The atmosphere was unimaginably disgusting, laden as it was with the most noxious and sickening odours.

It was a joy, wrote Roberts, to get out into clean air and open country. The ultimate aim of Greathed's column was to join the new commander-in-chief, Sir Colin Campbell – who had recently arrived in India – at Cawnpore. Its initial task, though, was to re-establish British rule in the country south of Delhi. This the column proceeded to do in a series of hard-fought engagements until – at Bijaigarh, nearly 100 miles south of Delhi – Greathed received urgent letters, imploring immediate assistance, from the beleaguered British garrison at Agra.

# IO

## CAMPBELL'S MARCH

At Agra the Lieutenant Governor of the North-West Mr Colvin – having in May disarmed the sepoys of the 44th and 67th NI – decided in June to move all Europeans and Eurasians into the famous Red Fort, taking up residence there himself on 4 July, by which time his health had almost broken down, from overwork. By this time Agra was a small island in a sea of hostile territory. The whole country between the Jumna and the Ganges was in a state of either rebellion or anarchy. Bundelkhand – to the west of the Jumna – Central India and Rajputana were being contested and communications were cut in every direction. Worse still, a large rebel force had gathered at the old, now abandoned Mogul capital of Fatehpur Sikri only 23 miles away. A committee of three men – a Mr Reade of the Board of Revenue, Major Macleod of the Engineers and Brigadier Polwhele – took measures, during the worst of Colvin's illness, to secure the British position. Firstly they ferried all the convicts in the city across the Jumna and then released them – rather than have a mob break open the gaol and unleash them on the city – and broke down the Bridge of Boats leading to the fort. By the time Colvin was on his feet again, two 'friendly' Native contingents – of Bhurtpore and Karauli – had defected to the enemy, and the rebel force from Fatehpur Sikri had advanced to Sassiah, only 5 miles from the fort. The British military commander, Brigadier Polwhele – mustering a force of 568 European infantry, a battery of six guns with European gunners, fifty-five Mounted Volunteers and fifty Volunteers, mostly officers of mutinied regiments – marched out to Sassiah to engage them.

It was generally felt, after the engagement, that the force under Pol-whele, some 742 Europeans, should have been adequate to disperse the enemy gathered at Sassiah had Polwhele adopted the traditional British tactic when confronted by Asiatic armies – a swift advance with the bayonet by British infantry. Instead, when the guns on the rebel left opened fire Polwhele settled down to a half-hour artillery duel in which the rebels' position behind rising ground, numbers – ten guns against six – and greater weight of shot were soon giving them the advantage. Before long they had blown up two tumbrils and British horses and riders were dropping fast. A threatened attack on Pearson's half-battery on the British left was repulsed by case shot and infantry fire – a similar attempt against D'Oyley's battery on the right was driven back by a charge of eighteen Volunteer cavalry under Captain Prendergast. Shortly after-wards both Pearson and D'Oyley on the right sent messages to Polwhele stating that their ammunition would soon be exhausted to no purpose unless he changed his tactics. Up until now Polwhele had been reluctant to commit the only British infantry between Agra and Bombay. At last – two and a half hours into the battle – he ordered the 3rd Europeans (later the 3rd Royal Sussex) to attack the village to its front. Despite heavy enemy fire the men attacked the village, drove the rebels from it and spiked two guns – but British losses had been heavy. Captain D'Oyley had been mortally wounded – after directing the fire of his guns in great pain he, at last, handed his pistol to the man beside him, saying 'They have done for me now; put a stone over my grave, and say that I died fighting my guns' – and Major Thomas of the 3rd Europeans was killed. With the British guns falling silent for lack of ammunition, the temporary advantage gained by the infantry could not be followed up – soon the rebels were threatening the village with infantry, cavalry and guns. Unable to defend what had been gained using infantry alone and with his communications with the fort threatened, Polwhele had no choice but to retire. The retreat was carried out in good order, covered by a small troop of Militia cavalry – mostly Eurasian clerks – and helped by the fact that the enemy, too, ran short of artillery ammunition and was reduced to firing copper coins as case shot. British casualties were forty-five men killed and 108 wounded or missing. The rebels, after burning Sassiah, marched off to Delhi where they were welcomed as the 'Victors of Sassiah'.

Like the battle of Chinhut in Oude, the defeat at Sassiah was a severe blow to the reputation of British arms in the country around Agra – in the city itself the town-crier, by order of the *Kotwali*, announced the following morning the inauguration of Mogul rule. Unlike in Oude, however, where the Residency garrison's dogged defence went a long way towards restoring British prestige, events in Agra dwindled into a half-hearted siege, until September and the despatch of the Delhi column under Brigadier Greathed.

Setting off on the morning of 24 September, the column crossed the Hindun and advanced on Bulandshahr, where it defeated a rebel force defending the town and demolished the fortifications. The last mine set failed to explode and Lieutenant Home – one of the party that had blown in the Kashmir Gate – ran, laughing, towards it. As he bent down to examine the fuse the charge ignited, killing him instantly. Greathed's column pressed on, via Aligarh – where they dispersed another rebel force and reached Bijaigarh on 9 October. Here it was that Greathed received the urgent request from the authorities in Agra to push on to their relief, as a strong body of rebels was threatening the fort. Greathed now sent his cavalry and horse artillery by forced march the 48 miles to Agra and, mounting his men on elephants, carts and camels, followed on behind.

In fact, the rebel forces – gathered from various parts of Central India, and by parties who had quit Delhi as the British gained control there – were nowhere to be seen when Greathed's troops started to arrive outside the walls of the Red Fort, and no one inside the fort had any clear picture of where they were. Among the garrison and their ladies there was much comment on the shabby appearance of the relief column. Bronzed, bearded, khaki-clad and covered in dust from marching 44 miles in twenty-four hours, the men made a stark contrast to the scarlet and pipe-clay of the 3rd Europeans and green of the Agra Volunteers. 'We presented, I am afraid, but a sorry appearance,' wrote Frederick Roberts, 'as compared to the neatly dressed ladies and the spick-and-span troops who greeted us, for one of the fair sex was overheard to remark, "Was ever such a dirty-looking lot seen?" Another lady assumed that the dreadful lot of men marching below her "must be Afghans"' – they were, in fact, HM 8th Foot. There was a feeling among the relievers that the relieved had hardly suffered at all, unless it was from boredom, and that their urgent pleas for assistance had been based on panic rather than any accurate assessment of the state of affairs prevailing in the surrounding country. 'We were not then aware of what soon became painfully apparent,' wrote Roberts, 'that neither the information nor the opinions of the heads of the civil and military administration at Agra were to be relied upon. That administration had, indeed, completely collapsed.' Roberts did not exaggerate. John Colvin had died the previous month and Brigadier Polwhele had been removed from command on the orders of the Governor General, shortly after Sassiah – although he had returned from the battle entirely unconcerned and satisfied that he had done as well as any man could have. Polwhele, of course, was no loss, but the men who took over after Colvin's death – E. A. Reade and Colonel Hugh Fraser – had done little to enhance the prestige of the British in native eyes. So low was it, that when news of the fall of Delhi reached the city – ahead of Greathed's column – the natives refused to believe it.

Roberts – a man generally charitable in his judgements – wrote of the council that ran Agra: 'There was no controlling authority; the crisis had produced no-one in any responsible position who understood the nature of the convulsion through which we were passing; and the endless discussion had resulted (as must always be the case) in fatal indecision and timidity. We could hardly be expected to know that the government of so great a province was in the hands of men who were utterly unfit to cope with the difficulties of an emergency such as had now arisen.' Typically, Roberts went on to point out that the men in question had – in quieter times – served their country well. He also added that their failures provided no excuse for what followed the arrival of Greathed's column.

Greathed was assured by the Agra authorities that the enemy was nowhere in the vicinity and had retired 12 miles beyond the Kari-Nadi, a tributary of the Jumna. Greathed, trusting this information, neglected to post pickets or to reconnoitre the surrounding countryside for himself and had ordered camp to be pitched on the brigade parade-ground outside the fort. The cavalry and artillery horses were picketed half a mile from the camp, where those men who were not putting up tents lay around sleeping until their wagons should arrive. The atmosphere was more like a fairground than a military camp, with European civilians from the fort and natives wandering round, keen to see the men who had captured Delhi.

Many officers had gone inside the fort for breakfast. Frederick Roberts was one of them. 'We had scarcely sat down, bent on enjoying such an unusual event as a meal in ladies' society, when we were startled by the report of a gun, then another, and another.' It had started at the guard of the 9th Lancers – four apparently unarmed native snake-charmers had wandered up and, on being told to go away, had produced swords from under their robes and cut down Sergeant Crews. Sergeant Hartington had rushed up to help and been cut with a *tulwar*, fracturing his skull, but despite this he had wrenched the weapon from the hands of his assailant and killed him with it, before wounding a second. As the Lancers' guard killed the other two natives, twelve guns opened up from the standing corn at the edge of the parade-ground – the force had, in Roberts' words, been 'caught napping'.

As Europeans and natives alike fled towards the fort, rebel cavalry galloped over the parade-ground, cutting down one gun's crew and preparing to carry it off. Captain French and Lieutenant Jones of the 9th Lancers charged with a troop and drove them off. French was killed and Jones received twenty-two sword cuts, mostly to his head and face. The Lancers' charge bought precious time – soon the Brigadier and his officers were hurrying out of the fort, fighting their way through a crowd of panic-stricken civilians. 'What a sight was that we came upon!' wrote Roberts. 'Independent fights were going on all over the parade-ground. Here a couple of Cavalry soldiers were charging each other. The game of bayonet *versus* sword was being carried on in real earnest ... Just in front, the 75th Foot (many of the men in their shirt sleeves) were forming square to receive a body of the rebel horse.' Among the 75th was Richard Barter, who heard the rebel sowars shouting to each other as they recoiled from the British square *'Arrah bhai! ye Diliwhale hain!'* ('Brothers, these are the Delhi fellows!') It was as well that they were – as veterans of Delhi Ridge, they were used to turning out quickly. Before long the infantry were advancing in the centre, Bourchier's battery and Remmington's horse artillery were firing from the gun park and, on the left, Colonel Ouvry with the 9th Lancers and Hugh Gough's Punjabis were driving the rebel cavalry before them. On the left, Lieutenants Probyn, Watson and Younghusband were leading their Punjabis round the enemy's flank. While Frederick Roberts was searching the battlefield for the Brigadier, he had a narrow escape: 'I was stopped by a dismounted sowar, who danced about in front of me, waving his *pagri* [turban] before the eyes of my horse with one hand, and brandishing his sword with the other. I could not get the frightened animal near enough to use my sword, and my pistol (a Deane and Adams revolver), with which I tried to shoot my opponent, refused to go off, so I felt myself pretty well at his mercy, when to my relief I saw him fall, having been run through by a man of the 9th Lancers who had come to my rescue.'

When Greathed arrived on the scene he ordered a general pursuit of the now flying rebels. There followed a delay while Lieutenant Colonel Cotton of the Agra garrison – technically Greathed's superior – arrived on the scene with his bandbox-smart garrison troops and assumed command. He took time to learn the details of the position before eventually agreeing with Greathed's order. Even so the pursuit soon overtook the enemy, overran their camp – only 4 miles away, further evidence of the Agra authorities' incompetence – and captured thirteen guns. British losses in the whole action were surprisingly light – twelve officers and men killed, fifty-four wounded and two missing, as well as twenty camp followers killed and wounded. Lieutenant Probyn of Probyn's Horse and Sergeant Hartington of the 9th Lancers were both awarded the VC, and the much-wounded Lieutenant Jones of the 9th survived to wear his – awarded for his capture of the gun at Badli-ke-Serai.

Exhausted by their forced march, the fight on the camping ground and the headlong pursuit – Roberts saw Punjabi infantrymen quenching their thirst in the Kari-Nadi having kept up with the cavalry for 12 miles – the force rested until 14 October, when it marched on towards Mainpuri. En route the force was overtaken by Hope Grant, who had been most indignant at being passed over for command by Greathed and had succeeded in getting the order rescinded. Hope Grant's arrival was a relief to many. Greathed – as Richard Barter punned – had proved to have 'no Great Head'.

The new commander-in-chief in India – since he arrived at Calcutta on 17 August – was Sir Colin Campbell. Born Colin McLiver, the son of a Glasgow carpenter, he had been educated at his maiden aunts' expense at the Glasgow High School, and obtained – in 1792 – an army commission at 15 through the good offices of their brother, a Colonel Campbell. Mistakenly gazetted as 'Colin Campbell', he retained the name – and went on to serve at Vimeira, Corunna, Barrosa, Vittoria and on the Bidassoa, and led the 'forlorn hope' in the disastrous assault on San Sebastian. Here he was wounded for a third time – when the previous two wounds had not yet healed. Having devoted the peacetime years after Waterloo to the study of his profession, he later served in China in 1842, the Second Sikh War and the North-West Frontier. His claim to public fame, however, was his command of the Highland Brigade in the Crimea, not least at the battle of Balaklava where at the head of the 93rd (Sutherland) Highlanders he held that port against an attack by Russian cavalry – an action that gave rise to the term 'the Thin Red Line' as a description of British infantry. Taking command of the 1st Division from the Duke of Cambridge, he was bypassed for command of the army in the Crimea on Lord Raglan's death, but made GCB and was granted an audience with the Queen. When informed – in London – of his appointment, and asked when he felt he might be ready to set sail for India, he simply said 'Tomorrow'.

On his arrival in India Sir Colin decided almost at once that whatever other problems faced him – Rohilkhand and Oude in rebel hands, Central India and the Punjab restive, Cawnpore fallen, Delhi not yet taken – the relief of Lucknow must be his priority. With 14,000 men coming from the United Kingdom, Campbell knew that a great deal of transportation – for men, baggage, ammunition and rations – would have to be assembled and to this he devoted his efforts. The necessary delay this imposed – he did not leave Calcutta until 27 October – led to him being nicknamed 'Sir Crawling Camel', but the failure of Havelock's first attempt at a relief had shown the difficulty of making such an endeavour with insufficient transport. By the time he set off for Allahabad Campbell had already pushed forward those troops that had been sent from China by Lord Elgin as well as the two detachments that were to form the Naval Brigade. These men were provided by two Royal Navy frigates, HMS *Shannon* and HMS *Pearl*, under Captain William Peel VC – son of Sir Robert Peel, and a hero of the Crimea – and Captain Edward Sotheby. The practice of using Royal Navy crews as foot soldiers – 'Bluejackets', as they were generally known – grew out of the fact that the British Army was small by European standards, and thinly spread. The British did not have military garrisons everywhere; what they did have, almost everywhere, were ships – these were the days when the definition of an island was 'A piece of land entirely surrounded by Englishmen'. When trouble broke out in remoter parts of the growing Empire it had become the practice to land parties of marines and sailors – most of whom were trained to fight with rifle and cutlass – to augment the land forces or even, on occasion, operate on their own. The sailors had distinguished themselves in the Crimea, where their purpose had been much the same as it would be in India – to man six 24-pound siege guns, two 8-inch howitzers and an improvised battery of Congreve rockets, which would give Campbell's column its biggest punch.

That communications on the 600 miles of the Grand Trunk road between Calcutta and Cawnpore were under constant threat was brought home to Campbell when he and his staff – travelling in bullock carts without escort – saw, near Benares, a party of rebels on fourteen elephants and twenty-five horses cross the road ahead of them. Already – at Kajwa, 20 miles west of the Grand Trunk road at Futtehpore – a detachment under Colonel Powell of HM 53rd and some Naval Brigade under Captain Peel had had a stiff fight with some two thousand sepoys from the Dinapore garrison and local villagers. The rebels had been driven off and three guns were captured, but Powell was killed.

Sir Colin arrived at Cawnpore on 3 November to find that the threats to the British position had scarcely changed since Havelock set off from there on his last march. Oude was still swarming with rebels – 45 miles away to the south-west the Gwalior contingent still threatened. As Havelock's had been, Campbell's communications with Allahabad were menaced by marauders from Oude; as Havelock had done, Campbell resolved to go forward. He had already ordered Hope Grant – who had superseded Greathed – to set up camp beyond the bridge over the Sai at Bani, only a few miles from the Alam Bagh, on the outskirts of Lucknow itself. There all the relief force's troops and transport were to concentrate and await his arrival. Leaving behind five hundred Europeans and five hundred Sikhs under General Windham – known as 'the hero of the Redan' for his gallant conduct during the final, unsuccessful, assault on that Sebastopol bastion – Sir Colin left Cawnpore on 9 November and joined Hope Grant on the afternoon of the same day. 'We were old friends,' wrote Hope Grant. 'Some years before, when he was in command at Peshawur, letters had occasionally passed between us, in one of which he wrote, "I have now one foot in the grave, and I am just remaining to scrape together enough of money to close the remainder of my days at home." On this occasion, after we had exchanged a cordial welcome, I said to him, "You little expected when I last heard from you that you would be appointed Commander-in-Chief in India." He answered, "I should as soon have thought to be made Archbishop of Canterbury."'

Inside the Lucknow Residency, Sir James Outram – lacking transport for the women, children and wounded of the garrison – not to mention the numerous wounded of the relief column – had concluded that he had no option but to sit tight and wait for Sir Colin Campbell. The extended perimeter of the Residency defences now included three palaces along the line of the river – the Tarawala Kothi, the Chattar Manzil and the Farid Bakhsh – which were occupied by men of the first relief column under Havelock. The all-important Alam Bagh – 3 miles away, on the other side of the city on the Cawnpore road (see map 6 on page xx) – he entrusted to the 78th Highlanders under Major McIntyre. The Alam Bagh – if it could be held – would provide a vital foothold and jumping-off point for Sir Colin's forces. In the event it could not be held and McIntyre had orders to withdraw down the road towards Cawnpore.

The six weeks' siege that followed Havelock's 'first relief' is more properly described as a blockade. The rebels made no attempt at an assault against the newly strengthened British garrison. The Residency's defences were strengthened and new batteries established. The fresh arrivals imparted an additional, aggressive spirit to the defence and sorties became more frequent. Three days after Havelock's relief a sortie was launched against Johannes's House – which had proved a constant thorn in the garrison's side. Private Henry Metcalfe volunteered, 'my former wounds being nearly well'. The storming party dashed forward and put two ladders against the windows of the house:

There happened to be a great tall soldier of the Grenadiers with the party ... We all rushed off together, and whether me being light or small or what, I reached one of the ladders just as the tall Grenadier reached the other, and it was a race between him and me, and although I reached every rung of my ladder as soon as he reached his, still he seemed to be higher than I was, and I never allowed for his height. However, I believe he got in at his window before I got in at mine, but when I got in I could not see anyone in my room. Consequently I concluded that the enemy did not wait for us but took to their heels as soon as we rushed forward. Well, I looked round the room to see if there was anything worth laying hands on in the shape of provisions etc. Well, there was a very large box, something about or nearly resembling a large flower bin. The lid was partly up so I threw it entirely up, and what was my astonishment to see three of my sable friends sitting on their haunches in this big box. Well, I shot one and bayoneted another, but the third was on me like mad and before I knew where I was he had hold of my musket by the muzzle so that I could not use the bayonet at him. So there I was, he chopping away at me with his native sword, and me defending myself the best way I could by throwing up the butt of my musket to protect my head and trying to close with him, which I knew was my only chance. In doing this I received a chop from his sword on the left hand which divided the knuckle and nearly cut off my thumb. Well, he had his sword raised to give me, I suppose, the final stroke, when in rushed the tall Grenadier. Tom Carrol took in the situation at a glance and soon put an end to my antagonist by burying the hammer of his musket in the fellow's skull, and when he saw me all covered with blood he shouted out a great hoarse laugh and said, 'You little swab, you were very near being done for,' and indeed, so I was. I then shewed him the box and its contents, and I can tell you it rather astonished him.

Pushed back by these sorties – for the most part beyond the effective musketry range – the rebels contented themselves with a protracted cannonade which, by regularly shifting their guns and lobbing balls and shells into the compound, proved very effective. F. C. Maude – now, with his battery, among the besieged – saw a round shot from an enemy battery across the river take the legs off a soldier who was standing beside him. 'I resolved to avenge him, and try and silence the gun. It was protected by heavy shutters on the embrasures, and they could distinctly see us as we went to fire our own guns; so they used to wait until we had done so; then they quickly opened their shutters, ran out their gun, and fired a more or less chance shot into our camp. One night I laid a trap for them, and mounted an 18-pounder iron gun in the embrasure of our dismantled piece. I also had an 8-inch mortar brought down into the battery.' In the early morning he stationed an officer in the Residency tower to watch for the enemy gun. 'We fired the usual four guns at the Mosque battery; and then we treated them to the novelty of a well-timed shell from the 8-inch mortar. While the latter missile was distracting their attention, I carefully laid the new 18-pounder. Shortly after the mortar shell had burst my friend in the tower called out: "They are opening the shutters!" I at once fired our reserve gun, and, as luck would have it, the shot went clean into the enemy's embrasure and knocked their gun over. They never fired from that place again.' An hour later Outram and some of his staff came down. 'The Bayard of India said, with a genial smile: "I have heard of your feat, Maude, and I now give you the highest reward it is in my power to bestow!" at the same time handing me a Manilla cheroot.' To Maude, a heavy smoker reduced to smoking dried tea leaves, it was a welcome award.

Maude also avenged a fellow officer, Lieutenant Graydon of the 7th Oude Irregular Infantry, who was shot dead at the post named after him. 'I happened to be passing when the body of poor Graydon was brought down ... I borrowed a musket, with half-a-dozen cartridges and copper

caps, and went up to "Graydon's post" to see how he had been killed.'
Maude hid in a fortified summerhouse and saw three sepoys creeping
towards the picket. 'I let drive with my "Brown Bess" at the leading man
and had the good fortune to bowl him over with a broken thigh. He
made two or three ineffectual attempts to rise, and I hoped to use him as
a sort of bait for the others.' The man's friends, though, used spades to
shovel earth in front of the man until he was concealed from view, and
then dragged him away. 'Poor fellow!' wrote Maude. 'I rather hope he
recovered. This was, I think, the only musket-shot I fired in the whole
campaign.' Although he clearly had an 'eye', Maude lacked the true killer
instinct of a sharpshooter, unlike Captain Edward Grant of the Madras
Fusiliers who, he wrote, 'used to go out every morning "sniping," as he
called it, carrying an Enfield rifle, with a supply of cartridges slung over
his shoulder in a game net, in the most approved sportsmanlike style. He
kept a regular "game book" in which he recorded his daily "bag".'

The underground war continued. 'I am aware of no parallel to our
series of mines in modern war,' wrote Sir James Outram of this second
phase of the siege. 'Twenty-one shafts, aggregating 200 feet in depth,
and 3,291 feet of gallery have been executed. The enemy advanced twenty
mines against the palaces and outposts. Of these they exploded three
which caused us loss of life and two which did no injury. Seven have been
blown in, and out of seven others the enemy have been driven; results of
which the Engineer Department may well be proud.' When the rebels
were heard mining towards a position, Crommelin's men – Captain
Crommelin was now Chief Engineer – would wait patiently for them to
break through into their countermine, then fire through the opening,
attack and capture the enemy gallery and then destroy it. Henry Kavanagh, who had procured an appointment as an assistant field engineer,
described this subterranean warfare: 'What a nervous moment was that
first crawl on all fours through a long, narrow, cold, damp mine, appalled
by the darkness, and a fancy that an enemy may have got in wishing to
blow out my shrinking brains, or that it might fall in and bury me alive!
It tried me considerably, and I had to say a great many encouraging things
to myself to calm my agitated heart, which vehemently panted for the
light again. Indeed it cost many efforts to appease my fears, and gain
confidence . . . At last I discovered that a resolute man was more dangerous
below than above ground.' His lesson was not long in coming. A mine
was detected approaching one of the Sikh positions, the Engineers count-
ermined but the noise disturbed the rebel miners, who fled. Kavanagh

had just relieved the officer on duty and 'went down with a revolver, conjecturing that the enemy would send in some one to see what had disturbed the miners. After waiting a while a sepoy descended with his musket, and advanced to my end of the gallery, where it was quite dark, whereas the light streamed down at his. I let him come in about his own length, and then shot him through the shoulder. I pursued him, and fired again, but the cap snapped, and he escaped roaring with pain. The enemy let water into the gallery, and an hour later it fell in.' On another occasion Kavanagh waited with loaded revolver for an enemy miner 'like a cat patiently waiting for her prey. Slowly and cautiously the enemy's miner lessened the partition of earth between us, and, in two hours, a too heavy stroke of his placed us face to face. His eyes glazed with fear as he spread out his arms screaming, and fell back mortally wounded into the shaft, where he lay moaning pitifully.' Kavanagh tried to retrieve the miner's tools but as he crawled through the enemy gallery he could hear the sepoys above debating who should go down. 'I began to think I had ventured too near, and was speculating on the probability of the pistol missing fire, when down came a Sepoy to solve the question by receiving a bullet in his stomach.' As Kavanagh pondered the fact that he had only one round left he heard another sepoy – above ground – boasting that he would come down and kill him. There followed an exchange of colourful insults until, after firing a volley down the shaft, the smoke of which nearly suffocated Kavanagh, the sepoys managed to hook their two mortally wounded comrades and drag them out. After further exchanges of insults, opinions and gossip, Kavanagh managed to grab the tools and bolt for safety amid cries of 'Well done!' from both his own Sikh escort and the rebel sepoys. These exploits gave Kavanagh the opportunity to distinguish himself, which he so desperately craved, but a greater opportunity, and greater danger, awaited him above ground.

One of Outram's first measures on taking over as Civil Commissioner was to organize communications with the Alam Bagh and, thus, with the relief column. With Campbell and the best part of five thousand men encamped around the Alam Bagh, Outram had sent, via a native messenger, a detailed despatch – drawn up by his chief of staff, Robert Napier (later Lord Napier of Magdala) – containing plans of the city and details of approaches to the Residency. 'Full and precise information is at all times valuable,' wrote Kavanagh, 'but when every moment's hesitation costs a life it is priceless. The chances and accidents of war no general can always foresee, and he who engages an enemy, ignorant of his whereabouts and of their resources, is sure to be embarrassed if compelled to alter his attack.' To save Sir Colin Campbell from such embarrassment, Kavanagh proposed to his friend Robert Napier that he, Kavanagh, should pass through native lines in the company of a messenger, Kunoujee Lal, in order to act as guide to the relieving forces. Kunoujee Lal, who regularly passed through enemy lines with ease, was appalled at the idea of attempting to do so in the company of a tall, fair-skinned, red-bearded Irishman. Napier was scarcely less so, but both were talked round by Kavanagh – Kunoujee Lal with the promise of a rich reward – and the idea was passed to Sir James Outram who, understanding the potential value of a European guide to Campbell, agreed. Dyeing his skin and disguising himself as a *badmash* in borrowed native clothes – he hadn't mentioned the venture to his wife as he left their quarters – Kavanagh presented himself to General Outram. 'Natives are not permitted to go into the house of a European with shoes on, nor take a seat uninvited. In order to draw particular attention to myself I did both, and the eyes of the officers, who sat at the General's table, were at once turned angrily and inquiringly upon the queer man who did such impudent things.' Kavanagh took this lack of recognition by men who knew him well as a good omen. Last minute adjustments to his disguise were made by Outram in person. 'I was daubed once more by the General himself, and, considering where I was going to, there was extraordinary hilarity in the whole proceeding, which was most beneficial to my nerves. My turban was readjusted; my habilments subjected to a close inspection; and my waistband adorned by a loaded double-barrelled pistol ... which was intended for myself should there be no possibility of escaping death at the hands of the mutineers, who would have done it in their own particular way.' At 8.30 in the evening Kavanagh and Kunoujee Lal were conducted down to the river Gumti by Captain Hardinge, who sent the Irishman on his way with the cheering words 'Noble Fellow! You will never be forgotten!'

Entering the water with his clothes, rolled in a bundle, on his head, Kavanagh began to have second thoughts. 'The first plunge into the lines of the enemy, and the cold water, chilled my courage immensely, and if the guide had been within reach I should, perhaps, have pulled him back, and given up the enterprise. But he waded quickly through the river, and reaching the opposite shore, went crouching up a trench for about three hundred yards, to a grove of low trees on the edge of a pond, where we paused to dress.' Soon they encountered a matchlock man on sentry duty:

'I thought it prudent to be the first to speak, and remarked, as we approached, that the night was cold, and after his repeating that it *was* cold, I passed on, observing that it would be colder bye-and-bye.' They encountered many more matchlock men – some accompanying people of rank in palanquins – until they reached the Stone Bridge, passed the sentry-post – Kunoujee Lal did the talking this time – and recrossed the Gumti. Soon they were in the main street of the city 'which to my great relief, was not illuminated so much as it used to be previous to the siege, nor was it so crowded. I shuffled and jostled against several men in the street without being spoken to, and only met one guard of seven Sepoys, who were amusing themselves with women of pleasure.' Not having seen green fields for five months, the fresh air at the edge of the city, when they reached it, was very welcome – 'I greedily sniffed at it all as I devoured a fresh carrot' – but soon they were lost in the area of the Dilkusha Park, and blundering about on the edge of the canal near the Char Bagh Bridge. At last they entered a native hut, whose occupants – two native women – put them on the right road once more.

By three o'clock in the morning they found themselves near a mango grove at the edge of a plain, where they stumbled upon a picket of sepoys, who questioned them closely. 'It was an anxious moment,' Kavanagh wrote. 'Kunoujee Lal lost heart for the first time, and threw away the despatch entrusted to him for Sir Colin Campbell. I drew their attention to his fright, and begged they would not terrify poor travellers, unaccustomed to be questioned by so many valorous soldiers.' He told the men they were going to Umroula, a village 2 miles from Campbell's camp, 'to inform a friend of the death of his brother by a shot from the British in Lucknow. They were greatly relieved on discovering that they had been falsely alarmed.' The two men moved on, losing their way once more and stumbling through a *jheel*. 'Indians rarely give expression to disappointment in curses, and the good fellow bore the interruptions more patiently than I did. Indeed he was once or twice disposed to laugh at the vehemence with which I abused every mutineer, every weed, every bit of mud, and every drop of water in the province.' After passing through a sleeping village, and a crowd of refugees fleeing the British who, they said, were murdering and plundering all around them, they arrived at 4 a.m. at the edge of another grove. Kavanagh was about to settle down for an hour's sleep when they were challenged in a native accent with the words 'Who comes there?' The sentry was a Sikh – they had reached British lines.

As the sun rose, the two men were brought to the quarters of the Commander-in-Chief.

As I approached the door an elderly gentleman with a stern face came out and going up to him, I asked for Sir Colin Campbell. 'I am Sir Colin Campbell!' was the sharp reply, 'and who are you?' I pulled off my turban, and, opening the folds, took out a short note of introduction from Sir James Outram. 'This, sir, will explain who I am, and from whence I came.' It was impetuously read, his piercing eyes being raised to my face at almost every line. 'Is it true?' he asked. 'I hope, sir, you do not doubt the authenticity of the note?' 'No – I do not! – but it is surprising! How did you do it?' I was tired, and anxious to be left alone to my thoughts, and I begged Sir Colin to excuse my telling the story then, and to be put to bed.

The next day – 10 November – Campbell consulted with Kavanagh. 'His Excellency kept me shut up with himself, repeatedly enjoining me to say nothing on the subject of the relief to the officers in the camp, who, he observed would endeavour to extract all I knew, and then form *their* notions of what was right and wrong ... He did me the honour of freely discussing with me the scheme formed by Sir James Outram for his consideration; and I was quickly struck by his quick perception of everything, and the promptitude with which he mastered the strong and assailable points of the city.' The plan decided on was to move on the Alam Bagh – and from there, make a right-handed sweep round the Dilkusha Park and cross the canal near its junction with the Gumti. Then, having secured the Sikandar Bagh, he would advance via the Shah Najaf and the Moti Mahal to link up with Outram (see map 6 on page xx). Outram would simultaneously break out of the Residency with all his forces, his wounded, women and children to join Campbell's column prior to a total withdrawal from the city.

Campbell's forces – some 4,700 men – were divided between six brigades. The Naval Brigade was commanded by William Peel; the Artillery Brigade – consisting of the batteries of Blunt, Remmington, Travers, Bridge and Bourchier – was commanded by Brigadier Crawford; Brigadier Little commanded the cavalry – two squadrons of the 9th Lancers and one each of the 1st, 2nd and 5th Punjab Cavalry and Hodson's Horse; Greathed commanded the 3rd Brigade – HM 8th Foot, a composite battalion of detachments from the three regiments in the

Residency, and the 2nd Punjabis; Adrian Hope led the 4th Brigade – his own 93rd, HM 53rd, the 4th Punjabis and a second composite battalion; the 5th Brigade – commanded by Russell – consisted of HM 23rd Fusiliers and part of HM 82nd. In overall executive command was Hope Grant: 'Sir Colin had previously raised me to the rank of Brigadier-General, and he very kindly told me that he would consider the whole force under my command, he himself merely exercising a general supervision over the operations.'

On the afternoon of 11 November Sir Colin Campbell reviewed his troops. Among the regiments on parade was a favourite of his – the 93rd Highlanders, who had formed part of his Highland Brigade in the Crimea, and with whom he had stood when they formed 'the thin red line' that defended Balaklava. They were a thousand strong, seven hundred of them wearing the Crimea medal on their chests. Among them was Corporal William Forbes-Mitchell:

The Ninety-Third formed the extreme left of the line in quarter-distance column, in full Highland costume, with feather bonnets and dark waving plumes, a solid mass of brawny-limbed men. I have never seen a more magnificent regiment than the Ninety-Third looked that day ... The old Chief rode along the line, commencing from the right, halting and addressing a short speech to each corps as he came along. The eyes of the Ninety-Third were eagerly turned to Sir Colin and his staff as he advanced, the men remarking among themselves that none of the other corps had given him a single cheer, but had taken whatever he said to them in solemn silence. At last he approached us; we were called to attention, and formed close column, so that every man might hear what was said. When Sir Colin rode up, he appeared to have a worn and haggard expression on his face, but he was received with such a cheer, or rather shout of welcome, as made the echoes ring from the Alambagh and the surrounding woods. His wrinkled brow at once became smooth, and his wearied-looking features broke into a smile, as he acknowledged the cheer by a hearty salute, and addressed us almost exactly as follows. I stood near him and heard every word. 'Ninety-Third! when I took leave of you in Portsmouth, I never thought I should see you again. I expected the bugle or maybe the bagpipes to sound a call for me to go somewhere else long before you would be likely to return to our dearly-loved home. But another commander has deemed it otherwise, and here I am prepared to lead you through another campaign. And I must tell you, my lads, there is work of difficulty and danger before us – harder work and greater dangers than any we encountered in the Crimea.'

After reminding them of the strength of the enemy, wrote Forbes-Mitchell, and the dangers that threatened them, Campbell went on: '"Ninety-Third! You are my own lads, I rely on you to do the work!" A voice from the ranks called out: "Ay Sir Colin, ye ken us and we ken you; we'll bring the women and children out of Lucknow or die wi' you in the attempt!" and the whole regiment burst into another ringing cheer, which was taken up by the whole line.'

The following morning the advance on the Alam Bagh began. At 9 a.m. the troops marched off and, after advancing for 3 miles, were attacked by some two thousand rebels with two guns. After the enemy guns had been silenced by Bourchier's battery, Hugh Gough – at the head of his squadron of Hodson's Horse – saw Hope Grant riding towards him. Gough and his men had not had an easy time under Hope Grant's command. An early mishap during picket duty had led to them being assigned to permanent rearguard duty and Gough had despaired of ever being able to distinguish himself – until the gallant conduct of his men when the rearguard was surprised by enemy cavalry restored their reputation. 'Hope Grant ... rode up to me, and desired me to take my squadron and see if I could capture the guns. He further gave me an order to spike them if I found I could not get them away; and to carry out this order I was provided with a hammer and spikes, or large nails. Of how I disposed of them I have not the slightest recollection, but I rather suspect I threw them away!' Gough decided a flank attack was the only way to get to the guns with small loss.

> With this object I made a considerable *detour*, and managed, under cover of some fields of growing corn or sugar cane, to arrive on the left flank of the enemy perfectly unseen. The guns were posted on a small mound, and a considerable body of the enemy had an admirable position in rear of this mound, in front of and amidst some trees and scrub. Between us and them lay a marshy *jheel*, with long reedy grass – an unpleasant obstacle, but which served admirably to cover our movements. I then advanced my men through this *jheel* and long grass at a trot, and so concealed our movements till we got clear, when I gave the word 'Form line' and 'Charge.' My men gave a ringing cheer, and

we were into the masses. The surprise was complete, and owing to its suddenness they had no conception of our numbers, and the shock to them and victory to us was as if it had been a whole brigade. My charger 'Tearaway' ... carried me like a bird, and I found myself well ahead. It seemed like cutting one's way through a field of corn, and I had to make a lane for myself as I rode along. The men followed me splendidly, and in a very short time the affair was over – the guns were captured, the enemy scattered, and the fight became a pursuit. Our loss was very trifling, as is often the case in a sudden surprise, but we cut up numbers of the enemy, and should have accounted for more but for the nature of the ground.

For this skilfully executed charge, Hugh Gough was awarded the Victoria Cross.

Having stacked all the baggage in the Alam Bagh and garrisoned it with the three hundred remaining men of HM 75th Foot, Campbell despatched a strong reconnaissance towards the Char Bagh Bridge – the route chosen by Havelock during his relief of the garrison – and farther west. Having thus distracted the enemy, he set off – on the morning of the 14th – on his intended route. His men marched eastward parallel to the route used by Havelock but $1\frac{1}{2}$ miles to its south. At the Dilkusha Palace the column came under heavy fire from infantrymen lining the park walls. The 4th Brigade – the 53rd, the 93rd and the 4th Punjabis – was halted while the heavy guns made a breach wide enough for the 93rd to enter.

Among the heavy gunners of Captain William Peel's Naval Brigade was Ordinary Seaman 2nd Class Joseph Hoskins: 'We unlimbered and commenced playing long ball with them [i.e., the rebels]. The 93rd Highlanders and 53rd were drawn up in rear ready for a charge we loaded the eight guns and charged the three rocket tubes the Captain gave the word fire and the troops charged through our guns.' It was here that Peel made a remark that was to become something of a catchphrase for the relief column. Reviewing the damage his first salvo had done, Peel, noticing a number of the infantry officers about to lead their men forward in charge, stopped them in their tracks with a languid 'One more broadside if you please, gentlemen!'

Waiting behind Peel's guns as they delivered their 'broadside' was Corporal Forbes-Mitchell of the 93rd. 'While we were halted,' he wrote, 'my company and No. 8, Captain Williams' company, were in a field of beautiful carrots, which the men were pulling up and eating raw. I remember ... a young lad not turned twenty, Kenneth Mackenzie by name, of No. 8 company, making a remark that these might be the last carrots many of us would eat, and with that he asked the colour-sergeant of the company, who belonged to the same place as himself, to write to his mother should anything happen to him. The colour-sergeant of course, promised to do so, telling young Mackenzie not to let such gloomy thoughts enter his mind.'

At last came the order to advance and the 93rd ran in through the breach and hastily formed line within the park.

The enclosure swarmed with deer, both black buck and spotted, but there were no signs of the enemy, and a staff-officer of the artillery galloped to the front to reconnoitre. This officer was ... Lieutenant Roberts, Deputy Assistant Quarter-Master General of Artillery, who had joined our force at Cawnpore, and had been associated with the Ninety-Third in several skirmishes which had taken place in the advance on the Alumbagh. He was at that time familiarly known among us as 'Plucky Wee Bobs.' About half the regiment had passed through the breach and were forming into line right and left of the two centre companies, when we noticed the staff officer halt and wheel round to return, signalling for the artillery to advance, and immediately a masked battery of six guns opened fire on us from behind the Dilkoosha Palace. The first round shot passed through our column, between the right of No. 7 Company and the line, as the company was wheeling into line, but the second shot ... ricochetted at almost a right angle, and in its course struck poor young Kenneth Mackenzie on the side of his head, taking the skull clean off just level with his ears. He fell just in front of me, and I had to step over his body before a single drop of blood of his had time to flow. The colour-sergeant turned to me and said, 'Poor lad! how can I tell his poor mother. What would she think if she were to see him now! He was her favourite laddie!'

The enemy's next shot cut down seven or eight men of the Light Company. 'Old Colonel Leith-Hay was calling out "Keep steady men; close up the ranks and don't waver in the face of a battery manned by cowardly Asiatics." The shots were now coming in thick, bounding along the hard ground, and MacBean, the adjutant was behind the line telling the men in an undertone, "Don't mind the colonel; open out and let them (the round shot) through, keep plenty of room and watch the shot."'

By now Frederick Roberts – on the staff of the Artillery Brigade – had ridden back from his reconnaissance and was soon bringing up guns. 'The artillery dashed to the front under his direction, taking the guns of the enemy in flank. The sepoys bolted down the hill for shelter in the Martinière, while our little force took possession of the Dilkoosha Palace.' The next move was against the Martinière. 'The Martiniere was situated near the river bank,' wrote Hope Grant,

> and was a handsome building, constructed like an Italian villa on a very large scale. The rebels had not expected to be attacked from this side, as General Havelock's force had entered the town and Residency by the main Cawnpore road . . . [and] had not consequently intrenched the south Martinière side with sufficient care, and it was evident that the building itself could not hold out for long. Our heavy guns were brought to bear on it from the plateau opposite the Dilkoosha; and after an hour's pounding a general advance was ordered. The position was easily carried, and several guns captured.

Two counter-attacks made on the British bivouacs between the Dilkusha and the Martinière were repulsed in the afternoon – during which time another reconnaissance was pushed forward – this time towards the Dilkusha Bridge. That night as the army settled to sleep tentless, their arms by their side, Kavanagh and another officer descended into the vault of the Martinière to see if the founder of the college – whose schoolboys were now manning the semaphore apparatus on the roof of the Residency – lay undisturbed. 'We found broken in two pieces the marble slab with the modest epitaph "Here lies Colonel Martin, who came to India a private soldier in 1760 and died a Major-General in 1800 AD".' Martin's bones had been disinterred and scattered. Kavanagh and his companion reburied them and then rejoined the Commander-in-Chief in his billet. 'Sir Colin lay on the cold floor, dreaming of the coming battle . . . I humbly lay by his side, and dreamt too.'

# II

# LUCKNOW RELIEVED

'Sir Colin Campbell is a short sleeper,' wrote Kavanagh, 'and he rises half dressed; his toilet is the shortest possible, and he is usually the first in the saddle.' After visiting the Lucknow outposts he climbed to the pinnacle of the Martinière. 'He . . . surveyed the city spread broadly before us, with its glittering domes, white temples, long tortuous streets, and embowered palaces; and he did not descend till minutely informed of the situation of the several positions intervening.' The army was on the march by 8 a.m. The rebels – having seen the British thoroughly scouting the canal line between the Char Bagh and Dilkusha bridges had come to the conclusion that Campbell's chosen crossing point would be somewhere between the two. To counter this they had dammed the canal to deepen the water there, which had the effect of draining the canal at Campbell's actual chosen crossing point between the canal and the Gumti. 'The enemy had been so completely taken in by the previous day's reconnaissance,' wrote Frederick Roberts, 'that they had not the slightest suspicion that we should advance from our right, with the result that we were allowed to cross the canal without opposition. About a mile beyond the canal we turned sharp to the left, and passed through the narrow street of a small village, coming immediately under fire from some houses on our right, and from the top of a high wall above and beyond them, which turned out to be the north-east corner of the Sikanderbagh.'

The Sikandar Bagh – Alexander's Palace – stood in a walled enclosure 20 yards square with bastions on each corner. At its centre was a two-storey building with a flat roof. The walls were loopholed and the approaches to it were blocked by abattis. The artillery of the advance guard – Blunt's battery of the Royal Artillery – now found themselves under a three-way fire, while their accompanying infantry – a company of the 53rd – were soon taking cover along the banks that lined the road. Sir Colin Campbell rode forward to assess the situation, Kavanagh beside him. 'A terrific fire of musketry poured from the high walls as some of the 53rd, with Sir Colin, reached the angle of the garden facing the river. The first man who attempted to pass under it was severely wounded in the hip, and lay with bullets ploughing the earth around him. I leaped from my horse, and dragged him by the arm into a hut close by, the poor fellow thankfully squeezing my hands.' A young volunteer staff officer – Lord Seymour, son of the Duke of Somerset – rode forward waving his sword and some men of the 53rd rose to follow him, but they were all stopped by Campbell's voice. Sir Colin had already – in the case of the younger Havelock – expressed his opinion of young staff officers placing themselves at the head of other men's troops. '"Come back!" Kavanagh heard him cry. "Come back Lord Seymour; you have no business there! I did not order it! I witnessed your gallantry with great pleasure. Consider yourself, my lord, as attached to my staff for the present! I admire your noble spirit and must take care of you!" The young nobleman returned abashed, and looking as if it was nothing to have escaped the hundred bullets directed at him.' Lord Seymour was lucky to have escaped one of Sir Colin's famous explosions of rage, where he would literally dance with fury while tearing verbal strips off his victim – being the son of a duke may have helped.

In order to get a better view of the position, Sir Colin and his staff rode up to the bank and placed themselves beside one of Blunt's guns. Frederick Roberts was among them. 'I heard the Commander-in-Chief exclaim, "I am hit." Luckily it was only a spent bullet which had passed through a gunner (killing him on the spot) before it struck Sir Colin on the thigh, causing a severe contusion on the thigh, but nothing more.' By now one of Towers' heavy guns and an 8-inch howitzer had arrived on the scene – dragged up by hand-ropes. They were deployed on the bank and their fire was soon directed at the point that Sir Colin had selected for a breach. Now also behind the bank were the remainder of the 53rd and Sir Colin's 'pets', the 93rd, among them William Forbes-Mitchell. In the village before the Sikandar Bagh, he wrote,

We saw a naked wretch of a strong muscular build, with his head closely shaven except for the tuft on his crown, and his face all streaked in a hideous manner with white and red paint, his body smeared with ashes. A young staff officer, I think it was Captain A. O. Mayne, Deputy Assistant Quartermaster-General, was making his way to the front, when a man of my company, named James Wilson, pointed to the wretch saying, 'I would like to try my bayonet on the hide of that painted scoundrel, who looks like a murderer.' Captain Mayne replied: 'Oh don't touch him; those fellows are harmless Hindoo *jogees* and won't hurt us. It is the Mahommedans that are to blame for the horrors of this Mutiny.' The words had scarcely been uttered when the painted scoundrel stopped counting the beads, slipped his hand under the leopard skin, and as quick as lightning brought out a short, brass, bell-mouthed blunderbuss and fired the contents of it into Captain Mayne's chest. His action was as quick as it was unexpected, and Captain Mayne was unable to avoid the shot, or the men to prevent it. Immediately our men were upon the assassin; there was no means of escape for him, and he was quickly bayoneted.

Like everyone else Forbes-Mitchell had his own opinion on where the blame for the Mutiny lay. 'Since then I have never seen a painted Hindoo, but I involuntarily raise my hand to knock him down. From that hour I formed the opinion (which I have never had cause to alter since) that the pampered high-caste Hindoo sepoys had far more to do with the Mutiny and the cowardly murders of women and children, than the Mohammedans, although the latter still bear most of the blame.'

Forbes-Mitchell and his comrades waited while the guns did their work:

As soon as the guns opened fire the Infantry Brigade was made to take shelter at the back of a low mud wall behind the guns, the men taking steady aim at every loophole from which we could see the musket-barrels of the enemy protruding. The Commander-in-Chief and his staff were close behind the guns, Sir Colin every now and again turning round when a man was hit, calling out, 'lie down, Ninety-Third, lie down! Every man of you is worth his weight in gold to England to-day!' The first shots from our guns passed through the wall, piercing it as though it were a piece of cloth, and without knocking the surrounding brickwork away. Accounts differ, but my impression has always been that it was from half to three-quarters of an hour that the guns battered at the walls. During this time the men, both artillery and sailors, working the guns without any cover so close to the enemy's loopholes, were falling fast, over two guns' crews having been disabled or killed before the wall was breached. After holes had been pounded through the wall in many places large blocks of brick-and-mortar commenced to fall out, and then portions of the wall came down bodily leaving large gaps.

While assessing the damage the guns had done, Sir Colin encountered an old friend in the ranks of the 53rd. Forbes-Mitchell witnessed the scene.

A sergeant of the Fifty-Third, who had served under Sir Colin in the Punjab, presuming an old acquaintance, called out 'Sir Colin, your Excellency, let the infantry storm; let the two "Thirds" at them [meaning the Fifty-Third and Ninety-Third], and we'll soon make short work of the murdering villains!' The sergeant who called to Sir Colin was a Welshman . . . Joe Lee . . . He was always known as Dobbin in his regiment; and Sir Colin, who had a most wonderful memory for names and faces, turning to Sir William Mansfield who had formerly served in the Fifty-Third, said, 'Isn't that Sergeant Dobbin?' General Mansfield replied in the affirmative; and Sir Colin, turning to Lee, said, 'Do you think the breach is wide enough Dobbin?' Lee replied, 'Part of us can get through and hold it till the pioneers widen it with their crowbars to allow the rest to get in.'

Knowing that time was of the essence, Sir Colin waved his cap and the bugles sounded the 'Advance'. 'The infantry had been lying down, under such slight cover as was available,' wrote Frederick Roberts, 'impatiently waiting for this order. The moment it reached them, up they sprang with one accord, and with one voice uttered a shout which must have foreshadowed defeat to the defenders of the Sikandarbagh.' The Sikhs of the 4th Punjabis gained themselves a 5-yard start by breaking cover the moment Sir Colin bared his head; Forbes-Mitchell watched them go:

The Punjabis dashed over the mud wall shouting the war cry of the Sikhs, *'Jai Khalsa Jee'* led by their two European officers, who were both shot down before they had gone a few yards. This staggered the

Sikhs, and they halted. As soon as Sir Colin saw them waver, he turned to Colonel Ewart, who was in command of the seven companies of the Ninety-Third (Colonel Leith-Hay being in command of the assault), and said: 'Colonel Ewart, bring on the tartan – let my own lads at them.' Before the command could be repeated or the buglers had time to sound the advance, the whole seven companies, like one man, leaped over the wall, with such a yell of pent-up rage as I had never heard before or since. It was not a cheer but a concentrated yell of rage and ferocity that made the echoes ring again; and it must have struck terror into the defenders, for they actually ceased firing, and we could see them through the breach rushing from the outside wall to take shelter in the two-storied building in the centre of the garden, the gate and doors of which they firmly barred.

The 4th Punjabis, now led by Captain Gopal Singh, and the 93rd reached the wall together. 'That was a gallant race,' wrote Henry Kavanagh, who was at Sir Colin Campbell's side. 'The Siekh was first – and dropped in dead! The agitated plumes of a Highland bonnet rose – the wearer stood for an instant in the breach, and fell forward. Another, and another! Two more struggled in the opening to die first.' The honour of having been first through the breach was to be debated for the rest of the century – as well as being the origin of a close regimental friendship between the 93rd and the 4th Punjabis. Frederick Roberts also watched 'that glorious struggle to be the first to enter the deadly breach, the prize to the winner of the race being certain death! Highlanders and Sikhs, Punjabi Mahomedans, Dogras and Pathans, all vied with each other in the generous competition.' In Roberts' view, 'A Highlander was the first to reach the goal, and was shot dead as he entered the enclosure; a man of the 4th Punjab Infantry came next and met the same fate. Then followed Captain Burroughs and Lieutenant Cooper of the 93rd, and immediately behind them their Colonel (Ewart), Captain Lumsden, of the 30th Bengal Infantry, and a number of Sikhs and Highlanders as fast as they could scramble through the opening. A drummer-boy of the 93rd must have been one of the first to pass that grim boundary between life and death, for when I got in I found him just inside the breach, lying back quite dead – a pretty, innocent-looking, fair-haired lad, not more than fourteen years of age.'

Among the first of the Highlanders through the breach was William Forbes-Mitchell.

I got through ... pushed up by Colonel Ewart who immediately followed. My feet had scarcely touched the ground inside, when a sepoy fired point-blank at me from among the long grass a few yards distant. The bullet struck the thick brass clasp of my waist belt, but with such force that it sent me spinning heels over head. The man who fired was cut down by Captain Cooper, of the Ninety-Third, who got through the hole almost with myself. When struck I felt just as one feels when tripped up at a football match. Before I regained my feet, I heard Ewart say as he rushed past me, 'Poor fellow, he is done for.' I was but stunned, and regaining my feet and my breath too, which was completely knocked out of me, I rushed on to the inner court of the building, where I saw Ewart bare-headed, his feather bonnet having been shot off his head, engaged in fierce hand-to-hand fight with the enemy. I believe he shot down five or six of them with his revolver.

The entrance being blocked, other men made efforts to break in elsewhere and join the fighting – the 53rd by a window to the right of the breach, and more of the 4th Punjabis via the main gate. The doors at the main gate were being slammed shut by the mutineers just as the Punjabis got there. Frederick Roberts watched as one of the Punjabis took a drastic step to prevent the doors being closed: 'The Mahomedan (Mukarrah Khan by name) pushed his left arm, on which he carried a shield, between them, thus preventing their being shut; on his hand being badly wounded by a sword-cut he drew it out, instantly thrusting in the other arm, when the right hand was all but severed by the wrist. But he gained his object – the doors could not be closed, and were soon forced open altogether, upon which the 4th Punjab infantry, the 53rd, 93rd and some of the Detachments, swarmed in.'

Inside the enclosure it was vicious close-quarter fighting. The sepoys, wrote Roberts, 'were now completely caught in a trap, the only outlets being by the gateway and the breach, through which our troops continued to pour. There could therefore be no thought of escape, and they fought with the desperation of men with no hope of mercy, and determined to sell their lives as dearly as they could. Inch by inch they were forced back to the pavilion, and into the space between it and the north wall, where they were all shot or bayoneted.' The Highlanders, according to Forbes-Mitchell had been instructed in advance how to conduct themselves in this hand-to-hand fighting. Before the battle, he wrote,

Sir Colin . . . addressed the men, telling us there was heavy work before us, and that we must hold well together, and as much as possible keep in threes, and that as soon as we stormed a position we were to use the bayonet. The centre man of each group of three was to make the attack, and the other two to come to his assistance with their bayonets right and left. We were not to fire a single bullet after we got inside a position, unless we were certain of hitting our enemy, for fear of wounding our own men. To use the bayonet with effect we were ordered, as I say, to group in threes and mutually assist each other, for by such action we would soon bayonet the enemy down although they might be ten to one, which as a matter of fact they were . . . He knew the sepoys well, that when brought to the point of the bayonet they could not look the Europeans in the face. For all that they fought like devils. In addition to their muskets, all the men in the Secundrabagh were armed with swords from the King of Oude's magazines, and the native *tulwars* were as sharp as razors . . . when they fired their muskets, they hurled them amongst us like javelins, bayonets first, and then drawing their *tulwars*, rushed madly on to their destruction, slashing in blind fury with their swords . . . As they rushed on us shouting '*Deen! Deen!*' (The Faith! the Faith!) they actually threw themselves under the bayonets and slashed at our legs. It was owing to this fact that more than half of our wounded were injured by sword-cuts.

There could be no question now, that the defenders of the Residency could hear that relief was at hand. 'Pipe-Major John Macleod,' wrote Forbes-Mitchell, 'struck up the Highland Charge, called by some *The Haughs of Cromdell*, and by others *On wi' the Tartan* – the famous charge of the great Montrose when he led his Highlanders so often to victory. When all was over, and Sir Colin complimented the pipe-major on the way he had played, John said, "I thought the boys would fecht better wi' the national music to cheer them."'

During the fighting, Forbes-Mitchell was witness to an extraordinary incident involving two men of his regiment, who had joined with a draft of volunteers from the 72nd Highlanders before the 93rd sailed from England.

Among the volunteers who came from the Seventy-Second was a man named James Wallace. He and six other from the same regiment joined my company. Wallace was not his real name, but he never took any

one into his confidence, nor was he ever known to have any correspondence. He neither wrote nor received any letters, and he was
usually so taciturn in his manner that he was known in the company
as the Quaker, a name that had followed him from the Seventy-
Second. He had evidently received a superior education, for if asked
for any information by a more ignorant comrade, he would at once
give it; or questioned as to the translation of a Latin or French quotation
in a book, he would give it without the least hesitation. I have often
seen him on the voyage out walking up and down the deck of the
*Belleisle* during the watches of the night, repeating the famous poem
of Lamartine, *Le Chien du Solitaire* ... Taking him all in all Quaker
Wallace was a strange enigma which no one could solve. When pressed
to take promotion, for which his superior education well fitted him,
he absolutely refused, always saying that he had come to the Ninety-
Third for a certain purpose, and when that purpose was accomplished
he only wished to die.

The second man 'was also a man of superior education, but in many
respects the very antithesis of Wallace. He was both wild and reckless,
and used often to receive money from some one, which he regularly spent
in drink. He went under the name of Hope, but that was also known to
be an assumed name, and when the volunteers from the Seventy-Second
joined the regiment in Dover, it was remarked that Wallace had the
address of Hope, and had asked to be posted to the same company. Yet
the two men never spoke to one another; on the contrary they evidently
hated each other with a mortal hatred.'

Incidents of second sight were by no means uncommon in the High-
lands and Western Isles at this time, as well as among the Irish. Nor were
premonitions of impending death uncommon – although usually on the
part of the man about to die. Forbes-Mitchell seems to have seen an
example of both.

Just about the time the men were tightening their belts and preparing
for the dash on the Secundrabagh ... Hope commenced to curse
and swear in a manner that Captain Dawson, who commanded the
company, checked him, telling him that oaths and foul language were
no signs of bravery. Hope replied that he did not care a d—— what the
captain thought; that he would defy death; that the bullet was not yet
moulded that would kill him; and he commenced exposing himself

above the mud wall behind which we were lying. The captain was just on the point of ordering a corporal and a file of men to take Hope to the rear-guard as drunk and riotous in the presence of the enemy, when Pipe-Major John Macleod, who was close to the captain, said: 'Don't mind the puir lad, sir; he's not drunk, he is fey [doomed]! It's not himself that's speaking; he will never see the sun set.' The words were barely out of the pipe-major's mouth when Hope sprang up on the top of the mud wall, and a bullet struck him on the right side, hitting the buckle of his purse belt, which diverted its course, and instead of going right through his body it cut him round the front of his belly below the waist-belt, making a deep wound, and his bowels burst out falling down to his knees. He sank down at once, gasping for breath, when a couple of bullets went through his chest and he died without a groan. John Macleod turned and said to Captain Dawson, 'I told you so, sir! The lad was fey! I am never deceived in a fey man! It was not himself that spoke when swearing in yon terrible manner.' Just at this time Quaker Wallace, who had evidently been a witness of Hope's tragic end, worked his way along to where the dead man lay, and looking on the distorted features he solemnly said, 'The fool hath said in his heart, there is no God. Vengeance is mine, I will repay, saith the Lord. *I came to the Ninety-Third to see that man die!*'

As soon as the assault began, Quaker Wallace threw himself into the fight 'like one of the Furies, if there are male furies, plainly seeking death but not meeting it, quoting the 116th Psalm, Scotch version in metre'. He was reckoned to have killed twenty-two men with bullet and bayonet, but remained unhurt himself proving, wrote Forbes-Mitchell, 'that, in a fight like the Secundrabagh where the enemy is met hand to hand and foot to foot, the way to escape death is to brave it'.

It was thirsty work, he wrote: 'By the time the bayonet had done its work of retribution, the throats of our men were hoarse with shouting "Cawnpore! you bloody murderers!" The taste of the powder (those were the days when the muzzle-loading cartridges had to be bitten with the teeth) made men almost mad with thirst; and with the sun high over head, and our being fresh from England, with our feather bonnets, red coats, and heavy kilts, we felt the heat intensely.' A number of Forbes-Mitchell's comrades, as well as men of the 53rd, went to a well below a peepul tree to draw water. Forbes-Mitchell's captain, Dawson, soon noticed a number of dead from both regiments strewn about the base of the tree.

After having carefully examined the wounds he noticed that in every case the men had evidently been shot from above. He thereupon ... called to Quaker Wallace to look up to see if he could see any one in the top of the tree. Wallace had his rifle loaded, and stepping back he carefully scanned the top of the tree. He almost immediately called out, 'I see him, sir!' and cocking his rifle he repeated aloud, 'I'll pay my vows now to the Lord, Before his people all.' He fired, and down fell a body dressed in a tight-fitting red jacket and tight-fitting rose-coloured trousers; and the breast of the jacket bursting open with the fall, showed that the wearer was a woman. She was armed with a pair of heavy old-pattern cavalry pistols, one of which was in her belt still loaded, and her pouch was still about half full of ammunition ... When Wallace saw the person whom he had shot was a woman, he burst into tears, exclaiming: 'If I had known it was a woman, I would rather have died a thousand deaths than harm her.'

Most of the rebels were pushed slowly across the enclosure towards the north wall – others took shelter in the pavilion in the centre or the bastions at the corners of the enclosure. 'Hoarse calls for help came from this side,' wrote Henry Kavanagh, 'loud and frequent orders to go in and bayonet from the other – curses, in the most awful words, mingled with imploring voices. A few ran wild through the combatants to end their misery by death. Hundreds were deliberately bayoneted and pitched, writhing in the agonies of death into a reservoir. The appalling sounds of cutting, hacking, and stabbing, were heard all round the garden, with the dreadful screams of the combatants.' The cries of the rebels 'Deen, Deen!', the Sikhs 'Jai Khalsa Jee!', and the British 'Cawnpore, boys, remember Cawnpore!', mingled with the wail of the pipes and the rattle of musketry.

Many of the rebels shut themselves up in the pavilion in the centre of the enclosure or the buildings clustered round the inner walls of the gardens. They fought to the death from room to room or floor to floor – tossed on the ends of bayonets like bales of hay to land in the flowerbeds below. When one door proved unbreakable a gun was wheeled into the enclosure – the door was soon blown apart and the infantry dashed in through the smoke to complete the work of slaughter. Lieutenant Colonel Ewart of the 93rd, seeing an enemy colour in one of the bastions ran into the room where he found it guarded by two native officers. Although both of them wounded him, he killed them and seized the colour.

At last the fighting was over – two thousand rebel dead lay in the enclosure. 'There they lay in a heap as high as my head,' wrote Roberts, 'a heaving, surging mass of dead and dying inextricably entangled. It was a sickening sight, one of those which even in the excitement of battle and the flush of victory make one feel strongly what a horrible side there is to war.' Seeing that the Sikandar Bagh was secure, Ewart, still clutching his colour, ran over to Sir Colin Campbell. Forbes-Mitchell saw their meeting:

> Colonel Ewart, seeing that the fighting was over, started with his colour to present it to Sir Colin Campbell; but whether it was that the old Chief considered that it was *infra dig.* for a field officer to expose himself to needless danger, or whether it was that he was angry at some other thing, I know not, but this much I remember: Colonel Ewart ran up to him where he sat on his grey charger outside the gate of the Secundrabagh, and called out: 'We are in possession of the bungalows, sir. I have killed the last two of the enemy with my own hand, and here is one of their colours.' 'D—n your colours, sir!' said Sir Colin. 'It's not your place to be taking colours; go back to your regiment this instant, sir!'

Needless to say, Colonel Ewart was not the son of a duke. Sir Colin's staff, however, cheered Ewart, and Henry Kavanagh, who also witnessed the scene, presented Ewart with a cap to protect his bare head. Ewart returned to his regiment much distressed at the Commander-in-Chief's reaction – Campbell visited him personally later in the day, apologized for his rudeness, and thanked him for his services. Campbell's direct route to the Residency ran from the Sikandar Bagh 1,500 yards due west to the Moti Mahal (Pearl Palace). Three hundred yards along this road was a small village with – about 200 yards on and to the right of the road – a large mosque, the Shah Najaf. With the sun beginning to set Campbell decided to close the day's operations with the capture of the Shah Najaf. This mosque – the mausoleum of the first King of Oude – was enclosed by strong, stone walls 20 feet high, which had been loopholed. Parapets for musketry had been constructed on top of the domed tomb. The doors of the mosque had been covered by a masonry outwork and to its east and west were houses surrounded by gardens and high trees. From these and the mosque itself an unceasing fire of musketry was kept up on the British as they advanced.

Blunt's battery was pushed forward – firing at the sepoys in the houses and gardens to the east of the main enclosure. Then Captain Garnet Wolseley, of the 90th Light Infantry – who had been wounded in the right leg in Burma in 1852, and in both legs in front of the Redan at Sebastopol in 1855 – was ordered to clear some huts from which the sepoys were firing on Blunt's gunners. These being seized and held by Wolseley's men, Sir Colin then called up the composite battalion led by Major Barnston, also of the 90th – ordering him to try and gain entry to the Shah Najaf and, if unable to do so, to come back and give a report of what he had seen, as the enemy's position was largely concealed from view by dense foliage. The composite battalion was composed of detachments from every regiment that had been destined for the China expedition and men from the regiments that had marched with Havelock, who had been left behind through sickness or wounds, as well as some men from Barnston's own 90th. 'Although a made-up battalion, they advanced bravely,' wrote Forbes-Mitchell,

> there were no scaling ladders, and the wall was still almost twenty feet high. During the heavy cannonade the masonry had fallen down in flakes on the outside, but still leaving an inner wall standing almost perpendicular, and in attempting to climb up this men were raked with a perfect hail of missiles – grenades and round shot hurled from wall pieces, arrows and brickbats, burning torches of rags and cotton saturated with oil – even boiling water was dashed on them! In the midst of the smoke the breach would have made a very good representation of Pandemonium. There were scores of men armed with great burning torches just like what one may see in the sham fights of *Mohurrum*, only these men were in earnest, shouting *'Allah Akbar!' 'Deen Deen!'* and *'Jai Kali ma ki!'* ['Victory to mother Kali!'].

Unable to break in, Barnston ran back to report to the Commander-in-Chief – returning to join his men, a shell prematurely exploding at the muzzle of one of Blunt's guns mortally wounded him. This, together with the enemy's heavy fire, caused some of them to fall back – they were rallied by Captain Norman and led forward again to seize some of the buildings to the east of the enclosure. To the musketry from the main rebel position was added artillery fire – the most effective of which was from a battery on the far side of the river Gumti. Sir Colin decided to bring up more of his own artillery – Corporal Forbes-Mitchell of the 93rd saw them arrive:

> At the word of command Captain Middleton's battery of Royal Artillery dashed forward with loud cheers, the drivers waving their whips and the gunners their caps as they passed us and Peel's guns at the gallop. The 24-pounders meanwhile were dragged along by our men and the sailors in the teeth of a perfect hail of lead and iron from the enemy's batteries. In the middle of the march a poor sailor lad, just in front of me, had his leg carried clean off above the knee by a round shot, and although knocked head over heels by the force of the shot, he sat bolt upright on the grass, with the blood spouting from the stump of his limb like water from the hose of a fire engine, and shouted 'Here goes for a shilling a day, a shilling a day! Pitch into them, boys, pitch into them! Remember Cawnpore, Ninety-Third, remember Cawnpore! Go at them my hearties!' and he fell back in a dead faint, and on we went. I afterwards heard that the poor fellow was dead before a doctor could reach the spot to bind up his limb.

Both Middleton's battery, firing case shot at the enclosures, and Peel's 24-pounders, firing at the walls, worked their guns under a heavy enemy fire. At one of Peel's guns all the crew were killed or wounded except Able Seaman William Hall – a black sailor – who continued to sponge, load and fire his gun single-handed, for which he later received the Victoria Cross. Hall's gun was no more than 10 yards from the wall of the enclosure, splinters from which proved as dangerous as the enemy's fire. 'It's no use, unless we are close up,' Captain Peel was heard to say, 'we must bring the place about our ears, and then get to close quarters.' In 'engaging the enemy more closely' Peel – displaying the cool head he had shown in the *Diamond* battery above Sebastopol – was true to the navy's Nelsonic tradition. 'Captain Peel behaved very much as if he had been laying the *Shannon* alongside an enemy frigate,' wrote Sir Colin in his despatch. One naval officer, Lieutenant Nowell Salmon of the *Shannon*, shinned up a tree with a rifle, from which position he brought down a number of sepoys – a sergeant of the 93rd, acting as his gillie, handed him up loaded rifles. Salmon, too – who, after dropping a sepoy who was throwing hand grenades, was shot through the leg – was awarded the Victoria Cross. Marines and Highlanders from Forbes-Mitchell's 93rd also did what they could to suppress the rebel musketry. 'After

Captain Peel's guns were dragged into position,' wrote Forbes-Mitchell, 'the Ninety-Third took up whatever shelter they could get on the right and left of the guns and I, with several others, got behind the walls of an unroofed mud hut, through which we made loopholes on the side next to the Shah Nujeef, and were thus able to keep up a destructive fire on the enemy.'

Among the defenders of the mosque were numbers of archers, as Forbes-Mitchell and his comrades had already observed. Now they encountered them at close range.

> One poor fellow of the Ninety-Third named Penny, of No.2 company raising his head for an instant a little above the wall, got an arrow right through his brain, the shaft projecting more than a foot out at the back of his head. As the poor lad fell dead at our feet, Sergeant White remarked, 'Boys, this is no joke; we must pay them off.' We all loaded and capped, and pushing up our feather bonnets . . . a whole shower of arrows went past or through them. Up we sprang and returned a well-aimed volley from our rifles at point-blank distance, and more than half-a-dozen of the enemy went down. But one unfortunate man of the regiment, named Montgomery, of No.6 company, exposed himself a little too long to watch the effect of our volley, and before he could get down into shelter again an arrow was sent right through his heart, passing clean through his body and falling on the ground a few yards behind him. He leaped about six feet straight up in the air, and fell stone dead.

By now both gunners and infantry had suffered heavy losses – even Peel was looking worried. 'Sir Colin was beginning to get extremely anxious, and no wonder,' wrote Frederick Roberts, 'the position was most uncomfortable, and the prospect was very gloomy. Three hours since the attack began! The day was rapidly drawing to a close, and we were no nearer our object . . . A retreat was not to be thought of, indeed, our remaining so long stationary had been an encouragement to the enemy.' Campbell turned to his 'own' regiment – the 93rd – to make one final attempt. 'Sir Colin, again addressing us, said that he had not intended to call on us to storm more positions that day,' wrote Forbes-Mitchell, 'but that the building in our front must be carried before dark, and the Ninety-Third must do it, and he would lead us himself, saying again: "Remember, men, the lives at stake inside the Residency are those of women and children and they must be rescued." A reply burst from the ranks "Ay, ay Sir Colin! We stood by you at Balaklava, and will stand by you here; but you must not expose yourself so much as you are doing. We can be replaced, but you can't. You must remain behind; we can lead ourselves."' This attempt was no more successful than the previous ones. 'The battalion of detachments had cleared to the front,' wrote Forbes-Mitchell, 'and the enemy were still yelling to us to "Come on", and piling up missiles to give us a warm reception. Captain Peel had meanwhile brought his infernal machine, known as a rocket battery, to the front, and sent a volley of rockets through the crowd on the ramparts.' Casualties soon started to pile up – even among Sir Colin's staff. 'The narrow path along which we were proceeding was choked with wounded officers,' wrote Roberts. 'Sir Archibald Alison, Sir Colin's Aide-de-camp, lost his arm, and his brother, (another Aide-de-Camp) was wounded. Adrian Hope's horse was shot dead – indeed very few escaped injury, either to themselves or their horses. I was one of the lucky few.' Peel's guns continued to hammer at the walls but with no effect – Campbell reluctantly decided that the attempt must be abandoned. Peel was ordered to fire another salvo of rockets, under cover of which Brigadier Hope would withdraw his men.

The aide who took the message to Hope, Captain Allgood, and Hope himself now decided to make one last attempt to find a way into the mosque compound. 'Assisted by a sergeant of the 93rd,' wrote Roberts, 'they set about their search, and actually did find a narrow gap, through which they could see that the enemy, terrified and thrown into confusion by the exploding rockets falling among them, were fast abandoning the building. The two friends helped each other through the gap, and, followed by some Highlanders they proceeded across the now empty enclosure to secure the only gateway, which was the one on the opposite side to that which we had attacked.' It is sometimes difficult to conceive – when one's own side is taking heavy casualties – how much the other side must be suffering. 'By the great pools of blood inside,' wrote Corporal Forbes-Mitchell, 'and the number of dead floating in the river, they had plainly suffered heavily.' Peel's rockets had tipped the scale and the Shah Najaf fell to the British just as they had been about to fall back. The sergeant, Paton of the 93rd – who had crawled through the gardens alone earlier and found the gap by which Hope and Allgood entered – nominated by his fellow sergeants, was awarded the Victoria Cross.

The relief column bivouacked that night where they halted. It was a cold, comfortless night and a short one. Shivering among his comrades in the Sikandar Bagh William Forbes-Mitchell could hardly sleep for their groans and shouts:

> The horrible scenes through which the men had passed during the day had told with terrible effect on their nervous systems, and the struggles, eye to eye, foot to foot, and steel to steel – with death in the Secundrabagh, were fought over again by most of the men in their sleep, oaths and shouts of defiance often curiously intermingled with prayers. One man would be lying calmly sleeping and commence muttering something inaudible, and break out into a fierce battle-cry of 'Cawnpore, you bloody murderer!'; another would shout 'Charge! give them the bayonet!' and a third, 'Keep together boys, don't fire; forward, forward; if we are to die, let us die like men!' Then I would hear one muttering, 'Oh, mother, forgive me, and I'll never leave you again!'; while his comrade would half rise up, wave his hand, and call, 'There they are! Fire low, give them the bayonet! Remember Cawnpore!' And so it was throughout that memorable night.

By sunrise on the 17th, however, morale was high. At the Shah Najaf, Lieutenant McBean, Sergeant Hutchinson and Drummer Ross climbed to the top of the Dome and with the regimental colour of the 93rd – topped by a Highland bonnet – signalled their position to the occupants of the Residency. The signal was answered – the Residency flag being lowered three times in reply. By now rebel gunners were firing round shot at the three men as they descended, but the drummer-boy ran up once more, played the regimental call, and 'Cock of the North' on his bugle. Ordered to come down by McBean the boy did so, but not until he had sung two verses of 'Yankee Doodle'. When the boy was questioned about his action, Forbes-Mitchell heard his reply: 'Ye ken, sir, I was born when the regiment was in Canada when my mother was on a visit to an aunt in the States, and I could not come down till I had sung *Yankee Doodle*, to make my American cousins envious when they hear of the deeds of the Ninety-Third. Won't the Yankees feel jealous when they hear that the littlest drummer-boy in the Regiment sang *Yankee Doodle* under a hail of fire on the Dome of the highest mosque in Lucknow!'

Campbell's plan was to take the Mess House – a large stone building halfway between the Shah Najaf and the Kaisar Bagh. After this the force would move on to the Moti Mahal, from which he could link up with Outram's garrison in the Residency. With an estimated 30,000 rebels still at large, Campbell knew that he could not hold the city and his intention was to evacuate the Residency. While the troops breakfasted and buried the bodies of nearly two thousand sepoys Sir Colin summoned Captain (now Brevet Major) Garnet Wolseley and told him that his company of HM 90th were to attempt to storm the Mess House and – if they failed – Wolseley was to report back to him what he had seen. He was to be supported by the composite battalion under Major Guise and a picket of the 53rd. The previous day's casualties had been heavy and Sir Colin – anxious to spare his men's lives as far as possible – ordered Peel's guns and Longden's mortars to fire on the Mess House until 3 p.m. before sending Wolseley's men in. After the hard fighting of the previous day it was hardly to be imagined that the enemy would abandon a strongpoint like the Mess House without a bitter struggle, but this – as Wolseley's men rushed in – was what they did, fleeing across the gardens to the Moti Mahal. Wolseley had captured his objective without losing a single man, but – not a man to give a flying enemy time to regroup – he led his men through the gardens, full of orange and lemon trees, and across a drawbridge in hot pursuit. His orders were to seize and hold the Mess House, but he saw before him a chance to seize the Moti Mahal by *coup de main*. Under heavy fire from the Kaisar Bagh and adjoining buildings – from which the men sheltered by passing up an arcade close to the main entrance of the Moti Mahal – they suddenly found themselves confronted by a 20-foot high wall. 'I got to the palace gate,' wrote Wolseley, 'and found it built up by a thick masonry wall, well loopholed. The fools had forgotten to dig a ditch outside, so after they gave us the first volley I manned the loopholes on my side, and there we stood, the enemy on one side and we on the other, both striving for the holes. I sent back for tools and in a short time we had a hole big enough for a man to get through, so in we went, one after the other, the niggers bolting to the river and trying to swim across . . . I had capital practice at them in the water. But I lost a number of my men at those infernal loopholes.'

Frederick Roberts, meanwhile, had been ordered by Sir Colin to place a regimental colour in one of the turrets of the Mess House. Borrowing one of the colours of the 2nd Punjab Infantry, he galloped to the Mess House, manoeuvred the long flagstaff up a narrow staircase and planted the flag on the turret nearest the Kaisar Bagh. 'No sooner did the enemy perceive what we were about, than shot after shot was aimed at the colour, and in a very few minutes it was knocked over, falling into the ditch below. I ran down and picked it up, and again placed it in position, only for it to be once more shot down and hurled into the ditch ... Once more I picked up the colour and found that this time the staff had been broken in two. Notwithstanding, I managed to prop it up a third time on the turret, and it was not again hit, though the enemy continued to fire at it for some time.'

Down in the courtyard of the Moti Mahal, Wolseley and his men were fighting a succession of small battles with groups of sepoys in outhouses and at loopholes in the main building, when a huge explosion at the western end of the courtyard covered them all with dust and smoke. As it cleared, Captain Tinling of the 90th emerged at the head of his company. These men had gone into the Residency with Havelock six weeks earlier. Inside the Residency Outram had been reluctant to incur further casualties by attempting a breakout until he knew Sir Colin was close. Seeing the British flag on the roof of the Mess House, however, he had ordered a sortie – and in this regimental reunion the relief column's link with the garrison had been made.

From the Mess House roof, Roberts and his companions – two of Sir Colin's staff officers – could see a British flag flying from the Engine House, only a few yards beyond the Moti Mahal. Four hundred yards of open ground – exposed to fire from the Kaisar Bagh – separated the relievers from the relieved. This Generals Outram and Havelock and their staffs crossed to meet Sir Colin and his staff. A number of officers – Colonel Robert Napier and three lieutenants – were hit and forced to turn back. Passing through the Moti Mahal gardens, Havelock was knocked off his feet by the blast from a shell, but clambered up unhurt. Soon, however, he found himself greeted by cheering men of his own regiment, HM 53rd. Hope Grant was with them. 'I had the satisfaction of being the first to congratulate him on being relieved. He went up to the men, who immediately flocked round him and gave him three hearty cheers. This was too much for the fine old general – his breast heaved with emotion and his eyes filled with tears. He turned to the men and said: "Soldiers, I am happy to see you."' Sir Colin Campbell, however, wasn't happy. Wolseley's exceeding his orders and pressing on to the Moti Mahal had sent him into one of his dancing rages – he had, he later said, 'never been so enraged by any man in [my] life' – but he recovered his equanimity as the two Generals approached him, and rose to the occasion. 'How do you do Sir James?' he said, doffing his cap and offering his hand, and turning to Havelock and 'How do you do, *Sir* Henry?' This was the first Havelock – who Roberts thought looked 'ill, worn and depressed' –

had heard of the award of his KCB and he brightened considerably. Outram by contrast, Roberts noted, seemed 'in no way broken down by the heavy load of responsibility and anxiety he had had to bear, or the hardships he had gone through'. Not everyone who had come out of the Residency stayed to witness the historic meeting. 'The meeting of the Generals', wrote Captain F. C. Maude, 'has been often described, and has been the subject of a stirring picture by T. J. Barker. My own share in it was somewhat ignoble. I accompanied Havelock, it is true, but a few paces behind him; and not knowing Sir Colin, nor having any particular *raison d'etre dans cette galere*, I sneaked off to get some tobacco, of which we were in desperate need, and of which we felt the deprivation far more than keenly than the want of spirituous liquors.'

Despite the arguments of some – including Hope Grant and Outram – that the Residency should be held, the Kaisar Bagh stormed and the rebels driven out of Lucknow, Sir Colin was insistent that the entire garrison of the Residency should be evacuated over the next few days. He did not feel that his force – lacking reserves and with its communications still under threat – was strong enough to hold the city. Preparations were set in hand to abandon the Residency.

That night Wolseley – who had been warned by General Adrian Hope to 'keep out of Sir Colin's way or you'll catch it; his orders to you were to take the Mess House only' – stumbled over a sleeping figure as he tried to find a place for himself to lie down. He passed a cold night, having lent his greatcoat to his friend Major Barnston, who was dying. On awaking he discovered that the person he had stepped on was no less than the Commander-in-Chief himself, who was also just waking. Sir Colin shook his fist at Wolseley, shouting 'How dared you attack the Moti Mahal without instructions?' The General, however, was smiling – he complimented Wolseley on his courage and skill, and promised him promotion.

The evacuation of the Residency began at 10 a.m. on 19 November, covered by broadsides from Captain Peel's guns – directed at the Kaisar Bagh – and canvas screens to shield the evacuees from observation. 'I turned my back on the Residency with a heavy heart,' wrote Mrs Inglis, 'for at that time I fancied a force might be left there, and that I was bidding farewell to my husband for some time.' Their route out took them first to the Sikandar Bagh, which according to Mrs Inglis 'was considered safe, except in three parts where the road was commanded by the enemy, and they were firing at intervals'. British sharpshooters in the

Shah Najaf and the Moti Mahal – among them Corporal Forbes-Mitchell of the 93rd – kept the enemy at a distance. 'From these two points,' he wrote, 'the enemy on the north bank of the Gumtee were brought under a cross-fire the accuracy of which made them keep a very respectable distance from the river, with the result that the women and children passed the exposed part of the route without a single casualty.' Arrived at the Sikandar Bagh they were met by the Commander-in-Chief in person. 'Sir Colin Campbell came and talked to me for some time,' wrote Mrs Inglis, 'he was very kind in his manner, and talked about us as dear creatures, meaning the ladies; at the same time I knew he was wishing us very far away, and no wonder!' Captain Birch, Brigadier Inglis's ADC, had helped Mrs Inglis by carrying one of the children. He then returned to the Residency to assist with the withdrawal – on the night of the 22nd/23rd – of its various 'garrisons'. 'First the garrison in immediate contact with the enemy at the furthest extremity of the Residency position was marched out. Every other garrison in turn fell in behind it, and so passed out through the Bailie Guard gate, till the whole of our position was evacuated ... The whole operation resembled the movement of a telescope.' Birch was sent back in to check that the last garrison had actually gone. 'The utter stillness and solitude of the deserted position with which I was so familiar, struck coldly upon my nerves; I had to go and I did ... I did not meet a living soul. I think I may fairly claim to have seen the last of the Residency of Lucknow before its abandonment to the enemy.' There was a question of etiquette at the Baillie Guard gate with both Outram and Inglis wanting the honour of being the last to leave. 'You will allow me, Sir,' said Inglis, 'the honour of closing my own door.' 'Let us go out together.' replied Outram and shaking hands the two men descended together. There followed a schoolboyish scuffle between their staff officers. 'The place of honour ... became the subject of a dispute between Captain Wilson and myself,' wrote Birch, 'but the former was weak from all the hardships and privations he had undergone, and could not stand the trick of shoulder to shoulder learned in the Harrow football fields. Prone on the earth he lay, till he rolled down the hill, and I was the last of the staff to leave the Bailie Guard gate.' They were not quite the last men out, though. Captain Waterman of the 13th NI fell asleep after his name had been called, and awoke to find himself alone. He escaped alive, followed his departed comrades through deserted streets and eventually caught them up, but, wrote Birch, 'the fright sent him off his head for a time'.

Sir Colin's troops, the evacuees and the Residency garrisons were all now concentrated round the Dilkusha Park where – by the evening of the 23rd – Sir Henry Havelock lay dying. He had contracted dysentery in Lucknow and this, combined with the stress and hardships of the previous months, had fatally weakened him. In Persia he had written that he dreaded the recoil on his constitution when rest should replace toil – now it had come to pass. He was 63, and before being summoned to India had been looking forward to retirement to 'a Tyrolese cottage, or a box on the Rhine'. He could no longer make out passages in his Bible, but his son Harry – with his arm in a sling – read to him from a hymnbook. To Outram he said, 'For forty years I have endeavoured to so rule my life that when death came I might face it without fear.' Just after dawn on the 24th he called to his son, 'Harry . . . see how a Christian can die' and passed away silently moments later. Havelock joined John Nicholson in the Imperial Valhalla. He was commemorated in paintings and statues – a book of his sayings was published, each pronouncement heralded by the words 'Havelock Speaks!' He was mourned throughout the English-speaking world – on the announcement of his death flags were flown at half-mast in New York.

Having despatched the women and children in the direction of Cawnpore – a dusty, ill-tempered, alarm-filled journey for most of them – Sir Colin was soon force-marching on ahead of them. He had left General Windham in command at Cawnpore to guard the Bridge of Boats over the Ganges and the entrenchment by the river. While supervising the evacuation he had received a letter informing him that Cawnpore was under attack – the Gwalior contingent, so long a threat, had struck at last. If the Bridge of Boats had been destroyed, Campbell knew, his army would be left isolated in hostile territory. Leaving Outram with 4,000 men to hold the Alam Bagh, he hurried his exhausted troops back to Windham's aid. 'I shall never forget the misery of that march!' wrote Forbes-Mitchell. 'We reached the sands of the river Ganges, on the Oude side of the river opposite Cawnpore, just as the sun was setting, having covered the forty-seven miles [in] under thirty hours. Of course the great hardship of the march was caused by our worn-out state after eighteen months' continual duty, without a change of clothes or our accoutrements off.'

To Sir Colin's relief the Bridge of Boats was intact – but beyond it Cawnpore was in flames. 'The first thing we saw,' wrote Forbes-Mitchell, 'was the enemy on the opposite side of the river from us, making bonfires of our spare kits and baggage which had been left at Cawnpore when we advanced for the relief of Lucknow! Tired as we were, we assisted to drag Peel's heavy guns into position on the banks of the river, whence the Blue-jackets opened fire on the left flank of the enemy, the bonfires of our spare baggage being a fine mark for them.' Windham – described by Sherer as 'handsome and debonair, very talkative, fond of a good story, dressy and fashionable' – had seemed the ideal man to secure Sir Colin's communications. If the final assault on the Redan at Sebastopol in 1855 had ended in failure it was no fault of Windham's, who had led from the front throughout and emerged a hero – 'Redan Windham'. When the combined forces of the Gwalior contingent and followers of the Nana Sahib – some 25,000 strong and led by Tantia Topi – had marched on Canwpore from the direction of Kalpi, Windham had marched out to meet them. He had only 1,700 men of his own – made up of detachments from various regiments, but believed that his policy of 'aggressive defence' was better than sitting in his entrenchment and awaiting events. Out-numbered, guilty of miscalculations of his own and let down by sub-ordinates – one colonel's conduct was described by Sir Colin Campbell as 'pusillanimous and imbecile in the last degree' – Windham was over-whelmed in three days' fighting and driven back to his entrenchment. Tantia Topi had added to his growing reputation and put a substantial dent in Windham's.

Sir Colin – having assessed the extent of the disaster – determined to attack at the earliest opportunity. Crossing the Ganges to Mangalwar, he pushed the convoy of women and children off towards Allahabad and – reinforced by 5,000 infantry, 600 cavalry and thirty-five guns fresh from England moved up to engage Tantia Topi. The rebels' position was strong on its left (which was protected by the Ganges) and its centre (in Cawnpore itself), but Sir Colin believed that its right could be turned by crossing the canal and the road to Kalpi, after which the whole position could be rolled up. On 6 December he attacked (see map 9 on p. xxiii) The rebels – deceived by a fierce bombardment of their centre and left – shifted reserves to meet the perceived threat. While Greathed demonstrated against the rebel centre, Walpole's, Hope's and Inglis's brigades moved against their right. 'It was a sight to be remembered, that advance,' wrote Frederick Roberts, 'as we watched it from our position on horseback, grouped round the Commander-in-Chief. Before us stret-ched a fine open grassy plain; to the right the dark green of the Rifle Brigade battalions revealed where Walpole's brigade was crossing the canal. Nearer to us, the 53rd Foot, and the 42nd and 93rd Highlanders in their bonnets and kilts, marched as on parade, although the enemy's guns played upon them and every now and then a roundshot plunged through their ranks or ricocheted over their heads; on they went without apparently being in the least disconcerted, and without the slightest confusion.' After a brief check at some brick kilns – where the enemy clung on tenaciously before being blasted out of them by one of Peel's guns – the Gwalior contingent broke and fled, losing its camp, its stores, its guns, and its reputation. The remainder of the rebel army – composed mostly of the armed retainers of rebel princes – fell back towards Bithur, pursued cautiously by General Mansfield. Short-sighted, and unwilling to trust the sight of others, Mansfield – a capable staff officer, but as he proved that day, no battlefield commander – allowed thousands of rebels to escape almost under his nose.

Hope Grant was sent in pursuit and, on the 9th, caught the enemy by the banks of the Ganges, scattered them and captured fifteen of their guns. Having secured his communications, dispersed the Gwalior contingent and avenged Windham's defeat, Sir Colin was keen to embark on the reconquest of the Doab – the land between the Ganges and the Jumna – but was forced to wait for his transport, now busy carrying the women and children of the Residency to Allahabad. It was not until January that he was able to begin his march on Fatehgarh. It was during this march that young Frederick Roberts – at Khudagunj – finally earned the distinction he coveted, which he had written to his mother was vital to secure his advancement in the service. He had attached himself to a squadron of the 5th Punjabi Horse, under his friend George Younghusband of that regiment. They were pursuing a body of mutineers who suddenly turned at bay. Hope Grant ordered – and led – a general charge of the cavalry, the 9th Lancers and Gough's, Probyn's and Younghusband's Punjabis. 'The chase continued for nearly five miles,' wrote Roberts.

We overtook a batch of mutineers, who faced about and fired into the squadron. I saw Younghusband fall, but I could not go to his assistance as at that moment one of his *sowars* was in dire peril from a sepoy who was attacking him with his fixed bayonet, and had I not helped the man and disposed of his opponent, he must have been killed. The next moment I descried in the distance two sepoys making off with a standard, which I determined must be captured, so I rode after the rebels and overtook them, and while wrenching the staff out of the hands of one of them, whom I cut down, the other put his musket close to my body and fired; fortunately for me it missed fire, and I carried off the standard.

Not all senior officers approved of the Victoria Cross, feeling – like Sir Colin Campbell – that it encouraged young officers to perform acts of recklessness. Fortunately for Roberts, his commander that day, Hope Grant, did not agree. 'The Victoria Cross has been a grand thing for making men and officers fight like Turks,' he wrote to a friend. '[I have recommended an] excellent young officer of the name of Roberts for the same distinction, and I trust H.M. will bestow it upon [him].' She did – Frederick Roberts was awarded the VC, the first step in a process that would eventually lead to him being the most decorated commoner in the Empire.

In Cawnpore, which he reoccupied on 6 January 1858, Sir Colin Campbell was contemplating his next move: the recapture of Lucknow, and the reconquest of Oude. Even as he did so, however, a campaign was opening – more than 200 miles to the south-west – aimed at clearing a territory which had been since the previous year's outbreak almost entirely in rebel hands, and which had been for Sir Colin a persistent thorn in his flesh – Central India.

# 12

## CENTRAL INDIA

What was known in 1857 as the Central India Agency consisted of six native states – Gwalior, Indore, Dhar, Dewas, Bhopal and Jawra – all of which were former members of the Maratha Confederacy, which had been defeated by the British in 1817. They were situated between the Nerbudda, Jumna and Chambal rivers, roughly 100 miles south-west of Agra (see maps 1–3). To the west was Rajputana (Rajasthan) and to the east Bundelkhand. The six states – four Maratha princedoms and two Muslim states that had acknowledged Maratha overlordship – were now governed indirectly by British agents, although their native princes continued to hold nominal power. They each had an army paid for by the prince, but officered by Europeans and controlled by the agent. There were besides a number of lesser feudal states that owed military service to their overlords, such as Maharajah Scindia of Gwalior. Also significant was Jhansi – on the river Betwa, a tributary of the Jumna.

After the outbreak at Meerut the insurrection had spread swiftly to Central India. Although the majority of the major rulers – Scindia at Gwalior, Holkar at Indore and the Begum of Bhopal – remained 'loyal', most of the smaller states rebelled, as did all the sepoy garrisons except one. By August 1857 the Grand Trunk road between Bombay, Delhi and Agra – and therefore Calcutta – was severed. With Delhi yet untaken, Cawnpore yet to be recaptured and the garrison at Lucknow yet to be relieved there was little enough the British could spare for the reconquest of Central India. Throughout Sir Colin Campbell's operations in Oude, therefore, Central India remained a threat to his rear (see map 3 on page xvi) and a refuge across the Jumna for defeated rebels.

It was not until November 1857 – with Delhi recaptured, Cawnpore in British hands and Lucknow relieved – that the British could turn their full attention to Central India. Some measures had already been taken. As soon as it had become clear that the Native troops of the Bombay and Madras Presidencies could be relied upon, columns were sent into Central India from the south-west and south-east. These columns united at Indore and – now designated the Central India Field Force – awaited their new commander.

Sir Hugh Rose arrived at Indore on 17 December. Rose was 56 – heir to a long line of politicians and diplomats, he was commissioned into the 92nd Highlanders and shortly afterwards transferred to HM 19th Foot. By 1839 he was a half-pay colonel, at which time he joined the team of advisers attached to the Turkish armies fighting in Syria against the Egyptian rebel Mehmet Ali. He remained in Syria as Consul General until 1848, when he became Secretary to the Embassy at Constantinople. He had been active in the preparations for the Crimean War, during which he served as a liaison officer at French Headquarters. Having volunteered for service on the outbreak of the Mutiny, he had been appointed to the Poona Division, a suitable post – with little likelihood of active service – for a man who had seen a number of battles and proved his courage under fire, but had never commanded troops in the field. First impressions were not favourable. Rose was considered a 'griffin' (newcomer to India), according to Dr Thomas Lowe of the Madras Sappers and Miners. Another doctor, J. H. Sylvester of the 14th Light Dragoons, thought him 'very effeminate, weak and I should think unable to rough it much'. Physically frail as he may have appeared, Rose was to prove a man of vigour, determination and high intelligence – and arguably the best general the British had in India at the time.

Rose's force consisted of two brigades, commanded by officers bearing the same name – fortunately spelt differently. Each brigade was based around a European battalion and a Native one. In Brigadier Stuart's 1st Brigade was HM 86th Foot and the 25th Bombay NI; in Brigadier Steuart's 2nd, the 3rd Bombay Europeans and the 24th Bombay NI. Each brigade also contained an infantry regiment and a cavalry regiment from the Hyderabad contingent, some cavalry – from HM 14th Light Dragoons and the 3rd Bombay Native Cavalry – as well as field artillery batteries and sappers. There was also a force of 800 men from the Bhopal contingent. These two 'contingents' – the Hyderabad and Bhopal – from princely states, had been, like the mutinous Gwalior contingent, trained by European officers and NCOs. Unlike the Gwalior contingent, however, they retained their European command structure.

On 16 January 1858 Sir Hugh marched with the 1st Brigade to Ratgarh; the 2nd Brigade marched on a parallel route to Gunah. Having invested Ratgarh on the 24th he discovered that the rebel Rajah of Banpur was advancing to the relief of the town and – on the 27th – marched against him and drove him off. The fort at Ratgarh was evacuated by its defenders on the 28th, and two days later Rose marched again against the rebel Rajah – who was now at Barodia – and completely defeated him. He then marched on Saugor where 170 Europeans – mostly women and children – had held out for eight months, although surrounded by hostile territory, largely due to the continuing loyalty of sepoys of the 31st Bengal NI. 'His troops marched through Saugor in a long line,' wrote one of the garrison of Rose's arrival, 'and you can imagine the impression their number made on the natives of the place. Such a thing as a European regiment had never been seen in Saugor, and we certainly never expected to see Her Majesty's 14th Dragoons. These men, and the large siege-guns dragged by elephants were a source of much curiosity and awe to the natives. You can hardly realise our feelings after eight months of anxiety and imprisonment.' At Saugor, Rose waited until he heard that a column under Brigadier Whitlock had departed from Jubbulpore to join him. This occasioned some delay – Whitlock was described as being like a bad revolver 'always going round but never going off' – before Rose could march on his main objective, Jhansi.

As well as being at the heart of the rebellion in Central India, Jhansi, situated as it was, represented a constant threat to the Commander-in-Chief's communications (see map 3 on page xvi). General Mansfield, Sir Colin's chief of staff, had written to Sir Hugh on 24 January: 'Sir Colin will be glad to learn if Jhansi is to be fairly tackled during your present campaign. To us it is all important. Until it takes place, Sir Colin's rear will always be inconvenienced, and he will be constantly obliged to look over his shoulder as when he relieved Lucknow. The stiff neck this gives to the commander-in-chief and the increased difficulty of his operations in consequence you will understand.'

There was more to it than mere strategy – the Rani of Jhansi had already become, and was to remain for the British, a hate-figure to vie with the Nana Sahib. Whether she was guilty as charged remains a matter of controversy – many among the British came to sympathize with, and even admire her. In modern India, she is revered; statues of her abound and her adventures are sold – in comic-book form – below the walls of her magnificent granite fortress at Jhansi. Lakshmi Bai – in her early thirties in 1857 – was the widow of the last Rajah of Jhansi, Gagadhar Rao, who in 1853, about to die childless, had adopted a boy from another branch of his family. It was his dying wish that the child should be recognized as his ultimate successor, but that the Rani should rule Jhansi for the remainder of her life. The British had recognized such adoptions before, but Lord Dalhousie, eager to extend the benefits of British rule had refused to in this case. He argued that Jhansi – unlike some other states – had never actually been independent, being a dependency, first of the Marathas and then of the East India Company. In March 1854, Jhansi was annexed. The Rani – described by a lawyer who saw her at this time as possessing a very intelligent expression, fine eyes, delicately shaped nose and remarkably fine figure – had been allotted a generous pension, was allowed to keep her city palace, and her 'son' was to inherit the dead Rajah's possessions. On annexation, she had declared 'I will never give up my Jhansi!' and she had – like the Nana Sahib – appealed first to the Indian Government and later to the British. By 1857, however, she seemed to have accepted the situation even if the British constantly irked her with petty financial restrictions connected with her husband's estate.

The outbreak of the Mutiny at Meerut in May 1857 had not, at first, caused alarm at Jhansi. On 5 June, however, commander of the garrison Captain Dunlop and two other officers were murdered by sepoys, who seized the small Star Fort that contained the Treasury and Magazine. Captain Alexander Skene, the political officer, thereupon gathered all the officers, women, children and Eurasian clerks – a total of fifty-five Christians – and lodged them in the fort. The rebellious sepoys having killed all the Christians they could find in the cantonment, had attacked the fort but been driven off by the Europeans – only four of whom had any military experience. A protracted defence of so large a perimeter by so few was out of the question, so on 8 June Skene asked the sepoys – who had now brought up two guns to face the fort – for terms for an evacuation. Receiving the assurances he needed, Skene marched his 'garrison' out. They were taken to a garden below the fort, known as the Jokhan Bagh, and there separated into three groups – men, women and children – and massacred; not a single European survived. The role of the Rani in all this remains uncertain – she claimed in letters to the British Commissioner at Saugor, Major Erskine, that she had been unable to assist the Europeans for lack of men and guns. The sepoys, she said, had demanded a large sum of money from her to pay for Jhansi's 'liberation', and had threatened to blow up her palace if she refused. Bearing in mind the conduct of the mutineers in Delhi it is not too hard to credit this claim. Certainly her position was a precarious one – the sepoys had already found an alternative 'rajah' whom they threatened to install, and Jhansi was soon invaded by two neighbouring states, Orchha and Datia, who claimed to be acting as allies of the British, but were in fact intending to divide Jhansi between them. Appeals for British help brought no response – it was clear that she was on her own. Casting her own cannon and enlisting sepoys to her aid, the Rani had soon defeated the invaders and placed the alternative 'rajah' under lock and key. She then claimed to be holding Jhansi for the British – as indeed Erskine, on his own responsibility, had begged her to do. Calcutta, however, had other ideas. With mutinied sepoys in the forces she had raised and strongly suspected of involvement in the massacre of Europeans, the Rani had already been cast as 'The Jezebel of India'. Whether she had planned to take advantage of the turn of events in the summer of 1857 or was a victim of those events left – like Bahadur Shah in Delhi – with little room for manoeuvre, she was now marked out by Calcutta for destruction.

After twenty-four days during which he gathered as much as he could in the way of goats, sheep and cereals, as well as elephants and oxen, Rose was ready to begin his march. The hot season was starting and the heat in 1858 was worse even than the previous year. 'The roads were dusty, the wells almost dry, the grass bleached and withered away,' wrote Dr Thomas Lowe. 'The winds began to blow as though they had just escaped from the hitherto-closed door of Pandemonium, and they swept over us, scorching up every pore of the body, and making the eyes feel as though they had been blistered.' At night the skies were lit by a comet – known as the Mutiny Comet – that for the natives presaged bad times to come, though not, any more, the end of British rule. 'The prostration of the whole Force,' wrote Rose, 'had become a matter of arithmetical calculation. So many hours of sun laid low so many men.'

When Rose reached Chanchpore – 14 miles from Jhansi – he received from Sir Colin Campbell an order to march to Charkori, 80 miles away, which was being besieged by nine hundred rebels under the leadership of Tantia Topi, who since his mauling at the hands of Sir Colin Campbell had been lying low at Kalpi. Simultaneously, the Governor General's agent with Sir Hugh – Sir Robert Hamilton – received a letter from Lord Canning to the same effect. Upon receipt of the letter, Sir Robert wrote back to Lord Canning that he had taken upon himself the responsibility of ordering Sir Hugh to continue with his operations against Jhansi.

The investment of Jhansi began on 22 March. The fort – $4\frac{1}{2}$ miles in circumference – is one of the most impressive even in India, with walls 6–8 feet thick and between 18 and 30 feet high. With flanking bastions equipped with batteries of artillery and a garrison of 11,000 men, the fort was defended by the Rani in person. By 29 March a practicable breach had been achieved, and preparations were on hand for an assault, when news arrived that Tantia Topi was back – this time with 22,000 men (including five or six regiments of the Gwalior contingent) and twenty-eight guns on the far side of the river Betwa, barely 6 miles away. Realizing that to break off the siege to face this new threat would revive the spirits of the defenders of Jhansi, Sir Hugh elected instead to maintain the siege and march against Tantia Topi with what men he could spare. This amounted to over 1,500 men of whom only a third were Europeans – 430 European infantry and 700 Native; 240 men of the 14th Light Dragoons and 200 Hyderabadis. He also took from his siege lines sixteen field guns and three heavy guns drawn by elephants. Marching to Bupoda on the river Betwa, it was his intention to lure Tantia Topi across the river so that the rebels would have to fight with the river at their back. At first light on 31 March, therefore, he began to withdraw his small force – the rebels' first line then crossed the river and by the evening of the same day they were encamped on the Jhansi bank of the Betwa. Sir Hugh drew up his small force in two lines and awaited the dawn; his men, like the enemy's, in his own words, 'slept on our arms'.

In the morning the rebels advanced, their line overlapping the British at both ends. In the opening artillery duel, the British guns – outflanked on both sides – proved the less effective, so ordering the horse artillery to his left, Rose directed it and two troops of the 14th Light Dragoons to attack the enemy's right, while he personally led his cavalry – Need's troop of the 14th and a troop of Hyderabad cavalry, under Lieutenant Clerk, against their left. Among the enemy's forces were large numbers of Afghan mercenaries – known in Hindustani as '*Valaitis*' (foreigners) a word that gives us the English term 'Blighty'. These unleashed a heavy fusillade on the advancing cavalry. 'The Valaitis jumped in hundreds on high rocks and boulders to load and fire,' wrote Rose in his dispatch, 'but before they could reload their matchlocks, Captain Need, leading his troop in advance, penetrated into the midst of them, and for a time was so hotly engaged that his uniform was cut to pieces, although, singular to say, he only received a slight wound himself.' In this charge the Hyderabadis did not distinguish themselves, as Rose later wrote to Sir Colin Campbell: 'The Hyderabad cavalry did not behave well ... Although led by a very gallant officer I could not get them to move against the left of the enemy and when at last they made an attempt to charge they did it badly ... when the Hyderabad Irregular Cavalry have had a tough job to do, they, except for a few brave men who are generally wounded or killed, do not like to face it.' Rose was fulsome, however, in praise of the 14th Light Dragoons, saying 'I believe I may say that what Captain Need's troop did on this occasion was equal to breaking a square of Infantry'. He scarcely mentioned his own part in the charge, but others were less reticent. 'It was a glorious sight to see them thundering along,' wrote Corporal Stent of the 14th. 'One minute, and they were among the enemy, and all that was to be seen was a confused mass of flashing swords and bayonets, struggling men and horses, and hoarse shouts of rage. From this seething struggling mass our men emerged victorious, for the result of the charge showed that an act of daring and personal bravery on the part of a leader (an act not often done – a Commander-in-Chief to lead a charge) will sometimes change defeat into victory as it did in this case.'

On the enemy's right, wrote Rose, 'The attack ... by the fire of Captain Lightfoot's battery and the charge of the 14th Light Dragoons were equally successful; and the enemy broke and retired in confusion.' The rebels centre now confronted by Rose's advancing infantry broke and fled the first line overwhelming Tantia Topi's second which was based on a ridge-line in the jungle. Even so, Tantia managed to extricate his men – setting fire to the jungle and withdrawing across the river covered by the bayonets of the Gwalior contingent. The pursuit by Rose's cavalry and horse gunners, however, proved relentless. Charging through burning jungle they cut down those who fled and those who tried to rally, capturing guns all the way. 'The 14th Light Dragoons and Hyderabad cavalry gallantly surmounted all opposition,' wrote Rose, 'and sabred the rebels who still held their ground.' At last a mile and a half from the river, they captured the eighteenth – and last – rebel gun. Without any artillery, and having lost 1,500 men dead and wounded, Tantia Topi decided against holding a threatening position on the Betwa and marched off back to Kalpi. Rose was now free to concentrate on Jhansi.

'I hope to conclude speedily the siege of Jhansi,' Rose telegraphed to Lord Elphinstone, Governor of Bombay, on the evening of the battle. In fact, Tantia Topi's intervention only delayed the assault on the Rani's fortress by forty-eight hours. Knowing the rebels' morale to be depressed by what they had hoped to be a relief column, Rose ordered a storm on 3 April. The attack was divided into two – the left attack consisted of two columns drawn from HM 86th Foot under Colonel Lowth and Major Stuart of that regiment; and the right, two columns drawn from the 3rd Bombay Europeans. At 3 a.m. the attacks marched into position and the assault began. The left attack quickly gained a foothold in the breach, and took the positions assigned to them, the right attack – intended to seize part of the wall by escalade – was hampered by its scaling ladders being too short. Lieutenant Joseph Bonus of the Bombay Engineers joined in this assault almost on a whim, having wandered down to watch the assault from the Brigadier's position. 'The ladder party was advancing to the wall,' he wrote to his parents.

> The enemy was on the alert and opened a sharp fire. There was some confusion. I thought I might be of use and so ran down to the party; I took charge of the ladder and with difficulty got it in position, then I called the men to follow and ran up the ladder, I did not see what other Engineers were doing but I was told afterwards that two more ladders were got up; the Engineers who led up there were both killed. As soon as I got to the top of my ladder I was assailed by a crowd of men; I managed to protect myself with my sword but I never thought of my revolver. Had there not been a man there I doubt if I could have got over the wall for the ladder was too short. I was not at the top for a very long time for a man to my left clubbed his musket and hit me a fine smack on my face, knocking me clean off the ladder, I fell on to the rock some 20 feet below; the subsequent proceedings interested me no more.

Bonus survived, after brandy and three days' bed rest – the other engineers in that party were all killed. Even so, the right attack managed to gain a lodgement for long enough for the successful left attack to come to their aid. Shortly afterwards the stormers gained the palace, where they found the silk Union Flag presented to the grandfather of the Rani's late husband as a reward for his fidelity. This they flew from the palace roof while the last defenders were driven into the town, where the 25th Bombay NI dispersed them. The Rani herself, however, escaped. Visitors to Jhansi today are shown a spot on the walls from which she is supposed to have jumped on horseback. Such an action would clearly have been suicide – however, a descent from the wall by ladder or rope to a waiting party holding fresh horses would seem practicable. Cordons of cavalry failed to prevent her escaping, but it was a close-run thing. Lieutenant Dowker of the Hyderabad contingent cavalry and his men, having surprised the Rani and her party at breakfast, 21 miles from Jhansi, pursued them for some miles killing forty of her bodyguard. Just as Dowker was overtaking her – by now she only had four attendants – he himself was wounded. After a hard ride of 100 miles, the Rani reached Kalpi where she was joined – the same day – by Tantia Topi, who had started from the Betwa River three days earlier. It was suggested by some that Native cavalry were reluctant to capture her, and therefore let her pass. Others have suggested that all the cavalry – British and Native – were too busy looting.

There can be no doubt that, as at Delhi and Lucknow, there was a great deal of looting and summary execution after the capture of Jhansi. The Central India Field Force, like all the other British columns, saw itself as an Army of Retribution. Almost before the force had begun its march, Dr Sylvester had witnessed terrible scenes in a village near Dhar. 'The men off duty and even some native soldiers but chiefly the 86th and Artillery were frightfully drunk having seized the native liquor shops. They then commenced looting and killing everything black, old men, young women and children!! This of course was to be deplored but I had anticipated this. They shouted Cawnpore, Delhi and down they went . . . Officers rushed down, the Provost Marshal and some Dragoons and they soon put a stop to it and destroyed all the liquor.' Officers could not be everywhere, however, in a newly captured town. 'The whole city looked like a fiendish burial ground,' wrote one native of Jhansi, describing the day after the storm. 'In the lanes near relatives maddened with sorrow were lamenting, mercifully sitting by the corpses of their kinsmen.' The following day, he wrote,

> Innumerable men were slaughtered . . . Even if a European was seen
> from a distance people hid themselves behind heaps of grass to save

their lives. Europeans used to set the heaps of grass on fire and compel the persons in hiding to die in the same. If, due to their fear, anybody tried to save his life by jumping into the well, they pitched themselves at the well with loaded guns. Then, either the poor man had to die in the water in utter suffocation or forced to fall a victim to the bullets of the Europeans in case he raised his head above the water. Several men took refuge in the fields. They were also searched out and shot.

On 25 April, leaving a small garrison in Jhansi, Sir Hugh marched towards Kalpi – 45 miles away – which had been a rebel base and arsenal throughout the Mutiny. Rose regarded Kalpi as the pivot of the rebel position in Central India and declared that as long as they held it they might boast that the East and West of India was British but the centre was theirs. Kalpi was now the headquarters of the Rao Sahib – the Nana Sahib's nephew. More than that, it and Lucknow were the two greatest rebel strongholds in India. Arrived in Kalpi, the Rani urged the Rao Sahib to reorganize his forces for the battle she knew would be coming. Tantia Topi was once again appointed commander of the force and chose Kunch – 42 miles south of Kalpi – as the place to stop the advancing British.

Kunch was a strong position, approaches to the town being surrounded by temples, gardens and woods, and the rebels had raised entrenchments in front of the solid town wall. Rose's scouts, however, informed him that the rebel position could be outflanked – Tantia Topi had once again left his flanks vulnerable. The flank march to the north-west that Rose now executed – a forced march of 14 miles – left forty-six men prostrated by sunstroke, eleven of them never to rise again. Even so, the next day Rose ordered a general advance, preceded by an artillery bombardment. After an hour his infantry had penetrated the northern part of the town, driving the enemy on to the Kalpi road. 'We should have destroyed the enemy,' Rose wrote, 'had not the dreadful heat paralysed the men ... I was obliged four times to get off my horse by excessive debility. The doctor poured cold water over me, and gave restoratives, which enabled me to go on again.' The rebel retreat was well covered by their skirmish line, largely drawn from the mutinous 52nd Bengal NI. Major R. H. Gall of the 14th Light Dragoon wrote to his brother: 'The enemy, chiefly the Gwalior Sepoys and Sepoys of all Mutineer regiments, retired in perfect order, throwing out a rear-guard in skirmishing order. This was overtaken by the 14th Light Dragoons and some Irregular Cavalry (with the latter

I charged) and was cut up to a man, fighting to the last with a valour that would have done honour to Leonidas. On several occasions I saw the fearless ruffians dash with their bayonets at our Dragoons after delivering their fire at two yards distance.' Another cavalry officer wrote that he would like to see a monument raised on the spot where they fell 'rebels though they were'.

By 15 June Rose was at Golowli, near Kalpi itself. His force had been reinforced – on the 5th he had been joined by HM 71st Highlanders; now at Golowli he linked up with a column under Colonel G.V. Maxwell consisting of HM 88th Foot (Connaught Rangers), some Sikhs and a 150-man Camel Corps formed from 100 Sikh Police and 200 soldiers of the Rifle Brigade. The rebel position at Kalpi had been well chosen. The ground was naturally suited for defence, being much intersected by ravines and therefore very difficult ground for cavalry and artillery. This the rebels had improved by entrenchment. It is a tribute to the strength of the position that Rose spent five days siting his artillery batteries before – on the 21st – commencing fire. The following day the attack began. Tantia Topi, who had concealed the bulk of his infantry in the ravines on his left and centre launched a feint attack with these troops – led in person by the Rao Sahib – before initiating his main attack on the British right. The enemy fought with greater determination here than at any time previously in the campaign. The heat had debilitated many of the European soldiers, and the Enfield rifles – which one officer reckoned the enemy feared as much as the artillery – became fouled and difficult to reload. The strength of this rebel attack against Rose's right seems to have taken him by surprise. Brigadier Stuart's men fell back – Stuart's staff drew their swords for self-defence and Stuart dismounted, placed himself by his guns and declared, 'We have nothing to do but die like Scotchmen.' As the British skirmish line – composed of men of the 3rd Bombay Europeans and the 25th Bombay Native Infantry – fell back, the rebel infantry were no more than 20 yards from the tents in the rear of the line, that contained men laid up with sunstroke. Once again Rose took a personal hand, leading the Camel Corps at a trot, dismounting them from their camels and leading them at the double to a small crest to the (British) right of the enemy's attack. After giving one of those cheers that, wrote Rose, 'all over the world have been heralds of British successes', the Camel Corps charged. It was one of those occasions where a well-timed counter-attack, by however small a number, can unsettle hitherto victorious troops. The rebel line wavered and then broke. At almost the same moment the Rao Sahib's column on the rebel right fell back. Pursued by the British horse batteries, some Camel Corps and men of HM 86th, they were driven into the ravines and shot or bayoneted, or into the Jumna where many drowned. Rose halted his force in front of Kalpi itself – preparing for an assault the next day. In the morning, however, it was discovered that the enemy had abandoned the city overnight.

As 24 May was Queen Victoria's thirty-ninth birthday the Union Flag was raised above the fort at Kalpi, an action which Rose believed should mark the end of the campaign. On 1 June he issued a general order that neatly summarizes the achievements of the force under his command. 'Soldiers! You have marched more than a thousand miles, and taken more than a hundred guns; you have forced your way through mountain passes and intricate jungles, and over rivers; you have captured the strongest forts, and beat the enemy, no matter what the odds, wherever you met him; you have restored extensive districts to the Government, and peace and order now reign where before, for twelve months, were tyranny and rebellion; you have done all this, and you have never had a check. I thank you with all my sincerity for you bravery, your devotion, and your discipline.' His health having suffered during the campaign, Rose now felt it was time to step down and leave what would surely be 'mopping up' operations to a successor. Accordingly he sent off a letter resigning his command, accompanied by the necessary medical certificate. On 4 June, however, news reached him of a development that, almost overnight, had restored the rebel position in Central India.

The rebel triumvirate – the Rao Sahib, Tantia Topi and the Rani of Jhansi – nothing if not tenacious, had been looking around for a new base from which to renew the fight. After some heated debate they had settled on Gwalior. After his defeat at Kunch Tantia Topi had stopped at Gwalior and having spoken to a number of the Maharajah's officers – as well as ex-officers purged by him because of doubts about their loyalty – decided that the remainder of his army was ripe for subversion. The majority of the officers and men, he concluded, as well as the nobles, had rebel sympathies and were unhappy with Scindia's adherence to the British. If Scindia's army could be won over, and Gwalior captured, the rebel cause would have a strong fortress as a base, money supplies, fresh troops and the opportunity to call on the so-far loyal Princes of the Deccan to rise in rebellion.

The Maharajah having proved deaf to Tantia Topi's appeals, the rebels – Tantia Topi, the Rao Sahib and the Rani – marched towards Gwalior with 7,000 infantry, 4,000 cavalry and twelve guns and, by 30 May had reached Morar, 3 miles north of the city. Convinced that the rebel army was demoralized by its defeats and short of supplies, Scindia marched out to meet them with 6,000 infantry, 2,300 cavalry, his 600-strong personal bodyguard and eight guns. Like Richard III before Bosworth, however, Scindia was already 'bought and sold'. The rebels advanced in lines of those skirmishers that had proved so effective against the British. When Scindia's artillery opened fire the skirmishers parted to make way for two thousand horsemen who charged and captured the guns. At this point almost the whole of Scindia's army went over to the rebels – his bodyguard fought bravely to enable him to escape, and with a handful of retainers he fled to Agra.

The rebels occupied the town and fort of Gwalior without resistance. The Rao Sahib proclaimed the Nana Sahib 'Peshwa' of the revived Maratha *raj*, with himself as his uncle's Governor of Gwalior. Looting was forbidden – Scindia's treasury was used to pay his own and Scindia's troops, celebrations were set in hand and letters were despatched to the Princes of Bundhelkhand and the Deccan calling on them to rally to the rebel cause. The Rani urged the Rao Sahib to make preparations for the British attack that would certainly follow this change of fortune, but as usual, her advice was ignored. Instead of marching into the Deccan to encourage the Princes there to rise, the Rao Sahib and Tantia Topi preferred to stay put and celebrate their latest coup. In so doing they fell into the error that was characteristic of rebel leadership throughout the Mutiny. Despite all the talk of driving the British into the sea, there was no real attempt at taking the strategic offensive. In all the main theatres the rebel strategy was to seize supposedly 'impregnable' strongpoints and simply wait for the British to attack.

They didn't have to wait long for Sir Hugh Rose, who decided against waiting for a successor and swiftly telegraphed the Governor General and resumed his command. Anxious to defeat the rebels before the rains came, on 4 June Rose sent Brigadier Stuart with his brigade in the direction of Gwalior, following with the remainder the next day. Catching up with Stuart on 12 June, he had marched on to Bahadurpur by the 16th where he was joined by Robert Napier – who had been Outram's chief of staff at Lucknow, and was now nominated as Rose's successor. Napier waived his right to take command and agreed to command Rose's 2nd Brigade instead. With Napier had come troops of the Hyderabad contingent, who had been returning home but had begged to be allowed to serve under Rose once more. Coming upon the rebels at Morar on the morning of the 16th Rose elected – despite the fact that his troops had already had a hot and tiring march – to attack at once. 'Morar looked inviting,' wrote Rose, 'with several good buildings not yet burnt; they would be good quarters for a portion of the force; if I delayed the attack until the next day, the enemy were sure to burn them. A prompt attack has always more effect on the rebels than a procrastinated one.'

Sending the Hyderabad contingent cavalry round to cut off the rebels' retreat, Rose – after a cannonade – launched the 71st Highland Light Infantry and HM 86th towards the enemy's left flank. There was hard fighting around a village on the enemy line and the *nullah* behind it, but after hard hand-to-hand fighting the rebels were driven back towards Gwalior. The Hyderabadis were delayed by ravines from preventing the rebels' escape, but two troops of the 14th Light Dragoons followed them for some way making, in Rose's words, 'great slaughter of them'.

Since Rose had arrived at Kalpi the nature of his campaign had undergone a significant change. Before Kalpi his column – like Havelock's or Sir Colin Campbell's – had operated in isolation. After Kalpi, having linked with Maxwell, and via him with Cawnpore, he could call on cooperation from other columns and launch a coordinated offensive. By the time he was nearing Gwalior a Movable Column from Agra under Colonel Riddell was approaching, bringing siege guns with it, and a brigade-strength field force from Rajputana under General Smith was close at hand. This force – composed of two squadrons of Bombay Lancers, most of HM 8th Hussars (who had taken part in the Charge of the Light Brigade), a battery of Bombay Horse Artillery, HM 95th Foot (veterans of some of the hardest fighting in the Crimea) and the 10th Bombay Native Infantry – was to fight an action on the following day that probably had a significance to the future of the rebellion out of all proportion to the numbers engaged. Smith's Rajputana Field Force arrived on the morning of 17 June at Kotah-ke-Serai, 5 miles from Gwalior. The rebels were in a strong position on broken ground, but the horse artillery soon drove the enemy's guns away and the 95th advanced, covered by skirmishers. The 95th – like many of the British infantry in this campaign – bore little resemblance to the red-coated figures who feature in the uniform prints of the period, as Lieutenant Crealock of that regiment recorded: 'The 95th – five hundred bearded sunburnt men, in once-white sea-kit smocks and tattered blue trousers – here and there bare feet, here and there native slippers – while for head-dress the Kilmarnock forage cap with a white cover did duty, sometimes assisted by a towel or a roll of coloured cotton.' The advance was briefly halted by a dyke across the rebels' front but, having crossed it, they pushed on. 'The men were too eager to try conclusions with the rebels we saw retiring before us,' wrote Crealock 'and required forcible Saxon to recall them from the fact that the fortress of Gwalior could not and ought not to be captured by them alone.' As the rebels were driven from the hilly ground they had occupied and on to a plain much-used by Scindia's troops as a parade-ground, Smith unleashed his cavalry.

The 8th Hussars had emerged on to the plain through a pass, covered by the Enfield fire of the 95th. The commander of the Hussars was Captain Heanage – a veteran of the Balaklava charge – and as soon as they had formed he led his squadron of ninety-eight sabres at the retreating enemy. Also present were two other Crimea veterans – the paymaster of the 8th Hussars, Henry Duberly, and his attractive blonde wife, Fanny. Fanny Duberly had attained a certain – and undeserved – notoriety on account of her Crimean adventures, and had been snubbed by the Queen at a military review. Alongside her husband she had marched 1,800 hot, dusty miles with the Rajputana Field Force. It was all a very far cry from the Crimea, where she had been fêted by British and red-kepi'd French officers, and courted by dashing Bersaglieri. Here, however, was something that appealed to her adventurous spirit. She had witnessed the Heavy and Light Brigade charges at Balaklava and she was not about to watch from the sidelines a third time. As the 8th Hussars and the horse artillery dashed forward her horse started to follow. She called to her husband 'I must go!' 'Go along then!' Henry replied, and so she did – one of very few women ever to participate in a British cavalry charge. More remarkably still, there was a woman among the rebel cavalry too. Clad in turban and trousers, and wielding a sword, the Rani of Jhansi tried in vain to rally her cavalry, until her horse stumbled and she was cut from the saddle by a trooper of the 8th. Some said it was a carbine shot that had killed her, and Private Timothy Abbott of the 95th later claimed that he had shot her with his Enfield. All that is certain is that Lakshmi Bai, Rani of Jhansi – almost uniquely among the rebel leaders in this war – died in the saddle, sword in hand, commanding her troops. 'The Ranee of Jhansi,' Rose later wrote to the Duke of Cambridge, 'the Indian Joan of Arc, was killed in this charge dressed in a red jacket, red trousers and white puggary; she wore the celebrated pearl necklace of Scindia, which she had taken from his Treasury, and heavy gold anklets; as she lay mortally wounded in her Tent she ordered these ornaments to be distributed amongst her troops; it is said that Tantia Topi intercepted the necklace. The whole rebel Army mourned for her; her body was burned with great ceremony under a tamarind tree under the Rock of Gwalior, where I saw her bones and ashes.' By the time Captain Heanage rode back from the charge 'very black in the face and unable to speak' – he was awarded the Victoria Cross for this charge – the rebels had fled the field, leaving five guns behind them.

Despite their success, Smith's men were in a precarious position. The Hussars were too exhausted by heatstroke to sit their horses – so Smith withdrew his men to the hilly ground and waited until Rose sent reinforcements. A squadron and a half of the 14th Light Dragoons, four guns and the 25th Bombay NI joined him that evening and the remainder of the force arrived with Rose the following morning – the 19th – when, on learning that the rebels were about to attack, Rose decided to forestall them. Sending Brigadier Stuart to attack the enemy's left with HM 86th and the 25th Bombay NI, he sent the 95th – in a diversionary attack – to attack a rebel battery on some hilly ground. The attack on the left drove the enemy before it, and the 95th made good practice with its Enfields – dropping the gunners round two rebel 18-pounders, one by one, until the guns fell silent. Soon the British were in control of all the high ground in front of Gwalior and Sir Hugh Rose was treated to the sight of the whole rebel army in full flight, abandoning their weapons. That night he slept in Scindia's palace.

With the death of the Rani the heart finally went out of the rebellion in Central India. The Rao Sahib and Tantia Topi fled – the Rao Sahib to begin a four-year period wandering as a holy man in the forests of the Punjab, followed by betrayal and capture. Tantia Topi was not finished yet, but would never again pose the threat that he once had to the British *raj*. The following afternoon the fort itself fell and Rose despatched Robert Napier – his designated successor – with 560 cavalry and a battery of horse artillery in pursuit of the enemy. He caught the rebels at Jaora Alipur on the 21st. They were 7,000 strong – Rose had already learned this and sent a message to Napier ordering him not to attack. It arrived too late and Napier launched his cavalry and horse artillery headlong at the enemy, who – supposing this to be the advance guard of a much stronger force – broke up and fled leaving behind 300–400 dead and all of their twenty-five guns.

Having restored Scindia to his throne Rose now felt at last able to resign his command. Gratefully handing over to Robert Napier, Rose returned to Bombay to take over as commander-in-chief there. Before doing so he had written to the Duke of Cambridge in London a letter that summarizes – with justifiable pride – his force's achievement in Central India. 'The rapid fall of Gwalior has had the happiest of political and military results,' he wrote. 'The Rebels are no longer an Army of combatants, they are disheartened fugitives, humiliated in their own opinion, and in that of their countrymen, by signal and repeated defeats, without Artillery, warlike stores or reserves. In a political point of view, it is better that Gwalior should have fallen into rebel hands and be retaken as it was. Before, English influence was extinct, and rebel influence was paramount in Gwalior. Now it is exactly the contrary. The political situation in Gwalior has been completely purified. Before it was Nana Sahib and the Peishwari Government. Now it is English power and grateful Scindia.'

# 13

## 'Mopping Up'

By the time Sir Hugh Rose had cleared Central India, Sir Colin Campbell had battered his way back into Lucknow. He had left Outram at the Alam Bagh with 4,000 men when he raced back to Cawnpore to confront Tantia Topi and the Gwalior contingent. Outram had held out there despite the efforts of the Maulvi of Faizabad – with 120,000 men at his disposal, of whom 27,550 were trained sepoys and 7,100 trained cavalry – to dislodge him. By 1 March 1858 Sir Colin was back at the Alam Bagh with a force of seventeen battalions of infantry, twenty-eight squadrons of cavalry and fifty-five heavy and eight light guns and mortars. All but two of his battalions were British and he was aided, this time, by the Gurkha troops of Jung Bahadur – de facto King of Nepal, who had thrown in his lot with the British. Sherer, who saw him at Cawnpore, described him thus: 'The Prince had a spare, active figure, unwearied as yet by his years or his habits; but the face was very Tartar – with the low brow, squab nose, and pointed eyebrow of his race. He wore goggles, too, partly for ornament I suspect, for he must have been well-accustomed to the sun.' At a *durbar* held in his honour Jung Bahadur told Sir Colin that if he had not seen England himself he, too, might have thrown in his lot with the rebels. Serving with the 90th Light Infantry, Captain I. S. A. Hereford was less than impressed with Jung Bahadur's men. 'True to their native instincts, they introduced themselves to us, as searching for plunder; in fact, the whole time they were with the force, until they were *escorted* with their 'loot' to their own country, they did nothing else; perhaps they disliked fighting for its own sake, or considered it only a waste of time in such a grand opportunity as the sacking of Lucknow! They were very short men, wearing loose blue trousers, red jackets, green turbans with brass crescents in front and were extremely dirty.' Even so, Campbell was glad of Jung Bahadur's contribution as his plan required numbers.

The rebels, having learned from previous British advances, had defended the city with three main lines of defence. One covered the Hazratganj where three roads into Lucknow converge; the second ran from the Imambara via the Mess House to the Moti Mahal; the third covered their main citadel the Kaisar Bagh (see map 6 on page xx). Campbell's plan was to blockade Lucknow from the south, attack it from the east and north, while leaving the west open. The plan had been drawn up by Colonel Robert Napier as being the easiest approach to the Kaisar Bagh – the heart of the rebels' defence – and because the ground offered the best positions for his artillery.

Sir Colin was to attack from the east, while Sir James Outram descended on the rebels' lines from behind, and Jung Bahadur and a division under General Franks advanced slowly north from the Alam Bagh. The attack began on 9 March – Outram, having crossed the Gumti and bypassed the city, now attacked through jungle towards the Chakar Kothi (Yellow House) on the racecourse, north-east of the city. He then advanced on the Badshah Bagh and set up batteries on the river bank to fire into the rear of the enemy's defences at the Martinière. When – under cover of Peel's guns – Sir Colin now attacked the Martinière from the front, the rebels fled across the canal after only token resistance. It had been a good day but not without a high profile casualty. Captain William Peel – by now appointed KCB and ADC to the Queen – while directing the fire of his naval guns as they battered the walls of the Martinière at close range, was wounded by a musket ball. He was carried off by his Bluejackets who – a few days later – prepared one of the ex-King's carriages for his conveyance. Disdaining such special treatment, he asked to be carried in a *dhoolie* like anyone else. The *dhoolie* in question, however, had been used to carry a smallpox patient – he succumbed to the disease himself and died at Cawnpore on 27 April 1858.

On the 11th, Campbell crossed the river and attacked the Begum Kothi. The Naval Brigade pushed two of their heaviest guns to within 50 yards of the walls and the 93rd Highlanders prepared to storm. Corporal Forbes-Mitchell was with them: 'No thought of unequal numbers held us back. The command was given: "Keep well together, men, and use the bayonet; give them the Secundrabagh and the sixteenth of November over again." I need not describe the fight. It raged for about two hours from court to court, and from room to room; the pipe-major, John Macleod, playing the pipes inside as calmly as if he had been walking round the officers' mess-tent at a regimental festival.' When the palace was taken Sir Colin did one of his dances – this time with pleasure. 'I knew it! I knew they'd do it!' he cried. 'I knew my Highlanders would take it!' Forbes-Mitchell witnessed the campaign's second high-profile casualty – and the passing of an Indian legend. While fighting from room to room he came to a room containing a number of rebels well armed with swords and firearms.

> I . . . sent two men back to the breach, where I knew Colonel Napier with his engineers were to be found, to get a few bags of gunpowder with slow-matches fixed, to light and pitch into the room. Instead of finding Napier, the two men sent by me found the redoubtable Major Hodson who had accompanied Napier as a volunteer of the storming of the palace. Hodson did not wait for the powder bags, but, after showing the men where to go for them, came running up himself, sabre in hand. 'Where are the rebels?' he said. I pointed to the door of the room, and Hodson, shouting 'Come on!' was about to rush in. I implored him not to do so, saying 'It's certain death; wait for the powder; I've sent men for powder-bags.' Hodson made a step forward, and I put out my hand to seize him by the shoulder to pull him out of the line of the doorway, when he fell back shot though the chest. He gasped out a few words, either 'Oh, my wife!' or, 'Oh, my mother!' – I cannot now rightly remember – but was immediately choked by blood.

Forbes-Mitchell placed him in a *dhoolie*, but he was already dying. Thus passed William Hodson – controversial even in his dying moments. It was soon being put about that he had been looting when he was shot. Forbes-Mitchell was adamant in his defence: 'The assertion that Major Hodson was looting when he was killed is untrue. No looting had been commenced, not even by Jung Bahadur's Goorkhas. That Major Hodson was killed by his own rashness cannot be denied; but for any one to say that he was looting is a cruel slander on one of the bravest of Englishmen.'

If Hodson wasn't after loot he was in a minority. For as the rebel strongholds in the city fell one by one over the next few days – the Sikandar Bagh, the Shah Najaf, the Moti Mahal, the Chattar Manzil and the Kaisar Bagh itself – Lucknow was picked clean. 'The city was in the hands of plunderers,' wrote Forbes-Mitchell,

> Europeans and Sikhs, Goorkhas, and camp-followers of every class, aided by the scum of the native population. Every man in fact was doing what was right in his own eyes, and 'Hell broke loose' is the only phrase in the English language that can give one who had never seen such a sight any idea of the scenes in and around the Inambara, the Kaisarbagh, and adjacent streets. The Sikhs and Goorkhas were by far the most proficient plunderers, because they instinctively knew where to look for the most valuable loot. The European soldiers did not understand the business, and articles that might have proved a fortune to many were readily parted with for a few rupees in cash and a bottle of grog. But the gratuitous destruction of valuable property that could not be carried off was appalling.

Forbes-Mitchell reckoned his own regiment got very little loot, especially after the prize agents took over. 'But it was shrewdly suspected by the troops that certain small caskets in battered cases, which contained the redemption of mortgaged estates in Scotland, England, and Ireland, and snug fishing and shooting-boxes in every game-haunted, and salmon-frequented angle of the world, found their way inside the uniform cases of even the prize agents.'

On 19 March Hazrat Mahal fled the city with her son – three days later the Maulvi of Faizabad abandoned the few houses he was defending on the edge of the town, and fled too. Lucknow was in British hands once more. Its fall, and those of Jhansi and Gwalior that followed, were death blows to the rebellion, but it was an unconscionable time a-dying. A series of small hard-fought campaigns – to call them mopping-up operations would be to do them an injustice – now began and it was not until December 1859 that order was fully restored. Of the leaders of the rebellion, Tantia Topi in particular proved a skilful and elusive guerrilla leader. Time and again British flying columns would bring him to action from which – by a skilful use of skirmishers to cover his retreat – he would escape to fight another day. Possessed of an amazing ability to raise fresh troops and acquire artillery, he kept large numbers of British troops constantly on the move in a nine-month campaign worthy of a volume of its own. It was not until April 1859 that he was captured, betrayed by Man Singh – a former rebel anxious to ingratiate himself with the victors. He was court-martialled, found guilty of treason and hanged. Also betrayed – and also hanged – was the Rao Sahib, the Nana Sahib's brother, in 1862. Of the fate of the Nana Sahib himself nothing is certain – having faked a suicide in the Ganges after his defeat at Cawnpore, he fled into Nepal and reportedly died of fever in September 1859. Doubles and imposters were sighted from time to time for the remainder of the century, but when in 1895 a young officer telegraphed to Calcutta, 'Have arrested Nana Sahib', he received the reply, 'Release at once'. Hazrat Mahal, the Begum, also fled into Nepal where Jung Bahadur allowed her to remain, though under constant threat of arrest. The Maulvi of Faizabad, after fleeing from Lucknow, waged a guerrilla war against the British in Oude with some success until attacking Pawayan, whose Rajah had refused to help him, he charged the main gate on an elephant. As the elephant smashed the gate the Rajah's brothers shot the Maulvi dead. The Rajah then cut off his head and took it to Shajahanpur to claim the reward. Finding the Magistrate and his friends at dinner, the Rajah – in a scene that surely inspired Kipling's 'Ballad of Bo Da Thone' – unrolled the bundle and spilled the head on to the floor.

The King of Delhi was put on trial in January 1859, accused of 'not regarding his allegiance as a British subject'. Mrs Muter attended the trial: 'At first he appeared alarmed,' she wrote, 'and his face wore an anxious expression; but by degrees it became more vacant, and he assumed or felt indifference, remaining apparently in a state of lethargy, with his eyes closed during the greater part of the proceedings.' He was found guilty of all charges and sentenced to be exiled in Rangoon. He was taken there in October 1859, together with his wife Zenat Mahal and a son by a concubine. Bahadur Shah, last of the Mogul Emperors, died in Rangoon in 1862.

# EPILOGUE

If the native prophecies had specified that 1857 would see the end of the Company's rule they would have been more accurate. Growing criticism in England – of the Company's handling of the outbreak and its causes, as well as its seizure of estates in Oude, its forcing of the pace of change and lack of respect for Indian customs – led to the India Act of 1858 whereby the rule of the East India Company was abolished. Henceforward India would be ruled by a viceroy, who would oversee everyday administration and law-making in Calcutta, and a Secretary of State for India, answerable to Parliament. In that year also the 'Queen's Proclamation' was read out in various languages in all the main cities and towns of India. In it the Queen assured the peoples of India that 'We know, and respect, the feelings of attachment with which the natives of India regard the lands inherited by them from their ancestors, and we desire to protect them in all their rights connected therewith ... and we will ensure that generally in framing and administering the law, due regard will be paid to the ancient rights, usages and customs of India.' The British Government would be careful never again to alienate the landowning classes. In addition, the Queen promised to treat all her subjects equally and respect all religions: 'We do strictly charge and enjoin all those who may be in authority under us that they abstain from all interference with the religious belief or worship of any of our subjects on pain of our highest displeasure.' The pace of change it was implied would be slow, but change there would be over the coming century. If the park containing the well at Cawnpore, where crowds of laughing boys play cricket now, is overlooked by busts of Tantia Topi and the Nana Sahib, it was to new men – of the type envisaged by Macaulay, Indian in colour and blood, but English in opinions and intellect – that the British would

349

hand over India in 1948. Mahatma Ghandi – the very incarnation of Indian spirituality – was a British-trained lawyer; when he visited England he stayed at the Dorchester.

A new India required new armies, and the Bengal Army – the three Presidency armies survived for most of the century – that emerged was a very different one. In future the army of the Bengal Presidency was to be formed of 'mixed' units – soldiers of various races and religions serving in regiments, as with the armies of Madras and Bombay. There was to be no artillery – except for five mountain batteries of the Punjab Frontier Force and four batteries of the Hyderabad contingent – and every garrison in India was to include British troops in a ratio of one to three. When the British Army struggled to meet that commitment, Indian numbers were reduced. The suspicion that the Mutiny had engendered in the minds of the British lasted well into the twentieth century, but Indian troops were soon proving their worth once more – in China under Hope Grant, in Abyssinia under Robert Napier. As the century progressed, there was a greater emphasis in recruiting the so-called 'martial races' – the Sikhs, Gurkhas and hill tribes who had helped the British reconquer India. These troops were regarded as the backbone of the army, though old Bengal regiments that had stayed true to their colours – there were seventeen of them – were included in the new order of battle, and officers of Maratha, Rajput or Dogra regiments would have disputed the claim. The three armies were merged into an Indian Army in 1895, and it was an army that was to serve the British Empire, and subsequently India and Pakistan, well. In the Great War, its soldiers served on the Western Front (where Frederick Roberts, now a field marshal, died visiting them in 1914) and in 1939–45, as the largest all-volunteer army in history, Indian soldiers – together with their British comrades-in-arms – inflicted on the Japanese Empire its only land defeat.

# VISITING THE
# BATTLEFIELDS TODAY

## DELHI

Many of the sites associated with the Mutiny have been swallowed up by modern Delhi and its suburbs, which have extended far beyond the nineteenth-century city limits. The Ridge itself is now mostly tree-covered parkland, but the British monument, erected on the site of Hindu Rao's House after the Mutiny, still stands. From the top of its tower one can (just) make out the Jamma Masjid mosque and the Red Fort. Although the old city walls are mostly demolished, some of the gates still stand – most notably the Kashmir Gate – scene of the mutiny of the 54th and 38th NI, Edward Vibart's leap from the walls, and the famous blowing of the gate by Lieutenants Home and Salkeld. The gate is in very good condition – it is still set aside as a national monument – and it takes very little imagination to visualize the dramatic events that took place there. Nearby is St James's Anglican church – built by James Skinner, founder of Skinner's Horse, who is buried near the altar. The church – with plaques commemorating individuals and regiments – is a must-see site for anyone interested in the military history of British India. The Red Fort and Palace are two of India's foremost tourist attractions and remain pretty much as they were in the 1850s. From the fort's walls, near the Diwan-i-Khas (Audience Hall) where Bahadur Shah first met the mutineers, one can stand where Captain Douglas stood and called down to the sowars who had ridden in from Meerut the morning after the outbreak. Outside Delhi, Humayun's tomb – where Bahadur Shah and his family took refuge after the storming, and where he, and later his sons, were taken into custody by William Hodson – is a magnificent example of Mogul architecture in a beautiful setting. To those familiar with the story the site has a certain melancholy – it is difficult not to sympathize with the last of the Moguls as he awaited his fate surrounded by reminders of the glories of his ancestors. The main British cemetery holds the grave of John Nicholson – prominent among countless others. Although preserved by the government, most British graveyards are, to a greater or lesser extent, overgrown, which can lend a 'treasure-hunt' feel to their exploration. The graveyard keepers generally know the whereabouts of the more famous graves, but with a good stick and a little patience there are many more discoveries to be made. Visitors are recommended to wear stout shoes and make plenty of noise to drive away snakes. Badli-ke-Serai – 6 miles to the north of Delhi – is now the site of the world's biggest vegetable market. A visit to the mound – site of the rebel battery captured by the 75th Foot – and the monument that still stands there involves a long walk through the kind of teeming crowds that only India can produce. Foreign visitors are rare here and touring groups soon attract a crowd of people, who will gather round and listen with intense and polite interest to a talk that few of them understand.

## MEERUT

The 40 miles between Delhi and Meerut can take a long time by road – on which buses and lorries compete for space with cars, bicycles and bullock carts – but is worth the effort. It is still a large cantonment whose barracks, with its lawns, cricket grounds, whitewashed stones and immaculate sentries, show that the Indian Army is still what it was. The square where the 3rd Native Cavalry was disarmed is overgrown with scrub now – but the house of its commander, Carmichael-Smyth, is still a senior officer's quarter. The Garrison church, though a little run down, is still in use and in the process of being restored. Like Skinner's Church in Delhi it is a gold mine for the military enthusiast, from the rifle racks attached to the backs of the pews, to the many memorials com-memorating actions, individuals and units from before, during and after the Mutiny. The Garrison cemetery contains most of the victims of the massacre of the night of 10 May 1857, including – perhaps the most poignant of all – Charlotte Chambers. The graveyard keeper, with his pet monkey, will show visitors to the most important graves, and to anyone interested in Victorian graveyards this one is worth several hours. As well as Mutiny victims the cemetery contains generations of British men and women who gave their lives to India. Some of those lives were pitifully short – the cemeteries of British India are full of babies.

## LUCKNOW

Lucknow is now a thriving industrial city – sometimes called 'the Manchester of India' – but many of the sites associated with the Mutiny remain. The Residency compound, preserved as a monument during British rule, is maintained as such today. The buildings – including the Baillie Guard gate, Fayrer's House where Sir Henry Lawrence died, the hospital and the Magazine – still stand in the condition they were in when the Mutiny ended, and the enthusiast would be advised to allow at least two days to explore it thoroughly. The Residency building, its upper floors razed by mutineer gunfire, houses an interesting museum of the siege. Behind the Residency are buried Sir Henry Lawrence and other well-known names from the siege – every gravestone seems to tell a story. The compound – a pleasant peaceful place of birdsong, manicured lawns and well-tended flower beds – is popular today with young couples, courting in that decorous Indian way that involves much hand-holding and eye-gazing. The Sikandar Bagh – the scene of some of the most brutal fighting when it was stormed by Sikhs and Highlanders – is unchanged, and as such is a very atmospheric site. Close by is the spot where Henry Kavanagh first met Sir Colin Campbell. On the outside wall of the garden – accessible through the entrance to the hospital next door (ask at the gate) – the 93rd's monument marks the spot where the regiment broke through the wall. On the outskirts of the city stands the Martinière, the Public School founded by General Martin – a Frenchman in the East India Company's service – whose schoolboys took an active part in the defence of the Residency. The structure is impressive, fronted by guns cast by the founder, General Martin, himself. In the trees near the school one comes across the grave of William Hodson. The boys of the school greet passers-by with that old-fashioned courtesy that used to be thought British. If E. M. Forster was right and the last English gentleman will be an Indian, there's a good chance he'll have come from the Martinière.

## CAWNPORE

At Cawnpore the site of Wheeler's compound stands beside a splendid memorial church built by the British after the Mutiny. The outline of the compound can be identified by marker stones set in the long grass. Around the altar of the church, stone tablets record the names of every victim of the massacres, many of whom are buried or commemorated in the churchyard. The well of the Bibighar – now level and capped with concrete – stands inside a public park. On most days it is used as a cricket pitch by small boys, under the gaze of busts of the Nana Sahib and Tantia Topi. Nearby, fallen now, lies the massive 'hanging tree' where hundreds of Indians – some of them possibly guilty – were hanged in reprisal by the British. The Satichaura Ghat, the scene of the first massacre, situated on the banks of the holy Ganges, is popular with newly married couples and their families, who go there to sing, dance and celebrate. Their presence creates a holiday atmosphere – a welcome relief after the Bibighar well and the hanging tree. Even so, it is not difficult, the site being largely unchanged, to visualize the awful scenes of that dreadful day in June 1857.

## AGRA

The Red Fort at Agra, the scene, many would have said, of a none-too-arduous siege – is beautifully preserved and a superb example of Mogul architecture. Of Mutiny interest is the grave of Mr Colvin, located in the centre of the fort. Sassiah – scene of one of the few British defeats – is situated 5 miles away on a busy road, the battlefield being largely taken up with an air force base to which access is forbidden.

## JHANSI

Jhansi is rather off the beaten tourist track and – unlike, say, Delhi or Agra – sees foreign visitors as something of a curiosity. The Rani's granite fortress is a gem – and a source of great pride to the locals. On the walk up to the main gate, boys sell comics in Hindi telling the story of the Rani, who is regarded – understandably – as a national heroine. The fort is well preserved, having been used by British troops until Independence. Inside the fort is a monument to a heroic husband and wife who manned a gun as the British stormed the fort, and fought until they were overwhelmed. The spot on the walls from which the Rani made her daring escape is pointed out by guides. In the town below is the Rani's Palace, with its audience chamber and private apartments, preserved as it was when Lakshmi Bai last occupied it. Across the town is the walled garden – now just a dusty yard – where the British captives were massacred. And nearby is the old Star Fort where the Jhansi mutiny began. The fort – containing nineteenth-century barrack blocks with verandahs – is still garrisoned by Sikhs of the Bombay Sappers and Miners, and access is restricted.

There is in India today a growing interest in what, to Indians, is the First National War of Independence. Statues of the Indian heroes of the Mutiny abound, as do monuments to those who 'achieved martyrdom' in the national cause; but British monuments are still treated with respect. A story from the dawn of modern India exemplifies this spirit – during British rule a Union Flag flew permanently from the roof of the Lucknow Residency. On the night India gained its Independence a crowd poured into the Residency compound intent on tearing it down, but were restrained by Nationalist leaders, who argued that such an act had no place in the new India. The crowd went home and the flag remained, to be lowered with dignity and ceremony at a later date. India has a long history of absorbing conquerors – keeping what it likes and ejecting what it doesn't. It did the same with the British. The Mutiny monument on Delhi Ridge carries two plaques – the original Victorian one, and a modern Indian one which politely points out that the 'rebels' referred to above were in fact 'martyrs' in the cause of Indian Independence. The sign is in English.

# INDEX